John Rigg was born and raised in
University of Cambridge with a degree in Economics, later completing a
Ph.D. He has worked as an economic consultant in London and in the Civil
Service in Scotland.

His sporting career principally comprised playing rugby league at
primary school, rugby union at secondary school and college, and cricket to
a reasonable club standard. *An Ordinary Spectator: 50 Years of Watching
Sport* is his first book on sport.

He is married with two children and lives in Scotland.

Find out more about John and his writing at:
www.anordinaryspectator.com

West Highland Way

April 2019

AN ORDINARY SPECTATOR

50 Years of Watching Sport

John Rigg

To Cheryl and Jillian

Best wishes

John Rigg

SilverWood

Published in paperback by SilverWood Books 2012
www.silverwoodbooks.co.uk

Text copyright © John Rigg 2012

If any copyright holder believes that their material has been used without
due credit, the author will make reasonable efforts to correct omissions
in any future re-printing.

Cover images © Trudi Wild, Jason Stitt, Patrimonio Designs Limited, Tiziano Casalta,
Naiyyer, Conde, Gmborden @Dreamstime.com

ISBN 978-1-78132-005-1

British Library Cataloguing in Publication Data
A CIP catalogue record for this book is available from the British Library

Set in Sabon by SilverWood Books
Printed on paper sourced responsibly

This book is dedicated to my father, William (Bill) Rigg

Contents

Preface

It is August 19th 1961 and I am sitting on my father's shoulders. We are at the back of the stand at Parkside, the home ground of the Hunslet rugby league football club in the industrial heart of south Leeds. The visitors are from Whitehaven, a place I am subsequently to learn is in Cumberland but of which, at this time, I have never heard. And because I have never heard of Whitehaven, the occasion is both exciting and frightening. Hunslet's opponents are adversaries from a strange place, who wear a different kit to the home side and who have arrived to do battle with my dad's team.

I am six years old.

The day will change my life. At the very least, it will set it on a course – of interests, of concerns and, at times, of passions – which it would not otherwise have followed.

The rain pours down. But I do not care. I am hooked, not only on the sport of rugby league – though that is certainly also the case – but, even after this first exposure, on the experience of the sporting event, viewed live and in the flesh.

Fast forward to August 21st 2011. I am sitting in the second tier of the South Leeds Stadium, the home ground of the Hunslet Hawks rugby league football club. The visitors are the Barrow Raiders, by a nice coincidence again from the north western provinces of the rugby league heartland, though the administrators now refer to the county as Cumbria. It is a warm summer's afternoon with a light breeze and a clear blue sky.

I am now in my mid fifties – I stopped watching rugby matches perched on my dad's shoulders long ago – and I have been a spectator at sports events for 50 years (and two days). This book describes my experiences as an ordinary spectator during this period. It relates my journey from

Parkside to the South Leeds Stadium – as the crow flies, a distance of less than a mile – and the various detours along the way.

The title of the book represents my status at most of the sports events I have been to see. I have been an ordinary spectator. In other words, for the overwhelming majority of the sporting occasions I have witnessed, from touchline or terrace or stand, I have paid my own way. To use an excellent phrase favoured by Americans, it has been "on my own dime". My perspective has been, therefore, not that of the professional commentator or the paid journalist, still less that of the participating sportsman/woman himself (or herself). Rather, it has been that of someone who has had to dip into his disposable income – whether from pocket money or student grant or take-home pay – in order to fund his spectating habit.

There was always a choice, of course. I could have spent my money elsewhere – on clothes or beer or foreign holidays – and, at times, needless to say, I did. In aggregate, these decisions are not either/or. But, at the margins, they are: a little more spent on this means a little less available to spend on that. And the choice is even starker when it is couched in terms of time: two hours spent watching this, rather than two hours doing that.

There have been two types of exception to this self-funding approach to sports spectating. The first and obvious one is the expenditure made on my behalf to travel and watch sports events when I was a young boy, mainly by my father, of whom more later. I will describe how, in some respects, even this funding regime did not last particularly long, whilst, in other areas, it was maintained over virtually the whole period I shall be describing. But initially, and for some time afterwards, the 6 year-old boy was subsidised from elsewhere within the family budget.

The second type of exception is represented by the limited number of sports events that I have not needed to pay to attend due to some form of corporate or other hospitality. These are genuine exceptions, however, counted on the fingers of one hand, and I shall identify them as they arise.

Having thus established the credentials as to my ordinariness as a spectator, the central questions arise. Why have I written this book? What have I attempted to achieve?

To answer these queries, I should first set out what I have *not* sought to do. This book is not intended to be a simple "I was there" catalogue of the sporting events – major and minor – at which I have happened to be present over the last five decades. Nor does the book present a list of results – "Yorkshire beat X by 150 runs and then lost to Y by 5 wickets and then drew with Z". Both options would have a very limited appeal for the writer and, I suspect, no interest at all for the reader.

My objective is altogether more subtle. And more difficult. It is to examine what it is exactly that I have derived from watching sport. What have been the emotions that I have experienced? What have I felt? Why have I been continually drawn back to watch time and time again? What have I been hoping for? What have I warmed to and what have I disliked? How have I adapted to the changing nature – and presentation – of sport itself? What have I learned about those whom I have watched – the winners and losers, heroes and villains, masters and apprentices, gentlemen and cheats? And what have I learned about myself in the course of watching the sporting contest? In summary: what is it that watching sport has meant to me over all these years? And does it still mean the same to me today?

In seeking to address these questions, I have been aware of two important points. First, the potential reasons for an individual's attraction to sport are already generally recognised as hugely wide in scope. Ed Smith has neatly summarised this range of motives in *What Sport Tells us About Life*: " An intellectual could spend his whole life like a sporting Thomas Aquinas... cataloguing sport's appeal and trying to prove what makes sport great. Or you can tune out the theory entirely and get swept along in the emotion, ceremony and sense of theatre. Scholastics or happy clappers – all are welcome in the sporting arena... Sport's polytheism is part of its colour, central to its magic. We go to the same event en masse and yet absorb it uniquely".

The task I have set myself is, I think, somewhat narrower in scope than that covered by Smith's point, though it remains challenging. I am not seeking to examine the appeal of sport *per se* or the validity of sport as either a philosophical concept or behavioural activity. Nor do I focus extensively on the motives of the participants, though this issue is of interest and is referred to on occasion. (Smith makes some particularly interesting observations about the motivation of elite sportsmen to continue performing long after fame and wealth have been attained). Rather, I wish to concentrate on the activity of spectating: that is, watching the live action in front of me, surrounded (or not) by other spectators doing the same thing, and absorbing (and interpreting) what I am witnessing.

Second, it follows from this that the questions I have posed cannot be addressed simply by recounting what I have seen. They also require me to set out what I have *observed*, which is not at all the same thing.

The concept of observation is one that I am happy with. It implies a detachment, an aloofness, a separation and – usually – an independence of perspective on the event at hand. I am entirely comfortable with that requirement. I am one of life's observers. For the purposes of this book, therefore, I must consider not only the actual events on the court or pitch, but the background context within which those events took place – the atmosphere, the other spectators, the hopes and fears of those closest to me who were caught up in the same events, the historical baggage surrounding the event itself. I should emphasise, however, that this does not necessarily mean a state of neutrality. For much of my early spectating life, as I shall describe, I would be passionately hoping that one of the two teams on view would prevail. But, even then, I was still an observer.

The book is largely written from memory. Where appropriate, I have checked all the factual points that I consider relevant – and for any errors or inaccuracies that remain, apologies – but the core of the text is based on my recollection of matches and grounds and players and incidents and results. This is an ambitious approach. Recollections – almost by definition – are selective and incomplete. And, of course, they can be "wrong", when set against the "facts" of what actually occurred. However, in a sense, this does not matter. If I am to attempt to answer the questions posed earlier, then my perspective for doing so can only be based on the memories I have. Indeed, they can only really be determined, not simply by my memory now looking back, but by my recollection of the thoughts I had – and the observations I made – at the time.

The accuracy of my recollections has been enhanced in three different ways. First, I have taken advantage of my innate reluctance to throw away any form of sporting memorabilia which has come into my possession. For the purposes of this book, this is mainly represented by the catalogue of programmes, scorecards, match tickets and other souvenirs which I have amassed over the years. I should report that I did not originally collect these items with any intention of using them as *aides memoires* at some stage in the future. But, having accumulated a stockpile of match programmes, in particular, it made obvious sense to draw upon it to trigger further memories and ideas.

Second, I have made a limited use of the growing list of video and DVD titles that include excerpts from some of the sporting events I have attended and of the highlights of "classic" sporting encounters that randomly find their way on to satellite television. These are selective items, of course, naturally focusing on the "bigger" matches which, in the context of this book, probably represent a minority of the events I shall describe. In these cases I hope I have been honest enough not to base my memory solely on the film clip seen many years after the actual event. Rather, these sources have been used primarily to inform or remind me of the background context: the size of the crowd, the markings on the players' kit, the condition of the pitch.

The third supplementary source of information is another burgeoning area of the sports media: the biographies and autobiographies of the participants themselves. I have drawn on these sparingly, partly because, as with the DVD and satellite television selection, there is a bias towards the bigger occasions, but also because of the variable quality of much of the content. However, the best of the books in this genre are excellent and, on the relatively rare occasions in which the author describes a sporting event which I attended, the participant's perspective is of considerable interest. Even though the player was on the pitch and I was in the stand, we were sharing the same moment.

The theatre of sport portrays glory, despair and drama. To give examples of each of these is an easy task, from which I shall not shirk in the chapters that follow. In this introductory chapter, however, I should say a little more about the last of these constituents: drama.

At one level, there is the drama of the full stage: the complete event, with its surrounding hype and atmosphere and gladiatorial engagement. Examples of these will be given throughout the period under review, from the Great Britain versus Australia rugby league test match at Headingley in November 1963 through to the Wales versus England Six Nations rugby match at the Millennium Stadium in Cardiff in February 2005. But there is also another type of drama, which probably occurs less frequently and is experienced over a much shorter time frame. It is the drama of the moment – of the micro-second – in which a defining characteristic of the contest is revealed. In some cases, the particular detail can determine the whole memorised experience. There is one such example in the Wales-England rugby match to which I have referred and I will report on this later.

Nor is this the full story. In many cases, though by no means all, the key to these dramas of the moment is not the incident itself – or the actual observation of the incident – it is in that split-second *before* the event occurs. It is in these moments that sport really makes the heart pound and causes the sharp intake of breath to be made. In short: it is often in the *anticipation* of the incident that the ultimate drama lies. It is at that moment when the observer – in this case, me – can see into the future. It is when we know – with absolute certainty – what is going to happen, not only before it happens, but before the rest of the spectators know it is going to happen and, probably, before the participants themselves.

I shall refer to these moments as "nano-dramas". The concept is attractive. In my dictionary, "nano" is a prefix meaning one thousand millionth. On a relative scale, it would represent the approximate ratio between the width of the nail of my little finger and the distance between

Lord's Cricket Ground in London and Candlestick Park in San Francisco. In the context of the sporting event, it is the ratio between the blink of an eye and what I referred to above as the "full stage" of the complete event.

In this book, I have identified a "First XI" of sporting "nano-dramas" and I shall describe them in more or less the order in which they occurred. It will be seen that some of them are very well known. Others will have long departed from the collective memory. A couple are very personal to my own spectating experience. And, of the examples given, at least five are characterised by the split-second of anticipation of the incident, as well as the actual incident itself.

This book contains its fair share of "big" events, particularly Test cricket matches, international rugby games – of both codes, union and league – and other rugby league showcase events, especially cup finals. But it is not a checklist of the usually perceived "highlights" of the sporting calendar. There are no Olympic Games, no Grand Prix, no FA Cup Finals. Some sports are not covered at all: there is no hockey or badminton or swimming. Nonetheless, I think that the broad catholicism of my sporting interests is captured. In addition to rugby, cricket and football – the main constituents of what follows – there are reflections, albeit some rather fleeting, on American football, basketball, boxing, golf, greyhound racing, marathon running, lawn tennis and volleyball.

The same comments apply to the named participants. It is hardly surprising, given the sports listed above, that we will come across the champions at the top of their professions: Geoff Boycott and Michael Vaughan, Gareth Edwards and Jason Robinson, Jack Charlton and Kenny Dalglish, Martin Offiah and Ellery Hanley, Lee Trevino and Tiger Woods. But, there will also be references to others on whom a lesser light shone but who, at one time, held the centre stage of my attention: Brian Gabbitas and Billy Langton (both of whom we shall meet shortly), John Waring and Howard Cooper, Keith Jones and Chris Parkes, Jamie Murray (footballer, not tennis player) and Alan Biley.

And again, in a similar vein, with the venues of the sporting events. Wembley Stadium, Headingley Cricket Ground, Twickenham and Murrayfield, amongst others, in addition to the magnificent Millennium Stadium already noted. Overseas locations as well: Madison Square Garden, Sydney Cricket Ground (for a rugby match) and the Olympic Stadiums in Munich, Moscow and Barcelona, as well as FedEx Field in Maryland and Soldier Field in Chicago. But the significant bulk of my spectating experience has been at more "ordinary" venues: the reader will be taken back to Parkside and to Lawkholme Lane, to Chandos Park and Grange

Road, to the Abbey Stadium and Plough Lane, to North Marine Drive and Hamilton Crescent. The truth is, of course, that these apparently humdrum locations are far from ordinary. Irrespective of their state of repair or the drabness of their location, they constitute the battleground of the contest. They are the arena. Moreover, in many cases – including at least a couple of those given above – they represent (or represented) a powerful legacy of sporting tradition that adds historical context to that contest.

It will be clear by now, therefore, that this book is on a totally different wavelength to the collected writings of those professional sports journalists for whom the alpha male competitive pressure to be the "chief", in the words of Simon Barnes in *The Meaning of Sport*, "take the form of a mania: you simply have to be present at every major sporting event that takes place anywhere in the world". As an example, Barnes refers to three other chief sports writers who, after covering an England game in the 2002 soccer World Cup in Japan, flew to Memphis, Tennessee, for a world heavyweight championship boxing contest and then returned to Japan in time for England's next match. Barnes himself, adapting a line from Hunter S Thompson's *Fear and Loathing in Las Vegas*, is quite clear on his preference: "When it comes to watching sport... I like the really big f...s". By contrast, the catholicism of my tastes extends to size as well as content: small can be beautiful.

The book follows a fairly inexact chronology in the sequence of sporting events that are described. I have eschewed the temptation to start at 1961 and progress through 1962 and 1963 and so on up to 2011 in a predictable and metronomic fashion. Instead, I have opted for a thematic approach, beginning with my childhood wonder at watching rugby and cricket and then moving through the various stages of my spectating career in what I hope is a reasonably logical and sensible manner. There is a certain amount of time-shifting, but not enough, I trust, to undermine the coherence of the overall narrative.

In developing this thematic approach, I have drawn on a useful template provided by another, earlier, writer. Not just any writer, it has to be said, but the greatest of them all. In *As You Like It*[1], William Shakespeare describes the Seven Ages of Man, beginning with the infant and progressing through the schoolboy, the lover, the soldier, the justice and the pantaloon until reaching second childishness. In preparing this book, it quickly became apparent to me that a similar model should be applied. Accordingly, my Seven Ages of Watching Sport provide the framework within which my spectating journey is described.

Some interpretation of this approach should perhaps be given here.

First, it should be noted that it is more than simply a literary conceit. In the context of this book, the concept of the Seven Ages reflects the obvious (but important) point that one's perspective of contemporary events – including the watching of sport – will inevitably change as one grows older. Put simply, the 6 year-old's analysis of what he sees in front of him will be different to that of the 16 year-old; likewise the 16 year-old and the 56 year-old. These differences will be determined not only by age and experience – though these factors are clearly significant – but also by circumstances and context. It follows from this that a given event will be viewed differently according to the Age of the observer.

Second, the Seven Ages that I have identified are, for the most part, different from those presented by the Bard. For example, the Awestruck Novice of my First Age is slightly more advanced than Shakespeare's infant "mewling and puking in the nurse's arms" (apart from the occasional bout of car sickness), and other variations are to be found throughout the range. The exception will probably come in the Seventh and final Age (when it is eventually reached). I fear that the characteristics of Shakespeare's second childishness and mere oblivion – "sans teeth, sans eyes, sans taste, sans everything" – might also be common to my Childlike Sage.

Finally, I need to emphasise the same point as that made above in connection with the "First XI" of "nano-dramas". The Seven Ages will also vary from one individual to another. Mine is a personal journey. It is unique to me and, therefore – by definition – so are my Seven Ages.

My Seven Ages of Watching Sport	
One	The Awestruck Novice
Two	The Youthful Explorer
Three	The Absent Player
Four	The Distracted Opportunist
Five	The Detached Traditionalist
Six	The Affluent Reflective
Seven	The Childlike Sage

There is, of course, an ever-changing cast list in the events that follow. The *dramatis personae* of the sporting stages of the early to mid 1960s have been successively replaced by the succeeding generations of actors through to those of the present day. It will be seen that some of the characters had an impressive durability, consistently featuring from one year to the next, before finally vacating the scene. For others – the majority – their appearance in the spotlight was much briefer, in some cases ephemeral. Yet others appeared at a given date and then, after apparently fading away, reappeared on a later occasion.

This last group is a particularly interesting one, I think, and I shall identify examples along the way. They represent part of a key characteristic of spectating life: that of echoes and repeats. From the dramatic perspective, the technique is one that is well known to the novelist or film-maker. It is the low key introductory reference to a character – or, alternatively, an incident or a place or a particular set of circumstances – that is later revealed to be of some significance. The outside observer is always interested in these networks of coincidence and repetition, and I am no exception.

I intend to say very little about my own sporting activity during the long period covered by this book. As background, however, I will report that my principal sports were rugby and cricket. The former was in the league code at primary school (St. Matthew's, Chapel Allerton, Leeds) and union thereafter (Roundhay School, Leeds, first XV; Trinity College, Cambridge, first XV; Cambridge University LX Club, two appearances). On the cricket field, I played for Roundhay School first XI, Trinity College first XI, Cambridge University Crusaders CC (four appearances versus Oxford University Authentics CC in the varsity second XI match), the first teams of North Leeds CC (Airedale and Wharfedale League), Saltaire CC (Bradford League) and Old Paulines CC (Surrey Cricket League) and the Thursday XI of Camden CC, Cambridge. At representative level, I captained the Leeds Schools Under 14s XI and played for the Yorkshire Senior Schools Cricket XI and the Yorkshire Cricket Federation XI (the county's Under 19s team).

I refer to this curriculum vitae of sporting representation, not to boast of its excellence, about which I will leave the reader to judge, but to illustrate the types of echoes that will reappear later. For example, the Leeds Schools Under 14 XI, which I captained in 1969, also contained a promising young batsman called Jim Love, later to play with distinction for Yorkshire CCC (which rewarded him with a benefit in 1989) and in one-day international cricket for England. The Yorkshire Cricket Federation touring team to the Midlands in 1974 was captained by Love and included at least four other future Yorkshire first team players. Similarly, the Normanton Grammar School first XV, against which I played for Roundhay School in 1971, contained Les Cusworth (later Leicester and England), Colin Lambert (later Harlequins) and Neil Tuffs (later Featherstone Rovers and Fulham RLFC); we lost by one point to a last minute try. Later, when I played for the Trinity College first XV in the Cambridge inter-collegiate cup (the quaintly named "cuppers") semi final of 1977 against a St John's College first XV, the opposition included Peter Warfield (England) and Alun Lewis (later British Lions); we got hammered by over fifty points. These players are mentioned here not for the purpose of some moderate name-dropping, but as examples of fleeting connections that will be re-made at a later date.

To conclude this introduction, there is one other person who must be brought forward at this early stage. My father: the late William (Bill) Rigg. He is a central character, not only in my early years of sports spectating, but throughout the whole period. In part, this is for the straightforward reason that we attended a significant proportion of sporting events together, especially rugby and cricket, and not only in my childhood.

More importantly, however, it was Dad who taught me how to watch a match – particularly a rugby match. How I learned to observe the sporting occasion, and what I observed – and my dad's role in providing this tuition – are key themes in the account that follows. It is for this reason that the book is dedicated to Bill Rigg.

For the record, in the August 2011 fixture, the Hunslet Hawks defeated the Barrow Raiders by 42 points to 12. Waine Pryce scored four of the home side's seven tries; Jack Latus kicked seven goals from eight attempts.

In the game played 50 years earlier, Hunslet lost to Whitehaven 7–12. The Hunslet try was scored by Brian Gabbitas; Billy Langton kicked two goals.

The First Age

The Awestruck Novice

I am slightly beyond Shakespeare's "mewling and puking" stage of infancy, but not by much. This is the age of my entry into a strange new world of allegiances and rivalries, of history and tradition, and of the emotional highs and lows of sports spectating. Through watching and reading about two sports in particular – rugby league and cricket – I begin my discovery of the principal actors on the sporting stage and their supporting cast.

Chapter 1

Parkside

For the chronicler of the story related in this book, it is a chastening thought that the narrative dates back as far as 1961. It is the distant past. For any spectator who has only come to sport in more recent times – and for whom the adrenalin rush of Twenty-20 cricket contested by named players in coloured clothing is the norm, or for whom the Super League is played on the lush green rugby pitches of summer, or by whom a legitimate tackle from behind by an advancing wing half on an opponent shielding the football has never been seen – the year of 1961 is bordering on the prehistoric. It would be another ten years before the first one-day international cricket match was played and the summer rugby of Super League was only introduced in the mid-1990s, by which time wing halves had long become an extinct species. When seen from today's perspective, the major sports dramas of 1961 – Richie Benaud's six wicket haul to win the Old Trafford test match for Australia, the length of the field try finished off by Tom Van Vollenhoven for St Helens against Wigan in the Challenge Cup final at Wembley, the Tottenham Hotspur double-winning triumph, Angela Mortimer's Wimbledon Ladies Singles Final win – are generally viewed in the grainy black-and-white film footage that captured the grainy black-and-white world in which we assume that these events must actually have occurred.

In the broader social context, when again viewed through our contemporary sights, 1961 might reasonably be seen as falling on the cusp between two eras. Britain had slowly emerged from the long period of post-war austerity and rationing to enjoy – or begin to enjoy – some of the benefits of a consumer society. It had been four years earlier that the Prime Minister, Harold Macmillan, had announced that "most of our people have never had it so good" and, by the turn of the decade, the growth in ownership of household durables such as televisions and washing machines, financed in part by expanding levels of consumer credit, was well under way. In this respect, 1961 might therefore be viewed as a staging post on the long haul of post-war reconstruction which the Atlee Government had commenced in 1945 and which successive Conservative administrations – Churchill, Eden and Macmillan – had continued in the 1950s.

The apparent disruption to the social order came later. In 1961, Macmillan would have two more years in office before Sir Alec Douglas-Home "emerged" – as leaders of his party did in those days – to lead the Conservatives to defeat against Harold Wilson's Labour party in 1964. 1961 pre-dated the Beatles' first hit record, the Cuban Missile Crisis, the first live transatlantic television link, *That Was the Week That Was*, John Profumo's resignation, the assassination of President Kennedy and Wilson's promise to exploit "the white heat of the technological revolution". These defining events of the 1960s did not occur until at least a year – or, in most of the cases above, at least two years – later. It seems persuasive to argue that, if a given year can belong to the old (rather than new) order, 1961 belongs to the former.

But it is not quite so straightforward, of course. In the international political arena, many of the central themes that would dominate the 1960s and 1970s – especially those relating to the various strands of East-West tension – had taken root by this time. 1961 was the year in which the Berlin Wall was built, Yuri Gagarin completed the first manned space flight and, late in the year, the first American "adviser" was killed in Vietnam. The years of the early sixties might nowadays be viewed in monochrome, but they can also be seen as firmly setting the stage for the decade of colour that was to follow.

Closer to home, a good friend of mine – Llyr James, of whom more later – has reminded me that, by 1961, in my very own part of the world, a significant movement of cultural forces was already shaping a new perspective on modern society. In particular, a succession of Yorkshire-born novelists was having a profound effect on the way in which northern Britain portrayed itself to the outside world. This rich seam included John Braine (born Bradford) and *Room at the Top* (1957) and Keith Waterhouse (born Hunslet) and *There is a Happy Land* (1957) and *Billy Liar* (1959) and would later extend to Stan Barstow (born Ossett) and *A Kind of Loving* (1962) and Barry Hines (born Barnsley) and *A Kestrel for a Knave* (1968). Modest extensions of the mediums and/or the geographical parameters would incorporate Alan Sillitoe (born Nottingham) and *Saturday Night and Sunday Morning* (1958) and Shelagh Delaney (born Salford) and Willis Hall (born Hunslet) and the first stage productions of *A Taste of Honey* (1958) and *The Long and the Short and the Tall* (1958). Waterhouse and

Hall combined to write the screenplay of *Whistle Down the Wind* (1961).

For my purposes, the key work of this period is, of course, *This Sporting Life* by David Storey (born Wakefield). The central character, Arthur Machin, is a professional rugby league player and the focus of the novel is on the difficult relationships he has with his colleagues, his family and, especially, his landlady and lover. Storey's descriptions of actually playing rugby league – as seen through Machin's observation of the violence around him and his own infliction of pain on opponents – are principally to be found towards the end of the book: "I developed a good hand-off – I banged each time at the tiger's nose with the base of my wrist, and the sound of that tiny crunch gave me the satisfaction a mechanic gets from the sound of machinery". However, the defining incident occurs on the very first page: "…before I could pass, a shoulder came up to my jaw. It rammed my teeth together with a force that stunned me to blackness…. I walk off with Dai shoving an ammonia phial up my nose…. [He] presses his fingers around my mouth and his thumbs roll back my lips. 'Christ, man', he says. 'You've broke your front teeth.'"

I can recall watching Lindsay Anderson's film version of *This Sporting Life* with my father on our black and white television when I was a boy. I was disappointed that Machin's team did not seem to have a fixture against Hunslet. At the same time, I was utterly captivated – and not a little unnerved – by the tension of Richard Harris's dramatic scenes with Rachel Roberts. Dad's response to the film was fairly non-committal, apart from generally scoffing at the weakness of the opposition's tackling when Harris ran some distance to score a try, although he was keen to point out that one of the extras in the team scenes, Ted Carroll, had been an actual player with Hunslet in his own right before becoming a respected actor.

In retrospect, the main point of interest is simply that the year of my first visit to Hunslet neatly straddles that of the publication of the novel (1960) and the release of the film (1963). If one wants to see a portrayal of professional rugby league at the precise time of my first exposure to it – a fictional portrayal admittedly, but one underpinned by Storey's own experience as a player – *This Sporting Life* stands as the permanent record. The game was then – and is now – tough and uncompromising. For my part, given that the huge critical successes of both novel and film coincided with my own early explorations of this captivating sport, I can reasonably claim to have been tapping (unknowingly) into the *Zeitgeist* of popular culture in 1961.

The Hunslet rugby league club – in full, the Hunslet Cricket, Football and Athletic Club – had a relatively poor season in 1961–62. They finished in

25th place in a league of 30 and were thus consigned to the second of the two divisions that were to be introduced in the Northern Rugby League, as it was then called, the following season. I was not particularly concerned about this. In the aftermath of my first visit, for the Whitehaven match in August, I was too busy cementing my allegiance to the club – its ground, its players, its colours, its history – and making sure that my knowledge was fully accurate in all respects. My father was adamant, for example, that the correct description of the colours of the Hunslet shirts was not green, yellow and white – as it might have appeared to the uninformed naked eye – but "myrtle, flame and white".

Hunslet was not my local club. Our family – parents, younger sister Rosemary, and me – lived in Moortown, in suburban north Leeds. If we were part of a rugby constituency, it was logically that of the Leeds rugby league football club, based at Headingley, and altogether more all-embracing and cosmopolitan. (The parliamentary constituency, incidentally, was safely conservative, with one Sir Keith Joseph representing us at Westminster). My friends at primary school, if they had any interest in rugby at all, supported the Leeds club. Moreover, for a local boy taking an interest in the sport for the first time, there was another reason for veering towards Leeds. They were the league champions, having won the play-offs for the trophy for the first time – a surprising fact, given the club's distinguished history – at the end of the previous season.

But my father had been born in Hunslet and had lived there, or in the neighbouring localities of Holbeck and Beeston, until he had joined the Royal Air Force at the age of 18 in 1939. His father – my grandfather, another John Rigg – had migrated from North Yorkshire to become a policeman in south Leeds before the First World War. After being badly injured in the war – and his life saved by the eminent surgeon Sir Berkeley Moynihan in an operation in Manchester – he had returned to the police force, becoming a desk sergeant at the station in Beeston. Dad later told me that John Rigg had been a good father to his four children – a strict disciplinarian, but kind and fair. He had also been a respected member of the local community, to whom people would come for advice and support.

The sense of local identity within Hunslet in the 1920s and 1930s – the years of my father's youth and adolescence – was a powerful one. It meant something to be part of a community in which people looked out for each other. Confirmation of this has been provided in the evocative recollections of some of my father's near contemporaries, who have made their names in wider fields. In *City Lights: A Street Life*, the writer Keith Waterhouse (born in Hunslet in 1929 and, therefore, a few years younger than dad) vividly describes the bustling locality of his childhood with its "tram-rattling arteries" lined by shops, warehouses, offices, breweries, foundries, factories and workshops. The industrial base of Hunslet ranged from "nook and cranny businesses crammed into small yards and down narrow alleys" through to the major sources of employment in clothing, engineering and printing. Waterhouse remarks on the extensive scale of the area's amenities, ranging from swimming baths and wash-houses, churches, chapels and mission halls through to temperance hotels, billiard halls, cinemas, stables and dog racing tracks. It was "a neighbourhood of great liveliness".

Waterhouse does not romanticise about the hard and dirty environment of Hunslet at this time, referring to "the soot and grime of industrial Leeds" and the blackened terraces which stemmed off the main roads. His description of the area echoed that of the distinguished social commentator, Richard Hoggart (born in Hunslet in 1918), who has noted that, in the years before the Second World War, this was one of the poorest districts in northern England. Although there were heavy duty jobs for men in glassblowing, railway engineering and the mills, with employment for women in the ready-made clothing factories, the environmental conditions were bleak. Hoggart described "the smell of heavy industry, chemicals and human sweat, especially in crowded tram-cars" and noted that "there was muck enough to blacken your lace curtains in a week".[2] In his seminal work on the culture of the locality – *The Use of Literacy* – Hoggart referred evocatively to "the miles of smoking and huddled working class houses". He also used his sociologist's perspective to detect "the great number of differences, the subtle shades, the class distinctions, within the working class themselves. To the inhabitants there is a fine range of distinctions in prestige from street to street".

Further evidence of life growing up in Hunslet during this period has been given in *Born on the Wrong Side*, the autobiography of Cec Thompson, who played for the local rugby league side between 1948–53, becoming a Great Britain international, before being transferred to Workington Town: "The poverty of Hunslet… was not only economic but also a poverty of culture and opportunity. Hunslet… was pretty rough".[3]

However, notwithstanding the difficult social conditions that were prevalent in Hunslet during their respective formative years, all three of the above accounts give an overwhelming impression of the strength of its local identity, Hoggart referring to "a hugely rooted sense of place, of belonging". My father would not have disagreed. He enjoyed his childhood in Hunslet, with his loving family and his small group of friends – "my little pals", as he later described them – with whom he shared the experiences of school and play. Most significantly, the values he learned from his family and the locality never left him. He lived in Moortown for over 50 years, but he was always a Hunslet man.

During my first season, I familiarised myself with the geography of the Hunslet rugby league club's ground – Parkside – very quickly. It had covered stands on three sides and an open grassy terrace at one end behind the posts: the "Mother Benson" end, named after the former owner of one of a row of nearby cottages. There was some seating in a stand running along one of the touchlines, but dad's favourite vantage point was at the back of the opposite stand somewhere between the 25-yard line and the half way line. The players entered the field near the corner of the pitch to our right, their changing rooms being an old wooden pavilion that overlooked the adjacent cricket ground.

Parkside was ideal for Hunslet's requirements. It had been the club's ground since the 1880s and was big enough for their most important matches – the record crowd had been nearly 25,000 for a cup match against Wigan in the 1920s. Whilst it was judged not to be of the standard of the Leeds ground at Headingley when it came to hosting representative matches (apart from a Challenge Cup semi final during the First World War and a Yorkshire Cup final replay in the 1930s), it had an atmosphere to which I was immediately attracted. It also had an excellent pitch. In his authoritative *The Grounds of Rugby League*, Trevor Delaney suggests that, in the early 1960s, "Parkside had arguably the finest playing surface in the game".

Of course, during the time of my early visits, I had had no experience of any other sports stadiums and, by definition, no reference points with which Parkside could be compared. With the massive benefit of hindsight, it is clear that the spectating amenities were fairly basic – if not, very basic – and that inadequate repair and maintenance was being applied. But I did not know that at the time. To the six year-old boy, Parkside was the big ground where my dad's rugby team played in front of thousands of people.

When he first started taking me to watch Hunslet, my father did not own a car. What he did have was a little green van, which belonged to the small building company for which he worked as a joiner and foreman.[4] The van was the means by which we travelled from Moortown through the centre of the city, across the river, and up the Dewsbury Road into south Leeds. As the crow flies, it is not a long journey: perhaps seven or eight miles. However, for the young boy, excited with nerves at venturing into a strange land, and struggling for breath against the van's heady aroma of petrol fumes and the dankness of old bits of timber, it was an epic undertaking. We parked in the open spaces of the car park outside the ground, an apparently boundless expanse of loosely bound asphalt, ash and gravel, my father being careful to avoid the large potholes that lay in wait to test the van's suspension.

At the match, there were three reasons for me to sit on my dad's shoulders. The first and most obvious was so that I could see the action on the pitch. The attendances were not very big – the *Yorkshire Evening Post*'s report of my first Hunslet versus Whitehaven game stated that the crowd was about 2,500 – but the close proximity of the spectators at the top of the stand would have been more than sufficient to impede my view, if I had been standing up.

The second reason, equally obvious, was so that Dad could explain what was going on. To begin with, this involved an explanation of the rules: what happened when someone dropped the ball, or scored a try, or kicked the ball into touch, or missed a penalty kick. I picked all this up very quickly. I also learned the scoring system: straightforwardly three points for a try and two points for any type of goal – penalty, conversion or drop kick. And I familiarised myself with the full repertoire of referee's signals: awarding the scrum, giving the penalty kick, penalising the scrum half for incorrect feeding, indicating the knock-on, pointing down to the place of touchdown for a try. All this was new information, which I absorbed with enthusiasm and ease.

The third reason was not so apparent straightaway, but became clear enough in time. It was so that Dad could explain what was really going on. In particular, it was so that he could explain the skills of the game. Initially, this involved describing the different roles of the players: the hooker in getting the ball from the scrum, the scrum half in distributing the ball as quickly as possible to his stand-off half, the winger in using his speed down the touchline, the lonely full-back acting as the last line of defence. There was a division of labour across the team (which, regrettably I think, exists to a much lesser extent in the modern version of rugby league). At the same time, all the players had to be proficient in all the skills: everyone had to be able to catch and pass and run and tackle. And there were no substitutes. If a player was injured, he either had to carry on as best he could, often by making up the numbers wide out towards the wing, or his side had to play with a man short.

Some of the players were particularly adept at particular skills and, as the weeks passed, Dad introduced me to the subtleties of the individual members of the Hunslet team. It was clear to me at an early stage, for example, that Alan Preece, the left centre, was an excellent tackler. He was not a very tall man, but he was solid and tough, and he would drive into his opponent with his head correctly positioned and his shoulder and upper arm braced for the impact at contact.

The other centre, Geoff Shelton, was a different type of player – smooth and graceful. Dad pointed to Shelton as the basic role model to illustrate the skill of taking the ball, drawing the man and giving the pass. It is one of the most fundamental of all rugby skills – in either code – and Shelton was an expert, to the considerable benefit of his winger and the team. Inside Shelton was the stand-off, Brian Gabbitas, who was another with good hands in taking and giving the pass, but who also had very quick feet and a devastating sidestep. It soon became apparent to me that Gabbitas was a favourite of dad's.

The full back and goal kicker was Billy Langton, who a few years earlier – in the 1958–59 season – had played and scored in every one of Hunslet's matches, a rare feat in those days as it had only once been previously achieved.[5] Langton was a slimly built man with a gaunt face and was not a particularly quick runner. But he seemed to me, even at that early stage and even if I would not then have described him as such, to be a meticulous professional. His goal kicking routine was unwavering and unblemished: the ball pointed upright or forwards towards the posts, depending on the length of the kick, three long strides back, and a smooth action and follow through. Langton kicked the ball front-on, with his toe, as was the almost universal preference amongst goal kickers in those days; the "soccer-style" kicker was a rarity. He was also a superb catcher of the rugby ball. It seemed that, in virtually every match, he would have occasion to retrieve a penalty kick by the opposition by standing next to the touchline, his feet fractionally in the field of play and his body leaning over the line, and catching the ball before it bounced. When the ball was safely gathered, he would twist and arch himself to remain in the field of play and then, his balance restored, set off on his return run.

In the forwards, Hunslet's best known player was Geoff Gunney. Earlier in his career, Gunney had toured Australasia with the Great Britain team in 1954 and had played in the 1957 Rugby League World Cup in Australia. Although he had been sought by bigger and wealthier clubs – notably Wigan – he had stayed loyal to Hunslet. Gunney would play a significant role in the later events at the club, on and off the pitch, but, at the time of my first visits to Parkside, he stood out as a big powerful man, equally adept at tackling and running, with a sledgehammer hand-off. When Hunslet were awarded a penalty, and if it was outside Langton's range to the goalposts, Gunney took the punts into touch: big booming kicks, delivered with a slow run up and a graceful swing of the leg. Gunney was also renowned as a gentleman on and off the pitch: a couple of years later, in 1963–64, he won the prestigious Windsor Trophy, voted for by a panel of referees, as the league's "best and fairest player of the season".

(I shall explain later why he did not repeat the success in 1964–65).

The Hunslet pack of forwards was to develop into a powerful unit within a relatively short period, but in my first season, in 1961–62, they often could not match the strength of their opponents. To the boy sitting on his dad's shoulders, they seemed to drop the ball a lot, particularly the big prop forward, Dennis Hartley, whose regular indiscretions caused the local supporters to shout their displeasure. At the time, I probably shared their disappointment and, whilst of course not replicating the worst of their curses, I would no doubt have joined in with the chorus of groans as another pass was spilled. It took me some time to appreciate the difficult role of the prop forward, who is charged with taking the ball into a defensive wall of usually two or three opponents with the aim of committing the tacklers and attempting to free his hands and slip the ball to a supporting colleague. Hartley was the unforgiven villain when the ball was lost in the weight of the tackle or stolen by an opponent. But his time would come.

The first season passed quickly and disappointingly as far as the results were concerned, though, with one exception, I do not recall being particularly upset by Hunslet's lowly position in the league table. I was more concerned with learning about the sport and the Hunslet players and the club's history. I was also absolutely fascinated by the concept of the league table.

The updated table of the 30 professional rugby league clubs was printed every Saturday night in the Green Post, the sports edition of the *Yorkshire Evening Post*. The Green Post was delivered to our local newsagents, just down the main Harrogate Road from my parents' house, at about a quarter past six. The newsagents was probably three or four minutes hard running from our house, but I would leave nothing to chance. On a winter's evening, I would set off well in advance – a quarter to six was not uncommon – so that I would be at the front of the queue when the delivery van arrived and the newsagent received the bundle of papers. On occasion, of course, the van was late – half past six, quarter to seven – and I would be left to wait even longer at the entrance to the shop, breathing in the cold air and stamping my feet with impatience.

In the 1961–62 season, the league table was always shown with a line drawn under the 16th club, as this was to be the cut off point for allocating the clubs to the following season's two divisions. For most of the season, Hunslet were well below the line, hovering somewhere in the middle of the lower section. Dad showed me what the columns in the Green Post's table meant – played, won, drawn, lost (there were no columns for points for and against) – and how this decided the number of points in the final column. I would pore over the table, checking which teams were at the top and bottom, where Hunslet were, where our next opponents were, which teams were on the same number of points, what would happen if we won our game in hand, where Hunslet would have been if we had won a couple of narrowly lost games (and remembering to deduct the points that those opponents had obtained). And, not least, I would be looking at the names of the other clubs and wondering where exactly these places were: would I ever go to Hull Kingston Rovers or Castleford or Batley or Workington Town? (For completeness, the tally currently stands at three out of four). I looked at the print on the page: the names and the numbers. It was like a Biblical text, to be studied in depth to reveal the ultimate truths.

After familiarising myself with the updated league table, I would revert back to the match reports. On most Saturdays, the Green Post's front page coverage would be of the Leeds United or Leeds RLFC matches, so that the report of Hunslet's encounter was usually to be found on the back page. My recollection is that it would be mainly a descriptive piece on the chronology of the game's main events with the scorers' names appearing in a prominent upper case typeface. If it had been a home fixture, that I had attended, I would cast my mind back to the action of earlier that afternoon. Was the account an accurate description of what I had seen? In due course, this process began to operate in reverse. I would observe a piece of action on the pitch at Parkside – a try, perhaps, or someone being sent from the field – and wonder how it would be written up in the chronicle that I would be poring over later that evening.

I also wondered how the Green Post could be produced so quickly after the completion of the Saturday afternoon's fixtures. I realised that the inside pages – containing review articles and special features, fixtures, and so on – would have been prepared in advance. But, even at an early age, I knew that the printing schedule for the front and back pages must have been tight: how could the report of a rugby match that finished at 4.30pm appear in a newspaper on sale at our local newsagents less than two hours later? After a while, I noticed that the coverage of the second half of matches was less extensive than the first half: in some cases, for the latter parts of matches, only the scorers and the final result would be given. And those football league games that kicked off at 3.15pm – why were they allowed to be different? – only had their final scores recorded in a hurried typeface in the Stop Press column.

I stored the Green Posts away at the bottom of the wardrobe in my bedroom for the purpose of further research on other days. Later, when the stock of newspapers was threatening to completely crowd out the space allocated for clothing, my mother insisted that they were transferred to the storage area at the side of the house in which we kept the gardening equipment. Needless to say, the combination of neglect and damp took their remorseless toll and, years later, when it came to clearing out the "side", the newspapers did not survive the purge. But, during that critical period of learning for the Awestruck Novice, the Green Posts had fulfilled their central role. I look back on them with affection.

The exception to my lack of concern about Hunslet's results occurred late in the season – on the last Saturday in March – when, in the normal way, Dad and I were watching the early evening television for news of the rugby scores. Our interest was focused on the reverse fixture to the one with which I had been initiated at Parkside the previous August. The result duly came through: Whitehaven 61 Hunslet 0.

I can vividly remember bursting into tears. Why, I am not sure. I don't think it was the humiliation imposed on my team. Or on dad's team. And, make no mistake, it was a humiliation – 61 points is a huge score in the modern game, but it was gargantuan in those days. I think it was the shock. How could it happen? How could a Hunslet team, with the players I had now seen perform several times, be beaten by such a score? My father, who I suspect was equally shocked, nonetheless seemed to take the result in his stride. He sat in his armchair, looking at the score on the television screen, and pursed his lips. "Something funny's happened there". After all these years, I can still remember him saying these words and shaking his head slowly.

The following Monday's short match report in the *Yorkshire Evening Post* noted the absence of some players through injury and illness and referred to a "lack of reserve strength and obvious weaknesses forward", though this did not really explain the huge margin of defeat. By then, however, I suspect that my attention had been diverted to the headline of the lead story on the newspaper's front page, as the now seven year-old boy tried to make sense of the unforgiving harshness of the wider world around him: "No Reprieve for James Hanratty". Hanratty was hanged for the A6 murder two days later.

Although he did not say so at the time, I think my father was pleased that his young companion had taken up this interest in watching rugby. He did tell me later that he had had no intention of forcing me to attend if I had not been interested. But he had been pushing at an open door. Likewise with the playing. Although it would be another three years or so before I played in an organised rugby match, Dad put me through a weekly practice of some of the basic skills on a Sunday morning at the Soldiers' Field in Roundhay Park. I was a more than willing pupil, duly attired in a proper rugby kit, including boots. The only obstacle to this routine was my obligation to attend one of the church services at St Matthew's, Chapel Allerton, thereby qualifying for that week's entry in my stamp book of church attendance and maintaining my eligibility, on the basis of an unblemished record, for a prize at the school's awards ceremony at the end of the year. A lengthy sermon from the vicar would merely add to the frustration of the delay to my training session. I think that I realised, even at that age, that the acquisition of the stamp was an act of some hypocrisy. I wanted to be practising my passing and kicking and, in the style of Billy Langton, perfecting my technique of catching the high ball.

An unexpected test came one particular Sunday, when I was practising diving over the line to score a try. It was not a difficult task: no-one was chasing or tackling me. Perhaps over-confidence was my undoing, as I completely mis-timed the manoeuvre and landed flat out with my stomach on the ball. It must have been the equivalent of being punched in the solar plexus. I lay on the ground, completely winded, wheezing desperately and, after the initial shock, with tears rolling down my face. My father came over slowly and asked me if I wanted to go home. I considered his offer for a few seconds and then replied that I wished to continue. Dad said ok and made me perform another dive, this time correctly.

The full significance of my decision was revealed some years later, when Dad told me that, had I opted to give up for the day, he would never have taken me to Roundhay Park again. This was not an idle remark: he meant it. I can only speculate on what the broader consequences might have been, but it is not at all certain that, without a continued interest in acquiring the basic skills needed to play rugby, the spectating interest would also have been maintained. My guess is that it probably would have been, though not to the same extent or with anything like the same commitment.

From what I have been able to gather, my father's own playing exploits had been relatively modest. He had played rugby (league) at school before leaving at 14 to go to technical college and, later, enter the seven-year apprenticeship that was required to become a qualified joiner. During the war, in the RAF, he had played a limited amount of rugby union. But that was about all. An obvious question, therefore, is whether he was looking to transpose a father's frustrated playing ambitions on to his son, so that he could bathe in any reflected glory that might accrue. I am quite clear that this was not the case. Had my reactions to either of my early experiences of spectating (at the Hunslet versus Whitehaven game) or playing (on that Sunday morning in Roundhay Park) been unfavourable, that would have been the end of the affair.

My father was also to tell me, though again this was much later, of his own experiences as a boy at Parkside. He had first gone there – aged 10 or 11

– with his maternal grandfather, a Scotsman called Peter McBride, and his uncle Willy McBride. Dad's father had rarely attended, as his duties as a policeman meant that he had to work on most Saturdays. It was Willy who was the keen Hunslet supporter, and the family group used to stand near the fencing at the corner between the main stand and the Mother Benson's end of the ground. After a while, Dad used to go to the matches with his pals – 7 or 8 in number – walking down from Beeston to the Parkside ground on a Saturday afternoon.

It would have been at about this time that Hunslet enjoyed one of their two great triumphs of the 1930s. Dad was 13 years old when the club won the Challenge Cup, beating Widnes at Wembley in 1934. The victory clearly left an impression on my father: he could recite the complete Hunslet team well into his old age. Four years later, Dad attended the famous match at Elland Road, when Hunslet defeated Leeds by 8 points to 2 in the Championship final. In later years, I was to lose count of the number of times he would to take the opportunity to describe how Leeds's most dangerous player – the powerful Australian stand-off Vic Hey – was tackled out of the match by his opposite number, the diminutive and brilliant Oliver Morris.[6] Dad would also recount the fate of these and other players, including his hero, the captain Jack Walkington, who returned after the Second World War to lead the club again, and the aforementioned Morris, who was killed in action in Italy in 1944.

The Hunslet rugby league club has always had a strong attachment to its local community. In the 1930s, this was particularly the case, as it also had been at Widnes, their opponents in the 1934 Wembley final. In *The Uses of Literacy*, Richard Hoggart recalled "the Hunslet rugby team bringing the Cup home from Wembley... coming down from the City Station into the heart of the district on top of a charabanc. They went from pub to pub in all the neighbourhood's main streets, with free drinks at every point". In the late 1950s, when his book was first published, Hoggart noted that in working class areas, "where rugby league is played, the home team is also an important element in the group life of the district. They are spoken of with genuine pride as 'our lads'". Cec Thompson, recalling the same period in *Born on the Wrong Side*, noted that, against the poverty and lack of opportunity, "the rugby club was Hunslet's proudest claim to fame".

On occasions, the linkages between rugby club and the local community could be quite imaginative, if not bizarre. Dad recounted the time when, in the 1930s, Hunslet sent out an appeal around the local schools for jam jars. At Far Beeston Council School, which Dad attended, the shed at the caretaker's house was duly filled to the brim with jam jars that were subsequently sold to raise money for the club. All the other local schools followed suit in aid of the club's finances. It was with a sense of pride, rather than embarrassment, that Dad recalled that the Leeds supporters referred to their local rivals as the "Jam Jar Team" for a long time afterwards.

From my earliest visits to Parkside, therefore, I had a sense of Hunslet's history, and of my father's long engagement with the club. The pinnacle of achievement had been long before Dad had been born. In the 1907–08 season, inspired by the captain Albert Goldthorpe, one of five brothers to play for the team over the period between 1885 and 1910, and with a pack of forwards known as the "Terrible Six", Hunslet won all four of the trophies at stake – Yorkshire Cup, Yorkshire League Trophy, Championship Trophy and Challenge Cup – the first time that this feat had been achieved.[7] The record-breaking season had culminated with wins over Hull in the Northern Union Challenge Cup Final by 14 points to 0 and over Oldham in the replay of the Northern Union League Championship Final by 12 points to 2.[8]

This was the club which my father had supported since he was a boy. This was the pitch on which earlier and greater Hunslet teams had played. This was the proud history of local heroes. And now I was part of it.

For my second season of spectating, Hunslet were in the lower of the two divisions of the Northern Rugby League. However, the early part of the season was marked, as it always was, by the Yorkshire Cup. As its name suggests, this trophy was competed for, with a neat arithmetic symmetry, by the 16 professional clubs on the eastern side of the Pennines – first and second division combined – on a knock-out basis.

To win the Yorkshire Cup, therefore, victory was needed in four matches: first round, second round, semi final, final. This feat had eluded Hunslet since the start of the four-trophy 1907–08 season: that is to say, for 55 years. The club had been runners-up a few times over this period – 5 to be precise, including in one of the emergency competitions during the Second World War – but actually winning the cup had proved to be a step too far, even for the powerful side of the 1930s. Meanwhile, no fewer than 11 other sides had won the Yorkshire Cup in the intervening half century, including Huddersfield 12 times and Leeds and Wakefield Trinity each on 8 occasions.

In the first round, in September 1962, Hunslet were drawn against Wakefield Trinity at Parkside. For me, at that time, the most glamorous teams in the league were Wigan, with their international right centre and wing pairing of Eric Ashton and Billy Boston, and Wakefield. The latter had won the Challenge Cup at Wembley in two of the last three seasons (and would go on to win it again in the current season, when Wigan were comprehensively defeated). The Wakefield champion was the massive goal kicking centre, Neil Fox, a member of a famous rugby league family, but they had a formidable presence throughout the side. The forward pack had a number of seasoned internationals, including Jack Wilkinson, Don Vines and Derek Turner, whilst the Wakefield three-quarter line of that time was populated by a number of dynamic South Africans. The names Skene, Prinsloo and Coetzer jumped off the pages of the weekly match reports given in the *Rugby Leaguer*.

In the event, Hunslet won comfortably – 34–9. Indeed, by the time the season was a month old, Hunslet were in the Yorkshire Cup semi final. I remember being excited about reaching this particular stage, but not at all hopeful, given that the opponents, Halifax, were another first division side and the tie was away from home. It was also a midweek fixture which, in the absence of the plethora of sports news bulletins which we now take for granted on radio and television or on the internet, meant having to wait until the following evening, when Dad brought home his morning paper, to find out the score.

Or so I thought. I can distinctly recall being in the kitchen of our house in Moortown on the morning after the game, just about to set off on the walk to school, when my mother mentioned the match. Dad had already left for work by this time. For some reason, I asked if she knew the score. To my surprise, she said that it had been a very close match and that Halifax had been winning 6–5 with a few minutes to go. I remember pulling an anguished face – after all these years, I can feel myself doing it – in anticipation of the news of a narrow defeat. Then Mum said that someone called Jeff Stevenson had dropped a goal and Hunslet had won 7–6.

Looking back, I know that my mother would have fully anticipated the excited response that her news would elicit. Nonetheless, she was probably more than slightly surprised when I proceeded to tell her all about Jeff Stevenson: a small, wiry scrum-half, then in the veteran stage, who had recently been signed by Hunslet, having been a well known player for Leeds, York and Great Britain. I was familiar with the career histories of all the Hunslet players and, accordingly, I informed Mum that Stevenson had done this before. In the Challenge Cup semi final of 1957, his injury time drop goal had taken Leeds to Wembley at the expense of Whitehaven. The words gushed out in the wild euphoria that filled the kitchen. I also gave Mum a short lecture on the value of the drop goal, worth two points, and how it was a crafty way of scoring when time was running short and the way to the try line was blocked. My mother took all this calmly in her stride. She was not an expert on rugby, but she fully understood the implications of this particular result and she knew what my reaction would be. I suspect that she might also have been tipped off by my father.

With hindsight, I do not think it an exaggeration to interpret my mother's provision of the news of Jeff Stevenson's winning drop goal and of my reaction to it, as relayed to each other in the kitchen on that particular morning, as a defining moment in my relationship with her during my playing and spectating career. She had recognised at an early stage that sport – rugby and cricket, in particular – would provide me with a great deal of enjoyment and, throughout her life, she was never other than wholly supportive of those interests and passions. I should emphasise that, in this context, "supportive" is not a word used lightly. It means providing encouragement or sympathy or showing interest or curiosity, as exactly required according to the circumstances of the moment. That is not to say that my mother did not have her own views on sport and its participants. Over the years, she would offer apparently random (and well informed) observations on various sporting matters – the skill of the French rugby union back division, the dourness of England's batting, the overpaid *prima donnas* on the football field – with which it was usually difficult to disagree.

Within the family arrangements, the division of responsibilities between my parents had been established and agreed, though probably also unspoken. My father provided the physical lead. He earned the family wage through his sheer hard work and long hours. He was the one who re-landscaped the lower part of the back garden or painted the window frames or, using tradesman's skills that I never came anywhere near to replicating, constructed a new coffee table for the living room. He also ran the family transport: the firm's small green van to start with, later to be followed by the luxury of a Singer Chamois (which Dad always made sure was not mistaken for its near neighbour, the Hillman Imp). The van rattled up the miles: in and around Leeds during the week, as Dad went about his work, and to Soldiers' Field in Roundhay Park on a Sunday morning, where, depending on the season, I would receive the latest instruction in improving my drop-kicking technique or playing with a straighter bat on my forward defensive. For the car, when it arrived, the major annual expedition would be for our summer holiday at the seaside, almost always for the week before the new school term started in September – Filey or Bridlington on the Yorkshire coast, Morecambe or St Annes on the west – in the preparation for which Dad would spend long hours on the previous Friday evening. The car would be washed and polished, the tyres and oil checked, the petrol topped up, as if we were about to engage in a long haul endurance operation. Which we were, of course: the tortuous pre-motorway route through York and Malton in one direction or Clitheroe and Preston in the other was not to be undertaken lightly.

In the meantime, my mother ran the household. She handled the family finances and made sure the pantry was adequately stocked and, when the need arose and a home visit was not possible, shepherded us over the two bus journeys that were necessary to reach the practice of our family doctor, Dr Silversides. In common with millions of her counterparts before and since, my mother saw to it that the rest of the family set off fully prepared for the events of the day. She was the one who rose in the cold darkness of a winter's morning to light the coal fire in the living room before preparing my dad's sandwiches and arranging my school uniform and sending me on my way with a bowl of cereal or porridge and a final run through of that day's spelling test.

My mother was not a Leeds girl: still less did she have any connection to Hunslet. She had been born in north London in 1922 and had moved up to Leeds when her father had obtained a post as a teacher of modern languages in the city. Although she had been christened Enid Peggie, she detested her first name and used the latter name throughout her life. Her father, Alfred Edgar Niblett – my grandfather – had been born in Osnabruck, Germany, in 1888, one of the ten children of an Englishman from Cheltenham, Charles James Niblett – variously described in the official records as a merchant or business schoolteacher – and his German wife (from Hannover). Critically, my grandfather had left it too late to travel to Britain before the start of the First World War and had been interned for the duration of the conflict.

Not that I knew any of this when I was seven years old, of course. I only learned the (incomplete) details of my grandfather's early life many years later from the small collection of his personal documents that eventually came into my possession. These include two editions of the *Ruhleben Camp Magazine* – dated Christmas 1916 and June 1917 – each of which runs to 60–70 pages of neatly printed articles and sketches, and which are now amongst my most prized possessions[9]. My grandfather's passport for 1935–40 includes the stamped permissions to visit Germany in 1935 and 1937, the print of which – notably of the swastika-bearing eagles – remains remarkably distinct to this day. These visits were to see his ailing mother, who died in Osnabruck in 1938. It was also only many years later, after I had arrogantly deluded myself that I had been the first member of my family to win a place at university, that I obtained a copy of the first part of the dissertation – *Grammatik der Osnabruckischen Mundart (The Grammar of the Osnabruck Dialect)* – that my grandfather had submitted in 1913, in German of course, for his doctorate from the University of Munich. He had previously graduated from the University of Birmingham in 1911. For these particular qualifications – Bachelor's Degree and Ph.D. – he only beat me to the punch by the best part of three-quarters of a century.

Some things I did know at the age of seven, however. I knew that my mother had a deep bond with her parents, whose home was only half a mile or so away in Moortown. Our regular Sunday visits would be signalled, from around this time, by my receiving the latest edition of *Look and Learn*, a task that I undertook with due gratitude and carefully disguised indifference. My maternal grandparents contributed to the family creed of good manners and correct behaviour and doing the right thing. This was supplemented, most obviously by my grandfather, by a belief in hard work at school and a painstaking attention to detail. For me, even at that age, all this seemed to fit together with the values and messages to which I was being exposed from my father's side of the family. I lapped it all up and was perfectly content.

The Yorkshire Cup final of 1962 was played between Hunslet and Hull Kingston Rovers at the neutral venue of Headingley. I thought at the time that Hunslet had done well out of the choice of venue, as Headingley was in Leeds and, therefore, fairly local. But I wasn't complaining. Besides, Hull KR were another first division side and the clear favourites. To give the game added spice, the Hull KR captain was a former Hunslet player, Harry Poole.

Dad and I went to the match with my uncles Bob Rigg (dad's older brother) and Vic Hough (dad's brother-in-law). This was the first time that other people had come to a game with us and, notwithstanding their familiarity as close family members, the feeling I had was of my uncles encroaching on to our territory. Watching Hunslet was our domain: it belonged to Dad and me, not to casual interlopers who only came along for the special occasion. This was grossly unfair, of course. In retrospect, it was clear that my uncle Bob, in particular, took great pleasure in sharing his nephew's excitement of the big day. But, for the moment, I held to my selfish view – a perspective that was to gain currency on a later occasion.

As we approached the Headingley ground, I stayed close to my father and uncles for safety. This was by far the largest crowd I had ever been part of – the records show nearly 23,000 – and Headingley was unfamiliar territory. We had seats on the right hand side of the North Stand, around the 25-yard line. The seating itself was entered from the back of the stand, which looks out across the cricket ground. I remember thinking how expansive the cricket facilities were – stretching across to the poplar trees at the far end of the ground – and how strange it was that the tarmacadamed cycle track around the boundary of the cricket pitch was used as a car park. Vic, who was a keen Leeds supporter, told me that he never parked there, because there was only room for two vehicles to be parked abreast and, if the drivers of the vehicles in front of you went for a drink after the match, you could be in for a long wait. He also patiently explained that the cycle track was only used as a car park for the rugby fixtures. This was in response to my puzzled query about the risks of the vehicles being hit by a cricket ball.

I do not recall being in any doubt that Hunslet would win the match. The team had already improved on the previous season's, as the core of the side not only became more experienced but was supplemented by one or two old hands such as Stevenson and the captain, Fred Ward. Dad took to Ward straightaway: a tough loose forward with good handling skills, and a born leader. A favourite Hunslet move near the opponents' try line would be when Ward took the ball as first or second receiver from the play-the-ball and, turning his back on the opposition to shield the ball, had the choice of passing to two or three oncoming runners. Dad knew – as Ward no doubt also did – that on most occasions, for his troubles, he would be subjected to severe assault on his back or shoulders either during or after his transfer of the ball.

In the event, Hunslet scored two tries, one of which was by the ever-improving Shelton, and Hull KR were squeezed out of the game. However, the *coup de grace* was little less than extraordinary. Towards the end of the game, the big prop forward, Dennis Hartley, received the ball in front of the Hull KR posts about twenty yards out – more or less in line with our seats – and swung his leg back to send a drop goal skimming over the bar. My recollection is that, at no point in its trajectory, was the ball higher than a couple of feet above the level of the bar. The crowd – including our party of four – was initially open-mouthed with communal astonishment until it realised the full consequence of what had happened. The sizeable Hunslet support was ecstatic. Dad, ever the technical purist, did wonder discreetly at the time – and, on occasion, for years afterwards – whether it had been a genuine drop kick rather than a punt, but the end result is firmly placed in the record books: two points towards Hunslet's winning score of 12–2.[10]

The 55 year hoodoo had been broken. The Yorkshire Cup had been won. Hunslet were my team, and they had just won a major trophy. I thought it was the most natural occurrence in the world.

There was further success later in the season. Hunslet lost only 4 matches in their schedule of second division fixtures and won the league by two points from their nearest rivals, Keighley. The decisive fixture was at Parkside, when Hunslet won 10–9. I recall two features of this game. The first was when a high, hanging drop goal attempt by a Hunslet player (not Dennis Hartley) was signalled by the Keighley full-back, the only player in the vicinity of the posts, as having fallen just short, the referee also being some distance from the ball. The full-back was crouching, staring at the cross-bar and waving his hands horizontally. The crowd near me jeered the action, implying that the player was not exactly a disinterested party, but I thought this reaction was unfair, even though I could not tell from my vantage point whether the kick had been good. Surely he was bound to be giving an honest opinion.

The second feature, which I thought strange at the time, was that the other Hunslet prop forward, Kenny Eyre, was playing against his own brother, Albert. I couldn't understand why, if they were brothers, they would not be playing for the same side. It became even more mystifying when I realised that neither was holding back in the ferocity of his contacts with the other. I was aware that these were professional players, of course – I knew they were playing for money, and they got more money if they won than if they lost – but I had yet to recognise what this meant in terms of the dispassionate setting aside of family ties.

One other match comes to mind during the later part of this triumphant season. In March 1963, Hunslet played host to Blackpool Borough: a reasonable side, later to finish fourth in the league. My recollection is not so much that Hunslet won comfortably – though I think they did – but that the elderly, frail-looking figure on the Blackpool right wing received very few passes. When he did get hold of the ball, he was either easily swamped by the Hunslet defence or crowded out into touch, on one occasion in front of us to the mocking cheers of the home support. However, I noticed that my father, whilst naturally content at his team's supremacy, did not share in the disrespect shown to this particular opponent. The winger was Brian Bevan, in the respected opinion of some – the distinguished actor and writer Colin Welland being one – the greatest winger ever to play the game.

Bevan had always looked elderly and frail – even in the sprightliness of his youth – but his speed and agility and devastating sidestep and swerve made him the most prolific try scorer in rugby history. He scored 740 tries for Warrington between 1945–62, before joining Blackpool for the last two seasons of his career. The 17 tries he managed in that period, plus the other 39 he scored in various representative matches, yielded a grand total of 796. In *Play to Win: Rugby League Heroes*, Maurice Bamford describes Bevan vividly: "He looked elderly, like someone's dad playing in a charity dads versus lads game – until he got the ball, then everyone had to look out". (For a tantalising illustration of Bevan in action, it is worth seeking out *Going for the Line: The Official Centenary Video – A Century of Rugby League*, which contains a short clip of him running the ball out from behind his try line in what looks to be the drawn Wembley Challenge Cup Final of 1954 between Warrington and Halifax. It is only a very brief excerpt, but it is a clear demonstration of Bevan's elusiveness and balance).

Dad knew better than to mock this great player. And so did I. By now, I had more than a passing familiarity with the major rugby league records. I shared my dad's pleasure at the Hunslet victory, of course. But I spent a large proportion of the match looking at the lonely figure on the Blackpool wing and making a mental note that I was watching the one and only Brian Bevan.

I do not recall the specific occasion when my father successfully persuaded me that I had outgrown the need to sit on his shoulders at the back of the stand. I should think it would have been before the 1963–64 season, when I was approaching nine years of age. I was not a heavy boy for my age, but there are limits. I was then confronted with a choice: to remain with Dad at the back of the stand and take a chance that my view of the pitch would not be obscured by the nearby spectators; or to walk down the terrace to stand at the front, behind the white fencing next to the touchline. The latter option was not without its advantages: for one thing, I was closer to the action and, when the play was directly in front of me, I could clearly see the various expressions – of pain, anguish, disappointment, anger – on the faces of the combatants. On the other hand, I lost most of the three dimensional perspective that the vantage point at the back of the stand provided: for example, in the particular way that a pass from Fred Ward or Dennis Hartley would open up a gap in the opposition's defence for Brian Gabbitas or Geoff Shelton to run through. In the main, however, I had little choice. Hunslet were in the first division, winning matches, and supported by a larger crowd than two years earlier. If I wanted to see anything of the games, the front of the stand it had to be.

The groundwork had been established for a successful year in the higher league. Hunslet finished in 11th place in the 16 team league and safely avoided relegation. As it happened, the sides finishing at the bottom of the division also avoided relegation, as the rugby league authorities decided, half way through what they had intended to be a four year experiment, to revert back to the single division for the following season. Hunslet also ran the touring Australian side close – albeit against the mid-week team – only losing by 13–17. This was not a match attended by me, my parents adamantly and unequivocally quashing any suggestion that I should be allowed to take an afternoon off school to watch the game.

Several other matches from this season flash back through the years. One was Hunslet's victory at Headingley against Leeds in September 1963. I recall being impressed by the striking colours of the Leeds shirts – blue and amber – and the presence of the bald player in the Leeds back division. This was Lewis Jones, one of the most talented Welsh rugby players of the post-war era and the holder of the most points scored in a rugby league season: 496 in 1956–57, according to my *Rothmans Rugby League Yearbook*. (Before checking this figure, I had a recollection of Jones's record being 505 points. Perhaps, like the height of Mount Everest, these measures are revised with the use of more accurate recording equipment). I do remember that Jones did not have the most comfortable of matches – this was his last season before emigrating to play and coach in Australia – and that some of the home supporters, with their short memories, were not forgiving of his mistakes. But my perspective was exactly the same as the one I had adopted for Brian Bevan at the end of the previous season: this was a famous player and I was seeing him in the flesh.[11]

Hunslet's success was frustratingly curtailed in the Challenge Cup, which was played, as usual, in the spring. In the previous season, the side had lost narrowly away at Warrington in the third round – one step from the semi final. This time, as an echo of the Yorkshire Cup confrontations in successive seasons, their path seemed immediately blocked by Wakefield Trinity, the holders, with whom Hunslet were paired at Parkside in the first round. This match was drawn, but Hunslet prevailed in the replay, thanks to a try by Geoff Gunney, who was later pictured in one of the newspapers stretching out from the tackle with his long arm and placing the ball on the try line. The next round saw a comfortable win away at Batley's Mount Pleasant ground, a match I watched, in the now familiar way, from the touchline with my father and my uncles standing further back on the terrace.

For the third round, Hunslet were drawn at home, this time to Oldham. It was a game I was confident we could, and would, win. The form at Parkside in the league had been good and a number of strong sides had succumbed there. But Oldham were a tough side, strong and niggly, their approach typified by the prop forward Peter Smethurst, a stocky man who, from memory, wore a distinctive headguard. The game turned into a long slog in the rain, wind and mud. Despite losing a man injured in the first half and playing most of the match with only 12 men, Oldham won narrowly, to the intense disappointment and irritation of the home supporters – including me – who chastised the referee for not intervening when Smethurst and his colleagues appeared regularly to be running offside or punching in the tackle or committing a myriad of other possible offences. My father saw the bigger picture, however. Smethurst was a splendid forward, committed and professional, and an abrasive leader from the front. Dad knew that he was a good player and that the stronger team had deservedly won.

The final match to recall here was played earlier in the season, again at Headingley, which I was growing to enjoy visiting for these big occasions. This was my first international match: Great Britain versus Australia in the third test. We again had seats in the main stand, this time on the left side, just inside the 25-yard line, close to the concrete ramp down which the players made their entrance on to the corner of the pitch. The coaching staffs walked down the touchline in front of us to reach their respective benches on the half way line.

In the jargon of modern parlance, there was a "context" to this match. For one thing, Great Britain had enjoyed a highly successful tour of Australia in the summer of 1962 when, if not for a touchline conversion in the last minute of the third test, they would have won the test series 3–0. I had read about this tour so often in my *Windsors Rugby League Annual 1962–63* (price two shillings and sixpence) that the pages had all come away from their binding. More relevantly, however, the Australians had already extracted revenge in the first two tests of the current tour, winning both games comfortably and scoring no fewer than 50 points in the second test at Swinton. This time, it was to be Great Britain's turn to attempt to avoid the whitewash.

Great Britain had made 10 changes from the side that had played in the second test, including dropping Neil Fox from the centre but introducing his brother Don Fox at loose forward. The game was one of unremitting ferocity, notwithstanding the stern discipline imposed by the referee, Eric Clay from Leeds, who sent off two Australians and the British prop, Cliff Watson. I remember sitting in the stand and being awed – and, it has to be said, somewhat frightened – by the violence of grown men. In amongst this, however, the finer points of the game continued to be revealed to me by my father and uncles. I have a clear recollection of Vic pointing out that, in broken play, when the Australian backs threw the ball across the line, their forwards stood behind them, out of the way. He was implying that this allocation of responsibilities had been carefully pre-determined and that any forward slowing the action down by being part of the movement would incur his coach's wrath.

The Australian backs had some talent, of course, one of the centres being the famous Reg Gasnier. I thought back to this match – and Vic's tactical tutoring – many years later, when I read the first volume of Clive James's autobiography, *Unreliable Memoirs*. James recounts, as a boy at Sydney Technical High School, being commandeered to provide practice opposition to Gasnier's first grade schoolboy rugby side. Gasnier was "the brightest schoolboy rugby prospect in years… He was all knees and elbows. His feet scythed outwards as he ran, like Boadicea's hub-caps… The way he shifted his weight in one direction while swerving in the other was a kind of poetry". James's account of his two brave attempts to tackle Gasnier provide a painful warning of the likely fate meted out to mere mortals by the rugby gods.

But, on that day at Headingley, Gasnier and his team did not prevail. The home side's tackling was more effective than Clive James's had been. Great Britain won 16–5 to avert the whitewash. The Australian frustration was demonstrated by one of their coaching staff who, walking back along the touchline to the exit from the field by the corner flag, threw the contents of a bucket of water over the celebrating spectators located in the section of the stand below us.

I should report here that it was not only through watching these matches that my enthusiasm for rugby was being satisfied. Although I had yet to play in an organised match – my debut, as a 10-year-old for Chapel Allerton Primary School against the Alwoodley Primary School "B" team, was not until the following season – I was already featuring in some important games. These took place in the small area running from the back door of my mother's kitchen through the connecting door and on towards the far wall of the compact living room of our house in Moortown. It was here that the various Hunslet matches would be re-played with me, of course, playing a prominent – or, more usually, dominant – role.

The games largely featured me kicking a small rugby ball up and down the available space and then, after picking the ball up, making a series of powerful runs through the two rooms. This was not without its hazards. In addition to the obvious dangers posed by whatever was boiling away at the top of the stove in the kitchen, it was in the corner of the living room that the large black-and-white television was kept. On the other hand, I was aided by two fortunate features of my parents' choice of interior design. First, the pattern on the large rug in the living room took the form of a series of rectangles: ideal for use as the touchline or try line, depending on where on the field of play a particular action was taking place. Second, the living room armchair had two firm wooden armrests and therefore, for the imaginative eight-year-old, it was a more than adequate replication of a set of goal posts.

When the weather was warmer, my parents usually joined forces to persuade me to play these games in the back garden. This was a far larger area than that available indoors and, naturally, I tended to favour it for the bigger matches such as cup semi finals and finals and, following my deserved selection, for internationals. The lawn was on two tiers – the top lawn and the bottom lawn, logically enough – separated by a low stone wall and a raised flower bed. The large blooming flowers usually to be found in the middle of this bed naturally took on the armchair's role as the goal posts to be cleared with any penalty kicks, drop goals or conversions.

The nature of the games would be the same outside as they were indoors, with me either kicking the ball up and down the garden or making a series of devastating runs through the bewildered (albeit invisible) opposition. When Hunslet scored a try, I had responsibility for taking the conversion. This tended to be when the main problems arose. For one thing, my father was not particularly impressed by his son's re-enactment of Billy Langton's goal kicking technique, which started by using the heel of his boot to dig a big hole in the turf in which to place the ball. In addition, on the frequent occasions when I scuffed the kick, the ball would usually career straight into the flower arrangement. I lost count of the number of times on which this happened when, after a delay of about a second and a half, there would be a furious wrapping on the kitchen window by my mother. It was not long before the anticipation of the rebuke was more painful than the rebuke itself.

This was a formidable Hunslet side. When all the players were fit, it was the same as the real team, with the exception of me being in the left centre position instead of the unfortunate Alan Preece: I saw myself as a cross between the stylish Geoff Shelton and the powerful Neil Fox. As the side rampaged through the season, I kept the scores in a series of exercise books, together with the names of the scorers and the weekly updates of the league tables. A glossy covered Cathedral exercise book (price one shilling and threepence), which I still have, records the first part of the season, including Hunslet's 46–3 victory over Leeds en route to winning the Yorkshire Cup. What I didn't realise at the time, though I was grateful for it subsequently, was that working out the league tables, including the columns of points scored for and against, represented a significant extension of my maths schoolwork. In subsequent years, both in school and afterwards, I was always comfortable with mental arithmetic and, although the direction of causality is not clear – did working out the league tables assist my maths, or was I good at maths and could therefore work out the tables? – my consistent and relaxed exposure to these important numbers obviously did me no harm.

The formal encroachment of my rugby interests into schoolwork took the form of the "project" which we were obliged to hand in at the end of one of the terms during my second year at primary school. Mine – no surprise – was on "Rugby League". Needless to say, I still have the document. It began: "Rugby League is a sport. It is a tough game. The ground is about 80 yards by 100 yards". I then proceeded to list various cup winners, league champions, names of the grounds, positions on the field and international match results and included a series of "action shots" culled from the *Yorkshire Evening Post* or the *Rugby Leaguer*. In a section entitled "The season of some Yorkshire clubs", I reported that: "The Hunslet team had quite a successful season. Towards the end of the season they had a lot of injuries. They reached the third round of the cup". That there is no record of the project being marked by my teacher does not surprise me. It is consistent with my recollection of the formidable Mrs Jowett – who was more used to projects on favourite birds or the discovery of America – being thoroughly bewildered by this particular submission.

For the record, my exploits in the back garden were not quite reproduced when I eventually took the field, playing at centre three-quarter, in my first real match for Chapel Allerton Primary School. We were beaten by Alwoodley Primary School "B" and I got punched on the nose for my trouble. However, in the review of schools' matches in the Green Post, I was reported as having provided "sound support" for our full back and captain, Martin Gray. My father proudly cut the paragraph out to show my uncles and then to store away somewhere safe.

Chapter 2

Wembley Stadium

For 1963–64, the season after the (real) Yorkshire Cup and second division championship wins, Hunslet changed the front cover of their match day programme – *The Parksider*. The previous photograph of the diving Dennis Tate scoring a try in one of the corners of the Parkside ground was replaced by one of the team and the club officials, with skipper Fred Ward holding a ball and the two trophies being proudly displayed. The other half of the cover continued to be occupied by the regular advertisement for a local scrap metal dealer.

The format of the remainder of the programme's eight pages remained unchanged. Most of them were taken up with a display of advertisements for other local businesses, the variation in which served to anticipate Keith Waterhouse's later observations about the diverse nature of economic activity in the area: structural engineers, a service station, a newsagents and tobacconists, launderers and dry-cleaners and even "S. Wolfson: specialists in Scandinavian furniture". The afternoon's teams were listed on the centre pages of the programme. The "club notes" section summarised the latest news and, after welcoming the day's visitors, invariably ended by reporting that it would be a hard match for Hunslet to win and that they would have to be on top form. The programme was printed in black and white – basic and functional – and, although it was only later that I was able to compare it with those of other clubs, I sensed its deficiencies. The absence of a full fixture list struck me as a glaring omission. And the lack of the league table was clearly a major sin.

Eight of the day's fixtures were listed in a section called "half-time scores". These were allocated letters from A to H, of which the Hunslet match was always A, the Leeds game B and the Leeds United fixture H. The letters corresponded to their counterparts shown on the small Parkside scoreboard, which hung on the fencing in front of the stand on the far side of the ground. (I assumed there was a similar scoreboard in front of our stand for the benefit of spectators on the far touchline). The A score was kept up to date with the placing of the individual numbers on the appropriate hooks by a tall elderly man with white hair, who, whatever the weather, always seemed to be wearing a long black coat. At some time in the second half, he would also put up the half time scores in the other matches. Sometimes this would elicit a murmured response from one of the spectators near to me – "Wigan's beating Leeds" – at which point I would check through the programme's code to see what the other games were and who was winning. Often, however, I was so engrossed in the match in front of me that it would only be when I found myself in dad's van, heading home, that I realised that I had forgotten to check the other scores. This caused me little concern, however, as I knew I would be reading the final results in the Green Post before too long.

The steady improvement in the Hunslet team brought significant rewards in 1965. The Challenge Cup run brought three successive home ties, against Oldham, Batley and then Leeds. The first two sides were seen off efficiently, leaving the local rivals as the barrier to Hunslet securing a semi final place. The match was all-ticket and Dad duly secured three: for him, me and uncle Vic.

Then, disaster. Two days before the game, I was struck down with flu and Dr Silversides ruled me out of the match.

On the lunchtime of the game, my uncle Bob bade me a cheery farewell, as he, Dad and Vic set off for Parkside, thanking me for my generosity in relinquishing the ticket. He knew I was disappointed and he meant well; I'm not sure that I fully reciprocated his bonhomie. I was cheered up later – when Dad told me of Hunslet's narrow victory, and of how nervous he had been as the closing minutes ticked by – though by then my spirits had already been raised from another source. It was that afternoon, lying in bed, that I started to read A.A. Milne's *Winnie-the-Pooh*. I thought the early paragraph beginning: "Once upon a time, a very long time ago now, about last Friday, Winnie-the-Pooh lived in a forest..." was the funniest thing I had ever read.

The draw for the semi final was made in the local BBC television studio on the following Monday evening. Two clear favourites remained: Wakefield Trinity and Wigan. The other semi finalists, Swinton, were not as strong as they had been in the previous couple of seasons. When Hunslet were paired with Wakefield, the latter's coach – the former Hunslet player, Ken Traill – remarked that it was good that there would be a final between sides from Yorkshire and Lancashire. Dad thought he was being diplomatic: what Traill really meant was that he was glad the two major clubs had been kept apart and that Wakefield had been drawn against the weakest of the semi finalists.

The semi final was at Headingley. Dad and I attended with Bob and Vic, four adjacent seats having been purchased in the main stand at twelve shillings and sixpence each. It was a hard game – tough and defensive – and, with less than a quarter of an hour to go, the score was still 0–0. I clearly remember Bob asking Dad at about this time – "Are we going to the replay?" – and I can recall thinking that this was looking to be the likely outcome, especially as the sides had drawn in the first round of the previous year's competition.

Then Hunslet had possession in the Wakefield 25. If my recollection is correct, they attempted one of those moves I described earlier, in which Fred Ward received a pass, stood with his back to the opposition, and looked to offload to an oncoming player. However, the move did not work, and the ball was spilled to the ground. What followed is the first example of what I labelled in the Preface as a nano-drama. The ball had not been knocked forward and was therefore still in play, rolling along the ground. Then, as the Wakefield defence momentarily hesitated, the ball was scooped up by Alan Preece who promptly scuttled under the posts to score a try. It was a match-defining moment: if I close my eyes and think about that semi final, the image that automatically comes to mind is that of Preece leaning forward and gathering the ball and thrusting himself over the line. I was to learn much later – when I had observed other similar incidents – that it is often when a pass inadvertently hits the ground that defences can be unlocked. The tackling line is thrown off guard or loses concentration, and the breach is made. Looking back to the Preece incident, it is highly likely that, had the move gone according to plan, and Ward had found his intended recipient, the Wakefield defence would have dealt with this particular attacking threat.

I joined in the general celebration by the Hunslet supporters in the crowd. It was not the prettiest of tries. But it was a try. And it was under the posts, with a routine goal kick to come from the reliable Billy Langton. It wasn't until Wakefield had kicked off again, and the Headingley score board had resolutely remained at 3–0, rather than the 5–0 that we had casually anticipated, that we realised that Langton had somehow missed the conversion.

But Hunslet were on a roll. The powerful Welsh winger, John Griffiths, scored a second try in the corner and, although Langton missed the difficult touchline conversion, he subsequently – and perversely – did succeed with a massive penalty goal from the half-way line. The final score was 8–0: Hunslet were in the 1965 Challenge Cup final. The scorers had included Preece and Langton, whom I had seen in my very first match against Whitehaven at Parkside. I stood and cheered as the players celebrated their victory before leaving the pitch. As I did so, a middle-aged Wakefield supporter, making his disgruntled exit up the pathway next to our seats, announced loudly to all within earshot that Wigan would thrash Hunslet in the final. He looked bitter and resentful. A nearby Hunslet supporter – an older brother of my father, to be precise – helpfully reminded him what the score had been in the game we had just seen.

For dad, whose boyhood Hunslet team had won the Challenge Cup in 1934, when he was 13, there had been a wait of over 30 years before Wembley had been reached again. My perspective was different. I was ten years old and my team had reached the Challenge Cup final. As with the Yorkshire Cup victory two seasons earlier, it seemed the most natural thing to have occurred.

There was never any chance of my going to the final, of course. The Wembley trip would be for grown-ups only and, sure enough, it was my father and uncles who made the journey. I was more than slightly aggrieved that, notwithstanding my loyal support of Dad and his team for the best part of four seasons, I was being excluded from the party, but, deep down, I knew that this was not just another fixture. Bob drove them down to London from Leeds, the three of them watched the match and then went for a meal at the Talk of the Town in the West End, and then Bob drove them home again in the early hours of Sunday. Dad slept for most of that day and then went to work, as normal, on the Monday morning. As a memento of the trip, I received a full-length cowboy uniform although, if the truth be told (and it wasn't) I was more than satisfied with the match programme and the coloured rosettes of Hunslet and Wigan.

Hunslet went into the match with a somewhat dour reputation, built around their solid pack of forwards, now comprising the dynamic young second row forward Bill Ramsey – a Great Britain tourist to Australia the following year – as well as the experienced Ward and Gunney and the maturing Hartley and Eyre. The hooker was another experienced player, Bernard Prior, formerly of Leeds and also to be capped by Great Britain during the following season. It was expected that this juggernaut pack – weighing in at a combined 90 stone – would seek to play the tight, conservative game that was much easier to do in those days before the limited tackle rule was introduced. In the event, both sides threw the ball around in the forwards and backs. Hunslet scored tries through Geoff Shelton and John Griffiths, but were never in front on the scoreboard: Wigan won by 20 points to 16.

In the years that have followed, I have seen only the briefest of video clips from this match. Nonetheless, certain incidents come back to me down those years from the memory of watching the game with my mother on the television at my grandparents' house. One was Hunslet's improper kick-off right at the start, which led to them immediately going 0–2 down when the resultant penalty goal was kicked from the half-way line. Another was an incredibly brave tackle by Billy Langton, only yards from the Hunslet try line, on the formidable Wigan winger, Billy Boston, as he charged down the touchline. And another was John Griffiths's vain claim to have scored a try when bundled over the sideline in a blur of defenders and corner flag; there were no video referees in those days, of course, and the score was disallowed. Griffiths (and thousands of others, including my dad) protested for a long time afterwards that an injustice had been done.

The video clip to look out for is that of Geoff Shelton's try, just before half-time, which brought Hunslet back into the match at only 9–12 down at the interval. It is to be found on *Going for the Line: The Official Centenary Video – A Century of Rugby League*, and it is majestic. Shelton takes a short pass from Brian Gabbitas at full speed about 40 yards from the Wigan goalposts. After breaking the attempted tackle by the opposing centres, he runs at the full back, feints to sidestep to his left and then swerves to the right, before straightening up and winning the race to the try line. Shelton demonstrates the lethal combination of grace, power and speed that he consistently brought to his centre play and, even in the grainy black and white of the reproduced television coverage, there is a poetic beauty to this particular try.

In rugby league circles, both at the time and in the long years since then, the Hunslet versus Wigan Challenge Cup final of 1965 is generally acknowledged to have been one of the best ever played. In his *The Rugby League Game* – which I selected as a form prize after my first year at secondary school – Keith Macklin includes the match in his "Great Post-war Games" chapter: "a magnificently thrilling game... a match of fine football, great tries and thrilling near misses... the dramatic greatness of this game... tremendous end-to-end stuff... palpitating second half... a superb, exciting match, one which restored faith in rugby league as a fast, open game to be enjoyed by players and spectators alike...". Macklin was a highly respected writer on the sport, and not one given to exaggeration or hyperbole. Nearly 40 years later, in *Play to Win: Rugby League Heroes*, Maurice Bamford stated that the match "has gone down in history as the best under the old unlimited tackle rule".

This view of the 1965 final seems to have been an unchallenged conventional wisdom, usually bracketed with the exceptional Hull versus Wigan final of 1985. The only revisionist interpretation I have seen is that provided in Dave Hadfield's *Up and Over: A Trek Through Rugby League Land* by the broadcaster and former international Phil Clarke, whose own father played in the match and is reported as having thought it "slow and useless". This remains a distinctly minority view and perhaps serves as a useful warning that those caught up in the euphoria of the successful Super League of the modern era might be prone to underestimate the strengths of the game in previous times.

Elsewhere in his otherwise admirable book, Hadfield makes some rather patronising references to the Hunslet song – "We've Swept the Seas Before Boys" – claiming never having to have met anyone who knew the words or tune: "it could be an introspective dirge for all I know". Hadfield might well be correct in his assessment of modern day knowledge of the song, but I suspect that the explanation is generational. My father knew the words and tune and, at Wembley that day, so did thousands of others. When he related his experiences to me late on the Sunday afternoon, virtually the first thing he reported was how vast sections of the crowd had been singing the song. Dad had found this to be both thrilling and moving, and I shared in his excitement, although it was of no surprise to me at all that the song had featured so prominently.[12] [13]

In the period between 1964–66, six Hunslet players represented Great Britain in at least one international – all of the first team pack, except Fred Ward, plus the centre, Geoff Shelton. Three players appeared in one match at Wigan against New Zealand, and Shelton and Ramsey were selected for Britain's tour of Australia in 1966. From my biased perspective, this seemed to be perfectly legitimate: these were good players, and they deserved their chance along with the famous players from the other clubs. It was a feature of those days, of course, that the best players were more evenly spread around the clubs than they are in the modern game, when the cream of the talent gets hoovered up by the three or four biggest clubs. In that three year period, players from no fewer than 22 of the 30 professional rugby league clubs played in at least one of Great Britain's 14 international matches.

This period – and, specifically, the Challenge Cup final of 1965 – also represented the zenith of the Hunslet team's performance. The side did reach the Yorkshire Cup final again that autumn, but they were beaten by the rejuvenated Bradford Northern, a club that had been disbanded only two years earlier before enjoying a dramatic resurrection. This final was also included in Keith Macklin's list of "Great Post-war Games" in *The Rugby League Game*. I suspect, however, that this was not so much for the quality of the match itself than for the fact that Bradford, thanks to an ambitious acquisitions policy that had established a glamorous team supported in huge numbers, had triumphed in a major final so quickly after re-joining the ranks of the professional clubs. I went to the final, again with Dad and Bob, but I can remember very little about it.

I did note, however, that the cover design of the match programme – including the typeface and the inked drawing of a rugby player holding the ball and evading a couple of tacklers – was identical to that which had been used for the Hunslet versus Hull KR Yorkshire Cup final three years earlier: only the colouring was different. Closer examination of the inside of the programme revealed that the structure of its contents was almost identical as well, comprising a short editorial, pen pictures of the players, photographs of the teams and a summary of the results in that year's competition, in that order. Moreover, most of the advertisements were the same, including South Yorkshire Motors Ltd on the inside cover and Fielding Walsh (a turf accountant in Castleford) and Windsors Fixed Odds Betting on later pages. As best I could, for a ten year-old, I grappled with the moral uncertainties surrounding all this. From a practical point of view – that is, for the compiler of the programme – it was an easy option. It also assisted the sense of continuity in a tournament that had dated from 1905 (when the first winners of the trophy were Hunslet). On the other hand, the similarities in the programmes seemed to detract from the special occasion that each final represented in its own right.

In terms of the action on the pitch, what remains in the mind much more vividly is Hunslet's semi final game against Castleford at Parkside. The Castleford team included Roger Millward, one of the finest rugby league players of the post-war period. Millward had come to a modest fame in a series of televised junior rugby matches that the independent channel showed on a Sunday lunchtime during the previous season. Now, at 17 years of age, and at his full height of five feet three inches, he was in the Castleford first team.

My match day programme for the semi final brackets Millward with Alan Hardisty, a Great Britain international, at the stand off position. However, my memory is of him playing on the wing and being absolutely mesmeric. For this match, unusually, Dad and I stood in the covered stand behind the goalposts, and every time the ball was passed across the Castleford line in Millward's direction, the sizeable visitors' support in the 10,000 crowd roared with anticipation. Of course, for me – the ten year-old Hunslet supporter – Millward was an opposition player, and I wanted his team to lose. I willed the Hunslet defence to close in on him and eliminate the attacking threat. At the same time, I also knew the significance of what I was seeing. With his speed and agility and devastating changes of direction – and notwithstanding his diminutive frame – this was clearly an unusual talent, and it was rewarded on this particular evening with two tries, albeit in a losing cause.

It is over 40 years since I watched the Yorkshire Cup semi-final of 1965, but my recollection of the crowd's excitement at watching the young tyro on the Castleford wing – and, in particular, of the nerve-wracking sense of anticipation about what might shortly happen, as the ball got closer to him – remains absolutely fixed. To describe the moments as thrilling does them a considerable dis-service. Accordingly, the memory of the Castleford backs passing the ball towards Millward constitutes the second nano-drama to be highlighted in this volume. It sounds routine, of course: and, at one level, it was. This was a professional rugby league side transferring the ball across the pitch and, as it did so, being challenged by a resolute defence. I can only report that – as with Alan Preece's try at Headingley in the Challenge Cup semi final the previous May – this particular image can be conjured up in an instant. And when it is, there is an immediate frisson of excitement, as well as the painful pang of nostalgia.

My assessment of Millward was not a difficult one to make, even for a ten year-old. Within five years, he was the linchpin of the Great Britain side that won the 1970 test match series in Australia, the last British side (at the time of writing) to win the Ashes. The video records – for example, on the *Century of Rugby League*, another production to celebrate the 100th anniversary of the break from the union code – capture the two tries scored by Millward (by then of Hull Kingston Rovers) in the second test and his decisive try in the final test, both in Sydney. In the latter match, incidentally, Great Britain's first try was scored when their prop forward charged down an Australian kick near the half way line and, after gathering the bouncing ball at full speed, held off the defenders in his sprint to score near the posts. The forward, by then of Castleford, was Dennis Hartley, the error-prone Hunslet player of my first season, but, by this time, one of the world's best front row forwards.

I got to Wembley a year late. In common with several other local schools, Chapel Allerton Primary School ran a school trip to the Challenge Cup final every season for boys in their final year. On a Saturday morning in May 1966, my dad dropped me off at Leeds City Station, my bag laden with sandwiches and pop, to meet up with my friends and my teacher – Mr Somes – in time to catch the 7.00am train to Kings Cross.

The day flashed by: train journey, coach tour of London, walk to the stadium, match, coach back to the station, train home. I can remember several things. First, as I had been captain of the school rugby team, I was regarded by my friends as the resident expert on the game. Accordingly, I was asked which team – Wigan or St Helens – was going to win. Given that Wigan had been good enough to defeat Hunslet in the previous year's final – and that the bulk of that side remained – I confidently predicted that they would retain the trophy. But what did I know? The final score was St Helens 21 Wigan 2, at the time the second biggest winning margin since the Second World War. The credibility of the expert had disappeared long before St Helens had begun their lap of honour.

Second, I recall using up my spending money on the match memorabilia: a programme, naturally, and a series of Wigan rosettes. I bought four of these altogether, of which one made it successfully back home. I can vividly remember wearing another one on my school blazer as we walked into a throng of spectators near to the Twin Towers, and then coming out of the throng on the other side with it having disappeared; another was stolen from my table on the train coming home by someone walking down the aisle.

Third, the announcement of the teams to the crowd. Dad had always thought that one of the most dramatic aspects of any Challenge Cup final was the peeling off of the players, one by one, from the team line up that had been introduced to the dignitaries, as their names were announced over the Wembley stadium loudspeakers. I agreed with him entirely and, as I watched the Wigan and St Helens players go through this ceremony, I thought – just I had when watching Wigan and Hunslet on television the previous year – how thrilling it must have been for each of the players concerned. Whatever the confusion of the team battle that followed, this was his particular moment of recognition by the watching multitude. Years later, I read what it had actually been like on this very day. In *My Kind of Rugby: Union and League*, Ray French, who played in the second row for St Helens, recalled the moment: "'Watson, Sayer, Halsall, Warlow...' the voice boomed out with its southern accent, so foreign on the northerners' day out. 'French'. I was jolted into action and strode to our side of the pitch, impatient to get started". It was a fulfilling moment to read this passage in French's studious book and to recapture the excitement of this part of the pre-kick off ritual.

Next, the view of the match itself. Or the lack of it. The schoolboys were given the rows of wooden benches near a corner flag and at ground level. The lack of elevation meant that any perspective on the game was lost – and this to someone initiated in his rugby viewing from the lofty perch of his father's shoulders at the back of the Parkside stand. Worse still, a group of grown ups then came along to stand right in front of us. I can remember shouting at them to move. Surprisingly enough, they ignored the squeaky voice coming from behind them and, to be honest, I was rather glad at the time that they did not seek to find out whose voice it was. Ultimately, however, I don't think I was that concerned. I had got to Wembley, at least.

The Wembley bowl was huge, of course. By the time of the kick-off, the mass of spectators stretched out into the distance as far as I could see. This was by far the largest crowd I had ever been in[14] and I looked across the vast army with a combination of trepidation and excitement. The far side of the ground looked a long way away – it was a long way away – and it was difficult to take in the obvious point that the distant spectators were about to watch the same match as I was. I took comfort in that which was familiar to me: Mr Somes and my friends. At the same time, I thought of my father, who I knew would be watching the game at home on television (still in black and white). I also knew that I would have a story to tell him when I saw him again. Nonetheless, as the match kicked off, I missed my dad.

And finally, the train journey home. Here I must report a stroke of genius by Mr Somes, who was clearly drawing on his years of experience of this occasion and his proven methods for dealing with a group of tired and yet boisterous eleven year-old boys. Sitting in the carriage, four to a table, we were instructed to write an essay about our day out. The bulk of the return journey was passed this way. I managed three or four sides in the best handwriting that I could manage on the jolting train. There was a short description of the London sights, but most of my essay was on the match itself, reporting on St Helens's dominance, based on their overwhelming share of scrum possession, and offering the view that their goal-kicking winger, Len Killeen, would have been my choice to win the Lance Todd Trophy as man of the match. After reading each essay very carefully, Mr Somes then announced that I had won three shillings for writing the best one. I have to say that this was a prize worth winning – the equivalent of three weeks' pocket money – so I was suitably pleased.

When I got home, the day's entry into my Lett's Schoolboy's Diary took its usual parsimonious form: "Arose at 5.30. Went to Wembley to see St Helens 21 Wigan 2. Toured London. Smashing experience. Bed 12.05".

The following morning, I read about the Challenge Cup final in my dad's *Sunday Express*. It reported that Len Killeen had won the Lance Todd Trophy. In my mind, at least, credibility was restored.

Chapter 3

Headingley Cricket Ground

I was interested in cricket for some time before I attended my first live match. My earliest memory of the sport is, as a seven-year-old, in 1962. In retrospect, it was only natural that the previous winter's fascination with rugby should be followed by a keen interest in the principal summer sport and the fortunes of the local team: in this case, of course, Yorkshire County Cricket Club. At first, it seemed strange that my loyalties should have to be attached to such a broad an entity as a whole county, rather than a local institution such as given by a rugby club. In the rugby league world, of which I was a veteran of one season, county status was the intermediate step for a player on the representative journey from club to country. However, in terms of the organisation of English cricket, I quickly grasped the essential concept of the county championship. I knew what a county was. And, of course, I had already assimilated the view that, of all the counties in England, Yorkshire was both unique and pre-eminent.

My father carefully explained what the county championship scores in his *Daily Express* and *Yorkshire Evening Post* actually meant and, in particular, what was signified by the mysterious letters – "c", "st", "b" and "lbw" – that denoted the nature of each batsman's dismissal. He also decoded for me the analysis that accompanied each bowler's name in the more detailed reports: the sequence of four numbers that denoted the overs bowled, maiden overs, runs conceded and wickets taken. It was a set of magical secrets to which I was being given the answers.

As with the league tables that charted the progress of the rugby league teams during the season, I became absolutely captivated by the cricket scores in the newspaper. My grandfather's *Daily Mail* was my favourite source because, in a different and more easily read typeface than the *Daily Express*, it would summarise the state of play of each championship match in a small paragraph above the scores: "Lancashire, with 7 seven innings wickets intact, lead Northamptonshire by 235 runs..." I would pore over these details, working out where this 235 run lead had come from: had Lancashire added to a first innings lead, or had they overturned a first innings deficit? In the meantime, continuing the pattern of the winter, my mental arithmetic skills were receiving further polishing.

There was some cricket on television – the test matches on the BBC and the Roses matches on the independent channel – though, to start with, I did not pay these a great deal of attention. The test match visitors in that first season were Pakistan, who were beaten 4–0. I can recall thinking how easy it was for England against this weaker opposition. The overwhelming nature of England's superiority was exemplified in one Pakistani batsman's dismissal, when he slipped and fell over when setting off for a run and got run out by the length of the pitch. The photograph of this incident in one of the newspapers perfectly captured the tourists' woes.

It seemed to be the natural order of things that Yorkshire would win the county championship – the only competition in those days – which they did under the captaincy of Vic Wilson. I did not give this much thought either. It was analogous to the feeling I would have only a few weeks later when Hunslet won the Yorkshire Cup: they were my team, and it was logical that they would prevail.

Yorkshire's most famous player – and the one whom Dad mentioned most often – was Freddie Trueman, who by then had been with the county for 13 years and who was still a test match player. Indeed, the year before, Trueman had taken 11 wickets in the Headingley test match against Australia. My father was never one for remembering the detailed facts and figures for any sport in which he was interested, but he had the full knowledge of local folklore. Referring to the 1952 test match on the same ground, when Trueman had been responsible (with some assistance from Alec Bedser) for reducing the opening of the Indian second innings to no runs for four wickets, he shook his head ruefully and said: "They were backing away... they were frightened of him".

The other player who interested me at that early stage was Ken Taylor. Not only did he play cricket for Yorkshire – and, indeed, he also represented England three times – but in the winter he played football for Huddersfield Town. I thought this was amazing. What a way to earn a living: playing sport all the year round. This type of dual sporting activity was not uncommon in those days, of course. The next Yorkshire captain, Brian Close, had played for Arsenal, Leeds United and Bradford City in his younger days and I was to learn before too much longer that the Warwickshire cricketer (and later England captain) MJK Smith had also played rugby union for England. Moreover, these sorts of occurrences were to be found for several years afterwards. But I was impressed with Taylor. This was serious sporting excellence. It also provided reassuring confirmation that my own ambitions to represent my country at both rugby league and cricket – and at rugby union and association football as well, come to that – were not entirely out of the question.

As with the rugby league interest, I started to delve into the background of my newly found heroes. This principally took the form of reading – and re-reading, several times – various well-produced little booklets that seem to have been regularly published at around that time. I obtained – probably from my father – *The Lifebuoy book of the test series: England versus Australia 1962–63*, an informative booklet *A Century of Yorkshire County Cricket*, which was edited by the *Yorkshire Post*'s cricket correspondent JM Kilburn and sold for two shillings in 1963 and, later, *Yorkshire County Cricket Club: American Tour*. The last of these reported on the post-season tour to the United States, Canada and Bermuda made by a full-strength Yorkshire side in 1964. For the games in Bermuda, the team was supplemented by a certain Gary Sobers, who appeared as a guest player. I thought that this was a good arrangement and wondered how it might be extended for the domestic season without compromising the Yorkshire-born only policy which (at that time) everyone associated with the county held so dear. I devoured these publications over and over again.

In addition to the booklets, I obtained a magazine called *1964 Cricket Spotlight*, which appears to have been a one-off publication outlining the counties' prospects for the coming (1964) season and reviewing the close season results of various touring sides. The latter included a summary of the MCC (i.e. England) tour of India in early 1964, including the scorecards of the five test matches, all of which were drawn. I looked through the Indian bowling figures with incredulity, wondering whether some of the England innings reflected staggering feats of concentration or performances of unremitting boredom, or both. In the first innings of the first test match at Madras, the Indian spin bowler RG Nadkarni bowled 32 overs, including 21 consecutive maidens, and conceded 5 runs. In the same innings, CG Borde bowled 67 overs for 88 runs. And so on throughout the series. In the five matches, Nadkarni bowled 213 overs and took 9 wickets for 278 runs.

I read through the statistics for each game and my imagination ran riot: the hot climate, the "overprepared and doctored wickets" (according to the magazine's report) and the inexorably long feats of concentration shown by the likes of Ken Barrington and Colin Cowdrey. In particular, I was captivated by the names of the Indian players. Why was it, I wondered, that, whilst most had the usual designation of initials and surnames – VL

Manjrekar, BS Chandrasekhar – others had apparently more complicated names or even titles. The nine year-old boy had no knowledge of the religions or politics or classes of India, of course; he did observe, however, that, in the fourth test match at New Delhi, Hanumant Singh scored 105 and the Nawab of Pataudi made 203 not out. I also wondered about the exotic sounding venues in which the MCC played some of its other matches: Bangalore, Ahmedabad, Amritsar. And, not least, I noted that, although Freddie Trueman was absent from the tour, three other Yorkshire players did feature in the test series.

By the time that the West Indian tourists arrived in 1963, I had graduated to following the domestic test match cricket closely on the television. Most people who watched them will not forget the dramatic closing minutes of the 1963 Lord's test, when Colin Cowdrey came out to bat with his broken arm in plaster to save the match. The following year, the Australians won the series in England thanks to their victory in the Headingley test, although I felt hard-done at missing the decisive action. At the time of Peter Burge's match-winning innings of 160, I was dancing round the maypole at my primary school's annual summer fete. It was not really where I or, I suspect, Dad (or, probably, Mum as well) wanted to be. However, there was some consolation at the Oval test, the abiding memory of which is Freddie Trueman obtaining his 300th test match wicket, the first time that this landmark had been reached. My recollections of this event are as clear as day.

By this time, I had become firm friends with the boy whose family had recently moved into the house opposite us in Moortown. His name was Timothy Kell and he was older than me by five years. Tim had been born in Rhodesia and was an outstanding schoolboy cricketer, later playing for the Yorkshire Schools team (which, unlike the senior side, did not impose any restrictions on the place of birth). Outside our houses, there was a wide stretch of road at the junction of two streets: an almost ideal, if irregularly shaped, oval in which to play cricket. Tim measured out 22 paces from the cardboard box he placed as a wicket in front of my garden gate and found that they just stretched to the pavement on the other side of the road, leaving room for an angled run up to the bowler's end for his left-arm deliveries.

Tim and I played our own series of test matches – England (me) versus South Africa (him) – with either a tennis ball or one of those harder sponge balls that seemed to bounce harder and faster on pitching on the ground. This was in the days before the boycott of South African sport by the domestic authorities, of course, so there was no interference from the politicians. Not surprisingly, given our relative ages (and, more importantly, respective abilities), South Africa tended to win emphatically, despite the fact that my England team had a disproportionately high number of representatives from Yorkshire. It should be noted that these were probably constituted games: 11 players each side (with Tim and I playing the roles of all 11), 2 innings each, all dutifully recorded according to the proper conventions of the scoring of cricket matches. (Learning to score was thus a further part of my cricketing education at this time). We played for hours, at weekends and evenings during the school terms and then all day in the summer holidays. In retrospect, Tim was getting the equivalent of long net practice from a willing batsman and bowler. I was getting expert tuition to complement the practice that my father would give me on Sunday mornings on the Soldiers' Field playing fields at Roundhay Park.

There were a couple of drawbacks to the test match arena on which Tim and I played in front of our houses. The first was that, if a South African batsman played a drive through extra cover, the pronounced slope of that part of the junction would take the ball into the far distance down the adjoining road. Three or four such shots in an over would make for a series of long trudges, during the course of which I would curse to myself and plot my revenge, invariably to no avail. To make matters worse, being a left-handed batsman, this was Tim's favourite shot. In the event that he drove the ball slightly straighter, the ball would not go all the way down the road, but, instead, disappear down the sloping driveway of one of the neighbours' houses. This did not present any succour for the England fielders, however, as these neighbours had a pair of particularly intimidating Chihuahuas. Looking back, there is no doubt that my longstanding dislike of all things canine dates from that time, when any attempt to creep into the garden to retrieve the ball would almost immediately be met by manic barking and the viciously aggressive approach of the two small white dogs.

The Chihuahuas represented one handicap to the playing arrangements. However, even they paled into insignificance besides our attempts to deal with the repercussions of one of Tim's powerful drives through straight mid off. Another sloping driveway lay in wait for the ball, this time belonging to a retired couple, whom we safely assumed had originally come from Germany. After all these years, I cannot be certain of the old man's name, though Kreitzmann is the one that comes to mind. Although by this time already in his seventies, at least, Mr Kreitzmann retained a imposing physical presence to accompany his shock of full white hair and harsh middle-European accent. The passage of time has only confirmed that he was undoubtedly one of the most unpleasant men I have ever encountered. Notwithstanding that no damage was ever done by Tim or me to his precious garden, and irrespective of whether we asked permission or not, any trespass on to Mr Kreitzmann's property to retrieve the ball was inevitably met by a sustained tirade of abuse. On the rare occasions when he left his house to walk to the shops or go on some other errand, he would also let fly with an almost uncontrolled rant about what would happen if we ventured into his grounds. I thought at one time that he might have some sort of mental illness and, on that basis, I was prepared to shrug my shoulders and give him the benefit of the doubt. However, it soon occurred to us that Mr Kreitzmann did not vent his anger on anyone else – postman, milkman, insurance collector – who walked past his house or crossed his threshold. It was with considerable satisfaction, therefore, that I was present on the occasion when the dreadful man was put in his place by Tim's father, who happened to have seen one of these outbursts and decided that it was beyond the pale. With the passage of time, of course, it is possible to see Kreitzmann for what he clearly was: an unreconstructed bully.

I learned very quickly from all this. In particular, I learned that it was a risky strategy to bowl to Tim on an overpitched length on or outside off stump, as the wide range extending from extra cover (long trek down the hill) through wide mid off (the Chihuahuas) to straighter mid off (Mr Kreitzmann) presented a complete spectrum of unpleasant consequences. As a result, the England bowlers tended to pitch just short of a length on middle or middle-and-off stumps, or else they would dig one in a bit shorter, knowing that a successful square cut by the South Africa batsman would either see the ball register a boundary against Tim's garden wall or, if luck were with the bowler, be halted by the raised kerb stone at the edge of the pavement in front of the wall, thereby restricting the scoring shot to just a single.

Tim and I had an efficient system in place for when cricket was sharing the television coverage with other sports, usually horse racing. The coverage would alternate between the two at regular intervals. When the horse racing was on, we would play our test matches in the street. However, when the cricket came back on, my mother was deputed to tap loudly on the window of the front room, so that Tim and I could rush into our respective houses to watch the action on our televisions. When the horse racing started again, we would hurry back outside to resume our duel. In retrospect, it is strange that we did not both go into either one house or the other, but that was the way it was.

Trueman took his 298th test wicket during the last over of a pre-lunch session in the Oval test match against Australia in 1964. He then took his 299th wicket with his next ball, at which point the players trooped off for lunch and Tim and I (and mum) had forty minutes to kill before seeing what happened next. We did not have any doubt that Trueman would get his 300th wicket, of course: the only uncertainty was whether he would get his hat trick as well. Tim and I spent the lunch break discussing this, and reached the conclusion that he might or he might not. Later, in the back garden by myself, I replayed the moment when, some time after the resumption, Trueman enticed the next Australian batsman, Neil Hawke, to give the crucial slip catch to Colin Cowdrey. As he left the crease, the generous Hawke had been the first person to congratulate Trueman. My reconstruction was slightly different: not only did I take the catch in Cowdrey's place in the slips, but I was also the first one to run up and shake the fast bowler's hand.

The real South Africans toured England in 1965 and, to Tim's only partly disguised pleasure, were far too good for the home side. Being a left-handed batsman, Tim had an affinity with the masterful Graeme Pollock, but his favourite player was his fellow Rhodesian, Colin Bland, also a batsman and, by common consent, the best fieldsman in the world. Bland fielded at cover point from where – with his speed across the ground, combined with his ability to pick up the ball on the run and then throw with deadly accuracy – he terrorised the English runners. I learned very quickly that it was not only his uncanny ability to hit the stumps that was so damaging – though this manifestation of fielding as an aggressively effective part of the game was bad enough for the batsman – it was the fear that he created in the batsmen's mind whenever they were contemplating even the safest run for a shot played out in his general direction. It was, in short, a lesson in the use of psychology as a sporting weapon, and I made careful note.

As with the rugby, I played my own games of cricket for Yorkshire and England both indoors and in the back garden. Most of the games were played outside, where I starred with both bat and ball. My nearest rival, in terms of all round ability, was probably Gary Sobers.

For the bowling, I pitched a set of stumps in the narrow flower bed at the bottom of the garden and delivered the ball at them from the top end of the lower tier of lawn. Needless to say, I opened the bowling alongside Freddie Trueman. This involved running down the top tier of lawn, leaping over the dividing flower bed, re-gathering my balance and delivering the ball towards the wickets. The backdrop was the side of the house, so, if I missed the stumps, the ball would usually rebound straight off the brick wall somewhere between the kitchen and the living room and back on to the lawn. I would then retrieve it and march back to the beginning of my run-up, rhythmically attempting to shine the ball on the side of my shorts in precisely the way that Freddie did.

I say "usually", because, for the more wayward deliveries, the ball would hit the glass window of one or other of the two rooms. This would prompt my mother to wrap firmly on her side of the kitchen window with a rather more agitated expression than she used when calling Tim and me in to watch the cricket on television. Her only consolation was that I would be using a tennis ball, rather than a "corkie". (This also rather undermined the attempts made by me – and Freddie – to raise a shine on one side, notwithstanding our furious polishing). When it was time for the fast bowlers to be rested and replaced by the spinners, I switched – Sobers-like – to bowl in tandem with Ray Illingworth or Don Wilson.

My batting technique was aided by the fact that the lower tier of lawn had a fairly pronounced slope. With the bat in my left hand, I would throw the ball up in the air with a bit of backspin so that, after it pitched, I could lean forward, holding the bat with two hands in the proper way, and play a stroke. This would either be a defensive block – modelled on the newspaper photographs or television shots I had seen of Geoff Boycott – or, more likely, a firm drive which hit the ball along the lawn so that it rebounded off the low dividing wall that separated the two tiers of lawn before speeding back past me down to the imaginary boundary rope at the wall of the house. This took some doing, as the garden wall was curved, but, with practice, I became sufficiently accurate, from a distance of seven or eight yards, to strike a particular group of stones in the wall so that the ball came straight back and regular boundaries were scored. Occasionally, however, the ball was overhit, and the flowers in the bed that separated the two lawns – or, at least, those that had survived my goal kicking exploits in Hunslet's colours earlier in the year – would feel the full force of the shot. I would put this down as being caught at mid off. Cue: more furious tapping on the kitchen window.

The surviving Cathedral exercise book – in which I also recorded my staggering points scoring feats for Hunslet in the kitchen and television room as well as the back garden – accurately records some of the cricket exploits that I undertook, as an eight-year-old, for both Yorkshire and England in the summer of 1963. It begins with a one innings Knock Out cup match at home to Gloucestershire, in which the visitors were bowled out for 55 (John Rigg seven wickets, Don Wilson two wickets, Chris Balderstone one wicket) and Yorkshire scored 56 for no wicket in reply (John Rigg 50 not out, John Hampshire 4 not out, extras 2).

This set the pattern for the championship season: Trueman and I bowled out Warwickshire for 62 and 42 after I had scored 143 not out; Hampshire suffered a similar fate (50 and 57) after I had made 192 not out; in the match against Derbyshire, I was actually out (for 184), but then took

15 wickets as the opponents were bowled out for 49 and 58; my season's top score of 288 was made against the unfortunate Gloucestershire, who were skittled out for 48 (JA Rigg 8 for 9, FS Trueman 2 for 30) and 51 (JA Rigg 8 for 8, FS Trueman 1 for 27, M Ryan 1 for 11). Yorkshire were merciless in crushing their opponents: Leicestershire were beaten by 507 runs (JA Rigg 242 runs and 16 wickets), Kent by 618 runs (JA Rigg 193 not out and 15 wickets) and Essex by an innings and 519 runs (JA Rigg 268 runs and 14 wickets).

After each match, my well-honed mental arithmetic skills would be applied to updating the whole of the Yorkshire team's batting and bowling averages. By the time the pages in the exercise book had run out, I had compiled 3,090 runs in 17 innings for Yorkshire at an average of 181 and thirteen seventeenths. (We had not yet done decimals at school). In retrospect, of course, I can see that I was mistaken in this calculation and that I was grossly in error. At the time, I did not realise that it was only the number of *completed* innings that counted in a batsman's averages. Given that I had been not out 10 times in my 17 innings, my correct average was actually 441.43 (or 441 and three sevenths). To confirm my value to the side, I had also taken 231 wickets for a total cost of 325 runs, at an approximate average of just under one and a half runs per wicket.

It all seems so ridiculous now, of course. But it was a great summer, playing in the garden at home in what seemed like endless sunshine and without a care in the world. The look – and feel – of the Cathedral exercise book, with its calculations and scores and averages and team lists and crossings out, bring back those joyful days in an instant.

The postscript to my Herculean feats came later – though not much later – when I started to read more widely about the history of Yorkshire cricket and some of the actual performances of the past heroes. George Herbert Hirst scored over 2,000 runs and took 200 wickets in 1906; Sussex were bowled out for 35 and 24 in 1878; Yorkshire were bowled out for 99 in 1900 and still beat Worcestershire by an innings; Wilfred Rhodes and Schofield Haigh bowled Nottinghamshire out for 13 in 1901; Australia were dismissed for 23 by Hirst and FS Jackson in 1902; Hedley Verity took all 10 Nottinghamshire wickets for 10 runs in 1932. And only seven years earlier than my back garden heroics, Jim Laker – a Surrey player, but still a Yorkshireman – had taken 19 of the 20 Australian wickets in the Old Trafford test match.

Moreover, not even JA Rigg's halcyon batting exploits of 1963 could match those of another earlier player, albeit a non-Yorkshireman, at Headingley. I did not manage any triple centuries, unlike Don Bradman, who followed up his 334 for Australia against England in the 1930 test match with 304 in the corresponding 1934 fixture and trifling efforts of 103 in 1938 and 173 not out in 1948. My exploits in the garden might have been the wistful exaggerations of a young and imaginative boy, but, in some previous instances, real life had not been that much different.

After loaning the county championship title to Worcestershire in 1964 and 1965, Yorkshire regained it the following season, which is when I made my first visit to the Headingley Cricket Ground. It had been decided by my father and uncle Vic that we would go to the second day of the Lancashire game. In the mid-1960s, the "Roses" matches remained key encounters in the cricket calendar, notwithstanding that Lancashire were considerably the weaker of the two sides. During this period, the rivalry on the pitch continued – though probably did not match – that of the inter-war period, when the northern counties dominated the county championship. Between 1922 and the outbreak of the Second World War, Yorkshire were champions 11 times and Lancashire 5, the other two title-winning sides being Derbyshire and Nottinghamshire.[15]

At the beginning of the day's play, Yorkshire were in a strong position, having bowled Lancashire out cheaply on the first day and moved into a first innings lead, with Geoff Boycott still at the crease. This last point was significant because, in his relatively short career to date, Boycott had already taken a shine to the Lancashire bowling, having scored three centuries off them in successive Roses innings. Our plans to go to Headingley were heavily predicated on the assumption that another Boycott hundred was in the offing.

The Headingley ground was 20–30 minutes drive from my parents' house, depending on how long it took to negotiate the traffic lights at the junction of Otley Road and Shaw Lane. We had not yet set off when – from the television coverage, I think – the shocking news came through: Boycott was out. This prompted a serious discussion about whether we should still go.

In the end, we did, for which I have been grateful ever since, because the day's events gave me the fix for watching live cricket that I have not been able to shake off. Yorkshire declared after 65 overs – as they were obliged to do, due to a curious and short-lived rule that applied in that season – and we sat back in anticipation of Freddie Trueman running through the Lancashire batting line-up in the second innings, just as he had in the first.

In the event, it was not Trueman who did the damage. Instead, a young fast-medium bowler called John Waring took seven Lancashire wickets to restrict the visitors' overall lead to just two runs by the time they were dismissed for the second time. In an action that, on much later reflection, I might have regarded as one of condescension towards their opponents, Yorkshire opened with their wicket-keeper, Jimmy Binks, and the left arm slow bowler, Don Wilson – rather than Boycott – and the pair knocked off the required runs.

Vic, Dad and I sat together on one of the wooden benches on the wide sweep of terracing on the western side of the Headingley ground. On that occasion – and for some time afterwards, until it became populated with the raucous beer-swilling test match crowds from the late 1980s onwards – I thought it was a great place from which to watch the action. We were square of the wicket, more or less in line with the crease at the Football Stand (i.e. rugby league stand) end of the ground, and sufficiently high up, about two-thirds of the way back, to get the three dimensional perspective that Dad had favoured from the back of the stand at Parkside.

The terraces were packed, with no spare seats as far as I could see from my vantage point between Vic and dad. It was also a hot day, with no shelter from the sun, and, not for the only time in my cricket spectating career, I found myself part of the communal wish to see a wicket fall or for some other break in the action, so that we could stand up and stretch our collective legs. The wickets fell regularly enough that day, especially to Waring, whose singular moment of glory this was; he subsequently faded from the Yorkshire scene.

I was absolutely captivated: by the Yorkshire players, as I tried to identify who was fielding in which position; by the speed of the quick bowlers, who appeared so much faster when viewed from the side, as opposed to from the front or back as on television; by how far back Binks and his accompanying slip-fielders stood when Trueman was bowling; by the ritualistic removal of the bails by the umpires before leaving the field at the lunchbreak; by the groans from the Members Stand, behind the wicket, as a Lancashire batsman played and missed outside the off stump; by the concentration of the crowd, watching the action and fully engaging with the progress that the Yorkshire team was making through the opposing batting line-up; and with the supporting cast of scorecard and newspaper sellers and ice cream vendors and, in the bar underneath our stand, the sellers of beer and light ales. Towards the end of play, Vic leaned across to tell us about the various items that the man on his left had consumed during the day: sandwiches, crisps, ice cream, pop, cakes, beer, chocolate, more beer... "This lad next to me has had everything", he said, *sotto voce*. I can still hear his admiring whisper.

After the day's play, Dad and I had arranged to meet my mother at her parents, a short distance from our house in Moortown. The intention was that there would be a dinner for the extended family, including my sister and me. I can remember, as if it was yesterday, lying down before dinner on the sofa in my grandfather's study and drifting into sleep. I was awoken by my mother, who said that I had a choice between continuing to lie on the sofa, if I wished, or joining everyone else in the dining room for dessert. As this was to be ice cream, I thought that I would get up. And then I thought that I would get up in a minute or so. Needless to say, I did not make it to the dining room. I drifted back off into sleep, exhausted by the sun and by the excitement of the day and by the convincing Yorkshire victory.

By the following summer, I was in my first year at grammar school and, as with the rugby, in the Under 13s cricket team a year early. My very first match was at Ashville College, Harrogate: a renowned cricket-playing school as well as, as it happened, the only school to have beaten (by one point) the Roundhay School Under 13 rugby side during the winter season. We batted first and I went out to open the innings with Mark Scholnick. I used an old Len Hutton bat that my dad had acquired from somewhere: it was a darkish brown and, facing the offside, had part of its lower edge missing. I edged my second ball to third man and we ran a single. Mark pushed his second ball directly at the short cover fielder and set off for a run. I was run out by about five yards. I optimistically looked across to the square leg umpire – our teacher, Mr Paine, from memory – to see his head shaking ruefully and his finger pointing upwards, and I dolefully walked off to the sounds of the Ashville boys congratulating each other and my cursed running partner murmuring "Sorry, John".

By later in the term, Mark and I had established a more reliable – if probably over-cautious – understanding for running between the wickets in our opening partnerships. We both had Geoff Boycott as our role model, of course, as reflected in our reasonably solid defensive techniques. However, our interests probably diverged in early June. At that time, Israel and the Arab states engaged in the Six Day War and Mark was almost certainly one of the sizeable number of Jewish pupils at our school who would spend their break and lunchtimes glued to their small portable transistor radios listening to each succeeding news bulletin. I, on the other hand – in common with a significant proportion of my non-Jewish friends – spent the lunch time breaks listening to our transistors for news of Boycott's progress in the Headingley test match against India. This was the famous innings in which he made 246 in a day and a half and was then dropped by England for slow scoring. I thought at the time that this was somewhat odd: after all, England won the test comfortably by six wickets, thanks largely to Boycott's performance. My father referred obliquely to conspiracies by the southern-based Establishment.

Boycott also scored heavily against the season's other tourists, Pakistan, when they played Yorkshire at Headingley: 128 out of an opening partnership of 210 with Phil Sharpe, who went on to make 197. Yorkshire declared at a massive 414 for 3 and then bowled Pakistan out for 150 before rain intervened in their second innings. I know the details, not from *Wisden*, but from my own detailed scoring of every ball of the match.

This was my new hobby. I had purchased a small pocket scoring book – the "Compactum" – and, beginning with this occasion, started to score every ball of the matches that I attended in exactly the way that Tim Kell had showed me. This meant, of course, that I had to see every ball: no problem for me for a three day game at Headingley in the summer holidays. It was a significant problem for Dad, of course, who was at work and who, with only occasional exceptions, dropped out as my companion at cricket matches at this early stage. Our partnership was not to be resumed for several years. Instead, I went to the Pakistan match with two of my schoolfriends, Brian Stevens and John Kirkland, both a year older than me and members of the school's Under 13 cricket team. We had a great day, which was only slightly dampened when, totally unexpectedly, Brian performed a prodigious feat of projectile vomiting on the single-decker number 45 bus taking us back to Moortown.

The scoring did present some practical difficulties. First, it soon became clear that the pocket scoring book did not have the capacity for large innings, such as Yorkshire's against Pakistan, on one page. I resolved this by using up the available space in the book and inserting extra pages for each innings's additional overs, as required. Second, using a ball-point pen meant that there was no room for error – an over incorrectly attributed to the wrong bowler, for example, or a mistaken catcher – if I wanted to avoid messy corrections and crossings out. Accordingly, I decided at that early stage that each day's play would be recorded on separate loose sheets of paper and then, for each individual delivery, carefully copied into the scoring book at home at the end of the day's play. This task was dutifully performed as a labour of love, with painstaking precision, as if I were a medieval monk transcribing the words of the Bible.

The same scoring procedure was adopted for my first test match the following year: England versus Australia at Headingley. As I recall, I went to a couple of days to see the play "live" and followed the remainder of the match via the ball-by-ball commentary on Radio 3. At the ground, I sat with my friends on the grass at the front of the Western Terrace, which was permissible in those days though it was not my preferred choice. This test match is mainly remembered for the unfortunate experience of Keith Fletcher – an Essex cricketer picked by the selectors in preference to

Phil Sharpe – who dropped some slip catches and made a duck in England's first innings. Other than that, and the novelty of seeing the cricketers of Australia in their baggy green caps for the first time, I did not find the test itself particularly exciting. Boycott was absent through injury and, although Ray Illingworth did take six wickets in the Australian second innings, the match petered out into a dull draw. Far more riveting was the final test at the Oval – again scored by me from first ball to last, though this time entirely through the medium of the radio – with its big innings from John Edrich, Basil d'Oliveira and Bill Lawry and the dramatic Underwood wickets on the last evening to win the match for England.

The 1968 Headingley Roses match – also carefully scored – followed a similar pattern to the corresponding game of two years earlier. Yorkshire bowled Lancashire out cheaply and then built up a big first innings lead, this time to win by an innings. For me, the striking thing about the Yorkshire innings was how, after a couple of the front line batsmen had made big scores – including a century by Doug Padgett – the middle order also weighed in with some heavy scoring. Ray Illingworth was a key figure here: the test match off spinner who could come in at number eight, as he did on this occasion, and play shots like a number three or four. I had the same impressed reaction to his dual skills, with bat and ball, as I had had with Ken Taylor's ability to play more than one sport at a high level. Illingworth's case was closer to home, however: my position in the Roundhay School under 13s was now as an off spinning batsman who also captained the side. I was not to know at that time – although, like everybody else, I did not have long to wait – that Illingworth's prowess as a captain would also be revealed before too long.

By the end of the 1968 season, therefore, I was something of veteran of cricket watching at Headingley. I had got to know the geography of the ground and had experimented with various vantage points, though the initial spot on the western side remained my favourite. I already knew that Headingley was not the most attractive of first class cricket venues. In particular, from the comparisons I had made from the television, it was clear that the quality and appearance of its functional pavilion were decidedly inferior, compared with its counterparts at Lord's or Old Trafford, amongst others. But I was struck by the sheer expanse of the arena. This was especially when I surveyed the ground from the edge of the Western Terrace, at the entrance to the passage leading down to the corner of the rugby ground, and looked across to the row of poplar trees behind the seating on the far side. It was such a huge playing area. How could a fielder possibly throw the ball in from the boundary all the way to just over the stumps? And how could a batsman hit the ball the vast distance required for a six?

I was also becoming more familiar with Yorkshire's historical association with the ground, dating from the turn of the century, when the centre of cricketing influence within the county shifted north from Sheffield, although it was not until a couple of years later that I came across the book that really captured my imagination on this. By then, the range of my cricketing library had developed from the Ladybird "Easy-Reading" Book *The Story of Cricket*, that I won as a prize at primary school in 1965, through to older books acquired from various sources – *How to Become a First Class Batsman* by Herbert Sutcliffe was sold in the Sutcliffe's sports shop in the Leeds arcades – and the heavy and glossy *Cricket: the Australian Way*, edited by Jack Pollard, that my father gave to me as a Christmas present.

John Marshall's *Headingley* is, in essence, a straightforward chronological description of the feats of the Yorkshire CCC and its players through to the end of the 1969 season. I lapped up the club's history, from Lord Hawke and Bobby Peel, Wilfred Rhodes and George Herbert Hirst through to Brian Sellers and Herbert Sutcliffe and on to Brian Close and Fred Trueman. Their prodigious feats jumped off the page. The book is written in a neat and simple style which, in my view, adds to the drama of the story it is telling. For example, there is a short, but poignant, description of the team's return from Sussex on the Friday before war was declared in September 1939: the journey that marked the break-up of the great Yorkshire side of the 1930s – "Final handshakes were exchanged in the Leeds City Square". This is followed by a summary of some of the players' fates – Hedley Verity killed in Italy in 1943, Bill Bowes taken prisoner of war – before Marshall moves on to provide a similarly moving account of the special burst of applause, taken up around the ground, as Len Hutton took guard against South Africa in the first post-war Headingley test match of 1947. When Hutton reached his hundred, "[t]he noise of [an earlier] thunderstorm was as a gentle rumble compared with Yorkshire's tribute to the Pudsey lad".

These passages registered profoundly with me when I first read them in 1970. They confirmed to an impressionable boy that, by watching Yorkshire and wanting them to do well, I was engaging with a sporting entity that had a noble tradition and a successful history. I knew that the club had been a touchstone for successive generations of cricket followers across the county, who had shared in the feats of the great players and teams and taken a pride in their achievements. I can read the same passages in *Headingley* today and still feel moved.

The Second Age

The Youthful Explorer

Although my father will continue to play a central role as a spectating companion for many years to come, this is the period in which I begin to strike out on my own or to attend fixtures with friends from school. My horizons are widened via the bus and train routes of West and North Yorkshire. New venues are explored, with rugby union and football added to the range of "live" sporting interests.

Chapter 4

Belle Vue to Borough Park

In September 1965, the Hunslet stand off, Brian Gabbitas, suffered a broken jaw in the league fixture away to Huddersfield. This was my first visit (of a total of two) to the famous Fartown ground and, because of Gabbitas's injury, it holds unhappy memories. My father saw the incident – a late and cowardly off the ball assault – and he told me later who did it. It was a serious injury and Gabbitas was clearly going to be out of action for some time; my uncle Bob suggested that he would probably look to get fit again for the first round of the new Challenge Cup campaign in the following February.

The Huddersfield trip was one of a series of journeys to Hunslet's away fixtures that Dad and I made at around this time. Sometimes Bob would come as well and, indeed, sometimes – if Dad had to work on the Saturday morning and could not get away in time – it was just Bob and me. My uncle had a senior position in the Leeds City Fire Brigade – second in command for the city, I think – but, by then, he would have been close to retirement with more available free time. Dad told me later that, having not been a particular close follower of the Hunslet club at any time beforehand, Bob had become enthused with the side's fortunes during their Wembley run. Like many new converts to a cause, he became fantastically keen.

Bob was the oldest of my dad's siblings – Dad came third out of four children in his family – seven years his senior. He had always been the adventurous and protective big brother. It had been Bob who had sorted out the kid at their school who had been bullying my father. In his youth, he had been the one who had started smoking cigarettes and who had bought the family's first car. Later, he had ambitiously taken his own family – his wife and two daughters – on motoring holidays through France and Italy or to Spain and Portugal. Afterwards, he would recount these exotic adventures during the occasional and (by me) eagerly anticipated Sunday evening showings of his 8mm cinefilms when, after dinner, both families would settle down in and around the sofa and armchairs in the spacious living room of my uncle's house to watch the flickering images of the intrepid travellers on the temporarily erected white screen. As a young boy, I admired Bob for his drive and energy, as well as his toughness and his optimism; I sensed that Bob thought that anything was possible, if one had the courage to attempt it. My father looked up to him and loved him.

Many years later, Dad looked back on these trips to the Hunslet away fixtures with some affection. "He used to take us all over", he would say as he recalled Bob chauffeuring us to various venues across Yorkshire as well as to Hunslet's local rivals, Leeds and Bramley. By now, of course, I knew the names of every ground in the rugby league – a knowledge base that was subject to regular testing by my father – and I took a keen enjoyment in visiting the locations that appeared in the match reports of the *Rugby Leaguer* or the *Yorkshire Evening Post*: Lawkholme Lane (Keighley), Wheldon Road (Castleford), Fartown (Huddersfield), Belle Vue (Wakefield Trinity) and Craven Park (Hull Kingston Rovers). In terms of mileage, these were not particularly long journeys, of course, but, to me at the time, they were exciting adventures to strange new places. On my first (and only) visit to what was then called Wheldon Road, I was both mystified and disconcerted by what seemed to be a huge expanse of soap bubbles stretching out by the side of one of the neighbouring roads, the locals either ignoring it or walking through and around it. Looking back, I assume that it was something to do with the discharges from one of the local chemical or other industrial sites: at the time, it was something from another – and harsher – world than the boy from suburban north Leeds was used to.

There were two downsides to these trips. The first was that I was a chronically poor traveller in the back seat of uncle Bob's car, notwithstanding that it provided a far more comfortable ride that my father's stuffy work van. Bob was a fast and confident driver, who almost always seemed to know the roads well, no matter which new place we were in. But the combination of motion sickness and the merest hint of petrol fumes was more than enough for me. I would spend each journey – there and back – attempting to overcome the desperate feelings of dizziness and nausea that would always come over me, by sitting next to an open window. The irony is that I do not recall ever actually being sick in Bob's car. But the regular experience of safe passage stood me in no stead at all when it came to the next journey.

The second problem was that the Hunslet's results were in decline. Their league position dropped to 17th in the season after the 1965 Challenge

Cup final appearance, a single but critical place outside the top 16 clubs that competed in the end of season championship play offs within the single divisional structure that had been re-established the previous season. All of the particular examples given above – Keighley, Castleford, Huddersfield, Wakefield, Hull KR – were from 1965 or 1966, and each resulted in defeat for the visitors.

This was frustrating for me, because I knew that the Challenge Cup final side would have been perfectly capable of winning all these fixtures. But the truth was that core of the Wembley team broke up very quickly: Shelton, Ramsey, Eyre, Prior and Hartley – all international players – were transferred; Ward and Langton approached retirement; others succumbed to injury or disillusionment. One or two good replacements came in – notably the Welsh half backs, Cliff Williams and Phil Morgan – but these were the exceptions rather than the rule.

For the season after the Wembley final, the cover of the Hunslet programme showed a photograph of the thirteen players who had played in that match, standing in a line wearing their cup final kit – white shirts with a chocolate "V" (rather than the myrtle, flame and white) with white shorts. The remainder of the programme was more or less unchanged: club notes, the team lists, and advertisements, including for the same scrap metal dealer on the front cover, although the A-H coded lettering for the half time scores was dropped. But the photograph only lasted a year before itself being replaced. I thought at the time that this was appropriate: by the beginning of the following season, over half the Wembley team had gone.

One of these was Brian Gabbitas, whose broken jaw at Huddersfield had brought about his premature retirement. Bob had been wrong. Gabbitas did not reappear for the first round of the 1966 Challenge Cup – a drab match against Whitehaven at Parkside, which Hunslet narrowly lost. By this time, I was firmly entrenched in my position at the front of the stand behind the fencing. As the Hunslet players took the field, I said to myself: "He's not playing then". Only, I was not just saying it to myself. I said it loud enough for the spectators immediately around to me to wonder who this gabbling little boy might be and what on earth he was talking about.

As the members of the Wembley squad started to go their separate ways – and were not adequately replaced – this marked the beginning of a long fallow period for the club. The Challenge Cup performance was a good barometer. In the nine years after the cup final appearance, Hunslet were beaten in the first round seven times and the second round twice. Some of these defeats were against fairly lowly opposition – the Whitehaven example is a case in point, as the Cumbrian team finished bottom of the entire league that year – which meant that, as my father pessimistically was always quick to point out, there was not even the compensation of the share of the gate receipts brought about by meeting one of the more fashionable clubs. By the time the first round of the 1967 competition came round – yet another home tie against Wakefield Trinity – only three players from the Wembley side of two years earlier were named in the programme: Preece, Gunney and Ward.

Dad, Bob and I continued our support at home and (occasionally) away. The trip to Wakefield in October 1966 saw an unfancied Hunslet team go into an unbelievable 17–0 half-time lead, before the inevitable fight back by the home side. This culminated in Don Fox dropping an enormous goal from just in front of the half way line in last minute to win the game for Wakefield by 18–17. I was devastated.

Hunslet's matches against Wakefield Trinity featured regularly in my formative years of watching rugby league, as the two sides' paths seemed to cross to a disproportionate extent: the first round Yorkshire Cup matches in 1962 and 1963, the first round Challenge Cup tie (with replay) in 1964 and, most obviously, the Challenge Cup semi final at Headingley in 1965. A league game at Parkside in February 1965 was memorable for another reason, however.

I watched the match from my usual vantage point behind the fence at the front of the stand. A few yards away from me, and to my left, Geoff Gunney was tackled by a Wakefield player. Something must have happened in the tackle because, obviously severely provoked, Gunney stood up and, instead of playing the ball, flattened his opponent with one of the best punches that the ground could ever have seen. At this point, the detail gets slightly hazy. My recollection is that it was a classic right hook; however, the following Monday's *Yorkshire Post* indicates that Gunney "felled Campbell, the Wakefield prop, with a straight left which Henry Cooper would have been proud to own". The record shows that Gunney was duly sent off by the referee, although this amounted to something of a technicality. He more or less condemned himself, walking straight in front of me towards the narrow exit from the pitch to the changing rooms and shaking his head ruefully to the referee as he did so. The crowd's reaction was utter amazement, first of all at the quality and destructiveness of the punch and then, when it had sunk in who had thrown it, in the stunned recognition of the perpetrator. I shared in this general reaction and coupled it with my own considerable disquiet at what I had seen. Geoff Gunney had been sent off. This was not consistent with my known view, firmly established at ten years of age, of how the world operated. Later, in uncle Bob's car on the way home, the full reality hit home: it was highly unlikely that Gunney would repeat his previous season's success in winning the Windsor Trophy as the league's "best and fairest player". (I was subsequently proved correct about this fairly safe prediction, although there was considerable consolation when the award went to Brian Gabbitas instead).

A happier occasion was in August 1967, when Dad had arranged the family's week-long summer holiday at one of the quieter west coast resorts – probably St Annes or Morecambe. By pure coincidence, I'm sure, this happened to be when Hunslet were playing their away fixture against Blackpool Borough. The home side were even weaker than Hunslet, though they did have one or two useful individual players. This was similar to Hunslet, who had replaced Billy Langton at full-back with a steady goalkicker called David Marshall, promoted a swift winger named Tommy Thompson from the reserve team and, most noticeably, recruited Phil Morgan from the stand off production line of Welsh rugby union.

Although Thompson was already in his early twenties, he looked a fresh-faced and somewhat frail youth and, notwithstanding the emergence of the much younger Roger Millward a couple of seasons earlier, he was probably one of the first players whose welfare I had concerns about on his transition from youth or reserve sides into the first team. I knew that this was a hard sport with its full quota of hard men. But appearances were deceptive. Thompson scored 28 tries during the season, a remarkable feat by someone playing in a side that lost more games than it won. He seemed to glide down the left wing and, at one stage of the season, it appeared that he would routinely score a try from long range, effortlessly beating his opposite number and outpacing the covering defence with a combination of speed and swerve. This seemed to happen with a remarkable frequency, as if part of a regular script: Hunslet forwards out-muscled; Hunslet backs attempt to make the most of limited possession; ball passed to Thompson in an unpromising position; long range try scored. However, notwithstanding Tommy Thompson's dashing tries, Dad and I both thought that Morgan was the class act in the Hunslet side – good balance, safe hands and a devastating sidestep – and he quickly became a favourite. His speed off the mark and ability to beat a defender marked him out as an exceptional talent and, as the inevitable corollary, a key target for the opposition. That his appearances were limited over the following years was due to the related combination of regular injuries and limited protection from the physical punishment received from superior packs of forwards.

On this particular day in Blackpool, standing on top of the grassy mound that provided a perfectly serviceable viewing area along one touchline at Borough Park, Dad found himself in conversation with an elderly supporter of the home side. It didn't take me long to realise that they were having a sensible conversation about the difficulties their respective individual favourites – Morgan, in dad's case – were facing, week after week, through playing in a relatively weak side. Each thought the other was thoroughly in agreement about his own player. The discussion was amicable and friendly, and it was not until later that I was bold enough to point out to my father that it had taken place on entirely parallel lines.

My enthusiasm for the sport – and for the Hunslet club's role in it – remained undiminished for some time. The beginning of a season was a period of unbridled anticipation. I can clearly remember receiving Hunslet's 1966–67 fixture card and devouring the names on it. The home fixtures were given in upper case and the away games in lower case and, at the top of the list, after the Lazenby Cup pre-season match against LEEDS, were listed HULL KR and BARROW. Great, I thought: two home fixtures with which to start the season, and an excellent opportunity to get some points in the bag for the league table. I poured over the rest of the list – CASTLEFORD, Keighley… WIDNES, York – and over the syllables within each of the names and then over the individual letters in each team. I looked at the gap between the home fixtures to see if, later in the season – and depending on the Challenge Cup draw and Hunslet's progress in the competition – there might be games at Parkside on three or four consecutive Saturdays.

The start of the season was also the time of publication of the *Eddie Waring Rugby League Annual*, which I first obtained for the 1963–64 season (price: two shillings and sixpence) and continued to buy (or to be given by my father) up until 1968–69 (price: three shillings). I read these from cover to cover several times, lingering on the first of the publications for the reports of Hunslet's Yorkshire Cup and second division championship successes from the 1962–63 season and the centre page article about Jeff Stevenson and on the 1965–66 edition for its extensive coverage of the May 1965 Challenge Cup final. The annuals always contained an interesting mix of articles on the history of the game, reviews of the previous season and prospects for the coming year. However, over time, there was a noticeable change in the tone of the subject matter of the photograph on the front cover. For 1963–64, the photograph was of the dashing Harold Poynton of Wakefield Trinity evading a Wigan tackler in the previous May's Challenge Cup final; a year later, according to the caption on the inside page of the annual, it was of Frank Collier of Widnes "tackling" Eric Palmer of Hull KR in the following year's final, though it was actually of Collier, with his large fist clenched, falling on top of Palmer and punching him[16]; for 1968–69, it was the face of Mr Waring himself, with his square jaw and wide grin, who was no doubt fully aware that, as the "television personality" duly described on the cover, he had cornered the rugby league market in the public consciousness.

I realise now that this was a critical period in my life as a spectator, not just with regard to Hunslet or even to rugby league in general, but in the context of watching sport *per se*. It was the last time that I was wholly passionate about the sporting fortunes of a particular team. From the end of the 1960s onwards, I don't think this ever happened again. Of course, I would continue to attend individual matches – rugby and cricket, especially – wanting one of the competing sides to win: Hunslet, Yorkshire, England, Great Britain, and so on. But there was never again the dedicated perspective of unequivocal one hundred per cent biased commitment that I had had in the period leading up to Hunslet's Wembley appearance in 1965 and in the couple of seasons that followed. Thereafter, I started the slow evolutionary process towards being the dispassionate observer – and outsider – that I described earlier in the Preface.

It is difficult to date precisely when this metamorphosis took place, but I would judge that the 1966–67 season represented the start of it. Hunslet lost the first game heavily to Hull Kingston Rovers – no great surprise in retrospect, as Hull KR were developing a powerful side (exemplified by the recruitment of the teenage Roger Millward from Castleford, who made his debut in this match), which reached the semi finals of the Championship play offs at the end of the season – and only drew with Barrow. So much for taking the opportunity to get some league points in the bag.

As an aside, the Barrow fixture was of interest for a slightly odd reason. Their stand-off was a player called Eddie Tees, who took his kicks at goal in what was then remarked upon as the "soccer style" or "round the corner" fashion. It was the first time I had seen this technique of goal-kicking and, whilst it was not entirely original – another Barrow player, Willie Horne, had adopted it in the 1940s and 1950s – it was certainly out of the ordinary. All the other leading goal-kickers of the day – Billy Langton, Cyril Kellett at Hull KR, Bev Risman at Leeds, Neil Fox at Wakefield Trinity, Len Killeen at St Helens – used the traditional method of the front-on approach, the strike with the toe of the boot and the straight follow through of the leg. (My viewing of the rugby union internationals on television revealed that this was also the approach used by the main goal-kickers such as Bob Hiller of England and Tom Kiernan of Ireland). It was Tees's style that would eventually become dominant, of course, and, although it took some time for the trend to be firmly established, it would be the "soccer style" – or variants on it – that became the norm. Within a couple of years, he had been joined in the professional game by David Watkins at Salford, who marked the end of his preparatory walk back from the ball with two or three exaggerated steps to the side so that he could approach his target from the correct angle and strike it with his instep. The

Yorkshire rugby union centre, Phil Carter, whom I was to watch a couple of years after that, seemed to adopt a hybrid approach involving a straight run up to the ball and then a strike with the instep; I never quite worked out how he did this.

I probably sensed that the Hunslet club was in decline some time around the middle of this particular season. When three winnable home fixtures presented themselves over the Christmas and New Year period – against York, Doncaster and Keighley, each of which had consistently ranked below Hunslet over the previous 3 or 4 seasons – Hunslet lost two and drew the other. For the whole of the season, I marked the scores in pencil down the empty right hand column of the fixture card after each game had been played. Then, at the end of the season, I worked out Hunslet's full record and checked it against the league table given in the *Rugby Leaguer*. They had played 34 matches, of which only 9 had been won.

By this time, my attendance at Hunslet's home fixtures was not guaranteed. For the present, this was not due to any disillusionment with the team's performances. Rather, it was because I was playing more often myself. I was now in the first year of grammar school and, having made the Under 13 XV, often found myself double-booked on a Saturday. This was not a problem if the school had a morning fixture, which was usually the case for the matches against other schools in and around Leeds. But, when the games were further afield, for example in Pontefract or Harrogate or Ripon – and, particularly if, as was usually the case, the Under 13s fixtures were bracketed with the Under 15s and the first XV for the away fixtures, and we were travelling on the coach together – the kick offs tended to be in the afternoon. Dad was adamant that I should play, rather than watch, and this was also my clear preference. For him, the dilemma of deciding which team to go and see – Hunslet RLFC or the Roundhay School Under 13 XV – was becoming more acute.

Initially, the prospect of double booking did not affect our seasonal planning. When the fixture list for the 1968–69 season was published, I studied it with the same intensity as before: LEEDS (Lazenby Cup), Blackpool Borough, YORK, HUYTON... though I noticed that it was smaller in size and printed on paper rather than card. My father purchased his season ticket for £5. My schoolboy season ticket was ten shillings, a cost that I had to bear in its entirety on the grounds, as determined by dad, that I would appreciate the purchase more if I had paid for it myself. I was by no means convinced by the logic of this argument and I argued my case with him, but he would not be moved, even by my final suggestion of a part payment. With the benefit of hindsight, it is clear that the family finances were stretched.

As the season progressed, I repeated my routine of marking the results in pencil in the margin on the fixture list. I still have the list today, carefully filed away in an album. It is perhaps instructive that my register of the scores stops in the first week in December, following a heavy defeat at Oldham. At that stage, Hunslet had won 6 out of 17 league fixtures.

My uncle Bob's enthusiasm for supporting Hunslet – and, indeed, watching any live rugby league match – remained undiminished, however. I have a clear recollection of us going to watch the other local side, Bramley, play Hull Kingston Rovers at around this time without dad. I can distinctly recall standing on a rough area of banked terracing, at the side of the McLaren Field pitch, and seeing the formidable Australian forward Arthur Beetson, who guested for one season at Hull KR, relish the physical confrontation with the home side. A search of the records shows that this was also in December 1968, the same month that I ceased the regular cataloguing of scores on my Hunslet fixture list.[17]

The full manifestation of my disillusionment with the Hunslet club came later, though not much later. By the early 1970s, the side – and the club – were in serious decline, both on and off the pitch. The response to a proposed cut in wages at the beginning of the 1970–71 season was a strike by the players and their replacement for a couple of games by local amateur players. Hunslet finished bottom of the league in two successive seasons and there seemed to be no further for them to fall. There was, of course, as was to be revealed shortly afterwards.

It was after one of my increasingly less common visits to Parkside – and a heavy defeat by Featherstone Rovers – that I announced, rather grandly, that I wasn't sure if I'd go to watch them any more, as they were making me depressed. This arrogant waffle was said to Dad in the kitchen, with my mother standing by the stove. I can recall the moment as if it were yesterday.

I knew, of course, as soon as the words came out that I had said the wrong thing. It was if I had stabbed Dad through the heart. His response was quiet and dignified. He thought for a few moments and then said, softly: "Well, I think I'll still go. I've been supporting them all this time". He was not being maudlin or self-pitying. This was just a simple statement of the truth, and of his intentions. By the time of the 1971–72 season, when I made the remark, Dad had been supporting his side for about 40 years. Even with the poor team they now had – Hunslet won two league games in the whole season – the club remained a fixed reference point from which he could not be separated. In the meantime, my mother gave me a piercing look: an unspoken statement that her fury could be added to whatever cocktail of inadequacy that I might now happen to be feeling.

It is reasonable to argue that the decline of the Hunslet rugby league club after the mid-1960s had its broader counterpart in the decline of Hunslet itself, albeit that the latter took place over a longer period. By the early 1970s, the "neighbourhood of great liveliness" that Keith Waterhouse identified in his childhood in the 1930s had long been replaced by an area of pronounced economic decline. During this later period, the economy of Leeds was beginning its major structural transformation, as the main components of the traditional industrial base – engineering, railway works, printing and clothing – were replaced as significant sources of employment by lighter industries and, especially, the burgeoning service sector. Hunslet was left behind. The process of de-industrialisation – the term used by economists to describe the sustained loss of manufacturing jobs – accelerated after 1973, as the combined effects of an oil price-induced recession and rapidly rising inflation took effect.

As economic change took hold, the social composition of Hunslet also shifted. By the time of his 1988 Channel 4 television programme *More Trees in Hunslet*, Richard Hoggart was reporting on the effects of the exodus of the middle class component of Hunslet's population – doctors, lawyers and other professional groups – who had evacuated the locality for the outer suburbs of Leeds; a clergyman quoted in the programme referred to "a community of the 'left behind'". The city planners also contributed to the area's demise. The notorious Hunslet Grange council housing scheme – a hideous block of architectural brutalism – had opened as recently as the 1960s, but had been demolished by the mid 1980s. In the meantime, there had also been the small matter of the M1 motorway smashing its way through the centre of Hunslet. Hoggart reported that the legacy of these various effects was the creation of "a wasteland... featureless, faceless, directionless, characterless". In *City Lights: A Street Life*, Keith Waterhouse described the street of his birth – Low Road – and recalled a dozen types of economic activity that had taken place, during the years of his childhood, on this main road into the centre of Leeds; by the time Waterhouse was writing, in 1994, the road had become an "urban desert".

The Hunslet club did have further to fall than the bottom of the league table, of course. It could fall right out of existence and, at the end of the 1972–73 season, that is what happened. The club's board of directors accepted an offer from a property company to sell Parkside and, in the absence of a replacement ground being found, the club was wound up and the proceeds from the sale apportioned to shareholders (i.e. mainly the board). It was a sorry end. The veteran Geoff Gunney – at the age of 39 – led the side in their final home match in April 1973. Les Hoole and Mike Green (in *The Parksiders: A Brief History of Hunslet RLFC, 1883–1973*) report the event sadly – "Geoff Gunney led his team on to the pitch for the last time. Despite a special effort, the young Hunslet side lost to York. Gunney was the last man to leave the field". The last page in Hoole and Green's book shows the photograph of the Hunslet side taken before the match with Gunney in the middle of the front row and his promising young colleagues – including the centre George Clark and the second row forward Phil Sanderson – seated or standing behind him. The hairstyles and sideburns of the players are of classic early 1970s vintage. In the background, the dilapidated wooden pavilion, with its rotten structure and missing timbers, provides the physical evidence of the club's demise.

I was not present at this match. My final game at Parkside – although I did not realise it at the time – had been the previous December, when Leeds had been the visitors. Looking back, this was entirely appropriate. Leeds had been a high-flying side for many years, having won the League Leaders trophy at the end of the regular season in five years out of the previous six through playing consistently attractive – and, at times, brilliant – rugby. During that short period, they won the Championship twice, the Challenge Cup (in the famous waterlogged final of 1968) and the Yorkshire Cup twice. In the final derby match on the Parkside ground, Hunslet fought bravely and, although Leeds won comfortably in the end, the home side was not disgraced.

There was a curious postscript to the Leeds match a short time later. I was still at school – by now in the sixth form – when I was invited to be one of two schools' representatives on the newly established Leeds Sports Council. This was a quango comprising local politicians and civil servants, and a heterogeneous collection of well-known local personalities from the world of sport. Plus me and another sixth former from one of the girls' schools. At the first meeting, I found myself, not entirely accidentally, sitting next to Geoff Gunney.

I can remember very little about my contribution to the meeting, largely because the said contribution was marginal, to say the least. But I can recall very clearly informing Mr Gunney that my dad had supported Hunslet for many years, that we had gone to the Leeds match, and that we thought the team had done well. Gunney responded kindly by saying that he thought they had had a moral victory. I duly reported this to dad, who was impressed – and, I think, slightly envious – that I had been in communication with the great man.

Notwithstanding the combination of Hunslet's desperate misfortunes and the undoubted brilliance of the Leeds team, there was not the slightest chance that either Dad or I would have changed our allegiances during this period.[18] Nonetheless, we were attracted to Headingley for some of the bigger fixtures, officially in a neutral capacity, though I suspect that my father usually tended to hanker secretly for the opposition to win. One such occasion was the championship play off match in 1968, when Leeds, the league leaders at the end of the season, lost to Wigan, a supposedly modest team that had finished the league season in eleventh place. Although they had let me down in front of my friends at the primary school day out at Wembley a couple of years earlier, I was still attracted to Wigan: their colours, their remaining stars from earlier years and their enthusiastic support all conspired to give them a noticeable vibrancy and glamour.

However, the biggest game at Headingley, every year, was on Boxing Day, usually against Castleford or Wakefield Trinity. These were full-bloodied affairs, usually with little in the way of Christmas spirit. In 1971, the Wakefield full-back, Geoff Wraith, was sent off after poleaxing one of the Leeds forwards in full view of both the South Stand and the referee. From our vantage point on the terraces behind the goalposts at the St. Michael's Lane end of the ground, we watched as the unfortunate victim was helped along the deadball line and off the arena into the changing rooms. His face was a bloodied mess: all that was missing was the shield on which the fallen warrior should properly have been carried. Wakefield also finished with 12 men in the corresponding fixture the following season, as the prop forward Mick Morgan was sent off after half an hour. Their numerical disadvantage therefore began to take on the status of an annual ritual, at this time of year, to sit alongside the Christmas Day editions of *Top of the Pops* and *Morecambe and Wise*.

The enormous crowds for these matches posed a problem for us in the earlier years, when my father and I obviously had to go into the ground through the separate adults and juniors entrances. One of us would invariably get in first and then have to look out for the other squeezing through one of the narrow turnstiles on the Kirkstall Road. It has to be said that the Leeds club did not seem to anticipate these huge attendances with any real foresight. For the 1969 Boxing Day match against Castleford, some of the turnstiles were closed and the marked frustration of the swelling masses outside the ground was only released when the main wooden gate, hitherto also closed, was smashed in by the sheer weight of numbers outside in the street. I was swept along by the surging crowd through the entrance and on to the designated spot where my father and uncles had arranged to meet me. At the time, I don't think any of us thought in any detail about the inherent risks in all this – it was many years before the Hillsborough disaster, of course, and, more analogously, still some time before the terrible loss of life at Ibrox Stadium at the end of a Rangers-Celtic match. My father remarked instead on my good fortune in getting into the ground without paying.

There was no alternation in the venue of these Boxing Day fixtures. Leeds were at home every season, although not always to the same opposition. This might have had something to do with the fact that, irrespective of the weather, the fixture was more or less guaranteed to be played – thereby avoiding a last minute gap appearing in the live television schedule – due to the Leeds club's much earlier foresight in installing an underground electric "blanket". In any event, as my father was again wont to point out, the Leeds club's coffers benefited significantly every season. There was no such luxury in the fixture planning as far as Hunslet were concerned.

The other annual attraction at Headingley during this period was the "sevens" competition at the end of the season. This was an afternoon-long tournament, arranged as a straight knock-out involving eight teams, that the WD and HO Wills company – "pacemakers in tobacco" according to the 1970 souvenir programme – began sponsoring in 1965 and which Dad and I attended, usually with my uncles Vic and Bob, in most years through to the end of the decade.

The competition was well organised with, in 1970, the first round ties scheduled to start at precisely 19 minute intervals. I was fascinated by the behaviour of the crowd and, especially, the way that certain sections of it in different parts of the ground suddenly came to life when their teams appeared for their opening ties. I was also captivated by the name of the sponsors, which sounded like a traditional firm of Dickensian lawyers rather than the manufacturer of mass produced consumer goods in the way of Coca Cola or General Motors. Accordingly, for this particular potential customer, the company's sponsorship of this sporting event unequivocally had its desired effect in terms of the subsequent brand recognition. For years afterwards, whenever I saw a reference to the Wills name, I thought back to those happy occasions watching the rugby league sevens on sunny summer afternoons at Headingley. The impact on my actual purchasing behaviour was noticeably less effective, however. I have only ever bought one packet of cigarettes in my life – and smoked two of its contents – and that was of Benson and Hedges.

Hunslet took part in the 1965 and 1966 tournaments, but were eliminated in the first round on both occasions and did not appear again. In the first three years, the honours were shared around, with the tournament being won by St Helens, Bradford Northern and Huddersfield. Thereafter, however, the star team was Salford, who were unbeaten in each of the competitions from 1968 to 1970. Their line-up in the last of these years was illustrative of the pace and skill that made them such a glamorous side. It included Mike Coulman and Colin Dixon in the forwards and Paul Charlton and Maurice Richards in the backs, with David Watkins at the centre of things as the creator and goal-kicker. Watkins was also the captain and official coach: I would not have been surprised if he had driven the team bus as well. I sat in the North Stand and was captivated by his play. He was outstandingly brilliant, with his speed off the mark and his jinking side-steps and the perfect timing of his passing to release his speedy colleagues. He was also hugely confident in his abilities – as he was entitled to have been, as a former Wales and British Lions fly half – and he was the dominant figure throughout the afternoon, as he orchestrated the Salford effort. Even the way that he wore his rugby shirt, with the collar lifted up around the back and sides of his neck, seemed to add to Watkins's lustre.

It occurred to me that, in addition to the individual talent at their disposal for this particular competition, Salford probably had an advantage in having a high proportion of their players – including Watkins, Richards and Coulman – with rugby union experience. The sevens format was not as common in rugby league as in union, and I deduced that, whilst it would of course have been in the different code, the union experience would have stood Salford in good stead when it came to pacing a match or, indeed, the afternoon as a whole. The final of the tournament was 10 minutes each way, which I would have imagined to have been a lifetime in the heat of a late May afternoon. In Hunslet's absence, Salford were the side that Dad and I (and Bob) were rooting for when they took part in the competition, and they did not let us down.

As the 1960s turned into the 1970s, I began to make some serious additions to my collection of match programmes, not only of rugby league games but of rugby union and football as well. To start with, this involved placing an advert in the section of the *Rugby Leaguer* that dealt with programme swaps and purchases. As I recall, I offered to swap Hunslet home match programmes for those of other clubs. In addition, I wrote a series of letters to the well known television commentators of the day, inviting them to send any spare old programmes that they did not want. I also wrote to the secretaries of various administrative bodies, ranging from the organisers of the annual Middlesex Sevens rugby union competition through to the secretary of the French Rugby Union, with requests for specific programmes of contemporaneous events or matches. At my mother's insistence, these requests were always accompanied by a stamped addressed envelope and separate postage stamps of the equivalent value of the programme.

The response was mixed, but, pleasingly, not without its successes. In both the illustrations given above, for example, I received the programmes more or less by return post: the Middlesex Sevens preliminary and finals matches (played on successive Saturdays) in 1970 and 1971 and the France versus Ireland rugby union international in the State Colombes in 1968. My mother then made me write back to thank the senders. In other cases, I received polite letters of acknowledgement which, in their own way – thanks to the signatures at the bottom – were equally valued: Brian Johnston, Denis Compton and Kenneth Wolstenholme were examples. Other commentators did not respond at all, and I made a mental note of their names.

The response to the *Rugby Leaguer* advert was harder to deal with. I was swamped with programmes from the supporters of clubs that I had not only not visited, but was also unlikely to visit, given that Hunslet's fixture list comprised predominantly Yorkshire opposition, with only a couple of Lancashire clubs featuring in any one season. Now I was inundated with programmes from Salford and St Helens, Leigh and Warrington, Workington and Widnes. A correspondent from Sydney sent four editions of the Australian *Rugby League News*. My difficulty, of course, was that I did not have enough collateral. My stock of Hunslet programmes did not contain any swaps, and I quickly realised that if were to meet my end of the range of bargains that I had now implicitly struck, I would either have to draw down my existing Hunslet programme collection or buy multiple copies at the forthcoming home games. In the event, both these routes were taken, in the case of the former not without some remorse, as I was reluctant to part with too many of the home collection. On balance, however, I was happy with the trade, given the wide spectrum of other clubs that were now represented in my collection: Barrow and Whitehaven, Rochdale and Swinton.

There were three reasons for my fascination with these match programmes from the other clubs. First, there were the differences in style and quality: the full range from the paper-based editions (Barrow, Dewsbury, Doncaster, Liverpool City, Whitehaven) through to the ones with glossy covers (Blackpool Borough, Hull Kingston Rovers, Rochdale Hornets, Swinton) and those with, in my view (though I would not have expressed it quite this way at the time) the highest production values (Leigh and Salford).

Second, I was intrigued to see that, for several clubs, the basic template of the programme was almost identical. They shared the type of front cover with which I was already familiar from my visits to Leeds: the name of the club at the top of the page; the name of the opponents and the date and time of the fixture in the bottom right hand corner; and a glossy surface with a broad stripe down the left half in one or more of the team's colours (Leeds yellow, Oldham red, Warrington yellow, York yellow and black). A quick check revealed that they all shared the same printer – Frisby, Sons and Whipple of Leeds – a company which, if it had not exactly cornered the market, was clearly exploiting various economies of scale in its production processes.

Third, there were the programmes for those matches in which Hunslet were the visitors. There were several of these, reflecting the generosity of thought of respondents to my *Rugby Leaguer* advert, who had assumed that these were the editions which I would really wish to possess. I was naturally interested in what the programme writers said about my club in terms of its history, its results against the host team and its players. The standard varied. A couple of programmes made virtually no mention of their visitors and, in retrospect, probably had their content drafted without knowing who the opponents would be. Others were much better: Blackpool Borough 1967 (with a nice tribute to Geoff Gunney), Leeds 1967 (reviewing the full record of the fixtures between the clubs) and Wakefield Trinity 1964 (summarising the clubs' post-war matches).

Viewed from today's perspective, these programmes provide an additional range of interests, of course, as we reflect on the everyday life of nearly half a century ago. A Blackpool Borough programme of September 1966 advertises Arthur Askey at the Grand Theatre, Arthur Haynes at the Winter Gardens Pavilion, Ken Dodd at the Opera House and the Tower Circus with Charlie Cairoli and his Company. The following year, when Dad and I saw Hunslet play at Borough Park, the attractions were Bruce Forsyth, Freddie Frinton and Kathy Kirby as well as Cairoli. The family went to see the great clown during our week's holiday. I thought he was fantastic.

One response from my trawl of sports commentators arrived some time after the others. I came home from school one day to find that my mother had taken delivery of a large brown paper package, which had been carefully and tightly wrapped. It was addressed to me and was waiting on the dining room table for my attention. It must have been a good twelve inches high.

I opened the package and immediately immersed myself in a collection of football programmes from the early to mid 1960s. The matches ranged from big games – such as England versus The Rest of World celebrating the Football Association's centenary in 1963, TSV Munchen versus West Ham United in the 1965 European Cup-Winners Cup Final, and the Manchester United versus Leeds United FA Cup semi final (and the replay) of 1965 – through to matches which will have drawn somewhat smaller attendances:

Barnet versus Preston North End in the 1965 FA Cup, Bradford Park Avenue versus Aldershot in 1966, Peterborough United versus Shrewsbury Town in 1966. The eclectic collection included the programmes for the England versus Czechoslovakia Under 23 international at Elland Road in April 1965, the Ireland versus England amateur international at Dalymount Park in Dublin in February 1965 and the Oxford versus Cambridge varsity soccer match at Wembley in December 1966. There were also several official football club handbooks, including Arsenal's for 1965–66 and Chelsea's for 1964–65. My attention was drawn to the Norwich City programme – for the home match with Crystal Palace in April 1966 – which used the same template for its core design as the rugby league clubs identified earlier. (In this case, there was a broad yellow stripe down the left hand side of the cover and a canary in the top right hand corner).

It was a treasure trove. I could not believe my good fortune. An accompanying note said:

Dear John

…I hope you will find that the enclosed make useful additions to your collection. There is, of course, no question of cost. I am only too pleased to be able to send the programmes on to someone who will appreciate them… Don't hesitate to come and say hallo next time we are at Elland Road.

All the best.

Barry Davies.

Barry Davies commentated for ABC Television in those days, although it was not long afterwards that he joined the BBC, where he worked until his retirement in 2004. I can honestly say that, whenever I subsequently heard one of his commentaries, I always thought back immediately to his earlier generosity. I hope he received my letter of thanks. My mother would have been furious if it had gone astray.

Chapter 5

North Marine Drive

With the perspective of the succeeding decades, and assuming that I were restricted to selecting one year only, I would judge that 1969 was my *annus mirabilis* for watching cricket. Two particular matches contributed to this and I shall come on to these shortly.

I was fortunate in that this was the first year of the new John Player Sunday League, the single innings 40 overs a side competition that, following the success of the Gillette Cup from 1963, provided a much-needed boost for the counties' finances. During term time, I was playing cricket for the school on a Saturday and going to see Yorkshire was frustratingly out of the question for most of the championship matches. But my Sundays were free and, with a 2 o'clock start and (usually) a 6.30-ish finish, I was able to venture around the county to watch the action.

In recent years, the Yorkshire club has drawn in its horns and focused its matches on only two home venues: Headingley and Scarborough. In those days, however, there was a much more even handed distribution of games to a variety of additional venues that, by definition, were closer to a wider spectrum of the side's support base: Middlesbrough, Hull, Sheffield, Harrogate, Huddersfield and Bradford. And so it was that, with my school friend and cricketing ally Brian Stevens – now thankfully less prone to unannounced vomiting on public transport – I became familiar with the bus routes and train timetables that would transport us from Leeds to some of these other places.

Having by now watched (and enjoyed) a number of three day games played at a studious – if not, snail's – pace, it was obvious to me at that early stage that the one day game was bringing some fundamental changes to the very nature of the sport and, with it, to the experiences and expectations of the (generally much larger) crowds. On one occasion, Brian and I took the train to Huddersfield for a Sunday League game against Sussex. Despite the fact that the first half of the playing time was lost to the weather, there was a huge crowd to watch a match reduced to 19 overs a side. I can clearly recall Boycott and Sharpe scampering a number of quick singles, each of which appeared suicidal when the batsmen first set off and each drawing gasps of astonishment from the spectators when it was successfully completed. Sharpe, a rotund figure whose nickname of "Toby Jug" more than adequately captured his body shape, would put his head down, stretch out his bat and hare down the wicket with his legs working like mechanical pistons. Yorkshire reached a total in the 90s that Brian and I thought would be more than enough. And so it was, though by a narrow margin, so that the crowd – including the Leeds contingent – went home happy. In the modern era of Twenty-20 expertise, any side would back itself to reach this relatively modest target within these available overs.

The success of the Huddersfield and other similar trips behind us, Brian and I became more adventurous. Given Yorkshire's lowly position in the county championship, it became evident that the key domestic match of the season would be the Gillette Cup semi final against Nottinghamshire at North Marine Drive, Scarborough. An added attraction was that Nottinghamshire were captained by the world's greatest all rounder, Garfield Sobers.

In those days, the road journey from Leeds to the east coast was a slow one, with traffic hold ups guaranteed as the A64 wound it way through York and Malton. Brian and I caught a full bus at a ridiculously early hour from Leeds City bus station in the confident expectation that we would be at the ground well in time for the start. And so we were. We arrived an hour before play began. The trouble was, so did thousands of other people, who now formed a long queue from the entrance to the ground along the main road and around the neighbouring Trafalgar Square. My recollection is that there was relatively little in the way of pre-sold ticketing for a match such as this. It was first come, first served, and, after our long journey, there was a clear danger that we would not get in at all.

In the event, Brian and I must have got two of the last available places before the gates were closed. We queued for two hours and eventually entered the ground an hour after play had started. We saw immediately that the rumours circulating outside had been true: Boycott was already out and Yorkshire were struggling. We found some space on the grass on the far side of the ground near the big white marquees that served as refreshment tents.

It was a fantastic day's play. Yorkshire reached a reasonable score, though not an overwhelming one, thanks to some sensible batting by Phil Sharpe and Doug Padgett and a few big hits by the tailenders. These included a towering six from Don Wilson that I followed on its full trajectory, as it nearly disappeared into the sky and then, as gravity took its toll, plummeted to land somewhere between us and the refreshment tents. It was a magnificent strike, characteristic of Wilson's potential for dangerous hitting, when, as a tall left hander, he would plant his right leg down the wicket and look to free his arms in a full swing. Thereafter the match hinged on whether Yorkshire could dismiss Sobers before he cut loose and won the game by himself. I watched entranced as Wilson bowled what appeared to be over after over at the great batsman, apparently tying him down for several minutes at a time with his accurate left arm spin, before Sobers would take advantage of a rare loose ball and send it crashing to the boundary. When Sobers was out, I thought that the roar would probably have been heard back in Leeds. The other Nottinghamshire wickets fell steadily – one to a running catch in the outfield by a young Chris Old – and Yorkshire had won. I could not have imagined a more perfect day.

Other one day matches took place either at Headingley or at one of the so-called "outgrounds". At the former, I watched in some disbelief as Richard Hutton ran through a Worcestershire side that included Tom Graveney and Glenn Turner to take 7 wickets for 15 runs. After all these years, this remains the best bowling analysis for Yorkshire in a one day game. When I got home and reported this amazing feat to my dad, his reaction was one that, I suspect, the unfortunate Hutton came up against throughout his career, even on the good days such as this: "He's not as good as his father was".

Brian Stevens must have persuaded his parents that we had had a good day out at the Gillette Cup semi final because they offered to take us back to Scarborough for a John Player Sunday League match later in the summer. The opponents were Leicestershire, now captained by Ray Illingworth, who had left Yorkshire at the end of the previous season when, as was the norm for the county in those days, he was not offered the security of a contract lasting more than one season. We sat in the raised stand that lies opposite the main entrance at Scarborough and provides a very good view of the proceedings. I don't think Brian's parents were particularly knowledgeable about cricket, and they were certainly mystified when I got out the loose sheets of paper from my school rucksack and started to score each ball of the match.

I watched Illingworth closely. He batted at number seven and made a quickfire 30. He bowled when he thought it was the right time and the Yorkshire batsmen would not score heavily off him. He positioned himself in the field so that he was not called on to do any acrobatic fielding. He switched his other bowlers cleverly and moved his fielders around so that the favoured scoring shots of the Yorkshire batsmen were cut off. Through his leadership, Leicestershire were always in control of the match and they won without being seriously threatened. Illingworth was the epitome of a professional cricketer, schooled in the Bradford League and the hard Yorkshire changing room of the 1950s, and, to me looking on from the stand, it showed.

In between the competitive matches played in the Sunday League, Brian and I attended another fixture at Headingley in July 1969. It was a charity match between the Lord's Taverners and an Old England XI in aid of the National Playing Fields Association: precisely the type of fixture that had been the main staple of the Sunday cricket diet until the John Player sponsorship came along to fund the counties' competitive league. Several of the players were from the Yorkshire team of the 1950s, whom I had heard about but not seen play, and so there was an immediate curiosity in watching the likes of Bob Appleyard and Johnny Wardle, albeit some time after their peak years. Similarly, I had read of the exploits of Bill Edrich and Sonny Ramadhin. "Heard about" and "read of" are understatements, of course: I knew many of these players' career details with some intimacy, particularly the Yorkshire contingent. Appleyard had taken over 200 wickets in only his second season (1955), before contracting tuberculosis and being sent to Switzerland to convalesce; Wardle, one of the long line of outstanding Yorkshire slow left-arm bowlers – dating back through Hedley Verity to Wilfred Rhodes and Bobby Peel – had been controversially dismissed by the county half way through the 1958 season. Other participants, reflecting the event's charitable status, had made their names in other fields: Colin Welland (Z Cars actor, not yet an Oscar-winning screenwriter), Gerry Marsden (without his Pacemakers), Bev Risman (British Lions rugby union and Great Britain rugby league).

Most of the former players were in their 40s, though a few more were in their 50s, with George Pope the oldest at 58. Perhaps not surprisingly, therefore, it was their batting skills which seemed to have lasted longer than their agility in the field. Old England reached 100 in an hour and declared at 295 for 7. In reply, the Lord's Taverners reached three figures in 40 minutes and their 200 in 80 minutes. Brian Stevens suggested very early on in the Lord's Taverners innings that the game would end with the scores level and, sure enough, the final score was 295 for 8. Given my belief that cricket was a game to be treated seriously, I felt curiously short-changed as the final stages were reached, especially when Gerry Marsden came in to bat and started to act the fool. This was a cricket match, I thought, not a pantomime.

Later on that evening, when I had had a chance to think about the day, my unwarranted priggishness disappeared as I reflected on my good fortune in seeing some of the famous names from cricket's past. Later still, in the middle of the night, my mother woke me up to tell me that the television pictures were coming through of the Apollo 11 space capsule on the surface of the moon, in which Neil Armstrong was preparing to take his small step and giant leap. I was 14 years of age and the world was full of wonder.

Yorkshire won the Gillette Cup final at Lord's later in the summer, thanks to the replacement opening batsman, Barry Leadbeater – Boycott was injured again – who bravely and skilfully saw off the potent threat of the Derbyshire fast bowlers, Alan Ward and Harold Rhodes. It was the second time they had won the premier one-day trophy (having also been successful in 1965) and, following their 5 county championship successes in the 7 years I had been following their fortunes, all apparently seemed to augur well for the future. However, all was not well. Although I did not realise it at the time, it was the routine Sunday League match against Leicestershire that was to set the scene for the following years. Yorkshire were not quite good enough on that day at Scarborough, and that was to be the story for many seasons to come.

I was not to know, of course, that Yorkshire's subsequent wilderness period would last for so long: it was to be 1983 before they won another trophy. But I did recognise the likely outcome of several members of a successful team leaving within a relatively short period of time. I had seen the Hunslet rugby league Challenge Cup final team of 1965 break up and not be effectively replaced. The same thing was happening again. After Yorkshire's successful defence of the county championship in 1968, Trueman and Taylor retired and Illingworth moved to Leicestershire; the wicket-keeper Jimmy Binks retired after the 1969 season. And then, to widespread shock – certainly within our household – the captain Brian Close was sacked at the end of 1970.

The response from the county authorities was that there was a stream of good young players coming through from the second XI and, certainly, Leadbeater's performance in the Gillette Cup final at Lord's and the consistent excellence of Chris Old suggested that this argument might have some merit. But the other counties were moving forward as well, especially as they reinforced their domestically raised talent with the cream of the test players from overseas, and Yorkshire's competitiveness – let alone the mid 1960s dominance – was seriously undermined. The promise of the "young lads coming through" was one that would be heard – without any effective delivery, in terms of championship or other success – for many years to come. To compound the difficulties were the stories – which were hard to avoid in the rumour-laden environs of club cricket within the county – of changing room unrest amongst the remaining senior players. The catalogue of intra-team rivalry, as interpreted some years later by Close's successor as Yorkshire captain in *Boycott: The Autobiography*, makes sorry reading.

The second major component of 1969 that made it such a great year for cricket spectating was the Headingley test match between England and the West Indies. On the Monday evening – the fourth day of the match – Brian Stevens and I caught the bus straight after school from Roundhay to Headingley (changing in Harehills) and, simply, walked into the ground to watch the best part of the post-tea session for free. It seems amazing now, but, in those days, before the modern era of zealous stewarding and all-ticket entry, this could be legitimately done. We found a great vantage point, leaning against a brick wall at the back of the small seated area between the pavilion and the passageway leading to the St Michael's Lane entrance.

The images come flooding back: the ground in an early evening sunlight; Basil Butcher scoring heavily, and making up for his ineffective earlier fielding on the boundary, when he had been unable to throw the ball because of an injury to his shoulder; a flurry of wickets, including Butcher's, falling to Illingworth and Underwood; Barry Knight's huge leap in his delivery stride before offering some relatively innocuous-looking medium pace; Sobers being bowled by Knight – edging on to his stumps, if I recall correctly – without scoring.

After the day's play, it was even better. Brian and I joined the jostling throng milling about for autographs, as the players left the back of the pavilion to go to their cars. I had not taken my autograph book, so the lined pages of a school exercise book, dug out from the bottom of my rucksack, served in its stead. It was a productive session. On various scraps of paper, which were later neatly cut out and pasted into the autograph book, I obtained the signatures of no fewer than nine of the match's participants, including Basil d'Oliveira, John Snow, Charlie Davis and Grayson Shillingford. There was a trade-off, of course: the quantity of autographs that could be obtained in the available time against the "quality" of the autograph, as proxied by the size of the surrounding scrummage of ruthless hunters. I do not recall that any of the players I asked refused my request. The rich haul matched the return I had had after the Lord's Taverners versus Old England fixture (Appleyard, Wardle, Pope *et al*) and gave me the bonus of adding John Edrich's autograph (on the page of the exercise book) to the more conventional offering previously provided by his older cousin, Bill.

In his *Headingley*, John Marshall describes the ground on the occasion of this particular match, specifically "the red brick vista at the Kirkstall Lane end... nicely mellowed by two platoons (each eighteen strong) of poplars, the ample foliage of which dances prettily in the breeze". He is quick to point out that the latter did not represent an attempt to create a rural idyll by the Yorkshire club, but, rather more prosaically, was its practical solution to the tendency of the inhabitants of the local terraced houses to watch the cricket over the wall for nothing. Later on, in his description of the occasion, Marshall captures the key characteristics of the Headingley crowd: "serious, but not entirely dour... unlike any other".

My father did come with me for another match at Scarborough – a Festival fixture between England and England Under 25s – in 1970. By a coincidence analogous to the one that had enabled us to see Hunslet play in Blackpool three years earlier, the family happened to be holidaying on the east coast at the time. It was another big crowd and, whilst there was no championship or test match kudos at stake, the fixture did count as first class and the players on each side presumably thought they had something either to prove or defend. I recall the young Bob Willis – a tourist with England to Australia a few months later – running in very quickly and bowling with considerable speed, only for John Hampshire to flick his wrists at one delivery and despatch the ball several rows back into the crowd. Later, as Dad and I walked around the ground, we passed a short stocky man coming the other way, smiling and pulling faces at the nearby spectators, who responded with bouts of laughter and affectionate finger pointing. My father remembered this incident with great affection for many years afterwards: the day we were at Scarborough and walked past Les Dawson.

My father's holiday planning had been less well organised the previous year. We had arranged to spend a week in North Wales and were scheduled to come back to Leeds on the Saturday morning, as usual. I spent most of the Friday evening trying to persuade my parents that it would be a good idea to set off very early – six o'clock in the morning would be about right, I thought – in order that I could make it back to Headingley for the start of the three day match against Somerset. My tantrums were to no avail. My parents were fairly down in the dumps after a rainswept week and a jellyfish-ridden beach in Rhyl and the last thing they wanted was to be hurried along by their impatient son. I spent the whole journey in the back of the car, looking at my watch and wondering how many overs I would miss: those up to the lunch interval, as it turned out. The Somerset overseas player was someone I had never heard of, but I judged that he was clearly something of a demon with the ball, as he took seven wickets in Yorkshire's first innings: he was a 21-year-old Australian called Greg Chappell. His scores of 43 and 32 suggested that he might be able to bat as well.

I can remember that, after this match was over, I knew that it would be the last one I would see in 1969, and that I was really disappointed that the season was about to end. There was an overwhelming feeling of anti-climax. When I got home, I worked out how many days there were until the beginning of the 1970 season – roughly, as the fixture list had not yet been published – and began the process of mentally ticking them off. I should think that this exercise lasted about three days: that is, until I had lost myself in the new rugby season and my attentions had turned elsewhere.

My other recollection of the Somerset match was that it was interrupted by at least one very heavy downpour. When this happened, I adopted the normal tactic of going over to the back of the pavilion and waiting outside the players' entrance on the offchance of collecting more autographs. Unlike for the test match, however, the number of others doing likewise on this occasion was relatively few, and I found myself at the front of a short queue trying to find some shelter next to the door at the bottom of the stairs leading up to the players' changing rooms. Almost immediately, I also found myself being summoned by one of the Yorkshire officials up to the home side's changing room, where I was asked by Phil Sharpe if I would mind running around to the newsagents to buy him a paper. I was given a shilling and despatched to do the job.

I don't think that I seriously considered the option of pocketing the shilling and going home, largely because – so I reasoned – this might have jeopardised my chances of successfully getting autographs on any future occasions. Therefore, I carried out the errand, as commissioned, and, after persuading the same official jobsworth at the foot of the stairs that I had legitimate business in the Yorkshire changing room, I returned to give Sharpe his paper and his sixpence change. Sharpe did not pay me much attention, as he was sitting at a sturdy table in the middle of the room studying his hand of cards, with Brian Close sitting opposite him demanding to know what he was going to do. But he was gracious enough to thank me and give me the sixpence as a tip. I felt suitably rewarded: this was surely a prize to beat any of the autographs that I had still to collect.

In the event, the autograph hunting at this match was as productive as at the Lord's Taverners/Old England charity match and the England/ West Indies test match: Chris Old, Doug Padgett, Mervyn Kitchen, Greg Chappell... And the prize one of all, carefully written in blue biro: Geoff Boycott. I was ecstatic at this last capture, as Boycott's mark was – supposedly – very hard to obtain directly from the man himself. After that: nothing. I think it is interesting, looking back, that the Yorkshire versus Somerset match was the last at which I collected any autographs at all.

It was as if, by capturing the prime scalp of Geoff Boycott, some psychological threshold had been reached. As a result, the succeeding pages of the book have remained empty to this day. The next time I would see an autograph book would be exactly 30 years later, at Disneyland in California, when my children were excitedly holding their books and waiting in line for the marks of Mickey Mouse, Goofy and Pluto.

When I got home from the rain-affected day of the Somerset match, I put Sharpe's sixpence in the top drawer of a cabinet in my bedroom, confidently deciding that I would keep it as a souvenir and not spend it. It was only on the following day that I realised that there were two other sixpences already in there, as well as a handful of other loose change. I kept the three coins for several weeks, before deciding that it was too much of a luxury to hoard them all and that they would have to join my limited stock of available spending money.

The next three or four summers followed similar patterns: test matches and/ or Yorkshire games at Headingley or one of the other grounds, occasionally with my father and sometimes with my friends – a classmate called Andrew Carter was by this time a regular partner – but often by myself. From Yorkshire's county championship matches during this period, my stock of scorecards reveals that I saw the likes of Lancashire, Leicestershire and Surrey, whose combined ranks of overseas players included Clive Lloyd, Farokh Engineer, Graham McKenzie and Intikhab Alam.

My routine during these matches at Headingley followed a series of well-established rituals: the single-decker number 45 bus ride from near my parents' home in Moortown all the way through to the ground; entry at the Kirkstall Lane side of the ground; the purchase of a newspaper from the small newsstand on the walk through to the tarmacadamed cycle track (not used as a car park for the cricket, as my uncle Vic had patiently informed me on a previous occasion); the surveillance of the complete ground as it opened up in front of me; and, not least, the inhalation of the particular smell of Headingley, more often than not of the dampness of the acres of wooden terracing on the western side, especially if the morning was dull or there had been overnight rain. Then, a crucial decision: the selection of one of the benches on the same Western Terrace. This required careful thought. Not only did I need to have a reasonably elevated perspective of the playing area, but the bench itself needed to be of the newer and cleaner wood that had been used in one of the periodic restorations of parts of the rows of seating in that part of the ground; it was certainly important to avoid the rotten seating, with its heavy splinters and little red insects, that covered much of the available terrace. (I consistently decided that the hire of one of the hard cushions that were available for daily rental either did not represent good value for money or fell exorbitantly outside my price range).

At Headingley, at the beginning of the second and third days' play, the new scorecard would be updated to include the full details of the completed innings and the wickets to fall during the innings in progress, though not the scores of the not out batsmen. This latter information would be given on the large scoreboard, erect against the backdrop of dark trees, which had registered the scores when play had stopped on the previous evening and had then retained them, unchanged, overnight. On these days, therefore, before the play was resumed, the scoreboard represented a time shift – back to 6.30pm the previous day – not only in capturing the individual and team scores at that particular moment but also, by identifying their respective numbers as given on the scorecard, in registering the two bowlers who were in action at the time. I was fascinated by the significant authority that the scoreboard thus possessed. The new day might present a new set of circumstances – refreshed players, different weather conditions, and so on – but, for the observer, the scoreboard ensured the proper continuity between one day's play and the next. It was both the lock on the state of the game when play had ceased on the previous evening and the bridge to the resumption of activity on this new day.

Part of the ritual of the day was established by the timing of the play itself, of course. The standard hours of play were quickly and firmly established in my mind: 11.30am until 1.30pm, 2.10pm until 4.15pm and 4.35pm until 6.30pm. This daily schedule has been brought forward in the years since then, and quite rightly so. I can recall wondering at an early stage why those sunny hours that were available before play started could be so casually forfeited, apart from on the last morning, when played started at 11.00am. Less significantly – but still somewhat annoyingly for the teenage pedant – it was also something of a mystery as to why the tea interval could not run for the 20 minutes from 4.10pm, thereby giving a perfect symmetry to the whole day. My abiding memory of the timetable, however, is of the number of occasions on which I waited patiently for the players to leave the field at lunchtime and then, after polishing off the sandwiches that my mother had dutifully prepared, looking across the Headingley ground to the pavilion clock. It invariably announced that it was 1.40pm – no later – thereby implicitly reporting that I would have to endure a long wait before the action would be resumed.

In addition to my sheets of paper on which to score the match, together with the usual provisions of food and drink, the contents of the rucksack I used for the visits to Headingley and elsewhere always included the current edition of the *Playfair Cricket Annual*. I still have the editions for 1970–73 – with their respective covers of John Edrich, John Snow, Geoff Boycott and Tony Greig – as well as a later edition (1996, Wasim Akram) which was bought for me as a Father's Day gift. One of my friends airily dismissed these publications at the time as "the poor man's *Wisden*", which might have been correct, but I didn't much care. The Playfairs gave me a huge amount of detail, including about the individual backgrounds of Yorkshire's daily opponents. They were also smaller and more compact and, most relevantly, within my price range: the 1970 edition cost 4 shillings, compared with the soft cover version of the *Wisden Cricketers' Almanack* at 30 shillings and the hard cover version at 35 shillings.

Some considerable time later, I reflected back on this purchasing decision. I decided that, had I bought *Wisden* in those years, I would almost certainly have continued to buy it in every subsequent year. Moreover, being the collector and hoarder I am, I might well have attempted to build up the collection of previous editions through second hand purchases. As it was, the first edition that I bought was that of 2002 and, only then, in recognition of Yorkshire's championship success of the previous year.

My father came with me to some of the Yorkshire days. I sat with him at an unfamiliar part of the Headingley ground, for us – the stretch of seating between the pavilion and the "coconut shy" behind the bowlers arm – as we watched the Yorkshire colt Andrew Dalton compile a stylish century in a championship match against Middlesex in 1972. The opposition's bowlers included the test player, John Price, a veteran of the 1964 MCC tour to India, the details of which I had devoured as a nine year-old in my treasured *Cricket Spotlight* magazine. Price had undoubtedly the most extraordinary run up I have ever seen. He started off somewhere around wide off, before running away from the batsman towards the boundary and then round in a wide arc until he straightened up to come in past the umpire. I had seen Price play on television several times – including earlier that summer in the Lord's test match against Australia – and I knew what to expect; Dad sat next to me, utterly dumbfounded. The crowd in the seats around us were also bemused and the catcalling was not long in coming, partly because Price would stop to glare at the batsman after practically every delivery, before slowly beginning the long trudge back to his mark. What I also realised, however, was that Price was a fine bowler – hostile and accurate, and rewarded by six wickets in the match – and it was an outstanding piece of batting by Dalton to make his score.

Yorkshire had to bowl Middlesex out after lunch on the last day to win. They did so through the efforts of their seam attack, led by Richard

Hutton and Howard Cooper, who took eight wickets between them, including the first four batsmen to lbw decisions. The umpires were Ron Aspinall and Arthur Jepson, both of whom, after an appeal, seemed to take an inordinately long time to make a decision: not a bad characteristic for an umpire, in my view. My recollection is that one of the Middlesex batsmen, on being given out lbw for the second time in the match, also took his time before departing from the crease, after carefully studying where his leg had been struck in relation to the wicket. His action (or inaction) did not affect the final reckoning in my scoring book, however: JM Brearley duly followed his first innings "lbw Nicholson 0" with a second innings "lbw Cooper 3". The umpires' regular answers in the affirmative were delivered by a slowly raised finger and, with a loud cheer of approval from the spectators, added to the enjoyment of Yorkshire's success.

I would judge that, of the John Player Sunday League games I saw during this period, Yorkshire won fewer than half. Many of the defeats came in the last over against sides that I would have expected them to beat: Glamorgan at the Bradford Park Avenue ground in 1970, Derbyshire at Harrogate in 1971, Hampshire at Bradford in 1972. Other losses were more comprehensive: at Headingley in 1973, Lancashire reduced Yorkshire to 35 for 8 and won with embarrassing ease. I went to this game with my father. We watched Geoff Boycott go through his pre-match ritual, about half an hour before the start, of walking out to the wicket, complete with bat and gloves though without pads, in order to stand in his guard and play a couple of practice shots against some imaginary deliveries. Boycott carefully examined the state of the pitch, looked around the ground to take in the overall environment for that day's contest and then exited the field back to the Yorkshire changing room. He was marking his territory, I thought: sending a subtle – or not so subtle – message to the opposition that this was his domain. A few minutes later, he was followed out into the middle of the ground by the Lancashire opening batsmen, Barry Wood, who always struck me as having modelled himself closely on Boycott – he was two years younger – and who had a good track record against his native county. Wood went through exactly the same routine: standing at the crease, playing some shots, studying the pitch and then withdrawing to the changing room with his mental preparation complete. In the game that followed, Boycott and Wood scored a total of 12 runs between them.

One opening batsman who did leave an impression was Gordon Greenidge, who formed a formidable combination with Barry Richards for Hampshire during this period. I can distinctly recall Greenidge facing Graham Stevenson, the Yorkshire seam bowler, in a Sunday League game at Bradford and, from my position on the main terrace, seeing him pull a short ball for four over to the narrow row of seating on the far side of the ground. It was the efficient dispatch of a poor delivery, but nothing particularly out of the ordinary for a batsman of the quality of Greenidge. Stevenson decided that his next delivery should again be short, but also, this time, quicker. Greenidge duly deposited it in exactly the same direction, the only difference being that it went over the whitewashed wall than ran behind the row of seating and out of the ground. I thought at the time – and I can picture the stroke to this day – that it was a shot of absolute contempt. This was a batsman who, even within the narrow context of a routine limited overs match, not only sought to dominate his opponent in the scorebook but also to impose some heavy psychological damage. I was to recall Greenidge's shot several years later when, in partnership with Desmond Haynes, his powerful driving and cutting contributed to an emphatic West Indies victory in a test match at Headingley.

Other matches, particularly late on in the season, were abandoned to the weather: for example Somerset at Harrogate and Middlesex at Bradford in 1970. For the latter, I paid my admission money to watch Brian Close, immaculately attired in his blazer and slacks, toss up with Peter Parfitt, who was dressed for the snug bar. Parfitt must have known what was coming: Middlesex scored precisely nought for no wickets, off seven deliveries, before the rains came. There was no chance of a refund, of course.

It was also at Bradford, in the early evening after a Sunday League game had been completed, that I wandered across from the main terrace to have a look at the pitch in the middle of the square. On this occasion – I do not recall which particular game it was – I had gone to the match by myself, following the familiar route of the bus journey from Leeds City bus station to Forster Square and then the walk up the hill to the ground. The umpires had pulled up the stumps and laid them out on the ground, in preparation for the groundsman's later work to tidy up the playing area. I put my rucksack down nearby. There were one or two other spectators casually strolling over the centre of the ground, but I was the only one on the pitch itself. I stood at the crease and – in the style of Boycott and Wood – imagined someone coming in to bowl to me from the football stand end. I probably played half a dozen shots, beginning with a couple of forward defensive pushes and then stretching my left leg a little further to drive through the covers. There was no bat in my hand, of course, but I could improvise without it, taking care to ensure my left elbow was in the correct position and my head was over the non-existent ball. At the same time, curiously, I imagined that I was also still on the spectators' terrace, away to my right, watching the action on the pitch. The pleasant excitement of this experience came to an abrupt end, however, when it was interrupted by someone banging furiously on one of the windows of the pavilion far away beyond the boundary edge and up at the top of the steep bank of members' seating. This was followed by a distressed shout, again from a long distance, of "Get off the bloody pitch". I was somewhat surprised at this. Was whoever was shouting aiming their instructions at me? I looked around: it could only have been me. What was the problem, I thought. Yorkshire's match was over and, in any case, I was only wearing soft-soled training shoes. But I took the (fairly strong) hint. I played one more forward defensive shot and then picked up my rucksack and walked back towards the main terrace, behind which was the exit I needed in order to take the main road leading back down to Forster Square.

Of the test match days viewed during these years, the dullest experience, by far, was the Saturday of the 1971 test match against Pakistan, when a grand total of 159 runs were scored in 104 overs over the course of the whole day. Ken Dalby's lyrical *Headingley Test Cricket 1899–1975* refers to the "mummified spectators, shrouded in gloom, and an arthritic scoreboard creaking wearily for six agonising hours". In reality, it was not as exciting as that. Far more enjoyably, two years later, I saw the first part of an immaculate Boycott century against New Zealand: Dalby reports that "the Yorkshireman treated the New Zealand bowlers like hired hacks, whipping the ball away with contemptuous ease". Both these games were won by England, with Illingworth at the helm.

The England-New Zealand match was Dickie Bird's first as a test match umpire. In *Dickie Bird: My Autobiography*, he describes how, leaving nothing to chance, he arrived at the ground at 7 o'clock on the first morning and had to wait for the groundsman to open the gates. "Once inside I went to sit at the back of the football stand and looked out over the empty ground... I had a cup of tea and a biscuit, wittered and invented all kinds of things to do... It was a tremendous thrill when I walked out... I felt even better after making my first lbw decision".

In between these games came the extraordinary – or infamous, depending on one's perspective – Headingley test against Australia in 1972. The tourists batted first and, sitting in my usual position on the western side, I can still hear someone shouting "Come on, Stackpole. Get them fair", as the Australian opener edged and snicked a series of fortuitous boundaries on his way to a scratchy half-century. After Australia had been dismissed cheaply and England had then lost seven wickets without overhauling their total, there followed the match's decisive – if somewhat improbable – century partnership between Ray Illingworth and John Snow.

Three memories remain of the England innings. The first is of one of the tailenders sending a huge skier to Bob Massie at long leg. The fielder circled around under the ball for an absolute age – all to the rising crescendo of the crowd's baying – before emphatically dropping the catch to a massive jeering cheer. The second is the Australian captain Ian Chappell giving himself a bowl and then putting on his brother, Greg (late of Somerset), in a desperate attempt to break the Illingworth-Snow partnership. It could have been the same voice as had advised Stackpole the previous day: "Put thee mother on". And the third – of longer duration – is of my huge enjoyment of the dour struggle, as England gained the ascendancy on the second day. Illingworth batted for four hours before, with some intended irony I suspect, registering his half century with a huge six over long on. In contrast with Pakistan's crawl the previous year, I was utterly captivated by the unfolding evolution of the match.

Illingworth and Underwood bowled England to another Headingley victory on the Saturday, when I was playing in a club cricket match. Their combined achievement of 14 wickets in the match was later attributed to the grass on the pitch having succumbed to a fungus. My less than objective interpretation at the time – which has not been significantly amended over the years – was that it was down to skilful bowling against batsmen who were not able to cope with the difficult conditions. Dalby refers to the "cunning psychological malevolence" of the two England spin bowlers.

This era of cricket spectating came to an end for me in the last week of August 1974. I had been awarded a place at the University of Cambridge and was about to live away from home for the first time. My father and I went to the second day of Yorkshire's match against Surrey at Bradford. Surrey were a useful side, with a selection of England and overseas test players and some promising newcomers, including the following year's Cambridge captain Chris Aworth. It was a fitting conclusion. We saw Boycott score an undefeated century to give Yorkshire a healthy first innings lead and then watched Phil Carrick take the first two of his six second innings wickets that enabled Yorkshire to win by an innings. One of his victims was Aworth, whom Carrick deceived in the air and bowled, throwing both arms jubilantly upwards as the bails fell to the ground. (My family will recognise this action as the one I make on the rare occasions that I answer a question correctly on *University Challenge*). I thought that I might mention this to the Light Blue skipper, if our paths crossed the following summer, though I also realised I would probably have to choose the right moment.

My hobby of recording each ball of cricket matches, ranging from test matches through to one day games, lasted only slightly longer. My last two games – both followed on radio and television – were the final of the first cricket World Cup between Australia and West Indies at Lord's in 1975 (including a century by Clive Lloyd) and a one day Prudential international between England and West Indies at Scarborough in 1976 (including a century by Viv Richards). In the latter match, England included the 20-year-old Ian Botham, who was dismissed for 1 and took 1 for 26 off his 3 overs; I thought he bowled too short and I was not sure whether he had a future in international cricket.

It was around this time, in an exercise that would be envied by the keenest train-spotter, that I devised my own *Wisden*-like list of cricket records from the matches I had scored. It was an impressive compilation. The century-makers ranged from respected names from my early cricket-watching days (Hanif Mohammed, Ken Barrington, Graeme Pollock, the last of these for the Rest of the World against England at the Oval in 1970) through to the modern heavyweights such as Lloyd and Richards although, ironically, the highest individual score I recorded was achieved in my very first scored game: Phil Sharpe's 197 for Yorkshire against Pakistan in 1967. The list of 5-wicket bowling hauls was dominated by Derek Underwood (against Pakistan, Australia and New Zealand), whilst the leading wicket-keepers were Jimmy Binks of Yorkshire and Alan Knott of England. There were 3 "pairs" (including Brian Luckhurst, whom Mike Proctor bowled out twice at the Oval in Pollock's match) and one hat-trick (by Ken Higgs for Lancashire against Yorkshire in 1968).

Looking back, I suppose that there are two interpretations of all this. One is that it was the sad pursuit of someone who (had the phrase not been inappropriate) needed to have got out more. Alternatively – and more positively – the scoring of the matches and the consolidation of the records represented my attempt to capture the times. Even in those days, I wanted to create a permanent and personal record of at least some of the games and the players that I had seen.

Chapter 6

Chandos Park

It was more than five years after I had first been to see Hunslet play rugby league that I attended a rugby union match. I had seen plenty of games on television, mainly internationals in those days, and I had already stored some famous tries in my memory bank – Richard Sharp's classic fly half's try against Scotland in 1963; Andy Hancock's length of the field effort for England, also against Scotland, in 1965; Keith Jarrett flashing on from the left of the screen to catch a bouncing ball and hare down the touchline in Cardiff to score for Wales against England in 1967 – but my father and I had never ventured to see a club game in the flesh. The irony was that the nearest club – Roundhay RUFC – played at a ground called Chandos Park in suburban north Leeds, less than a quarter of an hour's walk from where we lived.

My first game was not at Roundhay, however, but further afield, at Leicester: the English Schools versus French Schools (19 Group) international of 1967. This was a school trip, organised by the woodwork teacher and first XV rugby master, Mr Elliott. I persuaded one of my first year classmates to go with me and we travelled down on a bus packed mainly with older boys from the fifth and sixth forms. My abiding memory of the match is of being seated in the middle of a long row of spectators and, from virtually the opening kick off, being in desperate need of a pee. For some reason, probably fear of disrupting the older people around me, I sat cross-legged and in very considerable discomfort throughout the whole match: an experience that I have carefully sought to avoid ever since. For this reason, I probably paid less than my usual attention to the rugby match, notwithstanding that it was in an unfamiliar code with lots of kicking and frequent interruptions for line outs and scrums. This was a pity because the teams included some future senior players of distinction, including Keith

Fielding, Tony Neary and Robert Paparemborde. However, I did notice the heavy northern representation in the English side, with six players from Yorkshire schools and another four from Lancashire or Durham.

Dad and I picked a good game for our first venture to Chandos Park: Roundhay versus Headingley, played on a pleasant Spring evening in 1968. I could see right from the outset that this was more than a rugby match. This was a conflict about class and status.

The Headingley club – founded in 1878 – was one of the elite in the union code. Their fixture list boasted matches against many of the other nationally renowned clubs of the day – Coventry, London Scottish, Northampton, Wasps, Rosslyn Park, Richmond – as well as the stronger clubs in the north of England. The Roundhay club, on the other hand, was trying to break into this upper tier. Its formation was more recent (1924) and the fixture card was almost entirely drawn from the north: confrontations with tough sides such as Morley and Wakefield as well as the local fixtures with smaller clubs such as Old Roundhegians and Old Birkonians.

These were the days, of course, before any hint of meritocracy in the national club hierarchy. There was no formal league structure, or promotion and relegation. It was even before the advent of a national club knock-out tournament, which did not come into being until the 1970s. The only trophy contested by Roundhay was the annual Yorkshire Cup which, at this stage (maintaining the pattern of the previous half century) Headingley did not enter. Across England as a whole, the standing of any club was determined by two factors: its results on the pitch and, more significantly, the quality of its fixture list. The latter could only be improved – and, even then, only slowly – by sustained improvements, over many years, in the former.

I was not aware of any general animosity between the Roundhay and Headingley clubs. It was just that, from my limited reading of the pair's fortunes in the Green Post, there was little contact between them. Players did not seem to move from one to the other and, apart from their twice yearly meetings on the pitch, the clubs existed on more or less parallel lines. This April evening was, therefore, a rare opportunity for those lines to cross: the old guard versus the aspiring *arrivistes*.

My father and I took up our position on the banking of grassy terrace behind the goalposts nearest to the entrance to the ground in Chandos Avenue. It was a neat ground, with a small amount of seating in the stand to the right and a newly built clubhouse – to be officially opened that evening by the Lord Mayor of Leeds – in one corner. From our perspective, the pitch sloped down from right to left and also, slightly, towards us: I imagined that if a team found itself pinned down in defence in the near left hand corner, it would be quite difficult to force its way out.

Roundhay's match programme was also neat and well-presented, and not dissimilar to the one with which I was familiar at Hunslet: a page of club notes, the teams listed on the centre pages, plenty of local advertising and, an added bonus, the full fixture list with accompanying results. However, unlike the rugby league programmes with which I was familiar, there was also the novel feature of the designation of the special status of some of the players: a small sword or asterisk marking them as an international or county player, respectively. Roundhay had one county player, but Headingley had seven (including a certain I McGeechan at fly half[19]), one of whom – G Frankcom in the centre – was an international.

I remember the game as being tight and closely fought. Dad and I remarked afterwards that there had not been much passing of the ball amongst the threequarters. Rather, it had been a tactical battle with the respective half backs kicking for position: a fairly typical rugby union match of its time and, therefore, a good introduction for me. I enjoyed the tactical cat and mouse. The abiding memory, however, is of the Roundhay centre, Keith Jones – KHD Jones in the programme – bursting past his illustrious opposite numbers to cross the try line right in front of where we were standing and scoring behind the posts. This gave Roundhay a short-lived lead, and there was the serious prospect of the natural order of things being at least temporarily undermined, but Headingley came back strongly in the second half to secure a narrow win.

Roundhay's relative status for a local fixture was reversed during the following season when they were matched away at a club called Rodillians – the old boys of Rothwell Grammar School – in a Yorkshire Cup quarter final match. Brian Stevens and I went to see this mainly because one of our games teachers played in the centre for the home side. This involved two bus rides, one from north Leeds into the centre of the city and another on a red single-decker bus from the City Bus Station, but I was familiar with the route. It was the one I had taken many times on a Friday evening during the two previous winters, my rucksack of kit over my shoulder and my cricket bat firmly grasped in my hand, when I had attended the Johnny Lawrence cricket school in Rothwell. This was private tuition, paid for by my father, in the company of a handful of other boys and in the hands of a friendly and respected tutor. Lawrence's expert guidance to other (and more talented) cricketers has been generously and appropriately acknowledged elsewhere, not least in the opening chapter of *Boycott: The Autobiography*.

Although Rodillians were a long way below Roundhay in rugby's food chain, the game fell into what I now took to be the usual pattern of club rugby in Yorkshire at that time: a tough bitterly-fought encounter, this time narrowly won by Roundhay. However, my memory of this game is not so much of any of the events on the pitch, but for my position off it. Having over-estimated the waiting and journey times for the buses, Brian and I had reached the ground a good hour before the kick off and could have chosen anywhere from which to watch the match. In the event, I ended up standing on a low brick wall at the edge of the stand. It was only when the game was about to kick off, and the full crowd meant that all the other options for viewing had been closed off, that Brian pointed out that there seemed to be a loose sheet of metal hanging precariously off the roof of the stand above us.

In retrospect, I can say that this was one of the rugby matches that I have enjoyed viewing the least: not for the action (or lack of it) on the pitch, but because I feared for my safety from the expected falling masonry. Every time that the spectators shouted or jumped to their feet, the stand seemed to vibrate. I lost count of the number of times I looked away from the game and up to the edge of the roof. I was hugely relieved when the game was over and I could move away from the spot. It is interesting, looking back, that although I had been genuinely afraid of being guillotined by a rapidly descending sharp object, I did not cut my losses and move from my position on the wall. I had obviously determined to see as much of the game as I could before either being fatally injured by the falling metal or taking evasive action by jumping to safety.

Roundhay reached the final of the Yorkshire Cup in that 1968–69 season and, never having previously won it, no doubt viewed the final against Wakefield with a combination of reserve and expectation. This was an opportunity to demonstrate that they were (in Headingley's absence) the champion side in the county and, as a result, deserved greater recognition from the elite clubs. Wakefield were tough opposition, however, not least because they fielded a large bearded full back called Chris Parkes, who was a prodigious goal kicker. I went to the game, at Otley, on a Monday evening in late April with Brian Stevens and our rugby-playing games teacher. It was another fierce encounter, which, highly unusually for any sporting contest in those days, went into sudden death extra time. Parkes kicked a long range penalty and Roundhay's hopes were dashed for another season.

Following my usual routine, I searched the sports pages of the *Yorkshire Evening Post* over the next couple of evenings for a report and analysis of the match. I wasn't particularly hopeful: rugby union was the poor relation in the newspaper's sports coverage at the best of times and, true to form, there was only a single captioned photograph of the Wakefield captain lifting the trophy. It is only fair to point out, however, that, on this occasion, there was another sports story demanding attention. On the same evening that the destination of the Yorkshire Cup had been decided, Leeds United had fought out a goalless draw away to Liverpool to secure their first Football League championship title.

My father and I had no particular allegiance to the Roundhay club. They were our local side and, if Hunslet were not playing – and it was a reasonable afternoon or evening – we would take the short journey round to Chandos Park to watch a match. Accordingly, we saw a parade of northern club teams – Hull and East Riding, Preston Grasshoppers, Durham City, Vale of Lune, *et al* – most of which were defeated by the continuously improving Roundhay side. The arrangements for entry to these matches were relatively informal: sometimes, for the bigger matches, there was an admission charge (with a receipt in the form of a cloakroom ticket); on other occasions there was just a charge (with the assumed honest club official putting the money into his jacket pocket); and usually (and almost always if the match had been underway for more than a couple of minutes), we just walked straight in. Sometimes, there was a match programme; often, to my disappointment, there was not. Often, our arrival at the ground would coincide with the players leaving the changing rooms and walking straight past us across the small car park before they had to clamber under the metal railing that ran alongside the touchline at that corner of the field. It all added to the immediacy and informality of the event: the individual players wading their way between the parked cars, the irregular and ominous rattle of their metal studs on the tarmac and the haphazard entry of the two teams on to the pitch.

In keeping with the general arrangements for officiating these games, one of the touch judges would be a Roundhay member whose performance, I am bound to say on the basis of many viewings, was (almost) never other than completely impartial. The exception was on one occasion, when a dangerous opposition player received what appeared to be serious injury and the touch judge happened to be the one who, after running on to the pitch and attending to him, advised him to retire for the day. Later, after the player had made an apparently miraculous recovery that would have enabled him to resume, had he not changed back into his civvies, one of the opposition supporters stated that the decision to retire from the fray had been based on the views of the touch judge who, being a doctor, had given a firm medical pronouncement. Cue hysterical laughter from the nearby Roundhay supporters, one of whom could not resist correcting him: "Doctor? But he's a taxi driver".

During this period, my father and I also decided to pick our games at the Headingley club. This was not quite so convenient, as their ground was on the far side of the cricket ground down in Kirkstall, but we realised it was a good opportunity to view some of the international players we had previously only seen on television. It was with great anticipation, therefore, when we went along on the Saturday before Easter 1969 to see Cardiff.

As ever, I was fascinated by the Headingley programme, in which, again surrounded by a healthy amount of advertising copy, the club notes ran for five pages. These included a description of the long association between the two clubs, which dated back to 1911: a good illustration, if one were needed, of how the longevity of the contact within the select group of clubs was implicitly seen as a characteristic of the membership of that group and, therefore, something to be preserved. However, the particular point of interest – and a perfect indication of the relative status that Headingley considered that it had (and, indeed, did have), compared with its local rivals – was that the asterisks against certain players' names only referred to internationals; the county players were not worthy of designation. Headingley had one asterisked player (John Spencer) to Cardiff's five.

Two of the latter provided the principal reason that Dad and I had gone to watch the match. The Cardiff half back pairing of Barry John and Gareth Edwards was not only the current Welsh combination, but had appeared together for the British Lions in South Africa the previous year. I couldn't wait to see them. In the event, it turned out that I would have to wait a little longer. Although their appearance had been anticipated in the local paper, and their names were listed in the programme, neither John or Edwards played in the game. As Dad and I waited on the crowded open terracing next to the stand, just before the teams took the field from the clubhouse behind the goalposts to our right, the team changes were announced. The reserve half backs were playing. I had an immediate feeling of acute disappointment – shared, he told me later, by my father – and even though I recovered sufficiently to take in the occasion of seeing the famous Cardiff side in action, there was an inevitable sense of anti-climax. Many years later, I learned that, even in those distinctly amateur days, Gareth Edwards would pick and choose the "important" matches in which to play. This might help to explain his astonishing run of over 40 consecutive appearances for Wales. In attitude and preparation, his was a "professional" approach long before the formal change in status of the elite rugby union player.

Even without their absent stars, Cardiff were just too strong for Headingley, winning narrowly. In the programme for the following matches – a double edition to cover the Easter fixtures at home to Coventry (David Duckham, asterisk) and Gosforth (Roger Uttley, no asterisk at that stage), the editor quaintly reported that "we were beaten by a very fine side composed of delightful chaps".

In 1970, I got my chance to play on one of the most famous rugby grounds in the world. I was a member of the Roundhay School Under 15 team taking part in the Llanelli "sevens". This was an extensive and well-run event, comprising under 15 and open age schools competitions as well as plate tournaments for the first round losers in each. A number of venues were used and the luck of the draw meant that our second round tie was on the main pitch at the Llanelli club. We had a reasonable side, but little more, and we were beaten by Howardian High School. To be honest, although I played at fly half in the full fifteen-a-side version, the sevens game was not my *forte*: I could give and take a pass and I had a hefty boot, but my acceleration off the mark – indeed, my basic speed – left a lot to be desired. This is something of a handicap in sevens rugby. I can remember that the Llanelli pitch was both long and wide, and when one of our opponents picked up a loose ball in his own half and disappeared into the distance, it seemed even longer.

However, my greater disappointment was off the pitch. The organisers of the Llanelli tournament had produced a detailed programme, which contained the names and colours of all the competing schools and, for both age groups, all the players' names. Unfortunately, these team lists had had to be submitted several weeks earlier when, for some reason – I can only assume that my lack of blistering acceleration had had something to do with it – our rugby teacher had decided that I would not make the squad. I had thought at the time that this was unfair and, sure enough, I did make the first VII for the tournament. But when we got there, of course, my name was not in the programme – unlike the names of others who had ended up being nowhere near selection. A trivial issue, perhaps, but still a source of disappointment.

I have two other strong memories of the tournament. The first was on the first evening, when a number of the members of our squad – suitably bold on their *sojourn* away from home – entered a rather down-at-heel pub in the centre of the town. The locals looked quizzically at us, silently asking "You're not from around here, are you?" Having planned the expedition in advance, we dispatched our two biggest forwards to the bar to order six pints. I was excused this duty: as a fifteen year-old, who looked, at most, fifteen, I was trying to be inconspicuous at the back of the group, whilst desperately hoping that there were no policemen in the pub. The barman nodded in a friendly manner and asked if we were in town for the rugby. One of my friends confidently said yes were, we had come down from Leeds and were playing in the Under 15s tournament. The barman gave him a sympathetic but reproachful look, and we made our exits. Reflecting on this later, after we had settled for fish and chips and a can of coke from an equally down-at-heel takeaway shop, I thought of the scene in *The Great Escape* when Gordon Jackson is wished good luck by the German policeman and is condemned out of his own mouth when he answers in English.

The second memory is of the open age schools event, in which Roundhay reached the final. In the opposition – from Cowley School, St Helens – was the best schoolboy rugby player I had seen. John Horton played at fly half for the England Schools team and I could see why: he had the ability to read the play, speed off the mark, a bewildering sidestep and a strong kick. The only comparison I would make with Horton at this stage would be in the next competition I played in at Llanelli – two years later, by which time I had graduated to the second of Roundhay's open age sides – when another fly half, David Richards, won the competition for Neath Grammar School. These were the first of my contemporaries, or near contemporaries, to have stood out from the pack, metaphorically speaking, as considerable talents who could go far in the game. A few weeks after the final of the Llanelli sevens tournament, I pointed Horton out to my father when the St Helens rugby union team came to play a match against the Roundhay club at Chandos Park. Roundhay won comfortably, but it was clear that Horton was on his way up.

Dad and I were able to increase the frequency of our visits to watch Roundhay or Headingley matches when the rugby league authorities switched their schedules, including Hunslet's games, to Sundays. In one notable match, in March 1972, Roundhay defeated Orrell 21–7, the first time that the visitors had been beaten in 58 matches. The two clubs had much in common: both were successful and ambitious and keen to force their way up the club hierarchy. I had wanted to see Orrell for some time. Their name had been the one that had stood out in the rather curious table of the season's records of the northern rugby union clubs that was published every week in my dad's *Daily Express*. The clubs were listed in alphabetical order – perhaps 60 or 70 altogether – and their performances were given in the usual way: played, won, drawn, lost, points for, points against. There was no concession to the respective degrees of difficulty in the clubs' fixture lists and so the table actually gave no information at all on the clubs' relative strengths. Nonetheless, I studied the table as it was updated throughout the season, noting the diminishing number of clubs that had won all their games, until only one remained. However, after the Roundhay match, even Orrell had a lonely figure "1" in the defeats column.

The Headingley club also hosted some of Yorkshire's matches in the northern group of the rugby union county championship. Yorkshire consistently had a talented set of three-quarters – spearheaded by the Headingley partnership of Spencer and McGeechan – but the forwards were not so powerful, and the side usually came second best in the group to either Lancashire or Northumberland. Yorkshire also played a series of other matches at the same venue, and so it was that, in October 1972, Dad and I saw the great Willie John McBride lead out his Ulster side.

In *Willie John: The Story of My Life*, McBride has written movingly about how the surviving connections between rugby clubs in Northern Ireland and the republic of Ireland and, more generally, between Irish rugby and that in the rest of Britain helped to sustain the community in the north during the "Troubles" of the early 1970s. My personal view is that the story of the roar with which the Lansdowne Road crowd greeted the England team as it took the field in 1973, following the refusal of both the Welsh and Scottish rugby unions to play in Dublin in 1972, and of the response to the England captain John Pullin's introductory remarks at the post-match dinner – "We may not be much good, but at least we turn up" – is one of the most heart-warming sporting narratives of the twentieth century. The annual Yorkshire-Ulster fixture should be put in this context and, reading McBride's account of the importance of rugby to him and his province at that time, it is clear that there would never have been any doubt that he would turn out to play on that day at Headingley.

The Headingley ground was also the venue for the Yorkshire Cup finals of 1973 and 1974, both of which were contested by Roundhay and Morley and won by the latter. After the second match, in which the formidable Morley side recorded a 27–16 victory, the *Yorkshire Evening Post*'s verdict was characteristically provincial: Morley were "one of the best drilled and best equipped teams in the north of England". I can remember very little about these games except that the first of them was won by a superlative individual try in the closing minutes by the Morley scrum half, John Warren, and that both matches were contested with an unremitting ferocity. Years later, I was interested to read, in *Brian Moore: The Autobiography*, the former England hooker's comments, based on his experience of senior rugby in Yorkshire at the beginning of the 1980s, that the rivalries between the local clubs resulted in some "near-brutal battles" and that, by comparison with the harshness of the game at that time, modern day rugby is nowhere remotely near as dirty as it used to be. My view is that this assessment also holds for this earlier period in the first half of the 1970s, not only for the Roundhay-Headingley-Morley-Wakefield clashes, but also for the wider confrontations in the fledgling national knock-out competitions: the Morley versus Orrell and Headingley versus Gosforth games in December 1973 were examples. I watched these games with a grimacing fascination from the various touchlines and knew that I did not aspire to play rugby at this level.

Notwithstanding the ferocious nature of these club matches in Yorkshire at this time, I can only recall seeing one player sent off the field. This was in a Roundhay versus Headingley game at Chandos Park and, given the regular violence associated with this fixture, the circumstances were ironic, if not bizarre. I can still conjure a mental picture, as viewed from the touchline on the lower side of the ground, of watching a Roundhay player preparing to take a kick at goal from close to the Headingley posts, presumably a conversion or a penalty goal. One of the Headingley players must have said something to the referee, because he was called over and given a dressing down before being told to take his place behind the Headingley try line. I can only assume that he repeated the remark – in spirit, if not verbatim – because the referee called him over again and, this time, pointed to the touchline on the far side of the field. The player slouched off, directly to the touchline and then along in front of the main stand towards the changing rooms. The feeling in the crowd around me – a mixture of the two sets of supporters – was a combination of bewilderment and embarrassment, principally the latter.

The significance of the two Yorkshire Cup finals was twofold. First, I was fully aware of the unique history of the competition. With the exception of the Hospitals' Cup contested by London medical students, the Yorkshire Cup was the oldest cup competition in club rugby anywhere in the world, the list of winners dating back to the first victory by Halifax over York in 1877.[20] The reference to the "t'Owd Tin Pot" was the vernacular phrase to be found in the local newspapers each spring when the competition hotted up and the bigger clubs entered in the final rounds. The fact that a vibrant and respected club remained in Halifax added weight to the robust continuity that the competition represented. (Roundhay were to win the cup for the first time in 1975).

Secondly – and more immediately – it was from 1973 that, for the first time in the modern era, the winners of the cup could genuinely describe themselves as the best side in Yorkshire. In that year, Headingley re-joined the competition for the first time in over 50 years.

The timing of Headingley's re-entry was propitious. In April 1973, a week after they had played (and lost to) the Roundhay club in the quarter final, the Roundhay School rugby club held its annual dinner. As vice-captain of the first XV, my role was to give the speech welcoming the invited guests. The main guest was one Ian McGeechan of Headingley and (by now) Scotland, as he had made his first international appearance against the All Blacks during the winter. McGeechan had marked a distinguished performance in this match by dropping a goal, something which, in my role as the school fly half, I had the occasional success with myself. I intended absolutely nothing untoward when I remarked in my speech that, from the evidence of his international debut, it was clear that, like all great fly halves, Ian McGeechan was left-footed.

By this time, one or two of the recent old boys from the school side – who were also attending the dinner – had started to make their way in club rugby and the Roundhay club was the natural home to which they gravitated, if they decided not to pursue the more social rugby route of the Old Roundhegians. I consoled McGeechan on his side's loss to Roundhay: "Better luck next year". At that point, someone half way across the room immediately responded with "And the year after that", which was followed by a *Spartacus*-type canon of repeated calls "And the year after that", "And the year…" McGeechan – a schoolteacher himself in Leeds at that time – was a gracious and entertaining guest, and his participation at the dinner was illustrative of the serious attention that was given to the sport by the school.

Chapter 7

Elland Road

In the mid-1960s, one of the teachers at St Matthew's Primary School, Chapel Allerton, Leeds was a Mrs Revie. She did not teach me – there were two teachers for each year – though my sister was in her class some years later, when she got three out of ten for her end-of-year nature study test. I think it was because we always pronounced her name as if it had a double "ee" – "Reevie" – that it took some time for me to realise who her husband was.

As with the rugby union, my early exposure to soccer was limited to the few live matches that were shown on television – principally some of the internationals and the FA Cup final – later to be supplemented by the highlights packages on BBC's *Match of the Day* and the independent channel. The very first time I saw the game on television, I told my father that I thought it was much easier than rugby: after all, the players were allowed to pass the ball forwards in order to make progress down the pitch.

It would have been at about this time – at the age of seven – that I was given *The World Book of Football Champions*, a slim but lavishly illustrated volume with an attractive mixture of statistical detail and interesting articles. I pored over it, time and again. I was especially taken with its description of the recently completed (1962) World Cup – "Brazil triumph – and England flop once more" – which included all the results of the qualifying and final rounds. Only one thing puzzled me: in the results for the African zone qualifying group, Morocco were described as having "won on drawing lots". This was a new expression to me: for a long time afterwards, I thought it meant that Morocco had drawn several matches, which the editor of the book had not been bothered to list. I did him an injustice, of course. In its coverage of domestic football, the book went on to chronicle the championship successes that year of the "smaller clubs" in

England (Ipswich Town, a team built by their "astute manager Alf Ramsey [of] misfits and cast-offs from other clubs") and Scotland (Dundee). The league tables showed that Leeds United finished fourth from bottom of the old Second Division.

Sharing pride of place with the book of football champions was my collection of cards of Kellogg's International Soccer Stars. These were given away with the large packets of Whole Wheat Flakes that – so I persuaded my sceptical mother – were my favourite breakfast cereal. There were 12 cards in the set – in alphabetical order from Jimmy Armfield through to the (later disgraced) Peter Swann – to be mounted in a specially obtained folder; I managed to track down 11 of them, the only absentee being Bobby Charlton.

It would have been when I was slightly older – perhaps in the first year at grammar school and with the newly published edition of *Philips' Modern School Atlas* to hand – that I started to pay increased attention to the 92 clubs of the Football League. As with the beneficial effects on my mental arithmetic of working out rugby league tables or batsmen's averages, finding out the location of (most of) the clubs did wonders for my sense of English geography. I learned that Northampton was not near Southampton and, similarly, that, if Chester played Chesterfield, it would not be a local derby. I was struck by the sheer distances involved. I had thought that the journeys with my uncle Bob to watch Hunslet play at Keighley or Hull Kingston Rovers had been ambitious enough. What if I had been a supporter of, say, Gillingham and they were playing at Carlisle United, or York City (a better example, as York had a rugby league team) and they were playing in Torquay?

Paradoxically, notwithstanding the potentially huge distances that would require to be travelled before reaching some of the clubs, I also wondered about the potential opportunities for visiting some of these newly located grounds and watching, live, the famous sides that played there. These were the teams whose names featured in the fixture list in my dad's Saturday morning *Daily Express* and, later the same day, in the routine early-evening round-up of the results on the radio or television and then, slightly later still, in the Green Post sports edition of the *Yorkshire Evening Post*. It was about this time that I decided that, when I was only slightly older, I would get a decent bicycle and visit all these grounds in turn, beginning, sensibly enough, with those such as Bradford City and Huddersfield Town that were reasonably close to home. (For some reason, I thought that this plan should only apply to football league clubs. I had no thoughts of a similar arrangement to cycle to the grounds of those of the 29 other rugby league sides I had not yet visited – the vast majority, of course

– as I presumed that such visits would occur inevitably, over time, on the occasion of a Hunslet away fixture). I presented the idea to my mother, who looked at me with a fairly disdainful combination of horror and incredulity.

The detailed practicalities of the football ground arrangements, I also decided, could wait for a later date. For the present, I was concerned about locating those football clubs whose names did not appear to be linked to any of the towns or cities given in the index to Mr Philips's atlas. Where was Arsenal exactly, or Aston Villa or Port Vale? This particular problem seemed even more acute in Scotland. The index failed to list St Mirren or Raith, for example. Where was Heart of Midlothian? Was the St Johnstone club connected to the town of Johnstone in Renfrewshire? Further extensive research was clearly needed.

Don Revie's Leeds United side, having been promoted from the Second Division in 1964, quickly established itself as one of the leading sides in England and, from the following season, Europe. For reasons that have been extensively discussed over the years, they did not win any major trophies until 1968, when they beat Arsenal to win the Football League Cup at Wembley and defeated Ferencvaros over two legs to win the Inter Cities Fairs Cup. But, from their first year in the First Division, they were consistently in the hunt for the major trophies every season, usually on three or four fronts. The side was built around a formidable group of players, whom Revie moulded into a fearsome and ruthless unit, that, even today, still easily trips off the tongue: Sprake, Reaney, Cooper, Bremner, Charlton, Hunter... However, notwithstanding this local success story, my father had relatively little interest in going to watch any live football and, once I had emphatically bitten into the rugby offering, neither had I. I was approaching my fourteenth birthday before I went to see Leeds United play at Elland Road for the first time.

I went with a group of friends after school one evening in September 1968 to see Charlton Athletic in the second round of the League Cup. It was hardly the match of the season – although Charlton were top of the Second Division at the time – but I was amazed at the number of people who were there, both milling around the turnstiles trying to get in and then in the ground itself. We went on to the terraces that were situated in front of the Lowfields Road stand. On first entering the ground, we had to make our way up a steep incline before going over the top and down on to the other side in order to reach the terrace.

As we reached the top of the incline, before reaching the terrace, my first view of the ground was of about one third of the pitch, the remainder being blocked out by the stand. I was immediately struck by how green the grass was and how boldly the whitewash and the goalmouth stood out. (In those days, there was a sizeable gap between the goal and the crowd at that Gelderd Road end of the ground). I was also conscious that this was my first sight of the ground on which Hunslet had defeated Leeds to win the rugby league Championship final of 1938 – a match which Dad had attended as a teenager – though I did not mention this to my friends, because I knew that none of them would have been the slightest bit interested.

Although the crowd was sizeable, it was well below the capacity attendances that Leeds United were attracting in those days. (The ground record of nearly 58,000 had been set for a FA Cup fifth round replay with Sunderland, two years earlier). Nonetheless, it was hard for a 14 year-old of below average height to see without having to move and jerk his head around to find a line of sight between the heads and shoulders of the spectators in front of him. But when I did see the action, it was exciting stuff. Here were the famous Leeds players, with whom I had become familiar from the television: the snapping Billy Bremner, the powerful Jack Charlton, the skilful Johnny Giles, the uncompromising Norman Hunter. Each had his image to sustain, and was not reluctant to do so.

And here I was watching them in the flesh. Them and me, plus all these other people. But them and me. By this stage, my approach to recognising the significance of this contact was one that I had also been using extensively at rugby and cricket matches. I would look at the given player – focusing only on him – and take in the moment. It was my way of consciously registering the fact that I was now seeing this player "live". When the occasion allowed – say, during a warm up before a match or in a stoppage in play – I would run through the whole team, individually, in this way. Often, for the really well-known players, I would accompany this mental process with some physical sensation – a stamp of the foot on the ground, or a clenching of the hand so that a fingernail drove into the palm – to confirm my registration of the moment. I was seeing this player. Now. Live.

Once the match kicked off, I noticed that the spectators around me did not seem to have much patience with the Leeds team's efforts. They were not interested in fancy routines or intricate manoeuvres. They wanted instant results. Specifically, they wanted the ball to be deposited in the Charlton net, and when Leeds eventually put it there, it triggered a paroxysm of unbridled celebration from everyone on the terrace. It was the only goal of the game, but it was sufficient to meet the demands of the local supporters. It was clear to me that, even for this routine match, the crowd had a real passion and commitment. They identified with their team, and they wanted their team to win. After the match, my friends and

I walked back into the centre of Leeds for our fish and chips, before catching the bus back to Moortown. It had been a good evening.

The Leeds United programme for the Charlton match was more or less what I had expected: club notes, team line ups, fixture lists, advertising copy. Stapled within it was the Official Journal of the Football League – the *Football League Review* – which I assumed was attached to all clubs' programmes in a given week. It looked worthy and dull, and I didn't read it. Looking back on the programme, it is, as is often the case, the historical context that is its most interesting feature. In this edition, the club notes included a piece on how the arrangements for the second leg of the Inter Cities Fairs Cup final – the away tie of the Ferencvaros match – which had been held over from the previous season, were themselves now somewhat uncertain because of "the Czecho-Slovakia-Russian political events of the last few weeks". Exactly a fortnight earlier – on 21 August 1968 – the *Yorkshire Post*'s front page headline had been: "4.00am: Russians invade Czechoslovakia".[21]

At the time, however, the programme's most significant characteristic was the token – number 8 for the season – given on the front cover. These tokens took on the value of gold dust, if Leeds were to reach a cup final, because the possession of a certain number of them was the passport to a match ticket for the big occasion. My collection of Leeds United programmes in this period is, therefore, less than it could have been, as I ended up selling some of them to one of the older boys at school, whose token collection was not complete. His brother, who was in my class, chastised me at the time for only asking for the cover price of the programmes, rather than impose the sizeable mark-up that he knew the market would have borne.

My friends and I stood on virtually the same spot on the Lowfields Road terrace for the first leg of the European Cup tie against Lyn Oslo about a year later. The goals were rather more plentiful this time: ten of them altogether, all by Leeds. To start with – that is, for the first four or five goals – the crowd's reaction was the same as it had been for the goal against Charlton. These successive tides of euphoria suggested that the tournament itself was on the verge of being won. Thereafter – by the time Leeds reached eight or nine – the responses became more muted. Although I kept the information to myself – because I did not want to be called the smart arse that I undoubtedly was – I knew exactly what this phenomenon was. In the jargon that had been newly acquired in the first year of my "O"-level economics course, it was the "law of diminishing marginal utility". This is simply a common sense characteristic of consumer behaviour: that the additional enjoyment an individual obtains from consuming more of a good or service diminishes as the quantity increases. This did not apply to goal number ten, of course: the "law" breaks down if the consumption is addictive or if there is an additional benefit – in this case, the satisfaction of reaching double figures – to be obtained from further consumption.

A month later, my friends and I went to the big match against the newly promoted and high flying Derby County. The programme reported that "they are led by Mr Brian Clough, one of the most dynamic of the younger school of managers", who had done "right well" at the Baseball Ground. For this game – and against my father's express instructions – we graduated to the Gelderd End of the ground. This was the Leeds fans' "kop", though I always felt that they used the sobriquet with some half-heartedness, given that its brand ownership was clearly held by the Liverpool supporters at Anfield. It was the location for the loudest singing, the foulest language and the sizeable minority of local hardcases, looking for trouble, that attached itself to Leeds, as their counterparts did to every football team in the league.

Although there were a number of crush barriers distributed across the Gelderd End terrace, there was also a considerable distance between them, so there would be a regular flow of a mass of supporters down the terrace, often in rhythm to the action on the pitch. It is easy, in retrospect, to realise that this was incredibly dangerous. I have to say that I thought it was dangerous at the time, not least when one of my friends boasted of how, at a previous match, he had taken his feet off the ground and been swept along by the volume of bodies around him. We had a serious discussion, never satisfactorily resolved, about whether it was safer to stand behind one of the barriers, and be crushed on to it by the weight of the crowd pushing from behind, or to take up a position in front of the barrier and risk being seriously injured if the barrier gave way.

I did not confess to my friends that I was not really a Leeds United supporter. I was happy to go to their matches, of course, but it was usually in the spirit of the independent observation that was to characterise so much of my spectating activity in later years. Indeed, for the Derby match, my sympathies distinctly lay with the visitors. I thought that, rather like Leeds, they were an interesting team with a impressive combination of steel (Dave Mackay) and style (Alan Durban, Alan Hinton). Moreover, I had noted the name of their main striker, Kevin Hector, when he had been a prolific scorer for Bradford Park Avenue. However, in the present company, towards the top of the kop, I kept these views to myself.

The dynamic Mr Clough and his Derby County team came away empty-handed from this particular encounter, albeit probably with some sense of injustice. In *The Damned United* – the evocative fictional interpretation of Clough's short tenure as Leeds United manager in 1974

– David Peace reports the outcome of the earlier fixture from his subject's perspective: "There are 45,000 here… to watch them beat you 2–0 with two trademark Leeds United goals; the first from Clarke as the linesman flags for a foul throw from Bremner; the second three minutes later as Bates plays the ball forward to Clarke, who is at least three or four yards offside…" However, I didn't mind too much. I had seen the great Dave Mackay whose photograph, when a member of the Tottenham Hotspur FA Cup winners team in 1962, I had discovered in my beloved *The World Book of Football Champions*.

My ambivalent perspective of Leeds United has remained throughout the whole of the subsequent period, ranging through the successes of the late 1960s and early 1970s (including winning the league championship in 1969 and 1974 and reaching the European Cup final in 1975), the subsequent decline into the Second Division, the recovery under Howard Wilkinson to win the championship title again in 1992, the semi finals of the Champions League in 2001 and the ignominious fall out of the Premiership at the end of the 2003–04 season and then into League One (the old Third Division) for 2007–08. I have observed all this, if not with total indifference, then at best from a detached viewpoint.

Of course, this has not prevented me from adopting a wholly hypocritical stance towards my lack of attachment to Leeds United when it has suited me. I have regularly basked in the reflected glory of the club – and the city – when appropriate, whether as a student or when working or just meeting people for the first time.

"Where are you from?"

"Leeds".

"Ah. A Leeds United supporter?"

"Well, I tend to follow the rugby more than the soccer. But…"

The 'but' would be crucial.

"But I do follow the Leeds results, of course. They are doing really well/struggling a bit [delete as appropriate] *at the moment…"*

In the mid 1970s, when Andrew Carter and other friends and I were spending part of our summer holidays from university hitching or

Inter-Railing around Europe, the Leeds United connection was a trump card to play.

"We're from Leeds in Yorkshire". (Always with the "in Yorkshire", when we were abroad).

"Ah. Leeds United. Great football team".

This approach seemed to work consistently well with most of the Europeans we encountered, including those who spoke little or no English, whether it was the sullen car driver who was wondering why he had stopped to give us a lift, or the attractive Scandinavian students encountered in a youth hostel. Andrew had more honesty about this: he was a genuine Leeds United supporter. My view was that, if it gave these contacts something to relate to, it was no bad thing. And besides, they were more likely to have heard about the successes of Leeds United than the travails of Hunslet rugby league football club or Yorkshire CCC. It was only with some – though not all – American audiences, that the approach tended to be less successful.

"We're from Leeds in Yorkshire".

"Leeds?"

"You've heard of the famous Leeds United football team?"

"Football team? Football? Oh, you mean soccer, right?"

My father's detachment from Leeds United was more pronounced than mine. Indeed, it was to become decidedly antagonistic, for reasons I shall describe later. My ambivalence was determined, I think, not by anything in particular that I did not like about Leeds, but by my general preference for rugby over football. And, specifically, for my greater admiration for rugby players over footballers.

This is a generalisation, and I should expand on it. The football at Elland Road was always an enjoyable and interesting experience. I never went to a match and wished afterwards that I hadn't. The occasion was invariably one of drama and theatre. And I think that is largely the point. The play was often skilful – Leeds United were a superbly proficient side throughout these early years – but it was almost as if there was an element of pantomime and unreality about a match. Any match. By this, I don't mean that the play was half-hearted: certainly not, the vigour and crudity of much of the tackling would not survive any sort of scrutiny by the match officials of the modern day.

Rather, it was that much of the content of what I was seeing seemed shallow, if not dishonest: the diving of players, the mutual appealing for a throw in every time the ball went out of play and, especially, the incessant haranguing of the officials. Anything to gain an "edge" seemed to be acceptable, including the signals of displeasure that a player would invariably show to the crowd when a decision went against him. The crowd, for its part, would lap it up, adding a significant voice to the claim of unfairness.

I knew, of course, that professional football was a tough and competitive sport, with significant rewards for the winners and ultimate dismissal for the losers. Being professional meant "winning". This was emphatically confirmed by one of the key Leeds United players of this era in his autobiography, *Peter Lorimer: Leeds and Scotland Hero*: "From the day I walked into Elland Road as a young boy, Don Revie and Bobby Collins indoctrinated that winning mentality in me. Every tackle, every throw-in, every pass, every shot counts, because, as a whole, they make the difference between winning and not winning". (Just how far the Leeds United team of this era – and Revie in particular – were prepared to go in order to ensure that the winning mentality was reflected in the scoreline was only revealed at a later date).

I was fully aware that it was the "professional" approach that was adopted in football, and not only at Leeds United. It was accepted by everybody as a natural and inevitable part of the sport. And it had been for decades, since the balance of football power swung at the end of the nineteenth century from the gentleman amateur teams and the universities to the clubs in the industrial north of England. But I also knew that, in contrast, mine was a more puritanical approach – derived, I suspect, from several years of watching a sport in which a dissenting player was penalised by the referee marching him back another ten yards and in which, indeed, as I had been shocked to read in the *Yorkshire Evening Post*, a Dewsbury player had been banned *sine die* for pushing a referee. Of course, I knew that it was not quite as simple as that: I was certainly not blind to the fact that rugby league was also a tough and competitive sport and not without its own cheating and skulduggery. This was later confirmed – if confirmation were needed – in *Play to Win: Rugby League Heroes*, in which Maurice Bamford, contrasting professional rugby league in the period to the late 1960s and early 1970s with the modern Super League, states that "the downright brutality of the game as it was then was hard to believe without having seen or played it". But I did think that I recognised a different set of values in rugby, compared with football. And I was quite clear about which set of values I preferred.

And so, I picked my matches at Elland Road, and I enjoyed them all. I saw Liverpool in the second leg of a European Fairs Cup tie in April 1971, when Leeds successfully defended the single goal lead that they had carried forward from the first leg. Along with Derby, I liked the Liverpool side of this era, particularly the skilful midfield players, Brian Hall and Ian Callaghan, and the speedy Steve Heighway on the wing. In the same month, Leeds defeated Arsenal to give them what appeared at the time to be a marginal edge in the battle for the championship. My principal memory of this game is that a scrambled goal by Jack Charlton was followed by a furious protest from the Arsenal captain, Frank McLintock, who chased the referee back to the half way line, to no avail.

McLintock recalled the incident in *True Grit: The Autobiography* over 30 years later. He remembered that "playing away to Leeds was… the most intimidating fixture in football at the time" due to "the ferocity of their [Leeds's] assault and the blood lust of the crowd" and that this particular game – "a ferocious affair" – was no different. Charlton had scored "from a position which looked to me to be at least 6 yards offside". McLintock then goes on to describe a particularly interesting coda to the match which reveals much about the psychological dimension to these keen sporting rivalries, as well as his own leadership qualities. On the team coach returning to London, he started to plan how he would exploit the apparent injustice and the sense of grievance felt by his side to galvanise the players in the build-up to Arsenal's remaining league fixtures. Unfortunately, his thunder was stolen almost immediately when one of his team-mates, Bob McNab, volunteered the suggestion that the referee's decision had been fair and Charlton's goal had been valid. Over 30 years after the event, McLintock generously acknowledges that television replays had later confirmed that McNab's analysis had indeed been accurate.

The following autumn, West Ham United visited Elland Road for a third round replay in the Football League Cup. The Leeds crowd gave Bobby Moore a hard time, as I suspect they always did, given their obvious preference for Norman Hunter to play in his position for England. I watched Moore closely. He was immaculate. He gave a masterclass in the timing of his challenges, the crispness of his tackling and the accuracy of his distribution. This was only just over a year after his masterful display against Brazil in the Mexico World Cup and he was a player at the top of his game. Looking back – and at the risk of making a somewhat fanciful comparison – I think there was an obvious contemporary parallel with Ray Illingworth: both captains of their country; both with a mastery of their respective sport's essential skills; both in full control on the field of play.

West Ham fielded Geoff Hurst and Clyde Best in their forward line. Watching Hurst – as, indeed, with watching Mick Jones in the Leeds side at that time – provided a clear illustration of the benefits of seeing a game in the flesh rather than on television. These players ran for miles, creating space, drawing defenders, holding up the ball and, more often than not, getting whacked from behind for their troubles. Hurst was also a revelation.

But the really interesting character was Best, one of the first black players to make a serious impact in English soccer. I do not recall that the Elland Road crowd singled him out in any particular way – unlike at West Ham's own Upton Park ground some years later, when I witnessed some serious racial abuse against visiting players – but I did detect an underlying sense that, because of the colour of his skin, this was an unusual player. There was undoubtedly a feeling amongst the home spectators – of which, by association, I was one – that they were seeing something different. With the benefit of hindsight, it is clear that, in the racial stereotyping of the time, it was easier to accommodate the Leeds supporters' own experience of watching Albert Johanneson skipping down the wing for their side during the 1960s. Best was different: he played upfront, robustly, in the forward line.

I thought that Best played with dignity and athleticism. He was a real handful for the Leeds defence throughout the match and he was rewarded with the only goal of the game when, in the first period of extra time, he headed in a cross from Harry Redknapp.

The Absent Player

The years of my student life and early work experience are those in which I become the contemporary of many of the players in action on the sports field in front of me. It could be me on the pitch: but it isn't. They are the ones with the skill and toughness and dedication to take their place as the centre of attention.

Chapter 8

Grange Road
and Twickenham

In the autumn of 1973, my expertise in recognising the "law of diminishing marginal utility" – which I had identified five years earlier at Elland Road when Leeds United were rattling in ten goals in their first European Cup tie against Lyn Oslo – coupled with my answers to the interview questions that were posed on other aspects of economics, stood me in good stead with the University of Cambridge entrance examiners. It has to be reported that my interview, with an eminent economist called John (later Lord) Eatwell, got off to a shaky start. I turned up at Eatwell's rooms in Trinity College wearing my best suit – which was also my only suit – and my Yorkshire Senior Schools Cricket Association tie, hoping for some questions about my sporting interests and prowess. Eatwell, attired in denim jacket and trousers and with his feet resting on a low coffee table, proceeded to ask me how the determination of the price of new cars differed from that of vintage cars. In the event, everything turned out satisfactorily and, in December, I received a letter from the college's admissions tutor – "Dear Rigg..." – offering me a place for the following autumn.[22] The huge wave of euphoria which cascaded through the family on receipt of the letter was only tempered, for my mother and me in particular, by the regret that my grandfather – Alfred Niblett, the First World War internee in Ruhleben – had died only a matter of weeks earlier at the age of 84. There was no doubt that whatever academic qualities I might have possessed to satisfy the Cambridge examiners had been nurtured under his influence.

The letter from Trinity was the first of two personal successes in that month. A week later, playing for the North Leeds Cricket Club in the annual Boxing Day charity match against the Northern Cricket Society, my off spin proved too much for the England test cricketer, Chris Old, who tried to hit a delivery into Roundhay Park and was caught at mid-off by a delightful man called Tony Stone. "I was going to make damn sure I didn't drop that one", Tony said afterwards. As I ended up staying on in Cambridge to do a research degree, it was to be my home, apart from vacations in Leeds, until Christmas 1980.

After I arrived in Cambridge, I wasted little time in resuming my sports spectating career. One of my fellow students was a young man from Bridgend called Steve Evans – later a distinguished business correspondent with the BBC. On the second Saturday of the first term, we arranged to go and watch the Cambridge University rugby side play Cardiff at their home ground on Grange Road. Steve brought along another Welshman called Llyr James, who had arrived at Trinity to study history. It was a propitious occasion. Llyr has been one of my closest friends ever since that day: a thoughtful and kind man, whose opinions and values I greatly respect. In addition, his ability to analyse rugby players and rugby teams has been, alongside that of my father, one that I have always admired.

The Cardiff match was a good one with which to start. Moreover, it was one that set the pattern for most of the matches I saw at Grange Road over the next six years. The Welshmen brought a big physical side – including the international players Barry Nelmes and Alan Phillips in the front row and the future British Lion Roger Lane in the back row – and this obviously presented a severe test for the university's forwards in terms of winning anything like a reasonable share of possession.

However, once the students did win the ball, they certainly knew what to do with it. The half backs, Alan Wordsworth and Richard Harding, were both subsequently to play for England, as was the full back, Alastair Hignell. One of the wingers, Mike O'Callaghan, had played for the All Blacks and the other winger, Gordon Wood, for England Under 23s. In the centre was another England international, Peter Warfield, a player of considerable power and skill and the real linchpin of the side. A clear memory of this match is Warfield taking a crash ball at pace and driving back the three Cardiff defenders attempting to halt him: the visitors did not have the monopoly when it came to brute force.

The pivotal issue for the games at Grange Road, therefore – the key determinant of their outcomes – was whether the home side would win enough possession for their dazzling backs. And dazzling they were, in their ability to move the ball at speed and create scoring opportunities for each other. It was the pace at which they performed that really took the eye, together with the consistently excellent timing of the full back Hignell's entry into the three-quarter line. They were also aided by the speed of the forwards, whose advantage lay in their mobility around the pitch, their ability to re-cycle the ball from the break down and the imaginative ways

116

in which they secured possession at the line out with quick throws or shortened lines.

This rugby team was fit, as well as skilful. I mean: really fit. They played or trained six days out of seven during – and, indeed, before – the Michaelmas term in preparation for the Varsity Match against Oxford at Twickenham in December. In effect, without being paid of course, they were professional rugby players, in the sense of being completely focused on their objectives and devoting the time and effort to carrying out the various parts of their strategic plan. And their central objective was to win the Varsity Match. I remember that Llyr said that the Cambridge captain Steve Warlow, another Welshman, had told him that if they won all their other matches and lost to Oxford, the season would have been judged a failure[23].

Honours were even against Cardiff – 16 points each – the result setting the tone for a good term, with victories over Richmond, London Scottish, Blackheath and Harlequins. These were elite club sides, of course, who themselves no doubt trained two or three times a week. And they brought some good players to Grange Road: Alastair McHarg, Alan Lawson, Clive Woodward. But these sides were simply not as professional or as efficiently prepared as the university team. In the commentary for the Varsity Match programme that year, John Spencer (Cambridge 1967–69) referred to "the country's thirty fittest rugby players [who] are so organised as sides that they will be disappointed with the organisation of every side in which they subsequently play".

The average age of the Cambridge rugby side in my first term was, not surprisingly, two or three years older than me. The majority were, like me, undergraduates, though obviously further advanced in their courses. The others were doing postgraduates courses of various types, ranging from a Ph.D. in veterinary sciences to the one-year certificate of education. Indeed, the vet, O'Callaghan, was already 27 and was to play in the side for another three years. But the average age difference was only those two or three years. These players were not far away from being a team of my contemporaries, doing battle with mature club sides that did not take kindly to the thought of being run off their feet by a bunch of flashy students. If I had been of the required standard – which, of course, I was nowhere near – it would have been me out there on the pitch as well.

The only player younger than me in the side for the Cardiff match was Hignell, who had been the outstanding schoolboy sportsman of my year: captain of the English Schools Under 19 rugby side and a cricketer for Gloucestershire. He had had to convert from scrum half to full back at the start of term because his place in the university first team was blocked by Harding. However, such was his talent for the game that, by the end of the season, he had made the full England touring party for Australia in his new position.

In the first term, one of only three losses by the university side was to MR Steele Bodger's XV. This was an invitation side, run by the driving force behind the Barbarians club, which played the university each year on a Wednesday afternoon in late November. To my old school-friends in north Leeds, with whom I compared university notes at Christmas in the Chained Bull (and the Queen's Arms and the White House and the Regent…), this sounded like something out of PG Wodehouse. My response was that Mr Steele Bodger's standing in the game was such that this year's selection had included 10 internationals, including Mike Gibson, Andy Ripley, Tony Neary and Mike Burton. (Three other players, including Peter Wheeler, would win caps at a later date). Hignell missed what would have been the match-winning conversion in the last minute: a reflection of his inconsistent success rate for goal kicking, which I would see again at a later date and on a larger stage.

On the double-sided light blue card that served as the match programme, the status of visiting (and home) international players was designated, in the normal way, by the small cross against their names. The other designation was of the "Old Blues" turning out for the home (and visiting) sides. In the Steele Bodger XV, NO Martin (Harlequins and England) had both notations against his name.

On the second Tuesday in December, I went down to watch the Varsity Match at Twickenham with a small group of friends from college. We stood on the terrace under the West Stand roughly on the half way line. My expectation beforehand, having watched an attractive and successful side throughout the term, was that Cambridge would win easily. They had planned their campaign well: all but three of the team selected for the Cardiff match at the beginning of the term had survived to win their Blues. What I had overlooked, of course, was that Oxford's side would be as fit and as motivated as Cambridge's, and that the Grange Road experience of seeing off normal club sides through speed and skill was not likely to be repeated. In addition, the Cambridge fly half, Alan Wordsworth, was injured and did not play. And, not least, the Oxford side had some useful players as well: their captain, Charles Kent, was to charge through the Scottish defence for England on this ground two seasons later. Llyr James remarked that Kent was the only captain he had ever seen lead his side out on to the pitch whilst running backwards at full speed. I remember him getting thoroughly clattered by Warfield the first time he got the ball.

It was a dismal game, littered with mistakes, as neither side coped with the unremitting frenzy of the occasion and the blustery conditions. Cambridge won 16–15 by virtue of scoring two tries to none, one of which was when Warfield powerfully handed off a defender to score near the corner. Hignell, inconsistent as ever, landed the conversion from close to the touchline, but managed only two successful penalty goals from seven attempts. The Oxford points came from five penalty goals (out of ten attempts), one of which was awarded by the referee under the Cambridge posts when they infringed on retrieving the previous penalty attempt, which had just bounced off the crossbar. It was that sort of afternoon.

Of my group of friends down for the match, it turned out that I was the only one heading back to Cambridge that evening. I was going home for the Christmas break the next day, but the others went straight off after the game to their various destinations around the country. Steve Evans and I went for a coffee at the National Theatre and then he departed for Paddington. The evening was one of anti-climax, therefore: a disappointing match followed by a lonely journey back to college. But I had been to Twickenham, at least, and I knew that my father would soon be asking me all about it.

If Blues had been awarded for spectating, I would have won six consecutively between 1974 and 1979 for my successive appearances at Twickenham. On a couple of occasions (1975 and 1978), Cambridge did break free of the shackles to run up sizeable scores and they also won in 1976 (the first year that the match was officially sponsored), but Oxford reversed the results in 1977 and 1979. The scores would be dutifully added to the long list, dating back to 1871, that appeared in each year's match programme, together with the full catalogue of names of all the previous players to have won Blues.

I viewed all the games from the same spot on the terrace on the western side of the ground. One year, as the Cambridge side took the pitch – and a couple of pints having been consumed in The Cabbage Patch on the other side of Twickenham bridge – I shouted out "Come on, you blues", in a pitifully weak attempt at Footlights-type humour. My prattish remark was only topped by the self-important response of a thin wiry man standing in front of me, who turned around to point out that my message of encouragement could apply to either team: I observed loudly and boorishly to my friends that some of these Oxford chaps were a little deficient in the irony department.

The Cambridge defeats are recalled more easily than the victories. In 1977, Cambridge were consistently pinned back by an exemplary display of line kicking from Gareth Davies, who was close to winning his first Welsh cap, before the Oxford back row drove over the Cambridge line from a close range scrum. The 1979 match was probably the worst of them all – notwithstanding the Blues being won that day by some future internationals, including Nick Mallett and Paul Ackford – with some mediocre kicking from both sides, but particularly Cambridge. My disappointment in this match was exacerbated by the realisation that I had advanced to an age at which I was struggling to consider these players as my contemporaries: a salutary reading of the biographical details in the programme revealed that, with only one exception, I was older than every player on the pitch. The 1979 Varsity Match was the last that I went to see for over 30 years.

The autumn terms served up some consistently interesting rugby at Grange Road, though the university's results were obviously dependent on the quality of the successive cohorts of players. Some of the university's sides had some players out of the top drawer – Alun Lewis, John Robbie, Eddie Butler – and gave their opponents a hard time: I can remember a near full-strength Gloucester side, captained by Mike Burton, getting soundly beaten in 1975. By contrast, the teams in other years struggled against some of the first class opposition and received some drubbings of their own: by Cardiff and Leicester in 1977 and Northampton in 1978.

From my limited experience of watching them away from the familiarity of Grange Road, it seemed that Cambridge found it particularly difficult in the away fixtures against these top clubs. My friends and I travelled with some optimism – to Northampton in 1976 and Harlequins in 1978, for example – only to see disappointing Cambridge performances and anti-climactic defeat. Not that these losses counted for much by the time that the Varsity Match had been played later in the respective Michaelmas Terms; these were years of Cambridge success and, as seen, that was all that mattered.

As also noted, a consistent feature of the university side's games against the established clubs was the difficulty that the Cambridge forwards had in securing any set piece possession. The front rows would usually be compact and tight, and there was a succession of brave flank forwards who were adept at securing the ball at the break down, but if the games were reduced to a forward slog, then the lack of overall mass in the university pack was a clear disadvantage. Newport exploited their advantage in this area at Grange Road in a hard encounter in 1975. Occasionally, however, a player would emerge who could compete on his own terms: Ackford was one, as was Butler, who, drawing on his experience in the Pontypool pack, seemed to relish the physical confrontation for the ball. As one of my college team mates found out – playing for Trinity against Fitzwilliam in the college "cuppers" quarter-final of 1977 – Butler also practised a ruthless rucking technique on players who were lying on the wrong side of the ball.

The university side's fixtures – as with Oxford's at Iffley Road – attracted considerable media attention, at least amongst the London-based press. Although there was little danger of my father seeing much coverage in the *Yorkshire Evening Post*, there were full match reports in the *Times* and *Daily Telegraph*, together with reviews of the two sides' progress as the Twickenham encounter drew closer. Perhaps as a result of this, the clubs visiting Grange Road tended to bring their full strength sides although, in the pre-league era, there was no reason for them to do otherwise, as the games against the university were part of the regular fixture list. This meant that there was a regular stream of first class players on show: the young but powerful Terry Holmes, with Gerald Davies, for Cardiff in 1977, the speedy Nick Preston for Richmond in 1979. Other Steele Bodger XV selections also had no shortage of famous players with crosses against their names in the match programme, notably Ray Gravell in 1975, Andy Irvine in 1976 and Phil Bennett in 1978.

The university side's status in the hierarchy of English rugby was confirmed in 1978, when they were awarded a fixture against the touring New Zealand All Blacks. Matches against touring sides were nothing new – I had previously seen games against Japan in 1976 and the US Eagles in 1977, both narrowly lost – but I remember thinking that the arrangement of this fixture did rather confirm (if confirmation were needed) the importance of the university having the right connections in the rugby establishment. For the only time that I can recall at Grange Road, the match was all ticket, and I picked mine up from a small shop near the Arts Cinema. I was allocated to a section of terrace on the far side of the ground from my usual vantage point on the terrace nearest the entrance, and had to put up with some loudmouth a few places behind me who spent the whole game complaining about the Cambridge captain and Irish international, John Robbie.

In the event, after a nervous start, Robbie led his team with distinction and the final score of 12–32 fairly reflected his side's courageous performance against a group of players, led by Graeme Mourie, who were all out to secure their places for the international matches later on the tour. When one of the New Zealanders kicked the ball over the Cambridge try line and was obviously going to secure a touchdown, the player who gave him the most competition to win the race for the score was one of his own team mates. My other memory of the game is from before the kick-off, when the All Blacks did their traditional *haka*. Over the years, other sides have sought to counter this challenge (or intimidation, depending on one's viewpoint) in a variety of ways: by forming their own circle and ignoring it, or by advancing to meet the New Zealanders in a direct face-to-face confrontation, amongst others. The Cambridge team took a different approach: they stood in a line and, when the final leap was over, applauded politely.

In most years, Cambridge's last game before the Varsity Match was against the Harlequins. Each player would want to play in this game, in order to confirm his place for Twickenham and notwithstanding the risk of picking up an injury that would deprive him of his Blue. In the closing minutes in the 1977 fixture, the Harlequin wing Colin Lambert – a burly and fearsome player, who had been part of the Normanton Grammar School first XV that had beaten Roundhay School at the last gasp in 1971 – charged down the wing towards the corner and attempted to bounce the covering Alastair Hignell out of the way. Hignell timed his challenge perfectly, so that the collision took Lambert out of play over the touchline. I thought at the time that, whilst there was never going to be any hesitation on Lambert's part, neither had there been on Hignell's; he marked the moment with a clenched fist to himself as he took up his position for the subsequent line out.

I retired from playing rugby at the age of 24 in 1979, only three years younger than the great Barry John himself. My final match was for the Trinity College first XV against a visiting team from Harvard University, most of whom were schooled in American football and, therefore, brought an interesting repertoire of running, tackling and blocking techniques. In keeping with the Ian McGeechan tradition, I managed a left-footed drop goal to secure the win. After a good night in the college bar, we persuaded our visitors that it was the done thing to attempt the Great Court run – later featured in *Chariots of Fire*, of course – to the midnight chimes of the college clock. The slight difference with Colin Welland's Oscar-winning film script is that, in the Harvard version, those attempting the feat were entirely naked apart from their shoes and socks.

Before retirement, I had played a couple of games for the Cambridge University second fifteen – the LX Club – against the London Scottish second XV and one of the London hospital sides. The latter game was at Grange Road, so I was able to add that venue to Llanelli's Stradey Park as a first class ground on which I had played. My drop kicking skills let me down, however – I missed three in the two games – and I duly retreated back into the safer confines of college rugby. Somewhat to my amazement, however – and presumably due to a spate of call offs by others – I was invited to join the LX Club tour of South Wales that Easter. I declined the invitation, pleading pressure of work, having no great wish to be student bait for the back row forwards in the South Wales Police second XV.

Oxbridge university rugby has changed in the last three decades. The generous sponsorship now surrounding the fixture is allied to the full match coverage, complete with lengthy previews, on satellite television: the days of BBC1 breaking into its gentle Tuesday afternoon schedule once a year for a couple of hours seem to have gone for ever. For the elite clubs, the fixture at Grange Road no longer has the cache that it once had; their concern these days is to protect their players' welfare for the serious business of league and cup competition. And the universities' players themselves are different, with a greater proportion of postgraduate – especially overseas – participants. From now on, it will be a highly unusual occurrence for one of the universities to unearth an undergraduate of fairly immediate international potential, in the way that Rob Andrew, for example, burst on to the scene in the Cambridge side in the early 1980s. However, one constant will undoubtedly remain: the unshakeable desire of both sides to win the Varsity Match in order to claim that their season has been a success.

Chapter 9

Lord's Cricket Ground

Throughout the 1970s, Geoff Boycott was the central figure of English cricket. This applied whether he was actually in the England team or whether, as for nearly three years up to the middle of 1977, he was out of the side due to injury or self-imposed exile. At the same time, Boycott was also the key personality in Yorkshire cricket, having been awarded the captaincy after Brian Close's dismissal in 1970. In *Boycott: The Autobiography*, he describes how, after 22 years service, Close was called into a meeting with the chairman of the cricket committee and given the ultimatum of either resigning or being sacked. Boycott assesses this treatment of Close to have been "revealingly hideous". The political and mental challenges faced by Boycott in both his England and Yorkshire roles – exacerbated by the almost incessant coverage in the national and local media – are then described in a detail that makes uneasy reading.

I had met Boycott, briefly, when I was in the Headingley changing rooms preparing for one of the coaching sessions in the winter "sheds" to which promising cricketers across the county were invited each winter. I was one of a group of lads getting changed when Boycott suddenly came into the room and went around to introduce himself. I just about stumbled out an answer to his question about which schools we attended. The date is easily remembered: Boycott had his arm in plaster, having received a fracture towards the end of the successful England tour of Australia in the winter of 1970–71.

In most of the cricket teams in which I have played – at school, college and club – I was an off-spinning opening batsman. I suspect that it was almost inevitable, therefore, that my approach to batting would be based on trying to apply the principles that had been adopted by Boycott and expertly refined by him: watchful defence, sound technique and determined concentration. I do not think now – and nor did I think at the time – that this was my slavish following of a particular role model. It just seemed the most appropriate route for me to follow, if I were to have any success at my modest level of cricket. As I moved on from the unpredictable pitches on which our school cricket was mostly played and replaced them with the excellent pitches prepared by the college groundsmen across Cambridge, my batting improved whilst my bowling regressed.

It was also natural that, when I was a student, I would follow Boycott's scores in the papers, as part of the regular monitoring of Yorkshire's progress, or the lack of it. During this time, my regular telephone calls home to my parents would be characterised by my mother asking if I was eating properly and looking after myself and my father describing the latest report of the political in-fighting between the Yorkshire committees and the county captain. In terms of the "pro" and "anti" Boycott factions that the media seemed keen to promulgate amongst cricket followers – and, indeed, across the public at large – my father was firmly in the former camp. He judged that Boycott possessed the essential qualities for an opening batsman – "grit, guts and determination" – and, like many others across the county, he enjoyed the success by association when Boycott made another large score. By contrast, my father was generally less than enamoured with Boycott's critics on the Yorkshire committee, some of whom had had relatively modest playing careers, although he recognised that the opposition camp also contained some distinguished names from Yorkshire's past.

Boycott played twice for Yorkshire against the Cambridge University XI during my time at university. In 1977, after reaching an untroubled half century, he was clean bowled by a friend of mine, Charlie Bannister, who is probably still dining out on this triumph. Bannister bowled a series of wide deliveries outside Boycott's off stump, which he did not play a stroke at: there must have been seven or eight of these in a row over the course of a couple of overs. Then, Bannister sent down a quicker and straighter delivery which to universal surprise, including his own, Boycott missed. Charlie was a big heavy lad – 16 stone plus – and his leap of celebration at the sight of Boycott's broken wicket left an indentation on the square that required attention from the Fenner's groundsman for a long time afterwards. On his other visit to Cambridge, during the previous season, Boycott scored an unbeaten double century and then, when Yorkshire were chasing quick runs for victory, made an unbeaten 30 odd, scoring off every ball he faced, to secure the win. I thought the latter was an even more dominant display of batting than his first innings.

In the middle of 1977, Boycott announced that he was ready to play for England again. He returned for the Trent Bridge test match and scored a century against Australia, redeeming himself after earlier running out the local hero, Derek Randall. The next test was at Headingley and, before he played in the preceding county match against Warwickshire at Edgbaston, I could see what might happen. I said as much to my father. Boycott had scored 98 first class centuries in his career before going to Edgbaston and so, if he managed another one in the county game, that would leave him going to his home ground, Headingley, looking to score his 100th century. And in a test match against Australia. Boycott duly scored 104 against Warwickshire.

The rest is history, of course. I went to the Headingley test match on the first day and sat in my favourite position on the Western Terrace. Mike Brearley, wearing a somewhat sinister-looking skull-cap, was out third ball for nought[24], but that was an irrelevance for most of the spectators. The crowd around me cheered as Boycott hit his first four down to the boundary over to my left and then continued to offer a similar greeting – at least – to every one of his subsequent runs. When Boycott reached his 50, there was a massive collective roar from the terrace. The man sitting next to me stood up and shouted passionately, "Come on Geoffrey. Come on", punching the air vigorously as he did so. It was a personal plea from him to the player that, as far he was concerned, the player was bound to hear.

I was curious about all this. If Boycott were to be out next ball, the runs he had scored in the innings would mean nothing in the context of the personal achievement he was seeking. I interpreted the crowd's reaction to his half century as a combination of things: the release of the uniform tension across the ground, the recognition that he was half-way towards his target, and the growing realisation that he was on top of the Australian bowlers, including the fearsome Jeff Thomson and the decidedly quick Len Pascoe.

There was one moment of concern, when the Australia left arm spinner Ray Bright appealed forcefully for a catch by the wicketkeeper, Rod Marsh, down the leg side. Bright's body language suggested he was less than impressed when the decision went against him; he snatched his sunhat from the umpire in disgust. The crowd on the Western Terrace jeered. We were square to the wicket, of course, and in no position to judge the validity of the appeal. But we knew it was not out: it couldn't possibly be. The fates had decreed otherwise. From my own perspective, I thought that Bright was a scruffy cricketer – with an appearance not unlike that of the Richard Dreyfus character in *Jaws* and an ungainly bowling action – and certainly not the man to disturb the natural course of events on this particular day.

I was reminded of Boycott's innings several years later, when I saw highlights of it on a BBC video entitled *Cricket's Entertainers*, though, if the truth be told, I was already familiar with the *mise-en-scene*. It had been a bright warm day with, not surprisingly, the ground full to capacity. Boycott was immaculately turned out: shirt sleeves neatly rolled up above the elbows, shirt collar turned up at the back of his neck, England cap firmly in place (in this pre-helmet era, Brearley's skull-cap excluded). The crispness of his strokeplay was also confirmed: the square cuts off the Australian fast bowlers, the off drive for the boundary that brought up his 50, and the classical driving through the packed cover field when Bright strayed marginally off line.

And so I come to the third of the "nano-dramas" that I prefaced in the Preface and for which no reminder from the video is necessary. It was, of course, the shot that took Boycott from 96 to 100: the straight drive off the bowling of Greg Chappell that hurried down the slope and over the boundary in front of the members enclosure in the Football Stand. I knew as soon as Boycott hit the ball that it would be enough. Again, I was square of the action, and I could tell before the ball had travelled half way back down the pitch that it was moving at a sufficient speed to elude the bowler, provided that Chappell, falling away in his action, did not stick a boot across to intercept it. And, of course, he couldn't: the ball was too wide for him. I also knew that, once the ball had beaten the infield, there was no way that a chasing fielder could have caught up with it before it reached the boundary ropes. This particular nano-drama, therefore, is not so much in the boundary being scored, or Boycott raising his arms in the air, or some of the spectators running on to the pitch. It is in that split second, when I realised that the ball was on its way back from his bat and that the task had been achieved.

Boycott himself has written that his moment of realisation came even earlier. As he explained in his autobiography, "I saw it [the delivery] with an amazing sort of clarity… As soon as it left his [Chappell's] hand I knew I was going to hit it and I knew where I was going to hit it. Long before it pitched I knew exactly what I was going to do, as though I was standing outside myself, watching myself play the shot… As soon as I struck it I lifted the bat high in the air. In the millisecond that followed I realised what it all meant…"

At the end of the day's play, a large portion of the crowd gathered in front of the pavilion to applaud their hero and the rest of the England team as they came out on to the balcony. The roar rang out: "Yorkshire, Yorkshire". I knew that somewhere in that crowd was my neighbour from the Western Terrace.

The following day, I purchased the *Yorkshire Post* and the *Yorkshire Evening Post* to make sure that we had a permanent record of the historic achievement. My father bought the *Daily Express* just to be on the safe side. The headline on the front page of the *Yorkshire Post*'s "souvenir edition" was "The Magic Moment", with a photograph of Boycott playing the drive. The evening paper carried the full page photograph of Boycott standing in the middle of the ground, being congratulated by Graeme Roope, with three policemen making sure that no further intruders came on to the pitch. In the background, taking up half of the shot, the scoreboard shows 234 for 4 wickets with batsman number two on 100. The page is headed "Yorkshire's moment of history". My mother later went down to the *Yorkshire Evening Post*'s offices in Wellington Street to order a full size proper photograph, which she gave to me as a souvenir.

This was also, of course, the second day of the test match and, carried along by the general euphoria, England overwhelmed their opponents. Boycott took his score to 191 and was the last man out when the England total had reached 436. Then, in the Australian first innings, came another nano-drama.

The England selectors had introduced some new faces during the Ashes series, propitiously as it turned out, as several of the old guard had accepted the invitation to play in the alternative "circus" organised by the Australian media mogul, Kerry Packer. Two of these new players were Ian Botham, whose most famous exploits in a Headingley test match would come later, and Derek Randall. At the time, I regarded Randall as a batsman of above-average county standard who, though not a top class test player, was probably worth his place in the side because of the countless runs that he saved in the field. That view did not change over the years. With Randall, there was a clear echo of the South African, Colin Bland, who had toured England in 1965 and who had been my friend Tim Kell's favourite player. Like Bland, Randall's fielding was aggressive and dynamic. And on this particular day, it was, literally, mesmeric.

Where Randall differed from Bland was that he seemed to be an absolute eccentric. When any young cricketer is taught the game, he is told, when fielding in the outfield, to walk in with the bowler. Randall, usually fielding at cover point, would start by walking in and then shift to walking in very quickly and finally break into something that was not far short of a full out sprint. For any one delivery, including his walk back to his mark, he must have covered at least 60 yards. Allied to this was a propensity to keeping talking to himself and beat himself on his chest to make sure he was always fully psyched up. It was easy to understand why a batsman could be completely intimidated.

The Australians had already lost a couple of early wickets when their opening batsman, Rick McCosker, was run out by Randall. A delivery from Mike Hendrick was played defensively by David Hookes out into the covers on the far side of the pitch from us, with McCosker at the non-striker's end. There was no real hesitation or mix up between the batsman. It was just that, by the time McCosker had taken three or four strides down the pitch and then routinely decidedly to go back, it was too late. Although the ball had been placed some distance from Randall's original position, he had anticipated where it would go, swooped in on it, and, with a diving underarm throw, broken the wicket at the bowler's end with McCosker still out of his ground. Randall had triumphed, not just because of his speed across the ground but due to his speed of thought. It was sensational. It was if the Australian batsman was a rabbit caught in the headlights. And it was another wicket for England on their way to an innings victory.

Two years earlier, the England versus Australia test at Headingley had become famous for other, less positive, reasons. The visitors had thrashed England during the previous winter of 1974–75, when the captain Ian Chappell had unleashed Dennis Lillee and Jeff Thomson on the England batting line up. The sides came to Headingley for the third test with Australia again 1–0 up. England had the courageous Northamptonshire veteran David Steele making only his second appearance and Phil Edmonds (Phillippe Henri Edmonds, according to my *Playfair Cricket Annual*) on his debut.

Steele, in particular, had attracted my attention as an interesting character. He had been capped by his county no less than 10 years earlier, yet it was only now that he – along with the equally experienced Yorkshire batsman, John Hampshire – was being resorted to, in an attempt to see off the hostility of the Australian fast bowlers. His appearance and demeanour – glasses, grey hair, ambling gait – drew a range of colourful descriptions from the sporting media, of which "the bank clerk who went to war" struck me as particularly apt. In *Headingley Test Cricket 1899–1975*, Ken Dalby, never shy to use a colourful phrase, describes him as "looking for all the world like a bespectacled, baggy-trousered local vicar, going out to face the country squire's eleven on the village green". Over twenty years later, David Birley, in his authoritative *A Social History of English Cricket*, stated that England "discovered the kind of hero so beloved of tradition as to be part of the national self-image – the quiet, unassuming chap who stands up to the bully".

For the first four days, it was a conventional – and very interesting – test match. Lillee and Thomson tore in to the England batsmen, in their attempt to maintain their proven superiority, and I was captivated by their complementary styles. Lillee's sprint to the bowling crease – simultaneously smooth and menacing – was appropriately followed by the classical fast bowler's side-on action at the point of delivery. By contrast, Thomson's aggressive run up to the crease was driven by his basic athleticism and strength, with the release of the ball brought about by the dramatic uncoiling of the powerful muscles of his right shoulder and back as he hit his delivery stride. I had seen the pair on television, of course, including on the BBC's highlights packages during the previous winter. But here they were, live and in the flesh – and playing on my home ground – and it was thrilling.

Unfortunately for the Australians, however, it was a relatively benign pitch with none of the fungus-induced menace of 1972. Although Hampshire failed in both innings, Steele compiled two brave half centuries and I shared his and the crowd's disappointment when he was dismissed in the 90s in his second knock. Australia made a complete hash of batting against Edmonds's left arm spin in the first innings, when he took 3 wickets in his first 3 overs of test cricket and ended up with 5 wickets overall.

On the Monday, England chased quick runs in order to set up a declaration. Alan Knott came in and played a little cameo of an innings with some audacious hitting and running. His innings was ended, at 31, when he came down the pitch and ferociously cross batted a Lillee delivery so that it flew in a straight line above the head of the fielder at mid off. It was like a shell out of the barrel of a heavy gun. The fielder was Thomson, whom one might have expected to have been taking a breather, given the bowling exertions he was currently facing. Instead, Thomson leapt high into the air and twisted his arm so that the palm faced the oncoming shell. The ball smashed into his grasp. I thought at the time that this was the best catch I had ever seen. I don't think I have seen a replay of it since and, in a way, I hope that I never do. I remains in my memory as a fantastic piece of athleticism and skill by a player who was fully committed to helping his fellow fast bowler and his team. And, as such, it sums up the whole philosophy of Australian cricket over the period that I have been watching them play.

At the end of the fourth day, Australia, chasing the huge target of 445 to win, were making more than a reasonable fist of it at 220 for the loss of three wickets. One of the men dismissed was Ian Chappell, who was given out leg before wicket to Chris Old. In Dalby's view, this was the correct decision; he describes Chappell as "plumb in front". At the time, however, Chappell seemed to have a different opinion. He stormed off and, having rushed up the pavilion steps and entered the door directly opposite from us, slammed it so ferociously that the whole building seemed to shake. The taunting laughter of the crowd around us who witnessed this dissent was no doubt cheered by the reassurance that the full width of the cricket ground separated us from the irate perpetrator.

On the Tuesday morning, as I was assembling the contents of my rucksack prior to leaving for the ground, my mother suggested that I might wish to listen to the latest news broadcast on the radio. During the night, some supporters of a man in prison had dug up and poured oil on the test match pitch at Headingley. It was announced that, as the pitch was unfit for play, the test match would have to be abandoned. Mum queried this: surely they could just move a little further along the square and set up the stumps there. It was with some impatience that I explained to her that this could not be done. The enormous sense of anti-climax was taking effect already. I rang my friend Andrew Carter to cancel our plans for the day. Dalby ends his book with this event: "I wish him [George Davis] justice. Justice was not done to cricket-lovers at Headingley in 1975". As it happened, there was a steady drizzle and rain throughout the day, and it is doubtful whether any play would have been possible.

In addition to the Headingley test match at which Geoff Boycott scored his hundredth century, I saw the 1977 Australian tourists in two other matches. One was on the Sunday of a three day game against Yorkshire at Scarborough, when, for the only time, the whole of the family – mother, father, sister and me – went to a first class cricket match. We sat on the popular side on the banking in front of the main entrance and lapped up the sun; Boycott completed another century the following day.

The other was the first day of the Silver Jubilee Test at Lord's. I went with some friends from college and we sat in the lower tier at the Nursery End. Unusually, I can remember very little about the cricket, other than that England were bowled out cheaply on the first day after early half centuries from Bob Woolmer and Derek Randall. I was interested in watching Woolmer, who had initially come into the Kent side as a medium-paced bowler, but whose batting had developed so much that that was the principal reason he was in the England team. The influence of his mentor, Colin Cowdrey, was obvious: he had a calm presence at the crease and a pleasant array of classical strokes. He presented an intriguing contrast with Randall, who was all nerves and twitches and movement, though no less effective. The scorecard shows that Tony Greig was bowled by Pascoe. I cannot recall this exactly, but I assume that this was one of those several occasions when the tall England captain was undone by being unable to get his bat down on to a fast yorker.

Although this was not my first visit to Lord's, I was intrigued – as I would be on every visit – by the ground, not only the magnificent pavilion which stood at the far end from where we were sitting on this particular occasion, but those other parts of its geography – the Grandstand, the Tavern, the Mound Stand – about which I had heard countless references on radio and television. The pronounced slope, from right to left and especially down to the far left hand corner, about which the commentators also always referred, was clearly evident from our perspective. It was another of those occasions to clench my hand, so that the fingernails drove into the palm and I could register a physical recognition of my location. As with early visits to Headingley, I was also struck by the surrounding paraphernalia that accompanied the test match activity, particularly in the expanse of spare ground behind the stands at the Vauxhall End. And, not least, there were the ubiquitous MCC ties that seemed to be worn by every other spectator.

In truth, however, I felt that I did not really belong at Lord's. I was familiar, of course, with its history and tradition. I knew, for example, from John Marshall's *Headingley*, that Hedley Verity had taken 15 Australian wickets in the test match of 1934, including that of Don Bradman twice in one day. But there was something about the ground that made me uncomfortable which, in retrospect, I think was related to issues outside cricket. At that stage, I was a relatively infrequent visitor to London and, without quite being the country bumpkin, I recognised that Lord's represented that element of metropolitan living that I knew I would have to come to terms with in the not too distant future. More immediately, this somewhat alienated perspective was complemented by the various tradesmen around the ground – gatemen, scorecard sellers, cushion vendors – who seemed quick enough to take the spectator's money, but with a uniform brusqueness that was not exactly welcoming. My run-in with the jobsworth at the entrance of the pavilion was to come a few years later.

My first visit to the ground had come a year earlier when, again with friends from college, I sat in the Mound Stand to watch a day of the test match against the West Indies. We watched Steele and Woolmer bat for what seemed a long time without scoring many runs. Mere survival was no mean feat, it has to be said, against the opening bowling pairing of Andy Roberts and Michael Holding, but the speed of the action on the scoreboard – in terms of runs scored and overs bowled – was pedestrian. Even I – a self-declared connoisseur of the sport at this level – recognised that the play was unexciting. What wasn't slow, of course, was the velocity with which Roberts and Holding delivered the ball from one end of the pitch to the other. This was in the days when the England captain, Mike Brearley, was experimenting with his rudimentary skull-cap to give his head some protection, but when, otherwise, batsmen had relatively little head and body protection, certainly by today's standards. It can only have been great good fortune that a tragic accident did not occur somewhere along the line.

It was later in the series, at Old Trafford, that the scariest assault on the health of the English batsmen was made, when John Edrich and Brian Close bravely negotiated a period of violent short-pitched bowling in gloomy conditions. What we didn't realise, as we watching Roberts and Holding at Lord's, was that it would not be too long before the West Indies would supplement their attack by picking supporting bowlers – they were Bernard Julien and Vanburn Holder that day – who were equally as hostile as those taking the new ball. At the time, I simply thought that the view from the Mound Stand was very good: a full perspective across the ground.

Although the visits to Lord's were always interesting – I made the day trip down from Cambridge to watch Yorkshire win a tight Benson & Hedges Cup quarter final tie against Middlesex there in 1979,[25] thanks to a decisive innings from David Bairstow – I thought that the Oval was a much more welcoming ground. It was somehow less formal and, I suppose, more like the huge Headingley expanse to which I was accustomed.

This favourable impression was derived, despite the two disappointing experiences I had there at about this time. In the first, Andrew Carter and I saw Yorkshire bowled out relatively cheaply in the first innings of the Gillette Cup semi final against Surrey in 1980. Play started late, and Yorkshire were always at a disadvantage on an Oval pitch that was less batsman-friendly than it has been in recent years. When Boycott stroked a characteristically smooth square drive for four almost straightaway, we settled back for a sizeable Yorkshire total. However, they were undone by the hostile Sylvester Clarke and the reliable Robin Jackman.

Jackman struck me as an ideal seam bowler to have in your side: an willing workhorse with no little skill and a hurried skidding delivery. He certainly had a propensity to wind up the opposition and the opposition's supporters – and, presumably, a few umpires as well – by his style of appealing, which was theatrical, prolonged and frequent. At the other end, Clarke, notwithstanding an ungainly bowling action, exemplified the menace that surrounded so many West Indian fast bowlers of the time. In his thoughtful autobiography, *Playing for Keeps*, Alec Stewart described Clarke as the fastest and most intimidating bowler he played with or against. I clearly detected his threat, at the time, from the safety of the spectators' seats.

At the conclusion of the Yorkshire innings, there was no time for Surrey to begin their reply, which was held over to the following day (which I did not attend). As Andrew and I started to pack away our things before departure, I noticed that the nearby Yorkshire support was doing everything it could to improve the odds of their side succeeding the next day. This took the form, specifically, of a young man in the clearly identifiable colours of a Hull FC rugby league club shirt attempting to kick back the boundary rope an extra few inches towards the edge of the ground. Unfortunately, he did not meet with much success. The rope must have already been fairly taut, because when he pushed it back a short distance in one direction, it automatically tightened slightly – thereby encroaching on to the field – a little further along its path. It took him a few attempts before he realised that he was engaging in what mathematicians call a zero-sum game. Surrey reached their target the next day.

The second visit to the Oval was later in the same summer for the Saturday of the test match with the West Indies. I sat in more or less the same location, with the pavilion to my right, from which I had viewed Clarke and Jackman. This time, the prospect was of the West Indians – including Richards, Kallicharran and Lloyd – recommencing their shaky reply to the England first innings total of 370. Unfortunately for me and the rest of the spectators, the day was a complete wash-out. For the cricket authorities, things were not quite so serious, as there was no refund on any part of the full day's admission money.

My summer vacations at home from university provided only limited opportunity for spectating. During the week, I would take a short-term holiday job to refund the student coffers – I helped J Laing Construction Ltd to construct the British Home Stores building in Boar Lane in Leeds, and found that they had a mid-week cricket team, to which I was duly recruited – and I would be playing club cricket at the weekend. However, I did take the opportunity to see Mr Boycott score an exemplary century for Yorkshire in the Roses match at Old Trafford – another welcoming ground – in 1976, after which Geoff Cope bowled Lancashire out on the last afternoon to win the match. Yorkshire also defeated Lancashire on the last evening of the August bank holiday Roses match of 1979, though my principal memory of this match is of the sombre announcement over the public address system that Lord Mountbatten had been killed in an explosion on his boat and of the gasps of shock from the spectators sitting around us.

Two other memories are from John Player Sunday League games. In 1975 at Scarborough, Boycott and Hampshire put on a huge total for the first wicket – something approaching 200 – and I can remember the Gloucestershire team receiving some mocking cat-calls from some of the Yorkshire supporters as they left the pitch for the break between innings. I can also distinctly remember thinking, as this was going on, that it was not the size of the partnership that mattered, but the overall Yorkshire score. In the event, the Gloucestershire batsmen struggled and it looked as if

Yorkshire would win easily. Enter Alastair Hignell, batting fairly low down the order, who proceeded to strike three or four quick boundaries. One spectator near to me shouted mockingly, "He's going to win it himself, this lad" after the first couple of hits, but he soon fell silent as the Gloucestershire score mounted. In the event, Hignell and Gloucestershire fell short, but I recognised that it was a fair effort from someone who had just come back from an England rugby tour.

In the same season, Yorkshire played Somerset at Bradford, by now one of my favourite grounds. I continued to watch the games from the popular side, where the banking was quite steep, there was a regular stream of wit and jokes and, in the normal way, the boundary ran more or less right up to the first row of seats. On this occasion, I was ten or twelve rows back, when a Yorkshire player sent a huge skier towards the Somerset fielder, Phil Slocombe, who was on the boundary edge in front of us. Slocombe circled underneath it, lining himself up for the catch, whilst the crowd's jeering rose to a crescendo. Slocombe then dropped the catch, to widespread mirth behind him, and watched in despair as the ball trickled over the boundary for four.

Any professional cricketer would expect to receive a rocket from their captain for dropping such a catch, though probably in the confines of the changing room. Slocombe's particular difficulty was that Somerset's captain was Brian Close, who had been sacked by Yorkshire some years earlier, but who clearly would never want to waste an opportunity to put one over on his former employers. To make matters worse, the umpire signalled that the ball had gone for six. The umpire was quickly corrected by a combination of Slocombe and the crowd in the immediate vicinity, who pointed out that the ball had not carried the boundary on the full. At this, Close's ire rose even further and his distinctive voice, complete with unreconstructed Rawdon accent, was heard booming across the ground from his position close to the wicket. "What do you mean, it went for four? Why the bloody hell didn't you catch the bloody thing?" Slocombe's embarrassment was complete.

It struck me immediately that this was a prime example of the uncompromising and professional approach to cricket for which Brian Close was both respected and feared throughout the game. It was clear to me that he probably saw it as the only way to bring along the young talent at his disposal at Somerset: Slocombe was about my age and highly regarded, along with his contemporary Peter Roebuck and the slightly younger Ian Botham, amongst informed commentators. In *Head On – Botham: The Autobiography*, published in 2007, Botham confirmed the approach that his mentor had adopted: "I couldn't imagine Brian Close ever using soft words to get any of his players to perform. He'd tell them what to do... and give them a savage tongue-lashing if they messed it up".

This particular game turned when Viv Richards, basking in the glow of his participation in the West Indies's winning cricket World Cup Final performance at Lord's on the previous day, faced the Yorkshire medium pace bowler, Howard Cooper. After Richards had hit Cooper for a massive six, deep into the spectators at long on, he prowled around the crease with the characteristic demeanour that intimated far more acclaimed bowlers than Cooper over the years. I remember thinking that I did not envy Cooper the task of bowling the next delivery. But bowl it, he had to, of course, whereupon Richards edged the ball to the wicket-keeper, David Bairstow. As Richards departed the crease, he no doubt reflected, as I certainly did at that moment, on the facility of the sporting occasion to create a state of heady supremacy and then swiftly follow it with a lowering of the colours. For Brian Close, the afternoon represented a bad day at the office; he was dismissed cheaply and Yorkshire won by the narrow margin of 12 runs.

In many ways, this particular year (1975) gives a good representation of Yorkshire's chronic non-achievement over the long period following the break-up of Close's team of the 1960s. (It was non-achievement, rather than under-achievement, as the side was simply not of sufficient quality to compete consistently with the leading counties, whose ranks were bolstered with test match players from overseas). Andrew Carter and I saw them contrive to lose a low-scoring Gillette Cup tie against Leicestershire at Headingley when, after being bowled out for 109, they reduced the opposition to 86 for 9 before allowing the last wicket pairing to score the remaining 24 runs required for victory. I remember that the feeling of anti-climatic disappointment as we trudged home afterwards was difficult to shake off. As an aside, it did not escape my attention that one of the unlikely Leicestershire batsmen in that match-winning partnership was the veteran opening bowler Graham McKenzie, who was another player to have first come to my attention all those years earlier, in the 1964 edition of *Cricket Spotlight*, in a feature about that year's Australian touring party.

Things were slightly different in the county championship as, somewhat improbably, Yorkshire won 7 out the last 10 fixtures to finish up as runners-up. By the time the season reached its conclusion, Andrew and I were somewhere between the youth hostels of western Europe with our students' Inter-Rail cards, no doubt impressing those pretty Scandinavian students with our close association with the famous Leeds United. However, one match that we did see before we departed – and which Yorkshire did not win – was the August bank holiday fixture against Lancashire at Headingley. On the last afternoon, Yorkshire were set a target of 331 to win in what would turn out to be 60 plus overs. As might have been anticipated, it was not a particularly generous target, but the wicket was good and – or so it appeared to us – there was little chance of Yorkshire being bowled out. The challenge was not taken up, however. Yorkshire, showing little urgency, ambled to 219 for the loss of only one wicket by the time that stumps were drawn, with Boycott making 105 not out. In *Boycott; the Autobiography*, the match is dismissed as "an all-too familiar Roses bore and an inevitable draw". That was indeed how it turned out, but I did wonder at the time if, had Boycott led a more robust effort to chase the target, the draw would have been quite so inevitable.

In the final reckoning, the fact that Yorkshire drew rather than won the August 1975 Roses fixture did not represent the difference between first and second places in the final table. The champions, for the first time in their history, were Leicestershire, captained by the 43 year-old Ray Illingworth. But I think now – as I thought then – that that particular match captured in microcosm the controversy that Geoff Boycott generated both within Yorkshire and elsewhere. He was the best batsman in the Yorkshire side by far – his first class average was over 30 runs more than the next highest in that season – but the tension between his own personal objectives (and accomplishments) and the requirements of the side was always close to the surface.

Chapter 10

Elland Road Greyhound Stadium

The emblem of the Hunslet rugby league club, disbanded at the end of the 1972–73 season, was the phoenix rising from the ashes. It was highly apt. The New Hunslet club was established in time to take its place in the lower of the two divisions that were re-introduced for 1973–74. The stalwart Geoff Gunney was a driving force behind keeping professional rugby league alive in South Leeds. But Parkside had gone, of course. A new ground was needed and, for the next few seasons, it was found almost opposite the Leeds United soccer ground. New Hunslet RLFC played at the Elland Road Greyhound Stadium.

In comparison with Parkside, in terms of both the spectator facilities and – especially – the former ground's placing surface, the Greyhound Stadium was a poor relation. In *The Grounds of the Rugby League,* Trevor Delaney states the pitch was certainly the narrowest in the Rugby League at that time and extremely bumpy. Its main claim to fame was the use of American Football-style goal posts, which, as Delaney dryly notes, "did not exactly catch on with other clubs". But beggars couldn't be choosers, and this was the venue at which my father watched his favourite team until 1980.

It took my father a long time to get over the loss of Parkside, and I suspect that it was not until the 1990s that he ever really did. His consolation towards the end of the 1970s was that New Hunslet steadily built up a useful side. It was a difficult start, however. Although the registrations of the former club's players had been retained, not all were willing to re-sign: the full back David Marshall and the forward Phil Sanderson went to Leeds, for example. Nonetheless, after three seasons of gradual improvement, New Hunslet finished in fourth place in the second division in 1976–77 and, as four teams were promoted and relegated, went up to the first division for the following year.

It was obvious throughout this period – and frequently remarked upon by informed commentators at the time – that the rugby league authorities had still not hit on the appropriate format for promotion and relegation. The "yo-yo" effect was clearly evident. The same four teams (including New Hunslet) that were promoted in 1976–77 were immediately relegated back down to the second division in 1977–78. New Hunslet were then promoted again in 1978–79 and relegated again in 1979–80 (along with two of the other promoted sides, plus Wigan no less).

During these years, I went to the Greyhound Stadium probably no more than a dozen times in my Christmas and Easter vacations from university. There was very little terracing, apart from in front of the main social club; otherwise, there was only a view from ground level or, if not, from slightly below ground level, given the elevated nature of the playing surface in some parts of the ground. For me, this lack of atmosphere, due to the absence of a conventional and surrounding crowd, only seemed to add emphasis to the unremitting physical nature of the sport. The clashes between the players – the tackles, the confrontations – took place, if not in a vacuum, then in a stadium in which the sounds of the action seemed to echo back from the high walls of the surrounding licensed bars and restaurants within the ground. The effect was exacerbated by the narrowness of the pitch and the generally cramped nature of the playing environment. There were no wide open spaces into which the intimidated or the fleet-footed could retreat; instead, there was immediacy and claustrophobia.

One or two of the players stood out. New Hunslet purchased a powerful goalkicking centre called Mick Parrish from one of the local rugby union clubs. He took to the professional code well and succeeded in replicating Billy Langton's feat of playing and scoring in every one of the club's matches during the 1979–80 season. This was a considerable achievement, given that the Hunslet club (the old name having been re-established by then) was relegated from the first division. Just to prove it was no fluke, Parrish repeated the performance with Oldham, where he had been transferred, a couple of years later. The limited dimensions of the Greyhound Stadium pitch suited him, of course, in terms of the sizeable proportion of the playing area that was within his considerable kicking range. Other players to catch the eye were Allan Agar and Tony Dean, both experienced and tough scrum halves with good tactical brains, Gary Kemble, a young full back from New Zealand who played for the 1977–78 season, and Peter Muscroft, a strong and effective winger. These were all accomplished players who, as I could see from my occasional visits, gave hope to my father that the reputation of his beloved Hunslet team would be regained, following the sad days of the early 1970s.

Two particular games come to mind. The first, which I did not attend, was when Roger Millward brought his Hull Kingston Rovers side to the Greyhound Stadium a couple of weeks before they were to appear at Wembley in the 1980 Challenge Cup final. This was the same Millward, of course, that Dad and I had admired as a teenage prodigy with Castleford at Parkside fifteen years earlier. Dad was full of admiration again. He said that Hull KR had been on top form, as if primed for the forthcoming big occasion, and that Millward had been masterly in bringing his big strong running forwards into play. I could envisage them – Phil Lowe and Paul Rose in particular – causing havoc down the narrow Hunslet pitch. The other game – which I did attend – was a first division clash with Leeds in April 1980, which Hunslet won by 21 points to 7. The visitors had been clear favourites, as ever, but, on the day, they were distinctly out of sorts, the prop forward Steve Pitchford getting himself sent off. This must have been the last time that Hunslet beat Leeds in a competitive fixture.

During my Christmas breaks, the Leeds home league fixture on Boxing Day remained part of the annual ritual: Wakefield Trinity each year from 1974 until 1978, then Hunslet, then Featherstone Rovers. I can remember watching one Leeds versus Wakefield game – in 1976 – from the South Stand at Headingley, traditionally (and still today) the location for the most die-hard and vocal Leeds supporters. It was in this particular match that Leeds were absolutely shredded – there is no other word – by the Wakefield stand off, David Topliss. He swerved and side-stepped through the whole game, creating the openings for his bigger and more powerful colleagues to run through. Leeds just could not get hold of him. Topliss was almost like a boxer, drawing his opponent in close to make a move, before quickly jinking out the way, throwing his opponent off balance and creating the breach in the defence. It was absolutely captivating. A similar outcome occurred in 1980, when the rising star Steve Evans – the namesake of, but no relation to, my college friend – showed too much skill for the home defence, and the perennially unfashionable Featherstone surprised Leeds and secured an unexpected win. My father and I stood with my uncle Vic in the South Stand, neither of us particularly unhappy with the outcome.

A favourable characteristic of the Boxing Day match was that it had an 11.30am kick off. After the game, therefore, our quickly established ritual included a visit to one of the local pubs – usually the Original Oak in Headingley – to chew the fat. If Leeds had won, which they usually did, Vic would be keen to talk about the match and analyse the facets of his side's superiority, whilst Dad and I searched for alternative subjects for discussion. If the result had gone the other way – as in 1976 and 1980 – the roles were reversed. Either way, it was enjoyable and reassuring conversation which, without exception, always ended up with Dad and Vic casting themselves back to the matches and players of the past. For dad, this meant the 1938 Championship final, in which Hunslet had defeated Leeds at Elland Road. "You wouldn't remember Dolly Dawson, would you?", Dad would ask me after a couple of beers, referring to a distinguished Hunslet forward of this era. "No dad. It was before my time", I would reply politely. My father would then remind Vic, yet again, of the way that the slightly built Oliver Morris had nullified the attacking threat of the powerful Vic Hey. A third beer would be consumed. "You won't remember Oliver Morris, will you?", I would be asked. When Dad had moved on – as he inevitably did – to discussing Hunslet's Challenge Cup final victory over Widnes at Wembley in 1934, Vic would invariably refer to his longstanding friend, Cyril, with whom he had worked for many years. This was Cyril Morrell, who scored one of the Hunslet tries that day, breaking his collar bone in the process. Looking back, I suspect that the post-Boxing Day match discussion in the Original Oak followed more or less the same script every year, but I did not mind. There was a mutual affinity in a routine that was familiar and comforting and ours.

In most seasons, the other part of this winter schedule involved another home fixture for Leeds: the New Year fixture, usually against Hull KR. Dad and I went to the games in most of the years between 1976 and 1981 and, again, we took our places in the South Stand. For some reason, these games invariably seemed to follow the same pattern. Hull KR would arrive with an attractive and powerful side; one of the visitors' forwards would commit a foul in full view of the baying crowd in our stand and get sent off; and Leeds would run in a hatful of tries to win comfortably. It was not dissimilar to the earlier experiences with Wakefield Trinity in the Boxing Day fixture and, whilst it might simply be the faulty perspective of hindsight, this sequence of events seemed to happen almost every year: the rugby league equivalent of *Groundhog Day*. It certainly happened in 1976, when the Hull KR forward Paul Rose was sent off after ten minutes and Leeds won by 30 points to 5. In 1978, Rose lasted until the hour mark before being dismissed. The only difference to this scenario was in 1981 when, after once more losing a man relatively early in the game, Hull KR recovered to win the encounter. Somewhat bizarrely, my main recollection of this last match is that, for the whole game, a section of the home support in the stand chanted the tune from *Tom Hawk*, a song by a band called the Piranhas that had been in the pop music charts during the previous autumn. It was an annoying little tune at the best of times; these lads chanted it for the full duration for reasons that were not immediately obvious. My father – not a connoisseur of popular music trends – remarked bewilderedly towards the end: "They've been humming that song all match".

One player listed in the Hull KR squad for the New Year match of 1976 was Neil Fox, who, after playing for 19 seasons for Wakefield Trinity, moved to a succession of clubs during the last five years of his career. Fox had been one of the stars of the rugby league world when I had first started watching the sport in the early 1960s and a member of the formidable Wakefield side with which Hunslet had done battle in several cup ties during those years, not least the Challenge Cup semi final in 1965. Although Fox did not feature on this particular day, I did see him play in another match against Leeds at around this time – as a substitute for Bradford Northern in a January 1979 fixture, I think. By that time, he was 39 years old, but continuing to perform at the highest level, kicking goals and generally directing play for his side. (Fox went on to play for Bradford in their first match of the 1979–80 season, thereby achieving the feat of playing professional rugby league at the age of 40). His physical appearance had changed, mainly through the acquisition of a fashionable moustache that, from the distance of the South Stand, made him look like Gregory Peck in *The Gunfighter* and he had obviously lost some pace around the pitch. But his well-built frame and his distinctive style of running, with his high arms pumping across his chest, and his methodical goalkicking technique marked him out as the same player I had seen all those years before. I watched him with admiration. My *Rothmans Rugby League Yearbook* confirms that Neil Fox holds the record for the most points – 6,220 to be exact – in a rugby league career.

I continued the Hull KR connection in 1980 when, as noted, they reached the Challenge Cup final at Wembley. Their opponents were their fierce local rivals, Hull FC, and I went to the game with a friend from university who happened to be a Hull supporter. The memories from the day are very clear. First, when we were walking down Wembley Way towards the stadium and had just reached the top of the long ramp that led to the first of the entrances to the ground, the Hull team bus drove along the road below us. The concrete wall at the top of the ramp was quite high and I was asked by a short and squat middle-aged lady wearing a Hull rugby shirt and a Hull scarf if I could lift her up so that she could see her team. I could not refuse, of course, and so I undertook the commission at the cost, to myself, of some strain on my lower back and not seeing the team bus at all. The lady recognised my sacrifice, however. "Thank you. A lovely gesture" were her departing words.

On the pitch, a number of incidents. The most shocking was the late stiff arm tackle by a Hull player that broke Roger Millward's jaw. It was captured by the television cameras and can be seen in its unpleasant detail on the *Century of Rugby League* video. Even Eddie Waring was lost for words. We were standing quite high up behind the posts and I saw the offence as it was committed. More to the point, so did the referee, Fred Lindop, who, incredibly, merely let the player off with a warning. I sensed as soon as Millward was hit that there would be serious damage. He played on during the match, but, effectively, the injury ended his career.

Second, a much more pleasing moment: indeed, the next of my nano-dramas. This was the pass by the Hull KR prop forward, Brian Lockwood, that released his winger, Steve Hubbard, to score the game's first – and, as it turned out, decisive – try. It came after Lockwood had taken the ball at about second or third receiver and Hubbard came haring in from his wing behind him to take the pass at full speed and break through Hull's defensive line. Hubbard continued his arching run to go around the Hull full back, Paul Woods, and cross over for the try. The most amazing thing was the length of Lockwood's pass: it was probably, at most, about eighteen inches. And yet it was delivered with such exquisite skill and timing that the Hull players could not respond. It was, in short, a piece of rugby league class from a distinguished player. Lockwood had previously played in two Challenge Cup winning sides for Castleford at the end of the 1960s and was to return (with Widnes) in both the following two seasons.

Hubbard's try had an unusual coda. As he touched down, he was fouled in the act of scoring by Woods, another player for whom, it always seemed to me, the maintenance of on-field discipline presented a significant challenge. Lindop applied the unusual sanction of awarding a penalty from in front of the posts, in addition to the normal conversion, so that Hull KR scored a seven-point try. As they won the match 10–5, Hubbard's score turned out to have been more than sufficient to separate the sides. Quite right too: Lockwood's pass had deserved to win any match.

The other rugby league spectating I undertook during my visits home were for some of the bigger games at Headingley: that is, the Challenge Cup semi finals, the later stages of the John Player Trophy and one or two of the international fixtures. In 1980, Hull KR played Halifax in the Challenge Cup semi final and, having been the strong favourites to win, duly carried the day. The particular interest for the neutral spectator – as, of course, my father and I both were – was whether Roger Millward and another distinguished veteran, Clive Sullivan, could help Hull KR secure the win that would enable the two players to feature in the Challenge Cup final for the first time. Their success was widely recognised – except in Halifax – as the correct outcome. Three years earlier, Hull KR had lost to the strong Widnes side of that time. As we were leaving the South Stand on that occasion, I remember hearing a Widnes supporter greet a friend with "We're there again", in recognition of their success in reaching a third Wembley final in as many years. My thought at the time was that this supporter should make the most of this latest success as the cause of his triumphalism might not last for ever. It didn't, of course, although it still lasted for some time to come: Widnes also reached the Challenge Cup final in four of the next seven years.

One of these years was 1979, when the Headingley semi final was between Wakefield Trinity and St Helens. By then, my father and I had decided to go upmarket. Rather than stand in the South Stand, we – or rather he – invested in a couple of seats in the main stand on the other side of the ground. Dad bought these directly from the rugby league headquarters in Chapeltown Road, a habit that he maintained for some years afterwards when purchasing tickets for the big matches. It turned out that, for this particular game, the seats were just about the best in the ground. We were in a small area of seating near to the press gallery and with a close and uninterrupted view of the pitch. We felt like VIPs.

Wakefield's place in the semi final was a reward for their bold investment in some of the local rugby union talent. Keith Smith had played at fly-half for the Moortown and Roundhay clubs, as well as Yorkshire, and on the basis of his consistently excellent performances, particularly in a Roundhay fixture away at Coventry, had been capped by England. Mike Lampkowski was a powerful rugby union player, also capped by England, whose main deficiency, as reported in *Bill Beaumont: The Autobiography*, was that "he lacked that one ingredient that is so necessary to a scrum half: he couldn't pass a ball quickly and accurately". This was, to say the least, a major handicap for a scrum half in international rugby union; Beaumont refers to the England defeat at Murrayfield in 1976 when "passes were flying all over the place". But Lampkowski was a brave and determined competitor, and the Wakefield coaches had had the foresight to recognise his potential to be a highly effective rugby league loose forward.

The semi final was closely fought. Wakefield were winning narrowly, with only five minutes or so to go, when the announcement was made over the public address system that one of their forwards, Trevor Skerrett, had won the man-of-the-match award. I thought at the time – as I have often tended to think on such occasions – that the announcement was a little premature. And so it proved. Almost immediately, the powerful St Helens winger, Les Jones, forced his way over for a try in the right hand corner to regain the lead for his side. Hang on, I thought. On the basis that Jones had had the decisive input to the outcome of the game, wouldn't that now make him the man of the match and override the previous decision? Then, in the last minute, David Topliss made a final break from deep inside the Wakefield half and Keith Smith carried on the move before passing to the winger, Andrew Fletcher, who crossed the line for what did indeed turn out to be the winning try. Decision changed again, I reasoned. The final score was 9–7 to Wakefield. The man-of-the-match award should be given to Fletcher. Or to Topliss. I would have gone for the latter; Topliss's probing and skilful running had been a central feature of the match, not for the first time at Headingley, and, keeping his cool as the game seemed to have slipped from his side's grasp, he had crowned the performance with the match-winning break.

The other major rugby league competition at this time was the John Player Trophy. Although it did not have the status of the Challenge Cup, it was keenly contested by the big clubs. The rugby league authorities attempted to increase its aura by playing the semi finals on neutral venues, as with the Challenge Cup, which meant that Headingley often received some of these fixtures, if Leeds were not one of the participating clubs in these particular ties. On the other hand, what did not work in the competition's favour was its scheduling, as the closing stages were typically played between late November and early January, when the combination of inclement weather and live television coverage usually meant that the attendances were not significant.

My father and I went to the Bradford Northern versus Wakefield Trinity semi final at Headingley in November 1979. Our seats were at the back of the main stand: not as prominent as for our previous visit for the Challenge Cup semi final, but perfectly acceptable. The decisive try was scored by the Bradford centre, Derek Parker, who received a team mate's pass out of the tackle and, at speed, sold a subtle dummy and then stepped around the Wakefield full back on his way to the line. Dad and I agreed afterwards that the match had been compulsive viewing: hard, committed, fast and skilful. It was interesting that we reached this view independently, although it was perhaps not too surprising. I was on a weekend visit from university and, the Cambridge XV not being as attractive as some of its predecessors, was somewhat starved of decent rugby action; Dad had been watching a Hunslet team in the lower reaches of the first division. Our overall impression was that British rugby league was in a reasonable healthy state. The stark correction to this viewpoint would not be long in coming.

The feeling of satisfaction at seeing a good rugby league game was complemented when we got home and saw the brief highlights of the North of England rugby union side's victory over the New Zealand All Blacks at Otley. This was not just a win, but a comprehensive victory by a side that would form the core of the England grand slam team of later in the season. I have to admit that taking satisfaction from this outcome did reveal a certain amount of reflected glory in the North's performance on my part, as there were 10 Lancashire players in the team and only Alan Old from Yorkshire. Nonetheless, all in all, it was a good day.

Bradford won through to the final of the John Player Trophy, also at Headingley, against Widnes in January 1980. It was another tough encounter, won by Bradford 6–0, in front of a crowd of less than 10,000. However, my principal memory of the game is of two spectators, sitting five or six places in front of us in the main stand. They were father and son, both bedecked in Bradford shirts and scarves; the son also had a bobble hat in the team's colours. The man was probably aged between 35 and 40 and the boy was in his early teenage years.

The man shouted out at the top of his voice for the whole match, jumping up and down, berating the referee at every opportunity, gesticulating wildly with his arms, and complaining at the Widnes players every time they had the audacity to make a tackle. His son, not surprisingly, followed his example. "Come on, Golden Legs", shouted the man, as a scrum formed and the veteran Bradford hooker, Keith Bridges, attempted to win the ball. (Rugby league scrums were contested in those days, unlike the charade that passes for a scrum in the modern game). "Come on, Golden Legs", echoed the boy.

My father and I observed this performance, but did not say anything at the time. It was only when we got home that he asked me if I had seen the man in the stand in front of us. When I said that I had, he remarked that he was glad he had not watched the Hunslet games like that with me when I was a boy. I knew what he meant. It was not so much the public exhibition that he would have made of himself, though this in itself would have been more than enough to dissuade my father from acting in that way. It was the lack of knowledge that the boy – and, by implication, that I – would have accrued. "You would never have learnt anything".

I readily admit that there was – and is – an element of moral superiority in all this. The man and his son were enjoying the match. They were behaving themselves. They were certainly committed Bradford supporters. But whether they were followers of rugby league as a sport in itself, I was not so sure. In any event, I knew that my father and I were on exactly the same wavelength. My enjoyment of watching the Bradford-Widnes game was based on the earlier grounding I had received at Parkside, when my father and I had been supporting Geoff Shelton, Brian Gabbitas, Geoff Gunney and the rest, but we had also been observing Brian Bevan, Roger Millward and Peter Smethurst.

The Bradford captain, Len Casey, won the match of the match award at the 1980 John Player Trophy final. He was a tough and uncompromising player. Later in the year, in the test match against New Zealand at Headingley in November, he was involved in a fight with the opposition prop, Kevin Tamati, another hard man. Even by the physical conflict endemic in this particular sport, it was a vicious confrontation, with, at one stage, Casey holding Tamati in a headlock with one arm and pummelling him several times with his other fist. My father and I both winced at the nature of the clash, as also did many of the crowd around us. My recollection is that, as with the assault on Roger Millward in the Challenge Cup final at Wembley a few months earlier, the referee adopted a somewhat lenient approach, merely calling the players over and telling them not to do it again. Great Britain won narrowly due to two tries from the Leigh winger Des Drummond, a powerful and compact player who was very difficult to tackle: he always seemed to enjoy the confrontation with opposing players, who would invariably bounce off him if their challenges were not timed correctly.

Although Great Britain beat New Zealand on that occasion, it was only to give them a share of the three-match series, as they had drawn and lost the previous two games. Both sides were ranked behind Australia, who had convincingly beaten Great Britain in Brisbane and Sydney in the summer of 1979. In the previous Ashes series, in the autumn of 1978, the Headingley test had been the decider, as Great Britain, with Brian Lockwood to the fore, had won the second test at the Odsal Stadium. Unfortunately, Lockwood was injured for the third test and Great Britain, after holding their own for much of the game, went down 23–6. At one stage, after John Bevan had powered his way over to score a trademark try in the corner, it looked as if the home side might fight back for a stirring victory. Bevan certainly thought so, because, after scoring, he ran back down the length of the touchline in front of the main stand – in which we were situated – with his arm in the air and the crowd roused to a passion.

Australia were too strong, however. This was the touring side, captained by Bobby Fulton, which included Graham Eadie, Steve Rogers and Ray Price. I had seen the second test on television and Rogers, in particular, looked dangerous every time he got the ball. Their Headingley win was a staging post in their longstanding success in the Ashes series that has been unbroken since the victory of Roger Millward, Dennis Hartley and their colleagues in 1970. By a neat symmetry, the other try scored by the home side in the 1978 Headingley decider was registered by Millward, who was playing in his final international, 12 years after his first appearance for Great Britain.

Chapter 11

Cardiff Arms Park

My first international cap for rugby union spectating was for the Wales versus England fixture at Cardiff Arms Park in February 1975. Steve Evans (my fellow student, not the future Featherstone Rovers rugby player) and I travelled down from Cambridge on the Friday and stayed with his parents in Bridgend for the weekend. The train from Paddington was full to the brim with confident Welshmen going home to see the expected slaughter of the English. This was, after all, the Welsh team of Gareth, Gerald, Mervyn, JPR, JJ and the rest, all of whom, apparently, were on first name terms with the tide of homeward bound supporters.

Wales stretched out to a comfortable lead in the first 20 minutes and won the game, at a canter, by 20 points to 4. I had a good view from a small enclosed area of terrace in the North Enclosure, roughly level with the 25 yard line. England competed spiritedly, but did not seem to have either the organisation or the imagination to trouble their hosts. It was with some relief that the final margin of the Welsh victory was not larger.

For the crowd around me, the England match clearly took the form of a ritual: the travelling from the valleys (and from other points, east and west), the singing, the acclamation of their team, the identification with the individual stars and, in this game, the celebration at scoring three tries to one. The analogy has been used many times, but it was a religious gathering, with these particular idols and at this particular altar. I was the outsider, of course – the observer, looking on – though I suspect that, from my general silence and rueful shaking of the head, those around me knew where my sympathies might lie.

The combination of events on the field, where Wales controlled the game from start to finish, and the passionate and knowing superiority of the vast majority on the crowded terraces served, for me, to generate a feeling that bordered on claustrophobia. This was not a reaction to the physical proximity of those around me. Rather, it was, I think, a reflection of the limited mental space that I inhabited as a result of my minority (and losing) status. However, notwithstanding this somewhat uncomfortable sensation, the day was an unqualified success. I had visited Cardiff Arms Park, the famous citadel of Welsh rugby and, also, the venue of what might be considered to have been the best rugby match ever played: the Barbarians versus New Zealand encounter of January 1973.

And, at last – six years on from the disappointment of his not featuring in the Cardiff team that played at Headingley at Easter 1969 – I had seen the greatest rugby union player of my spectating era: Gareth Edwards. I will not dwell of the skills and attributes that he brought to the sport – the speed and length of his passing, the accuracy of his kicking, the devastating running, the tactical awareness, the leadership by example, and so on. Instead, I simply refer to that Barbarians-New Zealand match and a moment of skill shown by Edwards that would have been mundane had it also not been brilliant. This particular example is not when he scored the superlative first try or when he harried Sid Going into making the mistake that led to Fergus Slattery's score. Rather, it was just before John Dawes's disallowed try, also in the first half, when, on unexpectedly receiving a deflected kick inside the New Zealand 25, Edwards immediately side-stepped Bob Burgess, before passing inside to Slattery. No matter how many times I watch the tape, I am always amazed by the speed of Edwards's feet as he stepped around Burgess; he had no room in which to work, but his opponent still did not lay a hand on him. Unusually – and fortuitously – Cliff Morgan did the BBC commentary that day: "Oh, that fellow Edwards... What can touch a man like that?"[26]

My second visit to Cardiff was for the corresponding fixture four years later. I took my place in the South Lower Stand, almost diagonally opposite my previous vantage point. Wales had another fine side and England were even more comprehensively defeated: 27–3. One of the England players was Richard Cardus, then at the Roundhay club, who had gone to Foxwood School in Leeds. Foxwood were always Roundhay School's first opponents of the season – a fixture we never lost in my time at the school, although I doubt that I ever played against Cardus, who was a year younger than me. In the 1979 international, Wales took a long penalty kick at goal, which fell just short. As the ball was in the air, Cardus confidently shouted that he was going to catch it and readied himself in preparation, his eyes firmly on the oncoming target. He then promptly dropped the ball, before sprinting away towards the half way line, as if nothing had happened, whilst the referee and the rest of the players trooped over in preparation for the scrum under the England posts. The incident just about summed up England's afternoon.

All the Welsh players seemed to contribute to their overwhelming superiority in this game. In the match programme, one of the second row places was left vacant, as Wales had had a number of players injured in this position. The place was taken by the grey-haired veteran Mike Roberts, who proceeded to play a blinder. Then, in the brief period in which he was on the pitch as a replacement, Clive Griffiths made a searing break down the south side of the ground to set up another Welsh try. This probably added another £10,000 to his asking price, when the St Helens rugby league club signed him not long afterwards.

The intervening England-Wales match was played at Twickenham in 1978. The England fly half was John Horton, whose skills I had observed with some admiration at the Llanelli Schools sevens competition at the beginning of the decade. It was a hard game in which to play one's first international. The match was a dour slog from start to finish, typified by the uncontrolled free-for-all in the line-outs, that Wales won by three penalty goals to two. I stood in the South Stand – in those days, open to the elements and packed to crushing point – in the pouring rain, as the two packs of forwards hammered into each other, ripping up the long grass of the pitch as they did so. Alastair Hignell missed four penalty kicks out of six, including a straightforward one near the end that would have levelled the scores. It was an uncomfortable experience, not only due to the weather and the general level of play, but also because of the poor viewing facility provided by the terrace in the South Stand, the gradient of which was too shallow. Years later, in *Brian Moore: The Autobiography*, the former England hooker reported that this match represented his first visit to Twickenham at the age of 16: "…on a dark, filthy day… I can remember Gareth Edwards running on ahead of the Welsh team because it was his fiftieth cap [and] Alastair Hignell missing kicks for England…"

It was also from the South Stand that I watched England play New Zealand twice, in November 1978 and November 1979, losing on both occasions. In the first game, on a bright and cold day, England's continued line-out problems cost them dearly, as the All Blacks scored two tries in front of me after England throw-ins on their own line, albeit that one of them clearly followed a knock forward by Frank Oliver. However, I knew that New Zealand were not flattered by their 16–6 margin of victory; they had failed to capitalise on a couple of clear overlaps as well as missing a penalty kick from in front of the posts. One of England's scores was a drop goal by Dusty Hare who, with his back to the opposition, tapped a differential penalty to himself before swivelling round to take aim for the posts.

The second defeat to New Zealand was particularly galling, given that the North of England side had comprehensively beaten the tourists at Otley the week before. The North's victory had been on the same day that Dad and I had attended the Bradford Northern-Wakefield Trinity rugby league match at Headingley and had remarked afterwards about the high level of skills that the professional players had shown. I had been particularly struck that day by the centre play of Derek Parker, who had scored the decisive try for Bradford. By contrast, from behind the posts at Twickenham, I watched as the England centre, Nick Preston, managed a spurn the clear try-scoring opportunity presented by a two-to-one overlap by running towards the touchline and crowding out the space that his winger had to work in. This struck me as a simple illustration – and perhaps also an unfair one, as Preston had been an impressive performer when I had seen him play for Richmond against Cambridge University – of the difference in skill and awareness levels between the top practitioners in the two respective sports.

Of course, rugby union was still an amateur sport at that time. There were the usual stories of "professional" behaviour – players receiving brown paper envelopes or generous travelling expenses or sinecured jobs, for example – but the mindset within the sport, amongst players and administrators alike, was nowhere near the professional attitude adopted by their counterparts in the modern era. In *Bill Beaumont: The Autobiography*, the England captain of the late 1970s describes with depressing regularity the amateurishness – in the pejorative sense – of the approach taken by England at that time, not least in some of the team selections. He gives particular examples of the wrong players being chosen in key positions for the games against France in 1976 and against New Zealand in both 1978 and 1979, amongst others. The approach of the England authorities was exemplified by the build up to the first of these matches against the All Blacks: "There was virtually no preparation for a tilt at the best side in the world… We met as usual on the Thursday before the game… I was annoyed about the amateurish build-up to the game".

Following the second New Zealand match, I had therefore seen England play five times and lose every match. It was an increasingly familiar pattern of wrong selections, a lack of continuity in key positions, inadequate preparation and, on the pitch, uninspired and poorly implemented tactics. For most England supporters – including Brian Moore, an unknown spiritual soulmate at this time – there was an inevitable sense of resignation: "There was no real depression that England had lost. England supporters… were never overburdened with expectation".

The invariable feeling with which I was left after watching these internationals was one of profound anti-climax. I would look forward to each match with great anticipation, and this feeling would be heightened as, at Twickenham, I left the railway station and walked the half mile or so to the ground across Chertsey Road and past the lengthy queue milling around the final off licence. The tall stand on one side of the ground would come into view with the stark lettering – East – announcing its formidable presence. The final rituals – showing the ticket to the steward, passing through the turnstile, buying the programme, making the final visit to the toilet and hoping the bladder would then hold up for the next two hours – were undertaken with a keen eagerness and expectation. The sense of excitement would continue with the arrival of the England team on to the pitch in their unblemished (and, in those days, completely logo-free) shirts: pure white with the red rose – and with the disproportionately huge black numbers on their backs – against the red shirts of Wales or the all black of New Zealand. Then, the release of the national anthems. And then, from the English perspective, apart from the occasional piece of individual skill, a dull performance and defeat. Surely the best rugby union players in the country – and there were some very good players in each of these England sides – could do better than this?

When in Cardiff, there was the added prospect of enduring the long weekend of Welsh triumphalism – not, I hasten to add, from my friends and their families who were generous enough to act as my hosts – but, it appeared, from the rest of the country. The late 1970s represented the last golden era of Welsh rugby until the grand slam triumphs of 2005 and 2008. Cardiff city centre on the Saturday evening of the victories over England would be resplendent in red and cheered by the heady combination of success and beer. And also, it might be said, by an element of condescension towards the ranks of the defeated: this period represented the zenith of Max Boyce's appeal to his discerning audience as well as the (time limited) vindication for his comedy act.

In 1975, however, I did come across a refreshing exception to this general sense of unconditional exultation. It was to be found on BBC Wales Television on the Sunday afternoon, where the Llanelli and former British Lions coach, Carwyn James, was analysing some of the decisive action from the previous day's match. The sequence that I can still recall was when he described the misalignment of the English three-quarters, when they were under pressure on their own line, and how their jagged defensive formation had made it easier for the Welsh backs to penetrate and score a try. It was a technical analysis which was easy to follow and which, unquestionably, added to my understanding of what I had seen on the Saturday afternoon. Needless to say, it was also far superior to much of the waffle that passes for insightful comment on rugby on today's television screens (the estimable Brian Moore excepted). I was impressed, not only with James himself and his ability to communicate, but with the producers of the programme. They had done more than bring in a master for the analysis; they had respected their audience.

The other consolation after each of these internationals was that I had another match programme to add to the collection. In keeping with the norms for that time – as also applied, for example, for big rugby league matches until the late 1970s – the formats of the programmes did not change from year to year. The front cover of the programme for the England-Wales match at Twickenham in 1978, for example, was exactly the same as it had been for the corresponding fixture in 1966, apart from the date and the price – 25 pence instead of one shilling and sixpence. (I had acquired the earlier programme from one of my trawls of the television commentators). And very attractive it looked too, diagonally halved in white and red, with boldly printed typeface and emblems. For the New Zealand matches at Twickenham, the design of the cover was the same, except that it was in diagonally halved white and black with the New Zealand fern replacing the Prince of Wales's feathers. As with the Varsity Match programmes, there were weighty – and knowingly amusing – articles from representatives of the respective camps. For the 1975 match at Cardiff – behind a programme cover of vertical red and white bands – these were from the chief rugby writers of the *Western Mail* and the *Daily Telegraph*: JBG Thomas and John Reason. (The cover of the 1979 programme was identical to that for the 1975 match, apart from the bilingual presentation of the sides: Wales v England and Cymru v Lloegr).

I suppose the unchanging format of the match programmes was yet another reflection of the inherent conservatism within the administration of rugby union. But I didn't mind. I thought the programmes were collector's items and I read them from cover to cover. I respected the continuity and tradition that their format represented. From today's perspective, there is also now a historical dimension to their contents. The 1975 programme contained a half page advertisement for a Philips video cassette recorder which helpfully explained that: "With the Philips VCR you are able to record programmes from one channel whilst watching another channel". The price was £484, inclusive of VAT, the equivalent of over £3,000 in 2010 prices.

The most controversial of the rugby union internationals during this period was the England-Wales encounter at Twickenham in February 1980. Both sides were unbeaten in the Five Nations Championship at that stage with England, having beaten Ireland and France, half way towards a prospective first grand slam in 23 years. I took up my usual position on the terraces in the South Stand. In the match programme, Carwyn James wrote:

"I have a… sneaking feeling that England, at last, are coming good".

It was a horrible game, ironically reflecting the hype that had been prevalent in both sides of the Severn Bridge beforehand and, it seemed from my perspective, a considerable amount of antagonism between the respective sets of players. Even at the distance I was from the action, there was no mistaking the sheer violence of the rucking and the weight of collision at the scrums. Bill Beaumont described it succinctly in his autobiography: "It was an absolutely awful match from the first minute… [with] players from both sides behaving totally out of character".

The Welsh back row forward, Paul Ringer, was sent off after a quarter of an hour. My analysis of this incident was that it was a case of the red mist descending and a player being dismissed for dimness as much as anything else. After a series of incidents of foul play, the Irish referee, David Burnett, called both captains together and, by all accounts, warned them that the next player to infringe would be sent from the field. Ringer was that player for a late – and, it has to be said, less than vicious – tackle on John Horton. Beaumont acknowledges as much in his autobiography "I have seen later tackles and I have seen higher tackles, but his [Ringer's] sense of timing couldn't have been worse". That was precisely my opinion at the time. As soon as Ringer caught his man, I inadvertently muttered, "That must be him off" within the earshot of the posse of Welsh supporters around me. It wasn't a plea on my behalf to the referee; it was a statement of the inevitable which, to their consternation, the Welsh saw unfold in the next few moments.

Despite playing with a man short for over three-quarters of the match, Wales scored a second try to take an 8–6 lead late in the second half, and it looked as if my zero per cent success rate in seeing England win would be maintained. The frustration this time was that, notwithstanding the poor quality of the overall play, England appeared to have done enough to grind out a rare win over the Welsh and the apparently decisive try had only come about because the scrum half, Steve Smith, had been too slow in trying to punt the ball downfield and had had his kick charged down. However, Gareth Davies failed with the not-too-difficult conversion attempt, which meant that England could still win, if they could force their way down the pitch and secure a penalty kick. This thought occurred to me the moment that Davies's kick hit a post and bounced back. It probably occurred to him as well. Beaumont reports that it was certainly his view. And, sure enough, when, shortly afterwards, Terry Holmes infringed at a ruck, Dusty Hare coolly stepped up and stroked over the penalty kick, never looking as if he was going to miss.

Carwyn James's "sneaking feeling" had been correct: England duly completed the grand slam in the next and final match against Scotland at Murrayfield. I could not realise it at the time, of course, but the 1980 England-Wales encounter anticipated a set of circumstances that would be repeated exactly a quarter of a century later in the 2005 game at the Millennium Stadium – uncontrolled media hype in advance of the match; a close and tense affair between the traditional rivals; a narrow victory for the home side, brought about by a successful penalty kick in the closing minutes of the match; the victors moving on towards a grand slam – though with the roles reversed.

My return visits to Leeds during the university vacations provided regular opportunities to resume my observation of the fierce rivalries between the local rugby union clubs. An increasing number of these matches were in some formal competition. My father and I saw Roundhay play Headingley in an early round of the John Player Cup in October 1975 and we later picked up the competition again with Roundhay's quarter final against Gosforth in March 1976. Similarly, we saw Headingley against Morley in the Yorkshire Cup in March 1976 and Morley play Roundhay in the Yorkshire cup final of April 1980. Others were ordinary clubs games: Harrogate versus Roundhay in December 1977, Roundhay versus Pontypridd on a wet evening in September 1977. In some respects, the derby games have blurred into each other: they remained tough – sometimes brutal – encounters, usually closely fought, with occasional flashes of skill. These were the days long before the intervention of neutral touch judges or the post-match scrutiny of the all-seeing video cameras. The settling of longstanding local grievances was not for the faint-hearted.

We also resumed our trips to watch the prime fixtures at the Headingley club: for example, to see Coventry, London Scottish and Rosslyn Park – all with a significant presence of international players – in 1975. Headingley themselves were also able to field some impressive talent at around this time: the loyal Spencer and McGeechan, who had played for the best part of a decade, plus other England internationals in Andy Maxwell, Chris Williams, Mike Lampkowski (notwithstanding his uncertain passing skills and prior to his transfer to the rugby league ranks) and David Caplan. All of these players were behind the scrum, however. Headingley faced the same difficulty as the Yorkshire rugby union side (and, as previously described, the university team in Cambridge): that is, winning enough possession to allow these backs to flourish. The one player of personal acquaintance was Caplan, not through the rugby, but via his despairing efforts to keep wicket to my off spin during the half season we played together at Saltaire CC in the Bradford League. He was a talented sportsman and, moreover, a good bloke.

My father and I also continued to see a number of the representative games hosted by the Headingley club, including Yorkshire's fixture against Northumberland in October 1976 and the North of England's match with the touring Argentineans in October 1978. However, the game I can recall clearest was, unusually, played at Roundhay's ground at Chandos Park, where, as preparation for the forthcoming county championship series, Yorkshire played Edinburgh in September 1980. I went to this game by myself and stood on the banking on the lower side of the ground, just beyond the touchline.

The most striking feature of the match was the absolutely majestic performance by the Yorkshire fly-half, Alan Old. Although Edinburgh fielded half a dozen international players, the Yorkshire forwards gained a slight upper hand and this enabled Old to dictate the play. And dictate he did. Because I was quite close to the action, and also because the crowd was relatively sparse, it was possible for me to both see and, occasionally, hear Old giving directions to his team mates in the Yorkshire back line. I watched Old very closely. His technical skills were complete: running, passing and, especially, kicking. On one occasion, he gestured over to one of his wingers to indicate where he was going to put the ball, and then, possession having been secured, he put it there: it was if he had walked over and placed it on the spot. Throughout the game, Old performed the rugby equivalent of moving the pieces around a chess board. Moreover, his demeanour was one of total calmness: he was never rushed or flustered. I knew I was watching someone who played in my old position of fly-half – I had stopped playing by this time – and who was an absolute master at it. It was a joy to watch.

Chapter 12

Old Trafford to Minsk

One of my friends at school, Chris Lawrence, a keen Leeds United supporter, had a firmly held theory about the European competitions in which his team played in the 1960s and early 1970s. He argued that the Inter City Fairs Cup (later the UEFA Cup) was harder to win than the European Cup because there was a higher proportion of teams on their way up, rather than those teams that had peaked when winning their respective league championships and were now in decline. That is an argument for the football cognoscenti to debate. What is less controversial, I would suggest, is that by the time the formidable Leeds United team of the early 1970s did reach the European Cup final – in 1975 – they were indeed past their peak.

The exceptional side that Don Revie constructed was based around essentially the same group of players that remained at its core for the ten year period that Leeds United were consistently challenging for trophies. The subsequent autobiographies of these players have emphasised the intense and closely bonded family atmosphere that Revie created amongst the playing and non-playing staff at Elland Road. However, for what it's worth, I don't think Revie stands in the same pantheon of great managers as his two main early rivals – Matt Busby and Bill Shankly – who, after they had built up their winning teams, also had the courage and skill to disband them (in Busby's case, of course, through tragic circumstances) and then succeed in re-building new sides to replace them. Using this criterion of being successful with more than one group of players also places other managers above Revie, notably Brian Clough at Derby County and Nottingham Forest, Sir Alex Ferguson with different generations of players at Manchester United and, in the 1930s, Herbert Chapman at Huddersfield Town and Arsenal. Revie's reputation has also been badly damaged by the allegations of attempted match-fixing which were first published in the

Daily Mirror and the *Sunday People* in the late 1970s.[27]

This is not to say, of course, that the Leeds United championship-winning side of 1973–74 was not impressively formidable. I went to see them just once. It was the January 1974 fixture at home to Tottenham Hotspur and the main reason for attending was undoubtedly to see Pat Jennings in the Spurs goal. For as long as I had watched football highlights on television, the commentators – including my favourite, Barry Davies – had always referred to the size of Jennings's hands. It was an unavoidable cliché, used whenever Jennings made a spectacular save or, especially, when he demonstrated his command of the penalty area by claiming a high cross or corner floated over by an opposing player. On this occasion, right on cue, Jennings, closely viewed from my vantage point at the side of the Gelderd End stand, watchfully followed the path of the ball as it came across on a high arc from the Leeds right wing. He timed his leap to perfection, stretching up to caress the ball in his right glove and then, as he began his descent, bringing his left hand across to make certain that possession was securely gathered. It was an action that Jennings had perfected on countless occasions – probably thousands – for Tottenham and Northern Ireland. And here he was, repeating the performance in front of me. The crowd around me, with their narrow and blinkered preferences, berated the Leeds team for conceding possession. However, my perspective was different. As Jennings stood in his penalty area and considered his options for distributing the ball to a forward player, my thought processes took a different, though inevitable, turn: "Pat Jennings has got big hands".

Revie had left Leeds by the time they contested the 1975 European Cup final against Bayern Munich in Paris. In the revealing *Peter Lorimer: Leeds and Scotland Hero*, one of his key players has described how the period after Revie's departure was characterised by intense rivalry between the pro- and anti- Billy Bremner factions within the club. Thereafter, according to Lorimer, after Bremner and Norman Hunter had joined the list of departed players and the club had slipped to tenth in the league at the end of the 1976–77 season and ninth in 1977–78, the side became the Leeds United Social Club: "There was no ambition to win things. There would be a bit of training, but the main business of the day would be the extra-curricular arrangements and the social members would gather for an afternoon's drinking".

These were my student years when, not surprisingly, my visits to Elland Road were sporadic and mainly during the Christmas or Easter vacations. I went to the games – as I had to the Tottenham match – with my old schoolfriends, Andrew Carter and Charlie Woodward, and Andrew's father: all Leeds supporters and all knowledgeable and realistic about their team's declining potency. The opposition for these fixtures was always attractive – Manchester City in December 1976 and December 1977, Everton in December 1977, Wolverhampton Wanderers in March 1978 – with the well-known players of the age in evidence: Joe Corrigan, Joe Royle, Bob Latchford, John Richards, *et al*. However, although Leeds maintained a reasonable level of success in these matches, I could tell – from my more or less neutral perspective – that they were not the team that their predecessors had been. In short: they did not have the bite – or, perhaps, the desperation – of the Revie years.

As noted, our favoured vantage point was on one side of the Gelderd End stand, behind the goal and fairly low down, where there was an angled view on the events on the pitch. The crowd remained much as I had noticed it to have been on my first visit to Elland Road for the League Cup match against Charlton Athletic several years earlier: consistently vociferous and unashamedly biased. As before, the goals, when they came, were greeted by a paroxysm of wild celebrating across the terraces. I also confirmed that my feelings towards the overall spectacle had not changed much either. Invariably, it was enjoyable to watch, but it was still a measured – if not stereotyped – performance, with each of the actors playing his part, as if following a set text.

Some of the actors liked to play the part of the fool, of course. One of the Leeds forwards during this period was Duncan McKenzie, a sharp and talented footballer, who was frequently referred to in popular discussion as someone who could – and/or liked to – jump over Mini cars.[28] In one match, the referee blew for an infringement – offside possibly – against McKenzie, who took up a position standing next to the defender marking him near the half way line as the ball was kicked back for the free kick to be taken. As the ball rolled towards them, McKenzie bent down as if to stop the ball for the defender but, at the last instant, decided to re-adjusted his bootlace instead. The defender was left to look rather foolish, as the ball rolled past him and he had to run back a few paces to retrieve it. Needless to say, the crowd thought that this was hilarious. I reflected on this incident for a little while afterwards. If I had been the (slightly humiliated) defender, it would have been a reasonable desire to kick McKenzie very hard the next time he was anywhere near. From McKenzie's perspective, quite apart from the immediate success of getting one over on his opponent, there was always the possibility that such retribution might take place in the defender's penalty area in full view of the referee.

Other players were content to play supporting roles. I remember watching Norwich City in a match at Elland Road at around this time. It struck me that one or two of their players were content to play neat little passes to each other on the margins of the real action – near the touchlines, for example – but they did not seem too interested in carrying the fight to the heart of the Leeds defence. Their attacks were invariably and quickly broken up, and possession lost, before the penalty area was seriously threatened. They were playing, yes, and even performing, but not challenging, and it was clear to me from an early stage in that particular game that Leeds, the reputation of some of their players preceding them, would comfortably win the match.

Andrew Carter and his father's enthusiasm for the game took us to Maine Road to see Leeds beat Manchester City, thanks to a decisive Paul Madeley header. From our view high up in the stands, I was struck, not for the first time, by the overall movement and fluidity of many of the players. I followed one off-the-ball run by Paul Power, in which he must have been at full speed for 60 yards in order to reach a spot in the Leeds penalty area where a more alert colleague might have found him with a correctly timed pass. As it was, the move came to nothing and Power was left to quickly retrace his steps to get behind the ball for his defensive duties. I thought that this was a valiant effort: I would have cursed my teammate for not allowing me some reward for the energy I had expended. For Power, of course, this was his job: he was handsomely paid to be fit and to run up and down the pitch for 90 minutes, and to put in those 60 yards bursts if need be. Manchester City should have had at least a draw from this match, as one of their players rattled a point blank header against the Leeds crossbar with only the goalkeeper to beat. I was interested in Andrew's father's interpretation of this incident after the match: it hadn't been a lucky escape for Leeds, he said, because the Manchester City player should have scored and it was not Leeds's fault that he didn't.

My visits to see old schoolfriends at their places of study usually coincided with a decent football match in the locality. Chris Lawrence went to the University of Sheffield, and so it was that I saw a skilful dribble and shot by Tony Currie win Sheffield United the March 1975 fixture against West Ham United at Bramall Lane. My main interest on this particular afternoon, however, was seeing Jack Taylor, who had refereed the World Cup final between West Germany and Holland the previous summer. This was the man who had given a penalty – albeit an obvious one – against the Germans, the hosts of the tournament, in the first minute of the match. (Of course, Taylor did even things up by awarding another penalty – far less obvious to most neutral observers – to Germany later in the half). Andrew Carter was at the University of Manchester and, therefore, an obvious occasion on which to visit was for the Leeds United game at Old Trafford in March 1976. At the time, Leeds were still in the race for that year's championship, lying in fifth position with games in hand. But, in retrospect, their performance was a precursor of the general malaise, described by Lorimer, that would set in later. Manchester United, managed by Tommy Docherty, cruised into a 3–0 lead and were only troubled by an incomplete Leeds comeback in the last five minutes, when they scored twice.

Apart from Currie's effort in Sheffield, the best goal I saw during this period was by Manchester United at Elland Road. Leeds were defending a corner which Gordon McQueen headed to apparent safety. Unfortunately for him, instead of steering the ball to the side of the pitch, he headed it straight forward. The Manchester midfield player, Gerry Daly, promptly volleyed the ball from the edge of the penalty area straight back into the Leeds goal. It was an impressive piece of skill – composed and powerful – and I was struck by the speed of Daly's thought as the opportunity arose and was immediately taken. However, for me, there was nearly an unfortunate aftermath when, in a college football match later in the term – Trinity College 5ths versus Churchill College 2nds (the 5ths being the name that the college rugby team had taken on entering an inter-college soccer competition) – I attempted to replicate Daly's effort when a similar chance arose. I swung determinedly at the dropping ball on the edge of the Churchill penalty area. But the feel of the impact on my foot was not as I had expected. In the split second after I made contact with an opponent's leg, I was absolutely certain that I had broken it. I had attempted to blast the shot with my full power, only to feel the contact with the Churchill player's limb, as he stretched forward. It was a sickening moment. Fortunately, to my great relief, I must have struck a fleshy part of his leg, rather than a bone, as there was no serious damage. (For completeness, we won 2–0).

My international debut as a football spectator took place in May 1977 or, more precisely, on the Tuesday evening of the week of my Finals examinations – Economics Part II – when I took the train down from Cambridge to watch England play Wales at Wembley. As a means of providing a short distraction from the pervading atmosphere of exam tension within the college, it was later proved – when everyone's results were displayed, in the traditional way, on the noticeboard of the Senate House – to have been a sound decision. However, as a match – and an occasion – I found it distinctly uninspiring.

At one level, it was good to watch those well known players of the time that I had not seen before – Kevin Keegan, Peter Shilton, Leighton James. James, in particular, stood out with his grace and skill and it was his penalty, decisively taken into the goal in front of me after he had been fouled by Shilton, that settled the match. In the second half, England huffed and puffed but did not create much: I rather thought that Keegan's shoulder-length moppet haircut reflected their triumph of style over substance. The commanding figure was Terry Yorath in the Wales midfield, whose crude challenge on Brian Greenhoff early in the game clearly demonstrated his (and the general Welsh) intent to secure the visitors' first ever win at Wembley. On the long slow haul back to Cambridge, I reflected on my limited sense of involvement with the occasion and my lack of concern with the result. I had been to see England play football in a competitive international; I had been back to Wembley for the first time since the Rugby League Challenge Cup final eleven years earlier; I should have been fulfilled and exhausted. Instead, indifference and anti-climax.

And what about professional football matches actually taking place in the city of Cambridge at this time? I attended just one, and a cracking game it was too: Cambridge United versus the high-flying Queens Park Rangers at the Abbey Stadium in the old second division in December 1979. I am able to place the date, with confidence, through the association of this particular match with one of the pop songs in the charts at the time. Amongst the selection played by the ground's disc jockey in the minutes leading up to the kick-off was The Jam's *Eton Rifles*. After all these years, I can still recall two young girls – probably aged twelve or thirteen – jumping up and down a few yards to my right and bellowing out the chorus: "Eton Rifles, Eton Rifles…" If I hear the record played on the radio today – admittedly, a rare occurrence – my mind immediately jumps back to the shallow terracing at the half-way line in the stand at Cambridge United.

Although Cambridge were in only their tenth season in the Football League and had the smallest ground in any of the four divisions – their average home attendance for the season to that point had been just over 6,200 – they had made remarkable progress up the league standings. Nonetheless, on paper, this particular fixture seemed to be a bridge too far. QPR were top of the table, with Chelsea and Newcastle United just below them and the match programme listing Chris Woods, Stan Bowles and Clive Allen in their side. Their manager, by a neat symmetry, was Tommy Docherty, whom I passed as I walked around the ground before the match trying to decide on the best vantage point. Docherty, surrounded by young fans and other autograph hunters, was playing to the gallery in his usual flamboyant – and, from this evidence, friendly – manner. I'm not sure he would have been too receptive afterwards, however. Cambridge unexpectedly won 2–1 thanks to a superb strike on the turn by one of their forwards, Jamie Murray. I was pleased with my afternoon's viewing, having seen the home side's new strike force of Alan Biley and George Riley, about which the *Cambridge Evening News* had enthused at length, and added the Abbey Stadium to Maine Road and Bramall Lane and Old Trafford on my roll call of spectating grounds. A couple of seasons earlier, in April 1976, I had also added Filbert Street – for a late season evening fixture between Leicester City and Leeds United – when a Leicester-supporting cricketing colleague and I called in on the way back from playing in a match in Loughborough. Leeds's fortunes in this game took a turn for the worse when Terry Yorath was sent off; they lost 1–2 and I was obliged to take on the role of disappointed Leeds follower.

But that was the pattern. Occasional soccer games were taken in, complemented by rugby matches with my father – and, for the Boxing Day rugby league match at Headingley, my uncles – when I was at home during the university vacations. During the Christmas break of 1977, I rattled up the impressive tally of Leeds United versus Manchester City and Leeds United versus Everton (soccer), Leeds versus Wakefield Trinity and Leeds versus Hull KR (rugby league), New Hunslet versus Hull (rugby league) and Harrogate versus Roundhay (rugby union). I described this busy schedule with some pride to my friends when I arrived back in college for the start of the new term. Their reaction was total indifference.

The detail changed in one important respect during the following year. In the early summer of 1978, my uncle Bob – dad's brother and our willing chauffeur to various parts of Yorkshire to watch Hunslet during my early spectating years – came to visit me with his wife and one of his daughters, plus my own parents, in Cambridge. I have fond memories of it being a great day, three of the details of which remain with me still. I can picture Bob standing in my set of rooms in Trinity – K6 Great Court, one of the best in the college – and looking out of the window admiringly to the fountain in the middle of the court and the chapel on the far side; his subsequent nod of appreciation to me was in silent recognition of the place I had reached. I can also remember him buying everyone an ice-cream from the vendor on Queen's Road next to the entrance to the Backs of King's College. And I can recall, later, when I had successfully ensconced everyone in a trendy Greek restaurant on St Andrew's Street, Bob and Dad eschewing the national dishes in favour of steak and chips (which, it turned out, was not a house speciality). A few weeks later, I learned that Bob had been diagnosed with lung cancer and, a short time after that, that he had died. The suddenness of Bob's decline – as well as his actual loss – was a huge shock to everyone and to my father in particular. Bob had been a lifelong smoker and it was clear that this habit, combined with the prolonged cocktail of noxious fumes that he would have inhaled during his career as a fireman, must have done the fatal damage. However, the rationality of any explanation was lost on my father, for whom Bob's death left a long and painful void.

Compared with their non-reaction to my Christmas 1977 spectating achievements, there was generally more enthusiasm amongst my college chums to the suggestion of watching one of the more parochial sporting events when it was hosted at the Kelsey Kerridge Sports Hall in Cambridge: the Oxford versus Cambridge university amateur boxing match. I went to see it twice, in March 1977 and March 1979.

Within the Oxbridge system, in the major sports – rugby, cricket, football, rowing, squash – a sportsman wins a Blue by competing in the Varsity Match. That is all that is required. The aim is to get into the team – say, rugby union – and play at Twickenham. If someone plays for the whole term and is then injured for the big match: tough. Similarly – and this happened to one rugby player during my time at Cambridge – a player could find himself on the replacements' bench at Twickenham, having been unable to make his way even into the reserve team fixture (for the Cambridge University LX Club against the Oxford University Greyhounds) and, due to an injury on the pitch, end up playing for part of the match against Oxford and thereby winning his Blue.

The standing joke when I arrived at university – possibly a sporting myth, possibly not – was that the easiest way to win a Blue was to get into the boxing team and then be willing to be knocked out by a (presumably slightly more competent) opponent in the Varsity Match. However, at around this time, it was also reported that the relevant Blues committee that pronounced on these things had decided to implement the more meritocratic proposal that, in order to win a Blue, the boxer had to actually defeat his opponent. Otherwise, he was awarded a half-blue, which was the equivalent of representing the university at water polo or lacrosse. When my friends and I went to see the university boxing matches, therefore, there was a strong incentive for the protagonists to a) have a reasonable idea of what they were supposed to be doing and b) convert any expertise they might have into a winning performance.

There were nine main bouts during each of the evenings, ranging up the scale from bantamweight to heavyweight, with two supporting bouts in 1977 and one in 1979. In both years, it was clear that the standard varied considerably between those boxers who had had some experience in the ring, often from their pre-student years in the police or one of the armed forces, and those who had been novices at the start of their university boxing careers. Amongst the latter, in the Cambridge teams, were at least three boxers whom I recognised as useful rugby players. It was the inexperienced boxers who probably had the most difficulty in remembering that the two minute round is a long time in a boxing ring: a common feature of the bouts was how markedly the initially frantic action slowed down during the second minute. After the third and final round, if the bout lasted that long, the protagonists would invariably be out on their feet.

The military connections were strong. In 1977, each of the services was represented by one of the boxers, one of the referees was a colonel, the prizes were presented by a lieutenant-colonel and the entertainment before the match and during the interval was provided by a military band. There was also a clear sense of tradition. The programme for the 1979 match reported that Cambridge had won 40 of the 68 Boxing Matches (note: upper case) against Oxford since the CUABC had been founded in 1897.

It was also clear in both matches that all the participants were possessed of considerable courage. In 1977, this was evident in the very first bout, in which the bantamweights – eight and a half stone and under – stood toe to toe from the first bell and attempted to knock the living daylights out of each other. In this contest, the Oxford boxer was Colin Moynihan (Monmouth School and University), later an Olympic rowing cox and Minister of Sport and now a member of the House of Lords. It was his predecessor – Sir Berkeley Moynihan – who had operated on my grandfather in Manchester at the end of the First World War, before my own father had been born.

Unlike the amateur boxers of today, the combatants did not wear any protective headgear, instead taking the full force of any blows that were landed on their unguarded heads. In the 1977 contest, the effects of this were most dramatically seen in the heavyweight contest, when the Cambridge man NJH Bashall (Rhodesian Army and St John's) – who was probably fed up with well-wishers reporting that he had the perfect name for a boxer – was stopped by his formidable opponent S McKie (Christ's Hospital and Lincoln). Fortunately, the stewardship of the evening was in experienced hands. The referees seemed to be able to spot quickly when someone was out of their depth, even if only slightly. I thought that if, in defeat, Bashall was awarded only a half-blue, then it was markedly less than he deserved.[29]

It was, on both occasions, a highly entertaining evening. The venue was appropriate, just large enough to accommodate a sizeable crowd of raucous students, who were keen to exorcise their bloodlust without seeing anyone badly hurt and certainly without any danger of testing their own courage by standing in the ring themselves and waiting for the first bell. Needless to say, when I had extracted myself from the general noise around me, I found myself taking a more detached perspective. My sense was that these student boxers operated in a select – almost isolated – environment, in which they trained hard, maintained their self-discipline in their preparation and general lifestyles, respected the traditions of their clubs, and largely kept themselves to themselves within the inner circle. Whatever the validity of the sporting myth that circulated outside the group, it was clear that – on both sides of the varsity divide – no-one was treating their chosen sport as a joke.

In 1978, I was a spectator at part of the Women's World Volleyball Championships. This is what we were told, at least, and as the teams we saw during an afternoon's visit to the tournament included Belgium and Tunisia (3 sets to 0), Mexico and Holland (3–2) and Yugoslavia and Italy (3–0), it is difficult to see what else it could have been. "We" in this context were a group of 15 or so British students undertaking a "cultural exchange" in the Soviet Union. It was organised by the National Union of Students, although, fortunately for me, no student activist or even politically sympathetic characteristics were required to be selected for the trip. I had simply seen an advertisement in a student newspaper and decided that it might be an interesting way to spend a couple of weeks in August/September. We visited Moscow, Minsk and Smolensk.

Minsk is the dull and depressed capital of the republic we learned to call Byelorussia and which is now the state of Belarus. It rained for the whole time we were there. As we had anticipated, the organisers of the Minsk leg of the trip arranged a similar range of visits to those that we had experienced in the other locations: a combination of cultural events (broadly defined) and several potent reminders of the huge sacrifices that the Soviet Union had made during the Second World War. Hence, an evening watching the Byelorussian State Folk Choir – with their fast dancing and immaculate costumes and broad (if, probably, false) smiles – was followed by a morning at the Byelorussia State Museum of History of the Great Patriotic War: the largest such institution in the USSR, we were informed. The 1970s equivalent of Club 18–30 it wasn't, and, of course, neither had I expected it to be. Instead, bearing in mind that this was some time before the Berlin Wall had even looked like falling, it was an interesting time to be on the other side of the Iron Curtain.

After the morning in the museum – with its sole recognition of the Western allies' involvement in the war being a single reference to a second front being opened up in Normandy in June 1944 – we were taken to enjoy the main sporting constituent of the fortnight. The Minsk games in the volleyball championships were held in a cavernous and largely empty sports hall, in which our party took up its position at ground level in one corner, some distance from the rest of the spectators.

Our collective interest in the event lasted until about half way through the Mexico-Holland contest. My diary of the trip records that Mexico were leading by two sets to one and were ahead in the fourth set. At that point, we decided that Holland – near enough neighbours, after all – needed a bit of proper support. Accordingly, we then proceeded to cheer loudly and wildly whenever the Dutch players won a point. For the rest of the inhabitants of the hall, including the participants on the court, this was clearly something of a surprise. It did not take long before the eyes of everyone else were upon us. The rest of the crowd – or, at least, that unlikely portion who had seen *Butch Cassidy and the Sundance Kid* – were no doubt asking: "Who are those guys?".

I should emphasise that we were well behaved throughout: there was no choice language or threat to invade the playing arena. There were simply whoops and cheers of delight whenever Holland scored a point or Mexico made a mistake. As a result, through a combination of the Dutch gaining confidence and the Mexicans, perhaps literally, taking their eye off the ball, Holland fought their way back to level the match at two sets all. It was at this point that I sensed the value of spectator power: we were conducting a small-scale replication of the way that the Anfield Kop might have taken a losing cause into their own hands and set about securing a Liverpool victory through the volume and passion of their support. In the event, however, it was to no avail. The Mexicans regained their composure and won the deciding set.

I did not mention to my fellow *ersatz* Dutchmen that I was already a hardened veteran of international volleyball. One of the rather pleasant tasks that I had undertaken during my time as a schools representative on the Leeds Sports Council – in addition to discussing a Hunslet versus Leeds rugby league match with Geoff Gunney – had been to accept an invitation to attend the England versus Luxembourg international ladies volleyball match at the Leeds University sports hall in March 1973.[30] The supporting match was the Yorkshire versus Lancashire men's match.

Later, when I returned to Britain from the Soviet Union, I reflected on what I had seen – Red Square, St Basil's Cathedral, the Kremlin, Lenin's Mausoleum – and the people we had met. The latter included several individual Russian students, who had not been part of the Comsomol (Young Communist) delegation that had formally welcomed us, but who had introduced themselves to us separately and then daringly sought out our views on politics and travel and music and the other interests that students from anywhere always have. I also made a mental note to find out which country had become the women's world volleyball champions of 1978. I had seen the preliminary skirmishes of the competition and I was curious to find out the final outcome. Unfortunately, I cannot say that I took any active steps to find out the answer. The years – and then the decades

– passed until, for some reason, it reached the point at which this long overdue postscript to the event in Minsk started to take on an unexplained significance. There was a loose end of my spectating life to tie up: which team had won the competition?

Finally, in 2005, I found out the answer. It was really not that difficult. Twenty minutes surfing on the internet took me to an encyclopaedic reference to the volleyball world championships. The result is that I now possess information on the final rankings of each tournament since the inaugural events for men (in 1949) and women (1952). Cuba won the women's competition in 1978 and Japan were the runners up. Mystery solved.

The Netherlands came 17th.

I returned to the Soviet Union two years later on another NUS trip: Moscow, Riga and Leningrad (as it then was). It was at the same time of year as the first visit and, therefore, just after the 1980 Olympic Games. In Moscow, during some of the spare time which we had been allocated in our itinerary to visit a large *beriozka* – one of the shops for the privileged elite that sold high quality goods for western currency – I took the opportunity to wander off alone and walk down to the Lenin Stadium, which I entered and sat in for about a quarter of an hour.

I took up a place about half way up a vast bank of terraced seating. If anyone saw me, I didn't know: I was not challenged or asked to leave. I made a mental note of the interior of the stadium: the tartan track, the generally spartan seating, the posher orange and red-backed seats, the flag poles, the bowl for the Olympic torch, the green football pitch in the centre and the big screens at each end. I knew that Sebastian Coe and Steve Ovett had triumphed in this stadium to the generous acclaim of the massed ranks in the seats all around me. Mine was a much quieter victory, late in the afternoon, with the sun going down at the point directly behind one of the large square blocks of floodlights. It was a pleasant and personal little detour. The entry in my diary of the trip records that I was feeling quite exalted when I left the stadium, walked past the large statue of Lenin and headed down the main boulevard back towards the *beriozka*. I bought an elegant wooden letter-rack, complete with Olympic rings, which now sits on the top of a bookcase at home.

The Fourth Age

The Distracted Opportunist

The distractions come from the pressures and pleasures of everyday life: mortgage, career, marriage, family. However, the opportunities remain for sports spectating, mainly in London and Yorkshire. Within the eclectic range of events and venues to be viewed and explored, the set-piece occasions of the rugby league Challenge Cup final and the Headingley test match provide fixed and reassuring reference points.

Chapter 13

Craven Cottage to Walton Heath

I stated earlier that 1969 was my *annus mirabilis* for watching cricket. If I had to select one such year for watching sport as a whole, it would be 1981. This reason for this is the combination of the range and quality of the sporting events which I enjoyed: not only rugby, football and cricket, but golf, tennis and athletics.

Having left Cambridge at Christmas 1980, I spent a few weeks at home and then, in February, took up a one year contract as a research assistant in the economics department of Queen Mary College, University of London (as it was then called). I found somewhere to live just down the road from the college, near the Roman Road in Bow, where there was a spare room in a house at a cost of £18 per week plus the share of the telephone bill. In other words, I swapped the unreality of college life in Cambridge, where I had been for six and a half years, for the real world of living in the East End. Needless to say, it did me no harm at all.

Before moving to London, I had a soccer game and a few rugby matches to clear. The first of these was the Leeds United versus Coventry City FA Cup third round match at Elland Road in January 1981. It was the first Leeds fixture that I had ever been to with my father. We stood in my usual position in the bottom right hand corner of the stand at the Gelderd End and watched the match fizzle to life briefly and then peter out into a 1–1 draw. Coventry were not a bad side – they had the skill and exuberance of Garry Thompson and the teenage Mark Hateley in their forward line – but they should not have been a match for Leeds, especially after they had had a man sent off. But I sensed that Leeds were seriously lacking in confidence: even with the superiority in numbers, they did not seek to put Coventry under the type of unremitting pressure that the Leeds team of old would have done. And that was the point, of course: this was not the Leeds team of old. It contained some fairly average performers, who were playing in front of smaller crowds (24,000 in this case). The signs were clear. At the beginning of 1981, Leeds United's decline into the first division pack – and, the following season, towards relegation – was well under way. They were now a mid-table side, whose defeat in the replay at Coventry a few days later came as no great surprise.

My father enjoyed the afternoon, however, as he also did our other visit to Elland Road for a soccer match: the Leeds United-Liverpool fixture later in the same season. Liverpool brought a near full-strength side – Souness, Hanson, McDermott, *et al* – but seemed to have half an eye on their European Cup semi final tie with Bayern Munich later in the week. As, by this stage, Leeds were looking for any league points in their bid to reach mid-table respectability, the 0–0 draw seemed to satisfy both sides. I thought that it was a relatively tame affair, especially in comparison with the Leeds-Liverpool and Leeds-Arsenal clashes I had seen from the Lowfields Road terrace ten years earlier. There seemed to be something undercooked about the match, in which only about half a dozen fouls were committed during the entire 90 minutes. My father enjoyed it, however, struck by the novelty of the experience. He told me afterwards that he was particularly taken by the Liverpool forwards – led by David Johnson and Kenny Dalglish – with their close ball control and their willingness to attack the opposing defenders. He was to return to Elland Road on other occasions in later years, but this second visit for a football match also turned out to be his last.

The first of the rugby union matches at the beginning of the year was another Wales-England encounter at Cardiff Arms Park. I went with high hopes. Even though England had not won in Cardiff since 1963, they had all but two of the grand slam-winning side of the previous season in their starting line-up. And it seemed that they would indeed prevail as, in the closing minutes, they held a one point lead. However, at an attacking scrum just outside the England 22 line, the Welsh scrum half, Brynmor Williams, dummied to pass the ball and drew the England centre, Clive Woodward, offside: a move which is now contrary to the laws of the game.[31] Wales kicked the easy penalty and, even though Dusty Hare had the opportunity to repeat his previous year's heroics by kicking a subsequent long range penalty, it was not to be. I watched this game from behind the posts in the Lower East Stand and spent a fair portion of the match jostling against the nearby spectators for a decent view of the action. Wales won 21–19 and the familiar sense of post-match anti-climax quickly set in.

A week later, I was at Chandos Park with my father to see Roundhay play Leicester in the third round of the John Player Cup. This was my last weekend in Leeds before my permanent move to London, and the fixture was a nice bonus. We stood on the lower banking of terrace, opposite the main stand, roughly on the half way line. Not surprisingly, there was a sizeable crowd around us but, unlike the previous week, I had a reasonable view. Leicester were the primary club side in England at the time and, in truth, they were never troubled, winning 34–3.

During the game, as Leicester rattled up the points, I placed myself in the position of the Roundhay players. They were a useful side, having won the Yorkshire Cup the previous season, with seven county players in addition to the international, Richard Cardus, in the team. But every one of the Leicester side was at least a county player and six – including Hare, Woodward and Wheeler – had played for England. For some reason, as the forwards took their places for a line out in front of us, I focused on the Roundhay hooker, who was a teenager in his first (and, as it turned out, only) season with the club. I wondered what was going through his head, as he battled against these formidable opponents in a losing cause. Was he playing in what would turn out to be the biggest fixture of his career? I checked his name in the match programme: B Moore.

Brian Moore later won more than 60 caps for England and played 5 times for the British Lions against Australia and New Zealand. As one of his international appearances was in the rugby union World Cup final of 1991, the Roundhay-Leicester game was probably not the biggest match of his career. More specifically for this account, he has described – in *Brian Moore, The Autobiography* – not only what his own thoughts were during the Roundhay-Leicester contest, but those of his direct opponent, Peter Wheeler. Moore recounts with some pride how, despite losing one of his prop forwards through injury, he did not concede a single strike against the head to the England hooker. He also reports that, afterwards, Wheeler had told him that he had not struck for the ball on any of the Roundhay put-ins and that Moore, who had struck for everything on the Leicester put-ins, should have shown some respect. As I read this account in Moore's book some years later, I immediately thought back to the formation of the line out in front of the spectators on the lower terrace at Chandos Park and the pressures being faced by the young Roundhay hooker preparing to throw the ball in.

The day after the Leeds United-Coventry City FA Cup match, my father and I went to see the first rugby league game of the calendar year: Leeds versus Hull Kingston Rovers at Headingley. In 1981, this fixture took on an unusual pattern in that the visitors actually did themselves justice and won the match. We followed this up with a couple of other Leeds fixtures before I departed for London – against Salford and St Helens, both of which resulted in home victories – as well as the John Player Trophy semi final (not to be confused with rugby union's John Player Cup) between Barrow and Hull.

As ever, the Leeds match programme provided excellent value. Dad and I had a standing joke about the "some memorable matches from the past" feature, which, absolutely without exception, always seemed to recount a Leeds victory. In these three games, it was Leeds 26 Hull KR 13 (1968), Leeds 12 Salford 7 (1973) and Leeds 9 St Helens 5 (1972): I rest my case. The next time we returned to Headingley for a league match – for which the "memorable match" was Leeds 24 Bradford Northern 2 (1979) – it was for the evening fixture on Good Friday, when the visitors were riding high in the current table. Bradford needed to win to keep their hopes alive of retaining their status as first division champions, which they duly did by 26–18, the title being captured in their next and final match of the season.

I am fairly sure that it was after this particular Leeds-Bradford Northern game that Dad and I both remarked on the most devastating use of a rugby league substitute that we had seen. The Bradford coach, Peter Fox, introduced his huge replacement forward, Dennis Trotter, mid way through the second half, when the Leeds defence was tiring. Trotter tore Leeds to shreds, making yards as first receiver and distributing the ball out of the tackle to his supporting half backs. Then, on one occasion when Bradford were attacking the Leeds try-line, he was skilfully used as a dummy runner in a planned move that allowed another player to score easily under the posts. In those days, the rotation of players – the "interchange" – that features in the modern rugby league game was not allowed, and the use of substitutes had to be given much greater thought. Fox, widely recognised as an astute reader of the game, provided a clear and revealing lesson on how the correct use of this tactical facet of the game could be hugely productive.

The next time Dad and I saw Leeds play Bradford Northern was later in the year, for the second round Yorkshire Cup tie in September. With it being the beginning of the new season, the rugby league authorities had issued one of their periodic edicts on how the game should be played, in this case focusing on tightening up on the technical infringements committed by hookers at the scrum. Accordingly, shortly after one of the Leeds props had appeared to kick a Bradford player when he was lying on the ground and been let off with a warning, the two hookers were sent from the field for failing to heed an instruction from the referee about not binding properly on their prop forwards. Dad and I watched this with some incredulity from our position behind the goalposts at the St Michael's Lane end of the ground, from where we eschewed our normal position in the South Stand in order to take advantage of the bright autumn sunshine.

In retrospect, however, the game was more significant for another reason. My father and I were immediately impressed by the performance of one of the newer Bradford players, who created disquiet in the Leeds defence whenever he got the ball and who would have scored a try under the posts right in front of us had not one of his team-mates snatched for the same pass and knocked it out of his hands. The match programme described the newcomer briefly as "an exciting, coloured centre who has begun the season in style". It was our first view of Ellery Hanley, the best British rugby league player of the last 30 years.

Once having moved to London at the end of January, I did not have to wait long before watching rugby league in the capital. The Fulham club had started up the previous autumn with a famous win over Wigan in their inaugural second division match, and they were to finish the season as one of the four clubs promoted to the first division. My only difficulty was in working out how much time I should allow to travel by London Underground, on a Sunday, from Mile End to Putney Bridge.

It was well worth the journey. The Craven Cottage ground was a friendly home for a side that, in that inaugural season in the second division, was supported by a hard core of 6–7,000 exiled northerners, antipodeans from the environs of Earls Court and curious locals. For my first game – a first round Challenge Cup game against Wakefield Trinity, then second from the top of the first division, in the middle of February – a crowd of over 15,000 turned up. Fulham had a useful side – heavily populated by experienced and successful imports from the main Lancashire clubs, Widnes in particular – and they gave Wakefield a hard game. As I watched the visitors – who included the excellent David Topliss at stand off and Mike Lampkowski, complete with passing skills, at loose forward – win a tight match 9–5, I knew that spending Sunday afternoons by the banks of the Thames would become a regular occurrence.

However, by the second half of 1981, when Fulham were competing in the first division, the initial euphoria of the successful first season had passed, and the reality of playing consistently difficult matches against top grade opposition was clearly evident. Although Fulham secured some impressive wins during the season – notably against the eventual champions, Leigh, towards the end of the campaign – they were not quite good enough to avoid relegation. It was the Hunslet "yo-yo" syndrome repeated: promoted in 1980–81, relegated in 1981–82 and then promoted again (as champions) in 1982–83.

I looked forward to the long treks across London. There was plenty to read on the journey, of course, given the volume of Sunday newspaper material. Then, there would be the short walk from the Putney Bridge tube station through Bishop's Park and into the surrounding suburban streets. On a bright autumnal or spring day, this was an expedition of expectation and hope, with the outcome always retaining an element of unpredictability: Warrington (a resounding win), Featherstone Rovers (a heavy loss), Widnes and Wigan (narrow defeats), and so on. Once in the ground, I flirted between the long terracing running alongside one touchline and the higher terraces at either end, depending on the weather.

Fulham attempted to complement their northern-based professionals with some local players, though the principal issue the club faced – that of maintaining the attachment of the core of the side, who lived and were based in Widnes and other localities on the M62 corridor – seemed to be a continual difficulty. There was no doubting the commitment and skill of these players – Reg Bowden, Mal Aspey, David Eckersley, and others – many of whom had already achieving considerable honours with their previous clubs. However, even as they were winning some of their games, it was evident early in the 1981–82 season that the side, lacking strength in depth, would do well to stay in the first division, especially as promotion and relegation still involved four clubs going in each direction. The lessons of soccer in the USA in the seventies – a more extreme example, admittedly – showed the difficulties encountered by a sport in attempting to establish firm roots in an unfamiliar environment. The average attendance in Fulham's first division season was about 4,500, an ominous decline on the year before.

I watched the individual players with interest, particularly the new entrants whom I had not seen before. The crowd took to Hussein M'Barki, a Moroccan winger who had had experience in French rugby union. He had something about him, not only as a player with speed and agility, but also as an ambitious sportsman, facing the challenges of a new language and a new culture. He was the difference between the sides when Fulham beat Hunslet in an early round of the 1982 Challenge Cup. Another player in whom I was interested was Neil Tuffs, who had played briefly for a couple of the northern clubs, but who, more relevantly, had been my opposite number over several years when Roundhay School had played the strong Normanton Grammar School sides. Tuffs was a skilful player with an acute tactical awareness; at this level, however, his lack of penetrating speed was revealed.

And I also watched the opposition players, of course. The young Andy Gregory – Bowden's effective replacement as the Widnes scrum half – played at Craven Cottage in October 1981. Now he did have speed, to go with the confidence of youth and the skills of a future international.

He played quite wide out, often running in an arc towards the centres and looking to offload the ball to team-mates coming on different lines of attack; Fulham never really go to grips with him all afternoon. It was a similar story when John Woods, another international, played for Leigh, albeit on a losing side. I watched this game from the open terrace at the cottage end of the ground. A little way behind me, a Fulham supporter – clearly a Londoner, given his accent – spent the whole match berating the Leigh side in general and Woods in particular. He just yelled out the whole time: "Wally! Wally". He obviously thought this was either hugely amusing or off-putting or both. "Wally! Wally". I thought at the time that this was a shame. Here was someone who had bothered to come along to watch a presumably unfamiliar sport and to take an interest in the outcome of the match. What a pity that he did not spend a little more time – or, indeed, any time – admiring the creative skills and tactical prowess of Woods or the speed and strength of Des Drummond on the Leigh wing.

One of my colleagues in the economics department of Queen Mary College was a young man of about my age called Robert Gausden. He was a specialist in econometric modelling – the application of mathematical techniques in the analysis of economic issues – who was working on one of the faculty's other research projects. Looking back, it is a matter of some regret that the path-breaking research paper we discussed as a possibility to write together – a predictive model of football attendances in each of the divisions of the English and Scottish leagues – was never finished (or, indeed, seriously started). However, despite Robert possessing what seemed to me to be a slightly quirky list of favourites – Charlton Athletic, Kent County Cricket Club and Sandy Lyle – we immediately hit it off and started to plan our visits to the various sporting attractions that metropolitan life had to offer. At the top of the list were Wimbledon, the Ryder Cup, and the soccer World Cup qualifying tournament.

Robert and I decided that the Thursday of the first week at Wimbledon would be the best time to go, as there would still be plenty of activity on the outside courts involving some of the better known players. In the event – and I cannot recall quite how we got the tickets or, indeed, if tickets were needed – we ended up in the standing area of the Centre Court to watch the British hopeful, John Lloyd, play an Argentinean called Jose Luis Clerc, who was the number nine seed.

In this context, "hopeful" meant "very hopeful" or "unrealistically hopeful", of course. This was the era of Borg, McEnroe, Connors and Lendl (the top four seeds) and everyone recognised that Lloyd was not in their league, including, no doubt, Lloyd himself. But, on this occasion, he played a fine game and prevailed against an elegant opponent. I liked the match. It was played in a good spirit and with considerable skill. I admired the players' speed across the ground and the variety of their strokes. It was also a real eye-opener to see how hard the ball was hit and how low over the net most of the strokes were played: the latter feature of the game simply does not come across in any television coverage. In short, it was a good match to stumble across, especially for someone like me, who found the histrionics of McEnroe and Connors to be coarse and boring. This was to be McEnroe's year, however: he beat the admirable Borg in the final after the other good guys – Lloyd and Clerc among them – had gone home.

It was inevitable that I would see the whole Wimbledon experience as the epitome of genteel English snobbishness. And this was just what happened. The cover of the "official souvenir programme" captured this perfectly: the championships were "upon the lawns" of The All England Club. Robert and I wandered around the outside courts, catching up with some of the less familiar names and generally acknowledging the camp-following activities that accompanied the tennis itself: the merchandising, the strawberries, the Pimm's. The less familiar names would have included some of those playing in the junior championships – Pat Cash, Henri Leconte, Helena Sukova, Zena Garrison – who were probably totally unfamiliar to 99 per cent of the spectators that day, including us, but who would make their mark in the main Wimbledon events within a relatively short period of time.

Needless to say, I was fascinated by the souvenir programme. I was struck by its overall excellence and, in particular, how efficiently it had been produced to enable it to be right up to date for the start of the day's play. The full draws were presented for each of the events, with the results given up to and including the previous evening, and the order of the day's play was given for each of the courts. The programme also contained informed articles on the major players, a map of the grounds, the full lists of previous winners, and lists of the current players given alphabetically and by country. For the completely sad cases such as me, therefore, it was possible to work out quickly that the only Dutchman in the "gentlemen's singles championship" (Tom Okker) had lost in the first round and that, similarly, the only French competitor in the "ladies' singles championships" (Miss C Vanier) had also succumbed at the first hurdle, albeit to the number two seed (Hana Mandlikova). The glossy advertising took the official programme to almost 100 pages, but a good souvenir it certainly was: a fine reminder of a very pleasant day.

Our trip to the Ryder Cup – or to give it its full title, the 1981 Sun Alliance Ryder Cup – was organised (for Saturday, the second day) on a similar basis as that to Wimbledon. That is to say, Robert and I decided that, because the event was in the vicinity – in this case, over the course at Walton Heath in Kent – there was no excuse not to go. It was a philosophy that I would apply again, several years later, for an Open Championship.

The 1981 event was the second in which it was a European side that took on the United States, thereby boosting the previous efforts of the players from Great Britain and Ireland. At that stage, however, the non-British influence was not hugely significant, as only three players – Bernhard Langer and two Spaniards, Jose-Maria Canizares and Manuel Pinero – were added to the domestic players, though the latter included Peter Oosterhuis, who played on the American tour. The European side actually began the day leading by a point, but the USA team was formidably strong – Nicklaus, Watson, Trevino, Miller, Floyd, Rogers *et al* – and they were to retain the trophy comfortably, clinically taking 7 out of the 8 points available on the Saturday and eventually winning by 18.5 points to 9.5.

But it was another fascinating occasion. Robert and I studied the map of the course and decided on what might be the best places to see the matches coming through – the fourballs in the morning and the foursomes in the afternoon. Our identification of the players, from a distance, was aided by the distinctively coloured clothing that each side wore: yellow shirts, green pullovers and dark tartan trousers by the Europeans; pale blue shirts and pullovers, plus grey trousers, by the USA players. I was happy with our choices of sites: the viewing was generally undisturbed, apart from at the end of the day on the sixteenth green, where three of the afternoon matches finished and what seemed to be an army of official photographers and other privileged hangers-on blocked out the views of the *bona fide* spectators. By that time, the dull and breezy weather of the morning had changed into a steady drizzle and then blustery rain, the deteriorating conditions accurately reflecting how the European challenge had disappointingly fallen away.

I can particularly recall the start of the afternoon session, when we found a good position at the first tee. We were therefore in the perfect spot as the names of the players were announced. For one of the matches, three of the players – Peter Oosterhuis, Sam Torrance and Jerry Pate – stood nervously around, shuffling uncomfortably as they waited to be called, like condemned men marking time before the break of their final dawn. Then, the fourth player turned up. He was laughing and smiling, as he started to talk to some people in the crowd and to crack a couple of jokes. It was Lee Trevino. It was clear to me that he had immediately seized the psychological upper hand and, sure enough, when it was time for his pairing's opening shot, the drive was sent careering down the middle of the fairway. Trevino strode after it, his talking and laughing resumed. I thought this was really impressive. He and Pate won the match 2 and 1.

The "official souvenir programme" of the Ryder Cup was as impressive as its Wimbledon counterpart. This was as I had probably expected: the programme was acknowledging the full weight of the history and tradition of the event and of the excellence and drama of previous encounters. Accordingly, in addition to the detailed biographies of that year's players and the description of each hole on the course and the recollections of previous memorable Ryder Cup days, there was a full listing of all the individual match results since the first Ryder Cup match had been played in 1927 in Worcester, Massachusetts. However, when it came to the results of the second match, in 1929, I'm fairly sure that I had a major shock. It had been played at Moortown in Leeds, probably less than two miles from my parents' home. Thirty years after reading the programme, I cannot recollect whether this was news to me at the time, but I have a feeling that it was. There had been a major slice of Ryder Cup history on my doorstep all the time that I had been living in Leeds. I assumed that Moortown's role in this great event was recognised at the local level, but from a personal perspective – and in the context of the historical expertise I had built up on the championship-winning eras of Yorkshire CCC or the "All Four Cups" exploits of Hunslet RLFC before the First World War – it was somewhat disturbing to find that my knowledge of this piece of local sporting history was non-existent.

As with the Wimbledon programme, the official souvenir had an impressive array of glossy advertising, which was either directly related to the sport of golf or, in the advertisers' wishes, closely associated with the prestigious event we had come to see. The latter including a double-page spread from British Airways announcing that the US team had flown in on Concorde. For the golf-related adverts, it was impossible to get away from the European captain, John Jacobs, who could be found on different pages promoting the European team's choice of general golfing wear, sweaters, golf bags and trousers, blazers and suits. As he also appeared – complete with 23 photographs – in a three-page golf masterclass, his presence was ubiquitous to say the least.

One thing puzzled me about the play. And it still puzzles me, all these years later, when I see the Ryder Cup on television. I have never quite been able to understand why, in the foursomes, when one player is looking at the lie of his ball for a putt, his partner stands close behind him and gives advice. I can only assume that it has something to do with team building and the concept of a joint approach to the matter in hand. Even so, these are golfers at the very top of their game: the players who earn vast fortunes because of their individual skills and abilities during the remainder of the year. It struck me then – as it does now – that having a second opinion on the line or strength of a putt would be more likely to add to the confusion, rather than provide additional information. On the other hand, I am a hack golfer: what do I know?

I enjoyed the day because I always take pleasure in watching sportsmen and sportswomen at the top of their profession. And, especially – as will already be apparent from my views of Wimbledon – when their achievements are worn with proper modesty. There will always remain something that is warming about watching Nicklaus and Watson – or their modern day equivalents – play a shot up to the green and then genuinely acknowledge the applause of the gallery as they walk up to mark and clean the ball and, later, as they sink the putt.

Compared with Wimbledon and the Ryder Cup, the soccer World Cup experience was more anti-climatic. England played Hungary at Wembley in November 1981 needing a draw to qualify for the following year's finals in Spain. It was a position that they scarcely deserved. In a five team qualifying group – also containing Norway, Romania and Switzerland – from which two countries were to gain automatic qualification, England had managed to lose three of their away fixtures. They had succeeded only in Hungary, where Trevor Brooking's famous goal – in which the ball was left wedged against the stanchion at the back of the net – had put them on course for a 3–1 win. Fortunately, a series of favourable results amongst the other teams had left England – with 7 points from 7 games – able to move above Romania if they avoided defeat in the final match of the group.

The match programme contained the usual clichés. The England manager, Ron Greenwood, stated that "there are no easy internationals nowadays", whilst the captain, Kevin Keegan, pledged that "England's players are prepared to offer blood to achieve World Cup qualification tonight". This provided the reassurance we all needed. Watching from behind the same goal as I had for the England-Wales game in 1977, at no stage during the match did I feel that England would not succeed in qualifying for the finals. It was clear, almost from the outset, that this was not going to be a repetition of the Poland match in 1973, which I had watched on television, when England, needing to win, had fallen a goal behind and only drawn the match. Hungary, who had already qualified as group winners, never really threatened the England goal and, I suspect, were ultimately not too disappointed that England's place in the finals had been secured at the expense of Romania. When, after a quarter of an hour, the Hungarian goalkeeper made a hash of an England lob forward into the penalty area and Paul Mariner swept the ball into the net, the capacity crowd reacted as if the trophy itself was about to be lifted. I saw things rather differently: Mariner had merely confirmed the inevitable and put everyone out of their misery.

I reflected on these thoughts for some time afterwards. Perhaps I knew that the moment Mariner scored simply represented the start of a long period of unjustified hype about England's chances in Spain. Perhaps, also, I recognised that I would find myself caught up in that hype and more than willing to go along with it. Certainly, when, seven months later, Bryan Robson scored in the opening half minute of the first group match against France, I was fairly confident that that augured well for England's prospects in the tournament as a whole. However, I should have thought back to the second half of the Hungary match when, in steady drizzle, England missed several chances attacking the goal in front of me. One of these was when Mariner, set up by a neat Keegan dink, managed to head wide from six yards with an open goal and the goalkeeper absent. It was a portent of Keegan's later – and crucial – miss against Spain in the tournament proper. Not for the first or last time in following the fortunes of the national football team in major competitions, disappointment followed, albeit at a safe distance via the television screen.

The Hungary match was the second England international I had seen at Wembley in 1981. In May, they played Brazil in a friendly. Such was my normal approach to getting into these major events at the time that I just left work as usual and caught the Underground up to Wembley Park. It was only when I reached the stadium that I discovered the game was all-ticket, and that all the tickets had been sold. I suspect that, if it had been any other side but Brazil, I would have turned straight around and headed home. But it was Brazil, not quite the gold-plated version of 1970, but Brazil nonetheless, and the Brazil that would challenge strongly in the following year's World Cup finals in Spain until they were knocked out by Paulo Rossi's hat-trick for Italy. For the first and only time in my life, I bought a ticket from a tout. I paid £6 for a £3-50p ticket in the upper standing enclosure of the East Stand.

Brazil won 1–0, thanks to a goal by Zico, although England would have fashioned a draw had not the Aston Villa centre forward, Peter Withe, somehow managed to hit the post, when the ball came to him three yards out right in the middle of the goal in front of me. From my position in the stand, I also had the perfect view as a powerful and swerving free kick from Zico narrowly failed to beat Ray Clemence in the England goal. Higher up the stand, behind me and to my left, were the banks of Brazilian supporters – unlike the home crowd, many of them young women – chanting and dancing throughout the match, all attired in their national colours. Their movement and noise and exuberance dominated the evening. I had paid well over the official price for my ticket, but it was well worth the money.

For the general sports enthusiast, the year 1981 is probably best known for the Ashes cricket series and Ian Botham's famous exploits with bat and ball. I shall come on to the Headingley test match shortly. It is often forgotten, however, that Botham began the series badly. As captain, he had had two difficult series against the formidable West Indies side during the previous 12 months and, following a defeat in the first test match against Australia at Trent Bridge and a disappointing personal performance in the Lord's test, where he had registered a "pair", he had resigned the post.[32]

Robert Gausden and I sat in the lower tier of the Nursery End stand for the first two days at Lord's. It was Geoff Boycott's 100th test match and I wondered if, as a counterpoint to scoring his 100th first class century during the Ashes series four years earlier, he might mark this occasion in a similar manner. It was not to be, however, as an edged delivery from Geoff Lawson bounced off one slip fielder and was caught by another when Boycott's score was in the teens.

Apart from that incident, three things are recalled. First, I can remember being intensely annoyed by someone in the near – but indeterminate – neighbourhood, who had the radio commentary coming out of a transistor radio for much of the first day. The volume of the commentary seemed to rise and fall, so that, at times, it was barely audible, if not silent. At other times, there would be a crescendo as one of the commentators raised his voice with each delivery: "...comes in to bowl...", "...bowls to...", "...in and bowls..." In those days, the use of personal headsets was rare, and only lip service was paid to any vague requests made over the public address system to keep the volume of radio commentaries down. In any case, it only takes one radio to enable a wide sweep of spectators to pick up the sound.

I recognised this phenomenon as a classic example of what, in the jargon favoured by economists, is an "externality": that is, when the consumption behaviour of one individual (the transistor radio owner listening to the commentary) imposes a cost (intense annoyance at the unwanted disturbance) which is borne by someone else (me). Not that, in this instance, my ability to draw on the corpus of economic theory provided any consolation. It might have been only me, of course. Perhaps most, if not all, other spectators are indifferent to the unremitting background descriptions of what they can see for themselves. Perhaps, also, this is just another example of me being overly precious in my spectating preferences. Nonetheless, it remains the case that the overheard radio commentaries – or even the expectation of them – have been a recurrent source of anxiety during the test matches I have watched over the years.

The second item to recall is an incident during an impressive piece of seam bowling by Lawson, who took seven England wickets in the first innings. (His fellow opening bowler – one Dennis Lillee – completed the innings with analysis of nought for 102). At the time of one of the dismissals, there was the usual stoppage as everyone waited for the replacement England batsman to come to the crease. Lawson must have hinted to his captain, Kim Hughes, that he was a bit chilly. Hughes, seeing that the umpire holding Lawson's sweater was some distance away, simply took off his own sweater and handed it over to Lawson for him to wear for the brief period before play was resumed. I thought this was quite impressive: it was Hughes looking after his leading player at that particular juncture of the match, as well as indicative of the overall team spirit for which all Australian sporting sides are renowned. It would all end in tears, of course, both for the Australian team in the 1981 series and – literally – for Hughes who, a couple of years later, was unable to cope with the media questioning at a press conference announcing his resignation from the captaincy.

The third memory of this particular test match is of the complete lack of urgency shown by the participants – umpires, players and groundstaff – in attempting to resume play following breaks for rain and bad light. The sense I had at the time was that the authorities thought the paying spectators should think themselves privileged to be in the ground at all, irrespective of whether or not any play was taking place. This general approach to meeting the interests of spectators reached its nadir at seven o'clock on the second evening when, after four hours had been lost, the umpires Ken Palmer and Don Oslear judged that play should be abandoned for the day. It was bright sunshine at the time. I studied the playing conditions on my scorecard: "In the event of play being suspended, for any reason, for one hour or more on any of the first four days, play may be extended to 7.30pm on that day". The crowd took the umpires' decision badly, with hundreds of cushions being showered on to the pitch. In Lord's terms, this represented a state of near-anarchy.

In the jargon of the criminal underworld, the cricket authorities at Lord's had "previous". These events followed those at the previous year's Centenary Test (which I had not attended), when the long delays after rain interruptions had unprovoked unpleasantries in the Members' Enclosure. More relevantly from my own experience, they also followed on my whole-day wash-out, with no recompense, at the Saturday of the Oval test match against the West Indies, also the previous year. I was therefore less than impressed with the actions of Palmer and Oslear. If I had had a cushion, I would have thrown it.

The cause of the disgruntled spectator at the England-Australia test match was admirably taken up the next day by the cricket correspondent of *The Times*, John Woodcock. Under the headline "The day of the slow bicycle race", he wrote that: "Everyone behaved – players and umpires alike – as though they were much less interested than they ought to have been in putting on a show – in playing cricket, in fact". Woodcock was especially critical of the umpires, who had decided that the light was unfit "either with alarming insensitivity or ignorance of the playing conditions".

The test match was only one of several visits that Robert and I made to Lord's that summer. One was for the one day international, also against Australia, for which the England side included the Yorkshire batsman, Jim Love. This was the same Jim Love, whom I had captained in the Leeds Schools Under 14 side in 1969 and who, in turn, had been my captain on the Yorkshire Cricket Federation (Under 19s) tour of the Midlands in 1974. It was true to say, therefore, that Jim's career had progressed rather further than mine, though this particular day turned out to be its zenith in terms of representative honours. He was not quite able to take the fleeting opportunity that was offered at this level and the much sought-after progression from one day international to fully fledged test match cricketer never materialised. Amazingly – but, in a way, not surprisingly – this level of achievement has been given its own place in the annual *Wisden Cricketers' Almanack* publication: in the 2002 edition, Jim was listed as one of 20 England cricketers in this position.

The other Lord's visits were for Middlesex matches. One was a first class match, for which the opponents were the visiting Australian tourists. The irony here was that the Middlesex overseas player was Jeff Thomson, who had terrorised England and other test match sides in the mid 1970s, but who was not in this particular tour party. Thomson had a lengthy bowl from the pavilion end and, from our perfect vantage point in the Warner Stand, did not seem to be holding back against his compatriots. The other match was a one day John Player League fixture against Warwickshire, for whom Asif Din scored an elegant and match winning century. I had always thought that he was a stylish batsman although, like Jim Love, he did not make the final jump to the highest level. On that day, however, he just stroked the Middlesex bowling around the ground, as if it was a Sunday afternoon stroll (which, of course, it was).

The Headingley test match of 1981 has entered cricket folklore, quite rightly, for the performances of Ian Botham (with the bat) and Bob Willis (with the ball) in the England and Australian second innings, respectively. Having followed on 227 runs behind, England set Australia a target of 130 to win and bowled them out for 111. Botham scored 149 not out and Willis took eight wickets for 43 runs. I was not at the ground for any part of those two feats. But I have a startling and clear memory of one particular incident from earlier in the match.

Over the first two days, I watched Australia compile over 400 in the first innings on a difficult pitch. The weather was cold and blustery, and the breaks for rain did not cheer the home support. England spilled some straightforward catches, including two by Botham. Some of the crowd on the Western Terrace started to remonstrate with the bowlers; I don't think anyone was particularly impressed when, on taking a wicket, Graham Dilley raised his middle finger in a rather pathetic response. The Australian opening batsman, John Dyson, showed a sound technique and made an impressive century, which the Headingley crowd recognised as a sterling effort and generously applauded. Dyson responded by waving his bat at his colleagues on the pavilion balcony on the far side of the ground. I waited for some acknowledgement by the batsman of the applause being given in the rest of the ground, including from me. None came and so I stopped clapping.[33]

The incident that is seared upon my memory came at the start of play on the Saturday morning. It occurred at the resumption of the England first innings, which had only just begun on the previous day – Geoff Boycott was 0 not out overnight – and, 30 years on, its recollection instantly raises the hairs on the back of my neck. When Boycott received his first ball from Australia's champion bowler, Dennis Lillee, the ground was nearly full, which meant that there would have been about 18,000 present. I sat next to my father on the Western Terrace. As the delivery passed by the outside of the off stump, left alone by Boycott, and travelled through to the Australian wicketkeeper, Rodney Marsh, we could have heard the proverbial pin drop. All activity had stopped. There was not a single sound: not a murmur or a whisper or any movement at all. It was as if, apart from the players, every single inhabitant of the ground had been placed in a state of suspended animation. And then, after the ball had thumped into Marsh's gloves and he had passed it on to one of the slip fielders, there was the collective realisation that Boycott had survived his first ball. 18,000 people – minus a few Australians – breathed out a communal sigh of relief.

That incident – which lasted for that part of a second that it took for the ball to travel from Lillee's hand to wicketkeeper Marsh – is one of the most astonishing I have witnessed on the sports field, and it takes its place as one of the nano-dramas listed in this volume. Dad and I looked at each other immediately afterwards and made a mental connection of what we had seen. We only discussed the moment later, when we were at home and reflecting on the day's events. We were absolutely of the opinion that there had not been a breath of sound across the whole of Headingley until the ball smacked into Marsh's secure grasp. And we also agreed that that eerie feeling of complete suspense – and then relief – was only felt, in its purest form, for the first delivery that Boycott received from Lillee. A tension remained for the rest of the over – and, indeed, for the remainder of Boycott's innings over the next hour and a half (he was out for 12) – as the crowd watched the evolving proceedings with respectful attention, but the feeling was not quite the same as it had been for that unique delivery.

During the rest of the day, England's batsmen made a poor attempt at responding to the large Australian total, apart from Botham, who came in at number 7 to attack the bowling and, in a prologue to his later innings, make a quick-fire 50.[34] It looked like a series of routine Australian celebrations: Marsh taking a couple of catches from Lillee's bowling to break Alan Knott's record for the number of wicket-keeping test match victims; England following on; Gooch out immediately for nought, meaning that he had been dismissed twice in the day without scoring. And then, to add insult to sporting injury, the umpires refusing to take the available extra hour after 6 o'clock, when the ground was bathed in glorious early evening August sunshine, to make up some of the time lost earlier in the day. Clearly, the cricket authorities had learned nothing from the debacle at Lord's.

The rest is history, of course: Boycott setting out on the Monday morning to bat out the rest of the match but being dismissed a second time; Botham (helmetless in those days, of course) hitting Lillee, Lawson and Alderman to all parts of the ground, Dilley and Old providing valiant support; the Australian bowlers losing their discipline of line and length. Then, the following day: Bob Willis bowling a series of unplayable deliveries; Dilley taking a magnificent boundary catch to dismiss Marsh; and Willis charging off to the pavilion after uprooting the last batsman's middle stump.[35] By that time, I was back in Cambridge to follow up on some research for my dissertation before heading back to London. I was the person, therefore, who attended the 1981 Headingley test and failed to see the most famous instances of Botham's batting and Willis's bowling. But I had experienced that split second of drama, as Boycott survived his first delivery of the day from Lillee, the memory of which remains crystal clear.

I had not finished with the Australian cricketers in 1981. Robert and I went to three days of the final test match at the Oval. Although the Australians batted well in both innings, they seemed to me, by then, to be a spent force: England had already won the series. Boycott scored 137, his last test century in England, reaching his hundred with a glance to leg that an Australian fielder dived despairingly to stop but only succeeded in palming over the boundary rope. The main resistance in the field came from Dennis Lillee who, wearing a succession of brightly coloured headbands, returned his best test match analysis of 7 for 89. He also no doubt took some pleasure from striking Boycott three times with short-pitched deliveries, including once on the chin.

When Australia batted in their second innings, I have a clear recollection of Bob Willis, his tail up and the crowd roaring him on, charging in to bowl to Dirk Wellham, who was playing in his first test match. Wellham calmly stroked the ball through mid off for four runs and the crowd's roar quickly dissipated into a gentle round of polite applause. Wellham went on to register the notable feat of scoring a century on his test debut, though not without some cost to his side, as Mike Brearley reports in *The Art of Captaincy*. In an interesting section on the potential conflict between the team's interest and that of the individual player, Brearley relates how the Australian captain delayed his declaration for 25 minutes when Wellham was stuck on 99, thereby losing the opportunity to force the England openers to bat for an awkward period before the end of the penultimate day's play.[36]

It was on the Saturday evening of this test match, sitting in the sunshine in the Peter May Enclosure, that I heard from another neighbouring transistor radio that Swansea City, newly promoted to the first division, had beaten Leeds United 5–1 in the opening game of the football league season. Times had changed.

And so the year 1981 represented a rich selection of sporting events in terms of both their number and variation. In March, it included my walking the mean streets that stretched from the house I was sharing in Bow down to Poplar High Street at the top of the Isle of Dogs in order to watch and admire the participants in the first London Marathon as they approached the completion of their 16th mile. In April, my father and I saw Hull KR take on St Helens in the Challenge Cup semi final at Headingley. In the curtain raiser, the Colts challenge cup final between Hull and Castleford, I noted Lee Crooks as already looking a formidable player at the age of 18. In October, also at Headingley, we saw Bradford Northern take on Castleford in the Yorkshire Cup final, the former now with Ellery Hanley in the pivotal position of stand off and also including one of Hunslet's players from their last match at Parkside eight years earlier, Phil Sanderson, in their squad. The following month, a little further down the road at the Headingley club's rugby union ground, we saw a strong Lancashire side, led by the England captain Bill Beaumont, surprisingly beaten by Yorkshire in the northern group of the county championship. Dad and I nodded in admiration as

Beaumont, turning and retreating slowly following a Yorkshire drop out from their 22, accidentally impeded the progress of a chasing Yorkshire player in as subtle a way as is possible for a 18 stone second row forward. It echoed the street wisdom that Willie John McBride had displayed when playing for Ulster nine years earlier. Yorkshire had the last word, however: a smart interception try by the young Brian Barley upset the dominant platform that Beaumont and his colleagues in the pack had created for the visitors. Although we did not realise it at the time – and we would have been sad if we had – this was one of Beaumont's final matches, as the last in a series of concussive injuries brought about his premature retirement two months later.

The absentee from all this sporting activity, of course, was Hunslet rugby league club. By 1981, they were homeless, no longer having access to the Elland Road Greyhound Stadium, which was later demolished. In the 1980–81 and 1981–82 seasons, Hunslet played their home fixtures at the Mount Pleasant ground in Batley. As far as I am aware, my father did not go to watch them at all. I think, by this stage, he had probably and reluctantly written them off. He did not discuss this with me, however: nor the other – more serious – issues that he was facing at this time.

My *annus mirabilis* more or less coincided with my year at Queen Mary College, where my 12 month contract concluded at the end of January 1982. On that weekend, a friend from college rang me up, out of the blue, to suggest that we went along to Upton Park to watch West Ham United play West Bromwich Albion. The league table in the match programme showed that Ipswich Town and Southampton occupied the top two places in the first division. The programme also requested that spectators keep off the pitch at all times and avoid littering the pitch with papers. It all seemed eminently reasonable.

It was far from reasonable. We sat in the stand and listened to a sizeable proportion of the home supporters jeer and taunt the black players in the opposition side, Cyrille Regis and Brendon Batson, for the whole of the match. Regis and Batson were undaunted, both players going about their work in a way that reflected their status as professionals at the top of their game. I thought back to the similarly dignified performance by Clyde Best away at Leeds United over a decade earlier, albeit against a background that was nowhere near as hostile and unpleasant as the one at Upton Park. The irony was easy to identify, though still a sour one: Leeds's opposition at Elland Road that evening had been West Ham United.

Chapter 14

Plough Lane

In February 1982, a week after leaving Queen Mary College, I took up a post as an economic analyst in a London-based consultancy firm. I was to remain there for just over ten years. By the end of the decade, I had also married and started a family. As my domestic priorities changed, it was inevitable that the nature of my sports spectating activity should also evolve and become more selective.

To start with, however, things continued much as before, with my residence in London – in Bow until later in 1982 and then in Raynes Park – giving me the opportunity to take advantage of the range of different offerings in the capital city. An early evening out with some of my new work colleagues was to the greyhound racing at Catford: an interesting experience for any social observer. Over the course of the evening, with the races coming at precise 16 minute intervals, I graduated from choosing my bets based on the quirkiness of the dog's name or the colour of its coat through to adopting the more analytical approach of studying its form in previous races. Needless to say, my early winnings from the opening races were eroded as the later races took place. By the end of the evening, I had just about broken even: the rationalised pretence of every failed gambler.

There was an unavoidable excitement as the traps opened and the greyhounds raced away, and it was difficult to resist joining in the roar of the crowd in the main stand as I searched the field to see how my selection was faring. After the final bend was negotiated, and as the winning post approached, there would be a secondary roar, as those with potential winnings urged their dogs home. Then, a few seconds later, there would be the buzz of collective post mortem by winners and losers alike. I knew that this was foreign territory for me: a strange place, in which the odds given by the Tote would sometimes change suddenly – and, to me, mysteriously – as the race approached; and a shadowy world, as confirmed in the official race card where it was stated that: "We have our chromatography unit installed, enabling pre-race samples to be taken from all greyhounds running at this stadium every meeting. We thus provide an additional safeguard to your interests".

On another of the firm's awaydays – at the horse racing at Lingfield Park – the same outturn resulted from my personal betting strategy, though in the reverse way. My careful study of the horses' and jockeys' form in the early races resulted in consistent losses to the friendly bookmaker taking my money through the small hatch at the end of the corridor behind our box, before my financial equilibrium was restored with successes in the last two races, for which my choices were based solely on the names of the horses.

By the mid 1980s, the American football authorities of the National Football League were making serious attempts to stimulate interest in their sport in the UK, thereby following up the success of the regular weekly highlights programmes on Channel 4. As part of their pre-season warm up schedules, some matches were played at Wembley, including the Chicago Bears versus Dallas Cowboys in August 1986 and the San Francisco 49ers versus Miami Dolphins in July 1988. The matches were given considerable publicity and much hype.[37] The reality, however, was that these games were principally used by the respective syndicates as part of the process for deciding their squads for the forthcoming domestic season. As a result, the main players in each squad – Jim McMahon, Walter Payton and William "The Refrigerator" Perry for the Bears, Dan Marino for the Dolphins, and Joe Montana and Jerry Rice for the 49ers, for example – would tend to feature only relatively briefly. I did not mind this too much; it was good to see these players, even if only for a short time, and their truncated appearances were not a surprise to me.

Even though these matches drew large attendances – the Bears/Cowboys game attracted over 82,000 on a damp evening – I did wonder about the likelihood of American football taking root in the UK. In particular, I was not confident that British spectators would take to the rhythm of the game. Apart from the Superbowl, which was shown in its entirety, the Channel 4 coverage was of skilfully edited highlights. The reality of the sport, of course, is that it is packaged for American television, with frequent time-outs and other stoppages. It is totally different to the incessant rush and drama of a soccer match. Of course, I was not the only person to wonder whether this would be a fatal handicap in American football's bid to appeal to British tastes. I did appreciate, though, that the game has a drama of its own, particularly when time is against the quarterback and he is trying to orchestrate a drive down the field for the winning touchdown. I also liked the knowledge and enthusiasm of the American commentators, whose broadcasts were used by Channel 4. One of them casually described the sport as "a battle over real estate", which I thought was a perfect description. In the 1986 Superbowl, which was won by the Bears, one rush by Perry – 23 years old and tipping the scales at 308 pounds – was halted only when about six New England Patriots jumped on top of him. The laconic commentator merely reported: "Perry... [pause]... seems to be attracting a crowd".

In the same week that the 49ers and the Dolphins played at Wembley, Luciano Pavarotti gave an open air concert in Hyde Park. I had thought about going to this, but decided against and, as it happened, the rain poured down all evening, causing considerable discomfort to the VIP guests as well as the keener opera goers and the casual attendees, such as I would have been. But this was London: Joe Montana one day and Luciano Pavarotti the next. For someone earning a reasonable salary and with a willingness to seek out the attractions and to travel across the city, the benefits of metropolitan life were not to be underestimated.

When I joined the economic consultancy firm, my salary could not have been described as excessive. The firm was not based in the City and, in any case, this was before the "Big Bang" of City deregulation, which led to the rapidly accelerating pay arrangements in the Square Mile. Nonetheless, as I discovered later, my first monthly cheque was for more than my father was earning, after working as a joiner and foreman for the same building firm – the small concern based in the Armley district of Leeds – for over thirty years. Not that my dad would have minded. He was as aware as I was of the benefits of a university education. Besides, he had other issues on his mind. He was a skilled tradesman with a fine reputation as a conscientious manager of his workmen and a guardian of the high standards of the firm. However, at more or less the same time that I started my job in London, the firm for which he worked was taken over. After a brief honeymoon period with the new owner-manager, relations within the firm deteriorated. My father was subjected to what can only be described as systematic bullying by his new boss.

At the time, I did not know anything of the seriousness of his difficulties. My mother made some references to things not going too well at dad's workplace but, in essence, my parents shielded my sister and me from the detail of the appalling treatment that the new owner was meting out to his staff. My sister and I were both well into our twenties by that stage and could have coped with the news, however distressing. But our parents obviously judged that we had our own lives to lead and challenges to face without being burdened with theirs. Again, it was only many years later, when we were sorting out the papers left behind by our parents, that we fully appreciated the detail of what they had been going through at the time. When we did find out, their approach did not surprise us. We knew that our mother, in particular, had been a very strong character: a determined woman, with a clear sense of right and wrong. She would have been very protective of her husband.

The only doubt I had at the time was my suspicion that, for some reason, Dad seemed to be losing his confidence. He had always been a quiet man, certainly never one to thrust himself forward in any type of social gathering. But one or two little things did register with me which, unfortunately, I did not relate to any larger picture. For example, when he picked me up at the railway station in Leeds, he developed the habit of waiting at the side of the concourse, almost hidden, rather than standing in his usual location straight in front of the ticket barrier, and, whenever I arrived, it would take me a few moments to register where he was or, indeed, whether he was there at all. I thought this was slightly odd, but did not think to make any further enquiries about it of either him or my mother. I dearly wish that I had.

Among the benefits of working with my new office colleagues, quite apart from their generally friendly welcome, was an access to occasional tickets for the rugby union internationals at Twickenham: Scotland in 1983 and Wales in 1982 and 1984 were examples. The Calcutta Cup match is the one for which the recollections are the clearest. England began the game by kicking the ball dead, Scotland messed up their 22 re-start, and John Horton (ex Cowley School and a survivor of England's grand slam side of 1980) coolly dropped a goal from the resulting scrum. Here we go, I thought: a comfortable win for England coming up. Unfortunately, it didn't exactly work out like that. Scotland took the game to their opponents, the excellent Roy Laidlaw scored a try after one of his trademark arching runs and the tall second row forward Tom Smith caught a line out on the England line and dived over for another try. My somewhat inglorious record of watching England was extended. By the end of 1986 – by which time I had also seen them play and lose three times in Paris – it stood at played thirteen, won two and lost eleven.

In *Brian Moore: The Autobiography*, Moore, who came into the England team in 1987, suggests that the seminal game in England rugby history was the quarter final of that year's inaugural World Cup against Wales in Brisbane. England played woefully and lost a match they had been favourites to win. Afterwards, under a new management and coaching structure headed by Geoff Cooke, it became a priority to turn things around. By the end of the decade, things were different. England had a much stronger side, with better coaching and organisation, and they were starting to produce the results that, with their substantial resources, should have been forthcoming at a much earlier stage. In November 1990, they overwhelmed Argentina at Twickenham by 51 points to nil. The game is best remembered for the staggering punch with which the schoolboy Federico Mendez, playing in the Argentine front row, flattened the England second row forward, Paul Ackford. The lack of sympathy shown by Ackford's colleagues is evident in Moore's gleeful description of Ackford's newly acquired nickname of "Bambi on Ice", in recognition of the ways his legs were splayed as he was led from the field. Mendez followed Paul Ringer as the second player I had seen dismissed in a rugby union international.

At a more personal level, my other recollections of this game are based on two of the spectators in the newly reconstructed North Lower Stand. The man next to me was a Bath supporter, with what could only be described as a passionate hero worship of the England forward, Jon Hall. I thought that Hall was an excellent player – powerful and hard, with good handling skills – whose true worth was never really exploited by England. But my admiration for the player paled into insignificance compared with that of this spectator to my left and when, late in the second half with the match already won, Hall crashed over the Argentine line right in front of us for one of England's tries, the celebrations seemed to reach a form of ecstasy.

The second spectator was sitting a little way away, behind me and to my right, and I did not see exactly who he was. During the half time interval, he started a discussion amongst his friends of the previous week's Great Britain versus Australia rugby league test, which had been played at Wembley (and to which I will refer later). The man's accent was cut-glass home counties. It seemed all the more incongruous, therefore, when he described what he had seen: "That chap Ellery Hanley... He's a very fine rugby player". Too true, I thought, but fair play to you for recognising the fact.

By the time I saw my second Calcutta Cup match, in 1991, events between the respective countries' unions and players had moved on. After being heavily beaten at Murrayfield in 1986, England had played a very restrictive game to win the corresponding fixture in 1988 and had been heavily criticised by the Scottish coaching staff for doing so. Then, in 1990, Scotland had won the grand slam decider, also at Murrayfield, when England had been the clear favourites. Brian Moore has described the build up to the kick off for the 1991 match with some relish: "The focus when we lined up for the anthems was incredible. Not one England player smiled or moved... John Jeffrey was smiling and pointing. You won't be laughing for much longer, mate, I thought".

The England forwards took control and the home side ground out an efficient 21–12 win that constituted the second leg of the grand slam that did come their way that season. Simon Hodgkinson smoothly stroked over five penalties and a touchline conversion of the game's only try. Unusually for me at Twickenham, I had a seat in the East Stand, close to the front and roughly on the 22 line at the northern end of the ground: a school friend, Stephen Hunter, had obtained the tickets from his membership at the Roundhay club. We had an excellent view of the steely determination of the England forwards as they gathered for the line outs near to us, and also, on one occasion, of the immaculate skills of the Scotland full back, Gavin Hastings, as he rose for a high ball and gathered it safely, turning his body at the same time in the textbook manner. In another incident, on the far side of the ground, Jeffrey was clattered in mid air, when competing for another high ball following a long Scottish line-out: a tackle that was legal in those days, but has since been quite rightly banned as dangerous play. There was clearly not much love lost between the Scottish forward and his English opponents. The match is recalled with some poignancy at a personal level, however. Stephen was a good friend, with whom I played in our school's rugby teams at both primary and secondary levels, before he took up a place at the University of Manchester. He died the year after the Scotland match of a heart attack at the age of 37.

The most enjoyable rugby match I saw at Twickenham during this period was the Yorkshire versus Middlesex county championship final of 1987. At long last, Yorkshire had seen off the formidable challenges of Lancashire and Northumberland in the northern group and had negotiated their way past the quarter and semi finals. In the final, on a bright and blustery day, the key question was whether their workmanlike front five and dynamic back row would win enough possession for their three-quarters to show their paces. The answer was given in the opening two minutes. Yorkshire were awarded a free kick at a scrum on the half way line; the ball was quickly taken and recycled through all three of the back row forwards, before being released for the Yorkshire backs to stretch the right hand side of Middlesex's defence. It was precisely the type of quick-thinking, skilful play that I had seen successive Cambridge University sides adopt against physically bigger opponents all those years before. The connection is not a forced one: the Yorkshire fly-half was Rob Andrew, who had been through the Cambridge system and who, on this day, controlled the game immaculately.

It was a pleasure to watch. Yorkshire had the speed and guile of Rory Underwood and Mike Harrison on the wings, the steel of the young John Bentley in the centre and a sizeably raucous support echoing through the West Stand. Underwood scored two tries courtesy of an amazing catch and pass by Peter Buckton and a searing break, direct from a line out, by Andrew. Buckton, whose younger brother John was the other centre, was an immensely talented ball-handling forward, typically gambolling around the field with his sleeves rolled up and his socks down by his ankles, who was ideally complemented in the back row by Peter Winterbottom and Simon Tipping. Tipping was a hard blind-side wing forward who, in this match, produced the tackle in the Middlesex 22 which resulted in a hurried pass and lost possession and a try for the older Buckton. Winterbottom, interestingly, is described with awe by Brian Moore – who one would assume to be a reputable judge of these matters – in his autobiography as the hardest man he has ever met. Middlesex rallied strongly in the second half through the work of their pack and the swift distribution of their replacement scrum half, Floyd Steadman. But Yorkshire held on, and once John Buckton had scored the decisive try, the West Stand rang to the tunes of "Ilkley Moor Bah't 'At", as Yorkshire recorded their first county championship title win since 1963. It was enough to bring a tear to the eye.

Years later, I looked with interest in *John Bentley: My Story* to see what the player's recollection of the match had been. Not much, was the answer: "I was punched off the ball early on and played the rest of the match… in a daze".

Yorkshire returned to Twickenham for the county championship final of 1991, this time against Cornwall. The theme was the same: could Yorkshire's lighter pack win enough possession for the backs? This time, however, the outcome was different. Yorkshire were not quite the side they had been four years earlier – only three of the 1987 side remained in the team – and although they built up a sizeable lead going into the final quarter, the Cornish pack then took control. A Cornwall try in the last minute took the match into extra time, where the pattern of the previous 20 minutes continued and Cornwall ran out winners by 29–20. It was a brave performance, however: I was again impressed by the skill and commitment of Tipping and Buckton as the Yorkshire forwards were driven on to the back foot and by the robust determination of David Scully at scrum half. But it is the events off the pitch that remain longest in the memory. It was conservatively estimated that at least 30,000 Cornish rugby supporters made the journey to Twickenham. My father and I stood back in admiration, after we had reached the railway station and had begun our walk to the ground, as the tidal wave of Trelawney's Army swept by, bedecked in the black and gold of their team and complete with flags and banners and bands. The county championship finals were grand occasions: "Ilkley Moor Bah't 'At" and North versus South on one visit and "Ilkley Moor Bah't 'At" and Trelawney's Army the next, with not a hint of trouble from anyone attending the matches.

Top: "...so he could explain what was really going on".
My father, Bill Rigg, (in his Yorkshire CCC pullover) in 2002.

Bottom: The author in 2012.
(Photograph by Trevor Graham)

THE PARKSIDER

PRICE 4d.　　　　　MONDAY, SEPT. 27th 1965

700

Photo by J. Hickes

The cover of the programme for Hunslet RLFC's home matches in the season after the 1965 Challenge Cup final. The captain, Fred Ward, is fifth from the right. Alan Preece, the scorer of the first try in the semi-final, is on the far left.
(Photograph reproduced by kind permission of David Hickes)

The match programme as a document of social record, as illustrated by this full-page advertisement in the Blackpool Borough vs Hunslet programme in August 1967. The cast list included some of the top stars of the time – and one of today's.

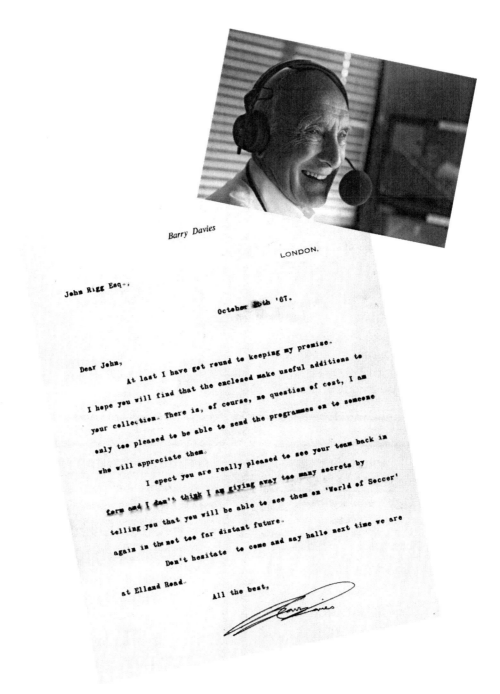

Barry Davies

LONDON,

John Rigg Esq.,

October 20th '67.

Dear John,

At last I have got round to keeping my promise. I hope you will find that the enclosed make useful additions to your collection. There is, of course, no question of cost, I am only too pleased to be able to send the programmes on to someone who will appreciate them.

I epect you are really pleased to see your team back in form and I don't think I am giving away too many secrets by telling you that you will be able to see them on 'World of Soccer' again in the not too far distant future.

Don't hesitate to come and say hallo next time we are at Elland Road.

All the best,

[signature]

Top: My favourite commentator (Copyright @ BBC Photo Library).

Bottom: The letter from Barry Davies that accompanied the parcel of football programmes sent to the 12 year-old collector in October 1967. I hope he received my letter of thanks. My mother would have been furious if it had gone astray.

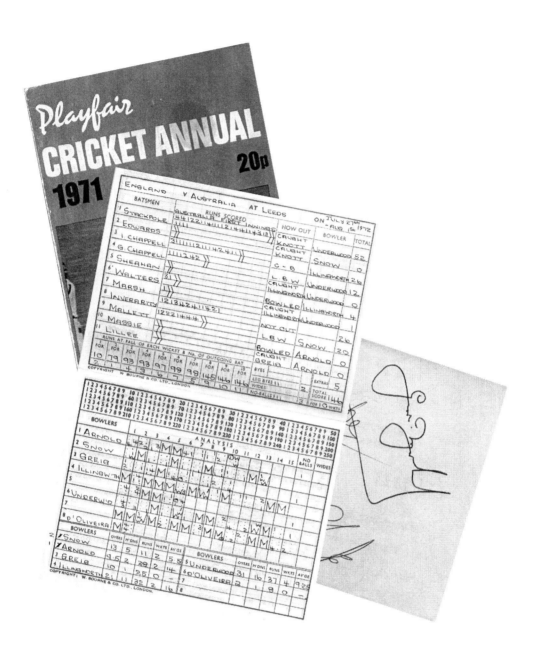

The main components of the young cricket-watcher's "toolkit" in the early 1970s:
"Compactum" scoring book, autograph book (with the prize entry)
and *Playfair Cricket Annual*.

Top: "Let us seek virtue" – the badge of Roundhay School, Leeds.

Bottom: The menu for the school's First XV rugby club dinner in April 1973. The guest speaker, Ian McGeechan, played for Headingley and Yorkshire and had just won his first cap for Scotland.

VIRTUTEM PETAMUS RS

1973 XV

ANNUAL DINNER
tuesday 10th april

C.H. GLOVER, ESQ., M.A.
J.G. CROSFIELD, ESQ.,

HEADMASTER.
CAPTAIN OF RUGBY.

- TOAST LIST -

- M E N U -

THE QUEEN.
PROPOSED BY THE HEADMASTER.

GRAPEFRUIT COCKTAIL
.....
CREAM OF MUSHROOM SOUP
.....
ROAST HALF CHICKEN
BACON AND STUFFING.
CHATEAU/CHIPPED POTATOES.
BRUSSEL SPROUTS.
.....
PEACH MELBA
.....
CHEESE AND BISCUITS.
.....
COFFEE.

THE GUESTS.
PROPOSED BY J.A. RIGG, ESQ.,
RESPONSE BY I. McGEECHAN. ESQ.,

THE 1st XV
PROPOSED BY THE HEADMASTER.
RESPONSE BY CAPTAIN OF RUGBY.

TOASTMASTER.
D.G. MORRIS., ESQ., B.A.

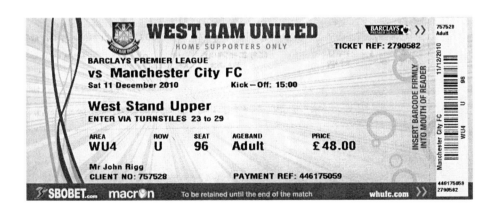

The rising cost of watching top-class sport:
Top: A ticket for a reserved seat in Headingley's Main Stand to watch the Great Britain vs Australia rugby league international in November 1963 cost the equivalent of 62½p.

Bottom: It was slightly more expensive to see West Ham United vs Manchester City in the Barclays Premier League in December 2010.

Three of the great stadiums of the world:
Top: The Olympic Stadium in Barcelona – the Lluis Companys Stadium – the then (2005)
home of the Espanyol football club.
Middle: FedEx Field in Landover, Maryland: the home of the Washington Redskins.
Bottom: Soldier Field in Chicago: the home of the Chicago Bears.

The threat of trouble was very considerably higher at any professional soccer match in London, of course. After I had moved to Raynes Park, I ventured a grand total of twice to Plough Lane, in neighbouring Wimbledon, to attend matches there. The ground was small and cramped, though that still did not mean that the games I attended – against Stoke City at the end of the 1985–86 season in which Wimbledon were promoted from the second division, and against Liverpool the following autumn – required any advance purchase of tickets. In the first match, Mick Mills – a distinguished England international and not a player I would have thought to make such allegations lightly – raced out of position and chased the referee the full width of the pitch to claim that he had been elbowed in the face by John Fashanu. The Liverpool match was distinguished by the entry of two visiting supporters into the home supporters' enclosure behind the goal – and disturbingly near me – and their efforts to provoke attack by the local hard cases who considered it to be their territory. The programme for the Stoke City game confirmed the rapid ascent that Wimbledon had made. In the "Looking Back" section, the featured match of only ten years earlier was a Southern League Premier Division fixture away to Tonbridge.

It struck me at the time that Wimbledon's experience was analogous to the position reached by Cambridge United when I had fleetingly observed them a few years earlier. They had been promoted on merit – as with all promotions through the leagues – but they had reached a status that was unsustainable in the long run. In Cambridge's case, they reached the giddy heights of eighth place in the old second division in 1979–80, the season I went to see them: an amazing achievement. Similarly, it turned out that Wimbledon lasted in the top flight longer than I expected – and, of course, crowned this achievement by winning the FA Cup in 1988 – but the decline, when it came, was not unexpected, given the level of resources with which they had to operate.[38]

As mentioned, it was a characteristic of the major football league matches in the 1980s that, on the vast majority of occasions, one could attend by simply turning up and paying at the turnstile, rather than having to order tickets in advance. A work colleague and I decided to go at such short notice to the Arsenal versus Manchester United fixture at Highbury in February 1985, thereby taking advantage of a flexibility which is largely not available today. We stood in the massed home support on one of the touchlines and could feel the consistent and unremitting venom with which the United players were subjected whenever they came into our vicinity. I tried to make sense of it. When one of the visitors stood on our side of the white line to take a throw-in, it was not simply routine banter that was being tossed in his direction: it was an outpouring of hatred. My colleague was a Manchester United supporter, but he fortuitously kept his counsel when Norman Whiteside slid in front of the Clock End to score the winning goal for the visitors.

Late in the second half, a flow of urine – weakening, but still discernible – reached our tier of the terrace from its sources higher up behind us. My one and only visit to the old Highbury Stadium was a quarter of a century ago and those are the recollections that survive: the dark passions around me, the goal, and the emerging sensitivity about where exactly I was putting my feet.

A similarly casual approach to planning attendance at football matches occurred some time earlier, in May 1982, when I happened to be staying with friends in Bishop's Stortford and one of them suggested – or, rather, pushed at the open door – that we go along to watch Ipswich Town play Nottingham Forest. With two games still to play, Ipswich were still in with an outside chance of that season's league championship title, although this depended on Liverpool faltering in their remaining games, and they were widely admired by the soccer neutrals for the style of their play and their ability to match the bigger and wealthier clubs in the first division. Forest had won the European Cup in successive seasons in the late 1970s, of course. They were managed by the same Brian Clough whom the Leeds United programme of October 1969 had described as one of the most dynamic of the younger school of managers, having done "right well" at Derby County.

Ipswich fell behind, and their need to chase the victory became ever more urgent. On one occasion, the ball ran out of play and an Ipswich player ran to collect it to take the quick throw in. Clough saved him the journey. He leapt up from his spot on the bench and intercepted the ball and rushed over to throw it back to the Ipswich player. The Portman Road crowd in his vicinity politely applauded his sportsmanship. In the event, Forest won comfortably – 3–1 – and it looked as if it were they who were challenging for the title, rather than treading water in mid-table. The quality of their play was exemplified by John Robertson. He hugged the left hand side of the pitch, taking up the ball as an outlet from his defence and midfield and relaying the ball inside to his supporting colleagues. I watched him closely for several minutes. He did not waste a pass: not one. Every time he received the ball, he used it to his side's advantage, whether with short passes inside or more penetrating passes to his advancing midfield or forward players. I came away from the ground feeling thrilled – as I always have done – at seeing a professional sportsman at the top of his game.

On the car radio, on the way back to Bishop's Stortford, we heard that Liverpool had beaten Tottenham Hotspur to clinch the championship title: Ipswich were to be runners up. A few days later, at the other end of the league table, Leeds United – whose season had begun so ignominiously at Swansea on the day I was watching the test match against the Australians at the Oval – were relegated into the second division.

The Sunday afternoon visits to Craven Cottage to watch the Fulham RLFC continued for another couple of seasons. Continuing its chronic "yo-yo" behaviour, the side was relegated at the end of the 1981–82 season, promoted at the end of 1982–83 and relegated again after 1983–84. Two games in particular stand out in my memory, both from the season in which Fulham were in the first division. The first was in October 1983, when I saw my first match under the newly introduced law which stipulated that sides had to hand over possession to their opponents at the end of the allotted six tackles, instead of the game being stopped for a scrum. I knew that something fundamental had changed when I looked in the match programme and saw that the visiting Leeds team had one of the Rayne twins at prop forward, the pair having always previously played in the second row. Within minutes of the match kicking off, it was clear to me that the game of rugby league had been speeded up immeasurably. The game could now be continuous, with a side usually opting to kick the ball on the last tackle in order to secure ground before their tackle allocation was completed, thereby setting up a new tackle cycle, this time with the opposition in possession of the ball.

One significant effect of the new law was that an entire generation of front row forwards – the hewers and carriers as far as the scrum was concerned – was made redundant, more or less at a stroke. It seemed that, within weeks, the traditional open-side prop forward – who had usually been a big heavyweight, required to give ballast to the scrum – was virtually nowhere to be seen. It was this law change – combined with the later introduction of complete laxity at the feeding of the scrum – that brought about the start of the much greater flexibility between positions on the field: stand off halves playing at loose forward and vice versa, scrum halves playing hooker, and so on. In some respects, that has been a shame, given the loss of specialisation and craft skills that it has implied. On the other hand, there was now no hiding place for any player not at peak fitness, especially in the front row.

Later in the season, Fulham were at home to St Helens. By this time, Fulham were in the lower reaches of the division and struggling with injuries and other absentees. I watched the game from the terraces running along one touchline in the company of a colleague from work and a friend of his, both supposedly knowledgeable supporters of the game. My colleague's friend then proceeded to loudly ridicule the St Helens side as they made their way on to the pitch. Admittedly, the visitors had affected a fairly bedraggled entrance, as if they not only were not bothered about the outcome of the match but had not been introduced to each other beforehand. Meanwhile, the skies behind the Eric Miller stand were turning black; it could have been a set for a Wagnerian opera. In fact, it was an object lesson in how appearances can be misleading. By the end of the match, St Helens had won by thirty points to nil and their initially ridiculed side – impressively led by the hard and skilful Kevin Arkwright – had demonstrated the full range of their professional skills.

After the end of the 1983–84 season, my rugby league viewing from London was much more selectively focused on the Challenge Cup finals (on which I report separately). The Fulham club left Craven Cottage at the end of the season and began a peripatetic existence that took them to the Polytechnic of Central London stadium in Chiswick and the National Sports Centre at Crystal Palace. The only game I attended was in north London – in Hendon, if I recall correctly – where Wigan gave them a heavy beating. However, a work colleague and I did go to a key match at Central Park in Wigan at the end of the 1984–85 season. The visitors were the high-flying Hull Kingston Rovers, who looked to have taken a match-winning lead with only a couple of minutes to go. However, Wigan hit back immediately and took the spoils thanks to a try by their charismatic winger, Henderson Gill. It was a long round trip for the day, but it was well worth it for my first and – as it turned out – last visit to the famous ground, and for a game of tension and passion in front of a capacity attendance.

By the end of the decade, other priorities had taken over to ease me away from the casual attendance at a sporting event: namely, marriage and the birth of a son. The competing claims are not incompatible however. A family weekend away in Bath in November 1991, for example, was notable for our visit to the magnificent Roman baths, the difficulties my 14-month-old son experienced when attempting to stand up and walk across the (sloping) living room floor of the our hired apartment, and my visit to the Recreation Ground to see the home side's rugby union encounter with Nottingham. (The parallel with my father's family holiday planning on the Lancashire west coast to coincide with a Hunslet match at Blackpool and on the east coast, when the Scarborough Cricket Festival was in full swing, will not have gone unnoticed). On this occasion, the match turned out to be a one-sided affair, as Bath had a fullish complement of their international players – Jeremy Guscott and Jon Hall, amongst others – and Nottingham were not quite the side they had been a few years earlier. The game also suffered from an unfortunate *longueur* in the second half,

208

when the action was stopped for what appeared to be a serious injury to a Nottingham player, though fortunately all turned out to be well. But it was another notable venue ticked off – alongside Highbury in North London and Central Park in Wigan and, to a lesser extent, Plough Lane in Wimbledon and Portman Road in Ipswich – as I continued my odyssey of sports spectating.

Chapter 15

Madison Square Garden to Sydney Cricket Ground

During the 1980s, my viewing of domestic sport was complemented by the events that I saw overseas. The start of this foreign experience actually predated the decade, not only through the Women's World Volleyball Championships in Minsk in 1978, but also the European Super Cup Final of 1975. This was the fixture played between the winners of the European Cup and the European Cup-Winners Cup: in this case, the first leg of the match between Bayern Munich and Dynamo Kiev. My school friend, Andrew Carter, and I were travelling around Europe on the students' Inter-Rail card at the time (at a cost for the card of £52 for the month) and, as luck would have it, we were in Munich when the fixture was played in September. The irony was, of course – particularly for Andrew as a committed supporter – that Bayern had beaten Leeds United in the European Cup final in Paris the previous May.

Thus, in the normal way, by buying our tickets at the turnstile on the day of the match, we found ourselves in the stadium in which the World Cup final had been played the previous summer (the game refereed, it will be recalled, by the same Jack Taylor who had handled the Sheffield United versus West Ham United game in March). We also found ourselves cheering loudly when Oleg Blokhin scored the opening – and, as it turned out, only – goal of the game mid-way through the second half. By doing so, we did put ourselves in a slightly vulnerable position, as there did not seem to be any other Kiev supporters anywhere else in the ground, although I think the people around us were more bemused than anything else. Despite the status of the occasion, I cannot remember anything else about the match although I am sure that I would have confirmed to myself – with the usual fingernail in the palm of the hand – which individual players I was seeing, particularly in the Bayern team: Franz Beckenbauer, Gerd Muller, Sepp Maier, *et al.*

It was also good to visit the stadium itself, with its long sweep of open stand. Later, when I returned to Britain, I searched in vain in the newspapers for any reference to the return fixture. (For the record, Dynamo Kiev won the second leg 2–0 a month later, both goals again scored by Blokhin).

The position of supporting the visiting sports team overseas was more conventionally experienced in the rugby arena in the 1980s, when I went to see England play France at the Parc de Princes on the three consecutive occasions in the Five Nations championship between 1982 and 1986. Needless to say, given my track record of watching England stumble to defeat on a regular basis, the home side won all three matches comfortably. The tickets came courtesy of my sister, who was living in Paris throughout this period.

In those days, England had not set out on the long run of consecutive victories over France – they were to lose in 1988 as well – that carried them from the late 1980s through to the World Cup third place play-off match in South Africa in 1995. France were all-conquering at home – particularly, in the clichéd but valid manner – when it was a warm day and they had the sun on their backs. 1986 was an example, typified by a move towards the end of the match, which started from a scrum in their own 22 and ended with Philippe Sella running behind the England posts to touch down. No-one – least of all the referee, Derek Bevan – seemed to mind that the crucial pass from Eric Bonneval to Denis Charvet, made directly in line with where we were sitting, was about four yards forward. This was in keeping with the liberal – if not completely absent – interpretation of the forward pass law which was prevalent in international rugby union at that time. England's cause that day was not helped when the scrum half and captain, Nigel Melville, received a poorly tapped ball from a line out and was thoroughly trampled by the French pack, necessitating his departure from the match. This turned out to be only the latest in the series of injuries that Melville received in England and British Lions shirts, the most serious of which was his horrendous leg injury against Ireland in 1988. Melville, by virtue of his ability to read a game and the speed and accuracy of his pass, was the best English player I have seen in his position and it was a great pity that his abilities were not fully exposed at international level.

The 1986 France versus England match had its other – more personal – compensations, however. My sister and I had taken our seats in the stand when, about 20 minutes before the kick off, a group of people started kicking a bunch of rugby balls into the ranks of the spectators. As one of the balls arrowed directly towards us, a spectator seated in the row in front jumped up to catch it. Unfortunately for him, the ball went straight through his hands and landed between my feet. I had not moved at all and yet, no doubt to the frustration of others around me, all I had to do was bend down and pick the ball up in order to claim it. This simple exercise took me about three attempts, at which point the man in front – a middle aged Englishman over for the match, who had clearly indulged heavily at lunchtime – demanded that we give the ball to him. I declined politely. He then offered to buy the ball, starting his bidding at twenty francs. I declined again. He had reached a high of *cent francs* by the time I had turned down his final offer. In truth, the ball was not that great: it was a cheapish imitation version with a plastic cover, albeit painted to look like the real thing used in internationals in Paris. But Rosie and I did not care. We had simultaneously decided that we wanted to keep it, and keep it we did. At one o'clock the following morning, we were kicking and passing it to each other down a side street near Rosie's flat in the Nation district of the city, where I re-enacted Sella's final dash to the try line near a lamppost. It was not until we cleared out my parents' house, almost two decades later, that the ball was banished to the rubbish skip in a poignant scene analogous to the one in *Badlands*, when Sissy Spacek reports that Martin Sheen decided "to shoot the football because it was excess baggage".

By 1984, my progress at the economic consultancy firm was beginning to yield some overseas visits to clients and other contacts. After I had accompanied my boss to New York for a week in September 1984, I stayed on to do the tourist run. One Saturday afternoon, after I had wandered through Central Park to watch the New Yorkers at leisure (jogging, cycling, rollerdisco dancing and playing volleyball and softball) – and after I had politely declined a smoke offered by one of the local hustlers – I exited the park just to the north of the Metropolitan Museum. I found myself at the start of the annual Fifth Avenue Mile road race, which ran due south and dead straight from 5th Avenue and 82nd Street down to 5th Avenue and 62nd Street.

In fact, there were six different races, beginning with the Men's Masters and finishing with the Women's Elite and the Men's Elite races. The last of these was won by the New Zealander, John Walker, who, ten years earlier, had been the first man to break 3 minutes 50 seconds on the track for the mile. I photographed Walker and his challengers as they ran past me a little way down the course. John Walker: one of the most famous athletes in an era of prodigious middle distance runners, whose longevity at the top of his event was astonishing. The elite women's field included the slim and attractive British runner, Wendy Sly, who had won the event the previous year, though she was beaten on this occasion. The front of the event programme announced that the races were conducted by the New

York Road Runners Club and – this being America – sponsored by the makers of the 5th Avenue candy bar.

On another visit to New York, at the beginning of 1987, a colleague and I took advantage of the basketball at the Madison Square Garden: the New York Knickerbockers against the Cleveland Cavaliers. Although the analogy might seem strange – if not perverse – I think, looking back, that there was a link to another sporting event that I had attended: not the two American football matches at Wembley, but the greyhound racing at Catford. The American football games were mainly attended by people like me: general enthusiasts or admirers of the sport, but not experts. By contrast, with the basketball – as with the greyhounds – I was acutely conscious that I was the outsider observer watching a totally foreign sport that had its own culture and traditions and about which I knew relatively little.

But it was hugely enjoyable evening. There is something balletic in the speed and grace of these big men and the skills that they possess. One of the Knicks – Patrick Ewing – was a mere seven feet tall. There would be the careful working of a position and then a sudden flurry of fast action as the scoring play was attempted and defended. I also liked the venue itself, with the brash and brightly coloured seating and its excellent views, and I listened attentively to the keen support of those sitting near us. On one occasion, a young man behind me berated one of the Knicks for losing possession and said to his friend that the player must be "brain dead". I don't think I had heard this term before – certainly not outside the formal medical context – and its use here was curiously shocking. Part of the attraction of the venue was the informality of the arrangements, including the ability to nip out to one of the nearby kiosks and come back with two beers and frankfurters to resume watching the action. It was a civilised experience: people were actually consuming alcoholic drinks and enjoying the sporting contest without any aggravation.

And finally – this again being America – I liked the total lack of inhibition with which the commercial world attached itself to the world of sport. The advertisement for Vidal Sassoon that covered most of two pages in the match programme contained endorsements for the company's range of products by the chairman of the Vidal Sassoon board, for the grooming gel by an Olympic swimmer, for the grooming mousse by a police officer and for the natural control hairspray – by a New York rabbi. I knew, of course, that the commercial and sports worlds were not just attached, but heavily intertwined. The contents page of the programme stated that the New York Knicks was a division of Madison Square Garden Center Inc, which was part of the Gulf and Western Company.

My earliest reading about international rugby league was the *Windsors Rugby League Annual, 1962–63*, which described Great Britain's test series success in Australia in the summer of 1962. My eight year-old imagination followed in the footsteps of Eric Ashton's team, as they trekked around exotic venues such as Rockhampton and Toowoomba as well as playing in front of huge crowds in Sydney and Brisbane. The text of the match-by-match reports set out the exploits of the tourists, ranging from their overwhelming demolition of some of their opponents (84–20 versus Wide-Bay Burnett) through to their ferocious battles against the tougher sides (6 players sent off – 3 from each side – in the game against New South Wales). The supporting photographs showed a series of action shots on the sun-baked pitches.

Sydney was the hot-bed of Australian rugby league, of course. Two of the three tests in that series were played at the Sydney Cricket Ground, which, as my father had informed me at an early age, shared with Headingley the distinction of being the only grounds in the world to host international cricket and international rugby league. In Sydney's case, this was actually on the same pitch. It had been here, in 1914, that Great Britain, without several of their best players through injury and reduced to 10 fit men in the game itself, had beaten Australia in the famous "Rorke's Drift" test match. Later, in 1970, the SGC similarly hosted two of the games in Great Britain's last successful Ashes rugby league series, including the decisive third match, when Dennis Hartley scored his vital try. The long list of cricket test matches hosted by the venue included two in the test series won by Ray Illingworth's England side in 1970–71, both of which England won, with Geoff Boycott scoring an unbeaten century to set up the victory in one of the games. For his part, Boycott had followed the lead given by his predecessors as great Yorkshire and England opening batsmen: test match centuries had been scored at Sydney by both Herbert Sutcliffe (1924–25 and 1932–33) and Len Hutton (1946–47).

One Sunday, in the summer of 1987, I took the hour's walk from my hotel in William Street in Sydney to the Sydney Cricket Ground and watched the home side, St George, get beaten 21–20 by Parramatta. The winning score was a long range drop goal in the last minute by one of the Parramatta forwards. I checked in my programme to confirm that it was John Muggleton, whom I had first seen playing in England on Australia's tour of 1982. I had remembered him then as a solid and uncompromising player; in Sydney, he launched a huge match-winning kick directly towards me as I sat in the covered stand behind the posts. The game itself was as hard and skilful as I had expected it to be, given the talented players on view, many of whom – including Craig Young, Peter Sterling and

Brett Kenny – were proven international players.

In one sense, it was pleasing that I was watching St George who, for me, had always been the most famous and glamorous Australian club side. In the years when my knowledge bank of the history of rugby league's honours and titles was being established – aided by scholarly works such as AN Gaulton's *The Encyclopaedia of Rugby League Football* – I had learned that St George had won the Grand Final of the Sydney First Grade Premiership for no fewer than 11 seasons in a row up until 1966. On the other hand, of course, I did not really mind which of the first grade teams I happened to be watching that afternoon. The main thing was that, whilst in Sydney – again on business commitments – I had taken the opportunity to sample a local sports event in the famous stadium.

From my seat, I took care to look around the stadium and try and take it all in, beginning and ending with the famous pavilion below me and to my right. The names of the stands – Bradman, Walters, Hill, Churchill – resonated with the powerful history of Australian achievements in cricket and rugby. Although the action on the pitch was a long way from my place in the spectators' seats – probably even further than at Wembley – I was conscious of the huge tradition, in both sports, that had been generated in the middle of the arena. I was here: live and in the flesh.

It was not all about tradition, of course. For the supporters of the two sides – colourful and keen – the action on the pitch was about the here and now, with the usual concerns about local bragging rights and the position in the league table. I also noticed that the game had attracted the local young toughs, for whom, I feared, the concept of bragging rights would be in danger of being taken too far after the match had finished. I did not hang about in the stadium to find out.

It turned out that my visit to the Sydney Cricket Ground was made only just in time. The Grand Final of the same (1987) season between Manly and Canberra was the last game of rugby league to be played there, as plans were completed for the major games to be played in the newly constructed Sydney Football Stadium. A couple of years later, in the excellent *At The George: and other essays in Rugby League*, Geoffrey Moorhouse wrote passionately about how the SCG had been "unforgivably vandalised" during its extensive modernisation as a cricket ground from "surroundings of elegance and grace" to the "mongrel mess" of a venue that was "charmlessly without character".

Before reaching Sydney, the earlier part of my visit to Australia had taken me to Melbourne. At that time, there was no professional rugby league in the city, where the dominant winter sport was – and continues to be – Australian Rules Football. I spent one of my spare afternoons on the tourist run – or walk – from my hotel in Collins Street to the Melbourne Cricket Ground. The journey took me past the cottage that had belonged to the first successful Yorkshire overseas captain, the building having been dismantled in England and sent out to Australia to be reconstructed stone by stone. This particular captain had predated Len Hutton and Ray Illingworth by the best part of two centuries: James Cook. Inside, the cottage was well preserved and I judged that it must have been a pleasant home in its time, though cramped by modern standards. I was struck by the smallness of the bed and (presumably) of the man who had slept in it.

I was able to walk straight into the MCG and sit in one of the seats at the front behind the railings. The ground was empty apart from the contingent of ground staff, with a perpetually circling lawnmower attending to the brilliantly green grass. The stands were huge and double-decked and, as in Sydney, named after the local heroes. I looked across at the one labelled The Ponsford Stand 1967 and trawled my knowledge bank: Bill Ponsford and Don Bradman had compiled a partnership of 451, a record for Australia for all wickets, against England at the Oval in 1934, having also shared in a partnership of 388 at Headingley in the same series. I tried to imagine the MCG full to capacity for a local Aussie Rules final or a Boxing Day cricket test match, but this was difficult to do on a warm sunny afternoon with the vast open spaces stretching around on all sides. Nobody seemed to mind that I was there, however. As with my detour to the Olympic Stadium in Moscow seven years earlier, I had been free to come in and sit down for a few minutes and look around at the famous sporting arena.

Attached to the stadium was a well presented Olympic Museum with its surprisingly small Australian Sport Hall of Fame. In those days, the hall of fame concept was largely an Americanism that was not widely adopted elsewhere. In my diary of the trip, I noted that I did not find it particular useful. I valued having sports museums and the opportunity these gave to see the match balls and playing kits and scorecards of the famous games of the past: it was the "hall of fame" bit that I considered might not be necessary. However, in the same notes, I also conceded that the Melbourne version played a role in emphasising the Australian sense of national identity, towards which sport in general has contributed so much. I knew that I should not forget that this was a young nation and that, elsewhere in the city, the transportation and re-building of a house of a mere 220 years of age (at that time) had clearly added a great deal to its sense of history.

Other business trips abroad did not lend themselves so readily to making the sporting connections. For example, in Beijing in 1986, I had to be satisfied with watching England lose to Portugal in the opening group match in the soccer World Cup on a scratchy black and white television. A few days later, on the flight home from Hong Kong, the captain announced that Bryan Robson had had to leave the field in the second match against Morocco (cue collective groan from the passengers) and that Ray Wilkins had been sent off (cue larger groan). A few minutes later, the captain came back on to announce that England had only drawn the match 0–0. This drew the biggest groan of all, signalling the collective conclusion that England's interest in the competition would be unlikely to last beyond the final group match, as well as what I sensed to be a generally assumed view that an England team – even with 10 men, or 9 or 8 men come to that – should have been capable of beating the likes of Morocco. I was not so sure: England were not yet out of the competition and, however unlikely, a good result in the third group match against Poland might be sufficient to take them through to the knock-out stages. In the event, my optimism was not misplaced, as Gary Lineker and his colleagues were later to prove.

The most remarkable of my overseas sporting connections during the 1980s was on a holiday in Nepal in 1985, when I was with a small group on a trekking tour near Annapurna. Although it was not an easy trip – we had three or four early days of incessant cloud and rain with not a mountain in sight, and we later camped above the snow line (when, according to my diary, I slept one night in nine layers of clothing and other protection) – it was undoubtedly one of the most memorable vacations I have ever taken. The mountains, the temples, the friendliness, the children: "Namaste, namaste, one rupee please".

Towards the end of the trek, after a long day's walk, on a bright and sunny day, we arrived at a delightful village called Birethanti. To reach our camp site, we had to cross a rickety bridge, which had gaping holes in its floor and only a chicken mesh netting on each side to prevent us from plunging into the river below. Once at the site, however, I was able to strip to my pants and, in the cold waters of the river, take my first bath for two weeks: it was absolutely glorious. At dinner that evening, sitting back with my first bottle of beer for a fortnight and staring around – yet again – at the wonderful mountainous landscape on all sides, it really did seem as if I was a long way from home.

The following day was a rare and much appreciated rest day. I took a trip over the bridge and into the village to find an elderly tailor, who I was told could put a patch in my old cords. His home was just a little way up the street, a very basic building of stone and mud with a rough thatch roof. The tailor's workspace was near the open door, looking out down the street, and I sat in the corner whilst he did the repairs. A bed took up most of the other half of the room, with the blankets loosely gathered at one end. The tailor was a frail, thin man with a rich brown complexion and tufts of grey hair on an otherwise bald head. He wore an old open shirt, shorts and no shoes. He used a footpedal on an old machine and chose the patch himself from a number of spare bits of cloth in a bag. The tailor's wife was a crotchety woman; she shouted down the street at a passer-by and seemed unhappy when I said that I did not have any cigarettes. When he had finished, the tailor proudly showed me his handiwork and I gave him a 5 rupee note.

On walking back through the village, I looked into one of the shops. Behind one shelf, as a type of wallpaper, there were several pages from an old edition of the *Hindustan Times*. I studied them closely and wondered for a moment what it was that seemed familiar. Then, I realised that, amongst the rest of the articles and other items, there was an action photograph from the Hull versus Featherstone Rovers rugby league Challenge Cup final of 1983: a match I had been to see at Wembley. I was, naturally, drawn into the shop. The man inside – probably in his late 40s – welcomed me in and, in excellent English, told me that he was visiting his family to mark a religious festival. He introduced me to his father and sister and told me how he read the *Daily Telegraph* whenever he could get hold of it, usually a week late. When I explained about the newspaper page on the wall, he nodded politely and said how he listened to Paddy Feeny on the BBC World Service sports news. He informed me that Manchester United were 11 points clear at the top of the first division – this was late October of the 1985–86 season – and that England had qualified for the 1986 soccer World cup finals.

The man said that he had been in a Ghurka regiment and had served for 13 years, including in Borneo in the early 1960s, when he thought that he would die. He had also been to Hong Kong and Singapore and Aldershot. He said that the people in London had been very friendly and I said the same about the people of Nepal. I was probably in the shop for about 20 minutes before we shook hands and said our farewells. The meeting was one of the highlights of an already memorable trip, and it was prompted by a photograph of a rugby league match played over two years earlier and thousands of miles away.

Chapter 16

Fartown

It is generally accepted that the defeat of the England soccer team by Hungary at Wembley in 1953 was a seminal event in the development of the sport in this country. England lost the game 6–3 before going on, six months later, to be humiliated 7–1 in Budapest. For the sport of rugby league, the visit of the Australian tourists of 1982 – and especially the first test match at the Boothferry Park ground in Hull – was every bit as significant. Thirty years later, the influence of this side, not only on the league code but on rugby union as well, remains devastatingly apparent.

Although Great Britain had not won the rugby league Ashes since 1970, there was a sense of optimism in the home camp as the first test approached. On the previous tour, Britain, marshalled by Brian Lockwood, had won the second test and the series had only been decided in the third game at Headingley. The fact that the first test match of 1982 was being played on Humberside was held to be an advantage for Great Britain, as the two local club teams – Hull FC and Hull Kingston Rovers – were, along with Widnes, the premier sides in the country. Moreover, the Great Britain coach was the widely respected Johnny Whiteley, himself a hero in the area for his playing exploits with the Hull club in the 1950s. Whiteley, interviewed on late night television on the eve of the game – my recollection is that it was on *Newsnight* for some reason – said that he thought Great Britain's size and power in the front row of the forwards would be the basis of victory. I was interested in this apparent departure from the stereotypical depiction of British guile and skill being the way to overcome antipodean size and power. I was also interested in one of the second row forwards: the same Lee Crooks who, barely 12 months earlier, had been playing in the Colts cup final for Hull against Castleford at Headingley.

I watched the first test of the 1982 series on television in the house

I was sharing in Bow. There were two defining moments. The first was when the Australian centre, Mal Meninga, handed off his opposite number, Les Dyl of Leeds, to score the first try of the match. Dyl was a talented player for his club and, in a longstanding partnership with the winger John Atkinson, had consistently posed a potent threat down the Leeds left flank. But Meninga was formidable: 15 stone, fast, skilful and with a sledgehammer of a hand off. He despatched Dyl with disdain, swatting him away as if he were a minor irritant, before striding away to touch down. The second key moment came in the second half, with Great Britain already well beaten. The Australian prop Craig Young was sent through a gap in the British defence in his own half and, after drawing the Great Britain full back George Fairbairn in the textbook manner, he released the supporting player to run half the length of the field to score a try under the posts. Fairbairn clattered Young with a late and high tackle after he had passed the ball, but it was a forlorn – and, I thought, rather pathetic – gesture. The Australian try scorer was Wayne Pearce, a second row forward who, in addition to contributing his share to the heavy graft in the pack, could run and pass like a three-quarter. Australia won the game by 40 points to 4, after which the BBC match summariser Alex Murphy – whose playing and coaching credentials would certainly have allowed him to recognise excellence when he saw it – described the tourists as having been "from another planet".

By the time the sides met for the third test match at Headingley, Great Britain were in disarray. Australia had already won the series, and the Great Britain selectors had introduced widespread changes throughout the team. Only 4 of the starting line up from Boothferry Park remained in the side. Amongst the new introductions were the scrum half Andy Gregory from Widnes and Mick Crane from Hull at loose forward. I had seen enough of Gregory to know that he was a player of international standard: tough, skilful and quick. Crane had always interested me, not only because he was another hard player or because of his excellent ball handling skills and his ability to open up the tightest defences. (Crane's crucial pass – all of two feet – in the build up to John Atkinson's decisive try for Leeds in the 1979 Challenge Cup final can be seen on the *101 Top Rugby League Tries* video released in 1989). Rather, there was something about his demeanour – indeed, his gait – around the pitch which was out of the ordinary, compared with other players. I could not pin down exactly what it was then, and I am not sure I could do so now, except to note David Hadfield's interesting perspective on the player, as set out in *Up and Over: A Trek Through Rugby League Land*. According to Hadfield, Crane embodied the philosophy of the "Three Day Millionaire": a reference to a local folk song in which the trawlerman is paid on a Friday, spends copiously over the weekend, and is back to sea in order to replenish his finances on the Monday morning.

Gregory and Crane added some spark to the Great Britain effort at Headingley, and the home side managed to hang on to their visitors until the beginning of the second half. Australia led only 6–5 after 50 minutes. But after they had scored again – and Crooks had been sent off for punching an opponent – the Australians pulled away, scoring 4 tries in the last 10 minutes. It seemed that, in supporting the ball carrier and running in the tries, any member of their side could be present: it had been Pearce in that example at Hull; at Headingley, it was the captain Max Krilich, who backed up a break made by one of his colleagues near the half way line and ran 40 metres to score under the posts. Towards the end of the match, Brett Kenny scored a very similar try. Kenny was the stand off and his try was of the type that might have been expected from a top class performer in his position. But Krilich? It was not in the script for him to score tries like this. He was the hooker.

Mal Meninga's contribution to Australia's 32 points to 8 victory was 7 goals, taking his total in the three match series to 21. I mention this to complete an aside introduced in one of the earlier chapters. Meninga was one of the last goal-kickers to adopt the front-on style – kicking with the toes, rather than the instep, and following the leg straight through the line of the ball – that had been the normal technique in my earliest years of watching rugby (league or union). From this time onwards, such practitioners would become the increasingly rare exception. The "soccer style" approach that I had first seen when Eddie Tees played for Barrow against Hunslet at the beginning of the 1966–67 season had become the norm.

Leaving the specialist skill of goal-kicking to one side, it was clear that the Australians had taken the game of rugby league to a higher level. It was not only a question of their mastery of all the required techniques of the game, particularly the handling and creative skills (where tradition had had it that Great Britain held the advantage), but in terms of their preparation, fitness and – in a word – professionalism. The initial perspective offered by Alex Murphy after the first test was confirmed in a more reflective manner by the 1983–84 *Rothmans Rugby League Yearbook*, which stated that "The Australians displayed a showcase of skill, strength and speed that… set alarm bells ringing throughout the 13-a-side code in this country". Like Murphy, I reached this conclusion after watching the first test. It was immediately clear that Great Britain would have a great deal to worry about for some time to come: Meninga was 22 years old, Pearce and Kenny were 21.

The 1982 tourists revolutionised the domestic game and Great Britain (and, latterly, England) have spent the period since then trying to catch up. The difficulty, of course, is that the target itself has been continually moving, as the Australian coaches develop their own game even further. The period since 1982, therefore, has been one of regular – often heroic – victories in individual test matches by Great Britain, but the inability to capture the spoils of a whole series.

By the time the Australians returned in 1986, their stand off and captain Wally Lewis was widely viewed as being the best rugby league player in the world. He had played on the 1982 tour without being a first choice for the test side, appearing as a second half substitute in two of the internationals. But he was now a formidable player, with his strength and kicking skills and, in particular, once a defence had been sucked into the middle of the field, his ability to fire out long flat passes to his three-quarters who, arriving at speed, could outflank their opposite numbers. The second test was played on a blustery day at Elland Road in Leeds.

My father and I watched this game from the West Stand. It was the familiar story. The big Australian forwards put Great Britain under severe pressure, prompted by the immaculately weighted kicking of the scrum half, Peter Sterling, whose uncanny ability to deposit the ball into the far right hand corner of the pitch on the Great Britain goal line was revealed three times in the opening minutes. Great Britain held on until the half hour mark, before the inevitable missed tackle on the huge second row forward Noel Cleal led to a try under the posts. In the second half, the floodgates opened and Australia won 34–4. I remember thinking that the Australians – bedecked in their dark green shirts with the two prominent gold "V"s, green shorts and broadly hooped green and gold socks – were wearing an outfit of superiority that matched that of the New Zealand All Blacks in the rival code.

It should also be said, however, that Great Britain played poorly in this game, repeatedly dropping the ball on the first or second tackles and giving every impression of having lost the psychological battle before they had stepped out on to the pitch. I checked the grim details on my video recording of the match, which I had made in the certain knowledge that I would wish to undertake some sort of forensic analysis of the game again when I got back to London. Great Britain lost possession of the ball on no fewer than 15 occasions before reaching even the third of their permitted six tackles. For completeness, I should report that, in a blurred still of one of the cameraman's long sweeps of the crowd, the video recording shows two particular figures in the capacity attendance in the West Stand looking down on the action and realising that the home side would not recover the widening deficit on the scoreboard. I still have the video at home.

The first test of the 1990 tour was played at Wembley. Great Britain won 19–12, the first time I had seen them defeat Australia since the match at Headingley in 1967. The star of the show was Ellery Hanley, whose skill and composure under pressure was clearly evident. In the second half, he set up the decisive Great Britain try with a deft chip and catch, which took him to within a few feet of the Australian line. Hanley's display at Wembley was widely commended, including by my neighbour in the North Stand at Twickenham during the England versus Argentina rugby union international the following week, his home counties tones ringingly endorsing the Great Britain's captain's display. In terms of the overall series, however, the victory came to nought. Australia won the other two tests and retained the Ashes yet again.

The other major rugby league playing nation is, of course, New Zealand, whose competitiveness with Great Britain was a feature of the 1980s. I saw the third test match at Headingley in 1985 just after I had returned from my trekking holiday in Nepal. On that trip, I had had a beer with a New Zealander from another trek, who had impressed upon me how the scrum half, Clayton Friend, would be too skilful for the home side. The third test was the decider, as the series stood at 1–1 at that point.

The series remained at 1–1 at the end of the match. Two abiding memories remain. The first was when an incident near us sparked off a mass brawl in which at least half the players on the pitch became involved. The referee was an Australian, Barry Gomersall, who was one of the first examples of a neutral official being appointed for an international rugby league match. At that time, the response of Australian referees to such incidents seems to have been to let the players get on with their dispute, and for those not involved to continue to play rugby. Accordingly, this was the approach adopted by Gomersall. And so, to the crowd's astonishment – including dad's and mine – the play continued with what could have been little more than 6-a-side for what seemed to be a huge period of time, though in reality it was probably half a minute or so. Fortunately, neither side scored during this time, so further controversy was avoided.

The second incident was right at the end of the game, when Great Britain were trailing 4–6. For some reason, the New Zealand centre Greg Prohm threw a punch in the act of tackling a Great Britain player, a foul seen by all of the crowd around us and, fortunately, also by the touch judge. This gave Great Britain a chance to level the scores with virtually the last kick of the match. The penalty was wide out on the touchline and some distance from the posts and the kick was entrusted to Lee Crooks. As he lined up the kick, Dad and I had the perfect view, our seats being directly in line with the mark and the goal posts. Crooks stroked the ball through the uprights as if it was a training session on an autumn evening. Skill and coolness under pressure: a replay of the Dusty Hare penalty goal that had taken England to victory over Wales at Twickenham in 1980. Several years later, I read that Crooks's effort had won some sort of award for the best rugby league goal kick of the 1980s: a somewhat strange accolade, although one for which we had had the perfect view.

New Zealand's test match with Great Britain at Elland Road four years later, in 1989, also had its drama, though this time right at the beginning of the game rather than at the end. Clayton Friend's successor as New Zealand scrum half was the feisty Gary Freeman who, in the first couple of minutes, was involved in an altercation with the Great Britain full back, Steve Hampson. Hampson settled the dispute by headbutting Freeman in full view of the officials. It was a senseless act of violence for which he was quite rightly dismissed. The crowd around me, after recovering from the initial shock of what they had seen, were immediately aware of the disadvantage that Hampson had placed upon his side. There was no sympathy at all for the player as he left the field.

It is remarkable how often a side that is one player short manages to win a match against the superior numbers, whether in rugby or football. In rugby league, in particular, having one fewer player is a significant handicap, given the speed of the game and the underlying strategy of seeking to create an attacking opportunity in which the defenders are outnumbered. In the event, Great Britain won this match relatively comfortably. I can recall being impressed by the control that Shaun Edwards exerted over the game through his tactical kicking and passing, whilst also struck by New Zealand's general ill discipline. Great Britain covered Hampson's absence by shifting the versatile Paul Loughlin from the centre to full back and moving Andy Goodway from the second row into the centre. Goodway was an immense player: big, strong, fast and skilful and an example of the type of all-round player through whom it was hoped that the Australian hegemony would be challenged. The Great Britain captain, Mike Gregory, was in the same mould.

Although the British game lagged behind the Australians at international level, the early 1980s were years of intense competition between the domestic clubs: this was the period before Wigan's overwhelming dominance. After meeting at Wembley in the Challenge Cup final in 1980, the two Humberside clubs contested the Premiership final in May 1981 and the final of the John Player Cup in January 1982, both at Headingley. The latter was a dour hard-fought game, won narrowly by Hull, which achieved some notoriety at the time for the amateurish way in which the

BBC put together the highlights package to show at the end of the Saturday afternoon *Grandstand*. There was also some controversy attached to the fact that the Hull captain, Charlie Stone, was allowed to go up and receive the trophy at the end of the match, having been sent off during the game itself. Not that the *Grandstand* viewers would have known, as his dismissal was edited out of the highlights.

It is extraordinary how, recalling matches such as this, played so long ago, certain individual incidents and comments are recalled. I think it must have been a typically brisk January day. Nonetheless, though the custom was not as widespread as in modern times, significant numbers of (many younger) supporters on both sides wore only their club colours, without jackets or scarves, no matter how inclement the weather. As my father pulled up at the Shaw Lane traffic lights as we neared the ground, and a couple of Hull KR supporters passed in front of us, he remarked on how foolhardy was this lack of protection against the cold. "They'll end up with arthritic joints, these lads". To this day, I am not exactly sure if dad's prognosis was soundly based in medical terms, but I can hear him giving it as if it were yesterday. The unfortunate irony is that it was his passenger – properly attired for the weather – who would be diagnosed with arthritis in later years.

My father and I sat in the main stand in our capacity as interested neutrals. Dad was probably leaning towards Hull FC slightly, as they fielded two ex-Hunslet players in their ranks: the stylish New Zealand full-back Gary Kemble, and the clever scrum half, Tony Dean. I was interested in the psychology of the Hull side just before the game started. Their massed ranks of supporters had taken over at least half of the South Stand, where the voluble Leeds supporters usually stood. At the end of their pre-match jog around their half of the pitch, the Hull players ran across – as a team – to their supporters to give them an acknowledgement that was clearly the result of some planned choreography. The roar nearly brought down the roof of the stand. It set the tone for the opening exchanges, in which Hull gained the decisive upper hand.

The close and intense rivalry between Hull FC and Hull Kingston Rovers was exemplified in their respective loose forwards. The Rovers had the hard Len Casey, who had played for Bradford Northern, when Dad and I had seen them beat Wakefield Trinity and Widnes on the way to winning the same competition two years earlier. Hull had the enviable choice between Mick Crane and Steve Norton, both of whom were skilful and creative players as well as able to look after themselves in the forward skirmishes. Norton sometimes played in the second row, although Hull also had the luxury of the young Lee Crooks and the goalkicker Sammy Lloyd (who, like Norton, had been recruited from Castleford at considerable expense) already available in that position. In any event, between them, Casey, Crane and Norton represented all that was tough, robust and skilful about British rugby league.

The other sides in the league found it difficult to sustain the challenge to the two Humberside clubs and to Widnes. At around this time, Castleford were a hugely attractive side to watch, with a fast three-quarter line led by the stylish centre, John Joyner, and a pack of forwards led by Barry Johnson. Johnson was always described as a ball-handling prop, which did scant justice to his ability to take on his opposite numbers and release the ball through offloads or passes to send a colleague through a gap. I always thought he was an enjoyable player to watch. Indeed, I thought the side as a whole was exciting, with a huge sense of urgency in the way that they played the game. The comparison I made at the time – this was the early 1980s – was that the Castleford side was the rugby equivalent of the pop group, Madness, who were of course very successful during this period. Under the leadership of Joyner and Johnson – and supported by the likes of the Beardmore twins, Robert and Kevin – Castleford were fast, energetic and skilful. Likewise the pop group, whose music was brisk and vigorous and for whom the movement on the stage of their lead singer, Suggs, was edgy and intense. This is probably the only analogy of this type that I have ever consciously made and, therefore, it appears as a strange insertion in this narrative. Three decades on, I think it was entirely appropriate.

But Hull FC had the edge on Castleford at this time, defeating them in the 1983 Yorkshire Cup final and in three Challenge Cup semi finals in four years, all witnessed by Dad and me at either Headingley or Elland Road. In the 1982 semi final at Headingley, the full-back Gary Kemble scored a majestic try, receiving the ball from a scrum near the half way line and arching his long-striding run over to the far right hand corner. He had skill, pace and courage: essential qualities at this level. A year later, his teammate, James Leuluai, took the ball at full speed and used a combination of direct running and subtle changes in direction to register the game's decisive try: it was not dissimilar to the way that Geoff Shelton had scored for Hunslet against Wigan in the 1965 Challenge Cup final. Kemble and Leuluai were two significant players in the Hull side of this era and, in these matches, were too much even for "classy Cas". The other incident that I can recall clearly was in one of the Headingley games after Malcolm Reilly, a star player in the 1970s who had enhanced his reputation in Australia with the Manly club, had returned to play with Castleford. By this stage, he had chronic knee injuries and he took exception to one of the challenges made by Lloyd, playing for Hull but ex-Castleford. It was not difficult to sense that there were some significant personal rivalries on the pitch to complement the contest between the two teams.

All through this period the Leeds club was unable to lift any of the major silverware: a hugely frustrating period of under-achievement for one of the wealthiest and most glamorous of clubs, probably made all the more galling for their supporters and officials when their ground was used as the neutral venue for so many of these big clashes involving other teams. They came tantalisingly close. In December 1982, Dad and I saw them narrowly beat Widnes in the semi final of the John Player Trophy at Fartown in Huddersfield. We stood on the massive open North Terrace which, although constrained by safety regulations from being used to its original capacity, still provided an open view of the whole pitch. For an earlier generation of spectators – especially in the boom years for rugby league attendances after the Second World War – the highly banked terrace had held up to 20,000 people and, according to Trevor Delaney in *The Grounds of Rugby League*, "the view from the top of the terrace was perhaps the most commanding in the whole of the Rugby League". I thought back to the previous visit that Dad and I had made to the ground – nearly 20 years earlier – when we had sat in the stand on the other side of the pitch and Brian Gabbitas of Hunslet had had his jaw broken in the late off-the-ball assault that ended his career. This time, as we drove home, my mood was lighter: Peter Ustinov was interviewed on an end-of-year sports review programme on the radio and gave a hilarious impression of a cockney supporter of the England football team giving his verdict on that year's World Cup: "We wuz robbed". Leeds could not sustain their form in the final the following month, however. Dad and I saw them beaten at Elland Road by a resurgent Wigan, then recovering from a period in the doldrums. Elland Road was also the venue of Leeds's tussle with Hull Kingston Rovers in the semi final of the 1986 Challenge Cup. On this occasion, even though they built up a healthy lead, they could not sustain their advantage and Hull KR came back to draw the match 24–24 and then go on to win the replay. Leeds were the bridesmaids again.

Apart from these important cup matches, seen during holidays or other trips back to Leeds from London, my regular visit to see Leeds play would be for the Good Friday evening matches at Headingley against Bradford Northern. Dad and I would take our places in the South Stand, both quietly hoping for an away win though generally keeping our counsel. In 1985, the strong Bradford side had their star player at stand off attempting to reach 50 tries for the season: the first time that this feat would have been achieved since the great Billy Boston of Wigan had done it at the end of the 1961–62 season. The player was Ellery Hanley, who had risen from being the raw and exciting talent that we had seen in the early season Yorkshire Cup tie in 1981 to being one of the leading players in the sport. I watched Hanley closely as he ran in his two tries that evening: both featured breaks made by other players and Hanley's ability to recognise that, with appropriately timed and rapid support, he would be in the ideal position to take the scoring pass. At one level, it was relatively simple: Hanley had met the fundamental requirement of supporting the colleague with the ball. On the other hand, it was immensely skilful: Hanley had seen the emerging opportunities before anyone else and arrived to take the ball at precisely the right point at the right time at full speed. At the end of the season, with 55 tries to his name during the campaign, Hanley signed for Wigan and his career path took on an even steeper upward trajectory.

On another Good Friday, again situated in the South Stand amongst the most diehard of Leeds supporters, Dad and I watched as a Leeds player took a high(ish) tackle from one of the Bradford team. The Leeds player went down in a crumpled heap to the sound of the crowd baying for immediate and terminal retribution to be meted out on the offending player by the referee. As the initial uproar died down, I suggested to Dad that the incident had looked worse than it was. Unfortunately, the volume of my voice was a little stronger than I had intended, and the comment was heard by everyone within the immediate radius of five yards or so. On the plus side, I don't think that anyone actually pinpointed who had made the remark and so, as the general reposts and other choice replies were bandied about, they were not directly aimed at Dad or me. One chap standing in front of us and slightly to our right was almost apoplectic at the injustice of my observation. Dad and I stood quietly and, when the furore had died down, I nudged him in the ribs and, nodding in the direction of this supporter, whispered to Dad that it was very risky for him to stand here and wind up these Leeds fans. He was virtually collapsing in silent laughter. In subsequent years, it became a standing rule, which we would agree on the way to the Leeds versus Bradford Northern games: we were not to stand behind any Leeds supporters in the South Stand and murmur provocative comments within their earshot.

By the end of the decade, Leeds had not really progressed. In February 1989, they were matched against Widnes in the quarter final of the Challenge Cup at Headingley and, although Widnes were a strong side, I sensed before the game that there was an aura of Leeds fancying their chances as a result of their home ground advantage and the big-name players in their side. The trouble was that Widnes had some bigger name players, including some high profile signings from rugby union – Jonathan Davies, Martin Offiah, Alan Tait – as well as an uncompromising set of forwards, led by the formidable Kurt Sorensen. Leeds were taken to the cleaners (losing 4–24) to such an extent that, in *John Bentley: My Story*, Leeds's own recruit from the international union code described this particular Widnes team, on their day, as the best side around during his career. Bentley was lined up against Offiah, with whom he had an uncompromisingly competitive battle over many matches. On this occasion, Leeds put a steeplingly high kick towards Offiah and Bentley sprinted down the wing in an attempt to clatter his opponent the split second he caught the ball. Unfortunately for him, he arrived a split second too late. Not very long, but long enough. In what seemed like a single movement, Offiah had caught the ball, turned away from Bentley, and sprinted outside him to set up the counter attack. Offiah did this without a hand being laid on him. It was an amazing piece of action.

Bentley writes interestingly about the general deficiencies of the Leeds team at the end of the 1980s, including the disruptive influence within the changing room of the competing cliques and personalities and the lack of an "enforcer" in the forwards: "They said that Leeds had no heart and when we went behind we would never come back. They were right".

It was at this game that I was pleased to see that the "Memory Lane" feature in the Leeds match programme had lost none of its objectivity in terms of portraying the club's mixed fortunes over the years. No fewer than four matches were reported, of which, surprisingly, four were Leeds victories: 7–2 versus Wigan (1950), 13–9 versus Bramley (1965), 17–12 versus Salford (1975) and 34–2 versus Warrington (1985).

As for Widnes, it was not just the individual skills of their players that were significant. In contrast to Leeds, they looked like – and played like – a team. They knew what they were doing and they did it quickly. If the ball was kicked out over their dead ball line, it would be retrieved and flung back immediately so that play could restart on the 22 line before the Leeds defence could re-group. I was really impressed and, after the match, I thought that Widnes were odds-on favourites to win the Challenge Cup. This was absolutely bound to be their year. They had invested heavily in their star players, but it would all turn out to be worthwhile as they would reach Wembley and secure the high revenues that the cup final appearance always brings. But what did I know? Widnes stuttered badly in the semi final against St Helens, had Richie Eyres sent off for a fairly innocuous tripping incident (though any trip is deemed to bring that mandatory punishment) and were defeated.

For the 1982–83 season, the Hunslet club found a new home: Elland Road. It was far too big for their requirements, of course – the spectators would typically be admitted only to the main stand and one other part of the terracing for most of their matches – but it was a fine pitch on which to play rugby and a regular home venue. My father – now retired, thank God – purchased his season ticket and paid his regular fortnightly visits as Hunslet sought to gain promotion from the second division (successfully in 1983–84 and 1986–87, the latter as champions), avoid immediate relegation (unsuccessfully in 1984–85 and 1987–88) and then resumed their second division rivalries against the likes of Bramley, York and Whitehaven. In the first division, Hunslet did not quite have the firepower to compete with the major sides, who were investing heavily in overseas (i.e. largely Australian and New Zealand) players: I saw Mal Meninga playing in one match during a season he played for St Helens.

In another match, against Castleford, the opposition responded to a late tackle early in the game by the young Hunslet forward Sonny Nickle by rushing in collectively to right the wrong and prompting a mass brawl by most of the players on both sides. The hapless referee, no doubt feeling he had to demonstrate some authority over the situation, sent Nickle from the field. I wondered whether this was a deliberate ploy by Castleford: had they not responded as they did, I suspect the referee would only have penalised Nickle, rather than impose the harsher measure. Hunslet played most of this game with 12 men and lost narrowly. I could see that Nickle was an intimidating player, even at the age of 18. After making a break from the half way line in one match against Leigh, he ignored the supporting players on either side by contemptuously charging straight through the opposition full back and scoring with ease. Together with his young contemporaries, James Lowes and Kelvin Skerrett, he would later become a Great Britain international, although this was after he had moved on from Hunslet. Nickle subsequently showed that his indiscretion against Castleford was no flash in the pan by getting himself sent off whilst playing for a number of other teams during his career.

One of Hunslet's most significant victories during this period – albeit one that I did not see – was that over Hull KR in the first round of the Challenge Cup in February 1983. Hull KR were the cup favourites and riding high in the first division; Hunslet were in the second division and out of the promotion race. Prompted by the skilful veteran John Wolford, Hunslet reached a 12–6 lead which seemed sufficient for the win even when Hull KR scored a try and conversation in the last minute to make it 12–11. Then, amazingly, Hunslet kicked the ball straight out of play at the subsequent kick off, allowing the Hull KR full back, George Fairbairn, an opportunity to kick the winning penalty from the half way line. Fairbairn was a fine goal kicker and the attempt was well within his range. I can only imagine the anxiety that would have been coursing through my father as he watched these events unfold having, in his normal way, made every pass and every tackle during the previous 80 minutes. In the event, Fairbairn missed, and Hunslet progressed to the next round. They were eventually defeated by Castleford at Elland Road in the third round, having again played with courage and skill against one of the first division's leading sides. The linchpin in Hunslet's effort was Wolford, who had had a short period in the top flight with Bradford, but most of whose career had been spent with lowly Bramley, for whom he played over 200 matches. His creative and leadership skills were widely admired – including by Dad and me in this game – and we could see that it was only his lack of extra pace that had prevented his wider exposure with a top club during his distinguished career.

One player who did have pace was the scrum half, Graham King, who loyally stayed with Hunslet throughout the 1980s, when a transfer to a bigger club would certainly have taken him close to a Great Britain place. King was another of dad's favourites and, on my occasional visits to Elland Road, I could see why, as he was invariably outstanding in both defence and attack. His speed resulted in some spectacular tries from long range. On one occasion, he received the ball well behind the scrum and on the retreat in his own 22 and, after beating two or three attempted tackles, hared away to score under the posts at the far end. My father rose from his seat when King broke through the first line of defence and cheered him every step of the way, his voice croaking with excitement. "He's a great little player, that King", Dad said afterwards, as he explained that such thrilling excellence was routinely provided by the player.

The Hunslet club did not have a happy tenancy at Elland Road. Predictably, the Leeds United authorities complained about the damage that the rugby games were doing to the pitch, although this struck me as a very weak line. The playing surface always looked pretty good to me, apart from the obvious areas around the football goalmouths where all the grass had been worn away, which was hardly the fault of the rugby players. In any case, I assume that someone told the football club that the style of football adopted by Leeds United at that time actually involved very little contact with the pitch in the first place, given the length of time that the ball was in the air.

My father began to report back on the lack of co-operation that Hunslet were getting from the football club, including the various little incidents that surrounded Hunslet's occupancy of the ground every other Sunday afternoon: doors being locked, keys unable to be found, no hot water in the baths, and so on. "Dirty tricks", he called them. He was at pains to remind me that it was not as if Leeds United were the landlords, as the football club's financial difficulties had previously meant that they had had to sell the ground to Leeds City Council. At the time, receiving these bulletins down the telephone in London, I wasn't sure whether Dad was picking up the stories from the local gossip in the stand or if they were being reported in the *Yorkshire Evening Post*, though I assumed that the latter source was unlikely, given the close relationship that that newspaper had always had with the football club. Then, years later, Dave Hadfield picked up the subject in his *Up and Over: A Trek Through Rugby League Land*: "Leeds United... always treated the arrangement as a grievous affront and were full of tricks (sic) like turning off the hot water on the Sundays when Hunslet were at home. That's why ... anyone with an ounce of rugby league about them should chuckle unashamedly at Leeds United's current [2004] plight". I don't think my dad ever read Hadfield's book, but there is no doubt that he had already intuitively taken his advice to heart. My father had never been a great supporter of the football club but, as the precipitous decline in Leeds United's playing and financial fortunes took hold from 2001 onwards, the word *schadenfreude* perfectly captured his soured perspective of the club.

The most significant club matches played at this time were, of course, the Challenge Cup finals at Wembley. It was no surprise that the 1982 final was between Hull and Widnes, given the prominence of these two sides in the domestic game at that time. My Hull-supporting college friend and I watched the Widnes winger, Stuart Wright, intercept a pass virtually on his own line and race the length of the pitch to score. Once Wright, a genuine sprinter, was in the clear, there was never any chance of the try being thwarted but, to his credit, the Hull player Dane O'Hara chased him back all the way and prevented him from running around and touching down behind the posts. This meant that the conversion attempt – by Widnes's makeshift kicker, Andy Gregory – was not as straightforward as it otherwise would have been: Gregory duly fluffed the kick.

Another Widnes try was scored after the second row forward, Les Gorley, had committed two tacklers close to the Hull line and then, with great skill, passed the ball around the back of the second man to his Widnes colleague, Eddie Cunningham, who fought his way over the try line. The try is included in BBC Enterprises's *101 Top Rugby League Tries* and is worth looking at again not only for the immensely skilful play by Gorley, combining power and finesse, but also for his reaction after Cunningham had scored. There were no scenes of histrionics or jubilant celebration: Gorley just turned around and started to walk back towards the half way line. The video confirms the strong impression I had drawn at the time. Gorley had recognised that his contribution to the try had been of the highest quality, no doubt, but, in his body language, he was also signalling that it was what he was there to do. It was just a part of his job. In the event, the two points saved by O'Hara were vital, as the match ended in a draw and the teams headed off for a replay at Elland Road.

My father and I went to this game and watched Hull win the trophy for the first time since 1914. We only had terrace tickets, but we found a small section on the Lowfields Road side of the ground where, because of the surrounding brick walls, we would not be crushed by the rest of the huge crowd. It was another titanic affair, which swung Hull's way when stand off David Topliss – whom I had previously enjoyed seeing when he had regularly terrorised Leeds defences when playing for Wakefield Trinity in the Boxing Day matches – bravely squeezed his way over the try line under the posts. At the game's climax, it is worth catching up with Ray French's commentary on this match for the BBC – on the *Century of Rugby League* video – for his quick-witted change of mind during mid sentence. As a Hull player is hauled to the ground, French states: "My word. If any man's won this game for Hull, it's… [suddenly, Lee Crooks picks up the ball near the Widnes line and bursts through a gap to score under the posts]… it's this young man, Lee Crooks".

Hull FC were back at Wembley the following season, this time against Featherstone Rovers, who had reached the final notwithstanding an indifferent league season, which had seen them narrowly avoid relegation to the second division. This was the first Wembley final after the Australian tourists' visit in the autumn of 1982 and I remember thinking that the time was right for some domestic players to push themselves forward as the type of all-round fast and skilful forwards that the likes of Wayne Pearce and Max Krilich had proved to be for Australia. Right on cue, the Featherstone forward David Hobbs took his opportunity, scoring two tries, including what proved to be the match-winner when he rounded the Hull hooker, Keith Bridges – a veteran hooker of the old school – near the try line. I suggested to my college friend – who had now seen Hull play at Wembley three times in four years without winning once – that Featherstone's victory was the biggest cup final upset since Sunderland had beaten Leeds United in the FA Cup final of 1973. I'm not sure that he found this to be much consolation, though he was polite enough not to correct me for forgetting about Southampton's win over Manchester United in 1976 and West Ham United's over Arsenal in 1980. In rugby league terms, however, I was probably right: the *Rothmans Rugby League Yearbook* for 1983–84 described Featherstone's win as the biggest cup final upset for more than

50 years. Two and a half years later, I would be reminded of the occasion – shock result and Hobbs's tries included – when I glanced into the small shop in the Nepalese village of Birethanti on the way back to the campsite after getting the hole in my trousers repaired by the local tailor.

For the 1986 Challenge Cup final – and for many years after that, apart from the 1987 match between Halifax and St Helens – a routine was established in which my father and I would attend the game with my uncle Vic: dad's brother-in-law, the keen Leeds supporter long exiled to Hampshire. Dad would stay with us in Raynes Park and he and I would meet Vic in the late morning in the bar at Waterloo Station after his journey on the fast train up from Bournemouth. We would then head off to Wembley more or less straightaway, usually arriving to see some of the Under 11s curtain-raiser that preceded the main event each year. The urgency was Vic's. He was always keen to do the next thing: to catch the Underground to the ground; to check out which part of the ground we were in; to find a bar for a quiet drink. Dad and I went along with this quite happily. However, we dragged our feet on the suggestion to rush away from the ground at the end of the match. Whilst Vic was always keen to join the long queue in Wembley Way stretching up to the Underground station, Dad and I always preferred to stay in the ground to watch the laps of honour and then generally to hang about until the stadium was virtually empty. There was something about savouring the occasion, including its dying embers, and thinking ahead to the following year's match. We had a final drink at Waterloo before seeing Vic on to his train.

Perhaps not surprisingly, from the perspective of today, the matches tend to blur into each other. But the key incidents are retained in the mind. In 1986, Castleford scored a try when the prop forward Kevin Ward received a pass in his half, pushed off an opponent and then, when two other players attempted to tackle him, freed his arms at just the right time in order to off-load a perfect pass to the supporting Tony Marchant. Marchant then used his winger, David Plange, as the ideal foil to cast doubt in the uncertain Hull KR defence and raced in himself to touch the ball down. It was a classic example of creating and finishing a rugby league try. I looked down on it and appreciated the continuity that Ward's skills had represented, as he followed in the footsteps of Dennis Hartley and Barry Johnson as a Castleford prop forward of the highest quality. I also recognised that the years were passing by: Alan Marchant – father of Tony – had been the Hunslet scrum half in the Challenge Cup final against Wigan in 1965.

Two years later, when Wigan won the trophy, it was for the first time in the long unbroken period of their successes in the Challenge Cup that would last until they were beaten by Salford in the quarter final of the 1996 competition. Their opponents were Halifax, who had won the cup the previous year, but who were now overwhelmed by the all-round excellence of Wigan, prompted by the speed and guile of Andy Gregory and Shaun Edwards at half back. After Wigan had scored one try and Halifax kicked off, Wigan immediately swept back again, the ball being carried by Joe Lydon with two or three supporting players on either side. It was as if a huge and irresistible cherry and white wave was unrelentingly sweeping forwards towards the Halifax try line and, especially, towards the veteran full back, Graeme Eadie. I had first seen Eadie play as a teenager for Australia against Great Britain at Headingley in 1973 and his long years in the game were now taking their toll on his speed around the pitch. However, whilst he was certainly not the fastest full back in the game, he knew how to handle himself. When Ellery Hanley crossed the line under the posts to score the try after Lydon's break, he delayed the act of touching down, perhaps savouring the moment (or show boating, depending on one's interpretation); Eadie clattered into him in a manner that displayed all his frustration with the position his side was in.

Hanley scored under exactly the same posts the following year, when Wigan overwhelmed the St Helens side that had surprisingly defeated Widnes – Davies, Offiah, Sorensen *et al* – in the semi final. This time, Hanley took the ball in a deep position on the left, his power and pace leaving a trail of missed tackles in his wake. I noticed that, when he crossed the line on this occasion, he didn't wait around before touching the ball down. As in the previous year's final, the opposing full back was given a torrid time; the difference on this occasion was that, instead of it being the veteran Eadie, it was the 17-year-old Gary Connolly, who endured a painful introduction to the game at the top flight. Connolly survived the ordeal, of course, later joining Wigan and playing a major role in their successes in the 1990s.

Chapter 17

Edgbaston

By the end of the 1980s, the annual routine involving my father and me (with Vic) for the rugby league Challenge Cup weekend at Wembley had its cricket counterpart in our attendance (without Vic) at the Headingley Test match.

On the first couple of occasions, Dad and I remained on the Western Terrace, using the same vantage point that I had favoured since my first visit to Headingley almost 20 years earlier. In 1984, we decided to go on the Monday (then the fourth day) of the West Indies test: a tactical error, as the game was wrapped up by the tourists by mid afternoon when they won by 8 wickets. Malcolm Marshall polished off the latter half of England's second innings with his customary quick and skidding deliveries, despite the fact that his left wrist was in plaster as a result of the fractured thumb he had received whilst batting. Then, Gordon Greenidge and Desmond Haynes opened the West Indian second innings with a century partnership containing a series of powerful drives and cuts. The former thrashed one Derek Pringle long hop to the offside square boundary with the same contempt that he shown the Yorkshire bowling in the Sunday League game at Bradford a decade earlier. England dropped a couple of easy chances – one of which, by Gower, provoked a predictably derisory reaction on the terrace – but the game was effectively lost by that stage. I thought that they looked ordinary, overpowered psychologically as well as on the scoreboard, and it was no surprise that the West Indies eventually won the series 5–0.

After the game, Dad and I joined the group of interested spectators who had wandered over the outfield into the middle of the square to examine the wicket. There was not much to see, apart from the usual scuff marks around the bowling crease; the pitch itself looked reasonable enough, from our untutored perspective, although Dad and I had a wry smile at each other when some of the other spectators, equally untutored, expressed their expert opinions.

Two years later, on a warm hazy afternoon during the test match against India, I was walking around the ground during the play when a section of the crowd attempted to start up a Mexican Wave, which, at that time, had been newly imported into the country following the World Cup soccer tournament in Mexico. After two or three false alarms, the wave took off and made its uncertain way around the ground, until it ran out of steam in its attempt to pass along the members' enclosure in front of the old pavilion. Such was its novelty at that time that the players – including the England team, who were in the field – stopped to watch. When play resumed, the Indian batsman Mohammed Azharuddin – his concentration clearly broken – was immediately dismissed leg before wicket by John Lever. Dad thought that he had been a little unlucky, but I took a harsher view: he was a test match cricketer, who should have been able to deal with the peripheral distractions and besides, coming from the sub-continent, he should have been used to the noises off. It was immaterial to the outcome, however: India won by 279 runs to clinch the series, with only two England batsmen registering more than 30 in either innings. As one of these was Bill Athey – formerly of the Yorkshire Cricket Federation XI (i.e. Under 19 XI, 1974 vintage) and, indeed, of the Yorkshire CCC first XI – I was quite pleased, as I had invested the princely sum of £10 (at odds of 7 to 1) for him to be the England top scorer in the first innings and his effort of 32 did the trick.

By the time of the 1989 test series against Australia, Dad and I had graduated to the Main Stand, usually called the Football Stand by commentators on account of the rugby pitch that is situated on the other side. We were glad to have done so. It was from about this time that the lager louts took over large sections of the Western Terrace with their rowdiness and drunken boorishness in such a way that Dad and I would have found intolerable had we still remained there. My earliest – and fondest – memory of the Western Terrace is of an open and generous part of the Headingley ground, from which the cricket would be watched by interested and knowledgeable spectators. By the end of the 1980s, this was no longer the case, at least for the test matches. The area was ruled by the sizeable minority who were principally interested in sitting in the sun, drinking all day, insulting the opposition, littering the ground with torn-up newspapers, and leering at any female who had the misfortune to walk around the cycle track in front of them.

If this view is perceived as snobbish, then so be it. Dad and I looked down from the Main Stand – literally and figuratively – and thanked our lucky stars that we had anticipated what would happen and had not inadvertently bought our tickets for that part of the ground. I offered this silent prayer in every year that followed. As I did so, I reflected with complete sympathy on those fathers, who had not been familiar with tribal geography of Headingley, who had brought their sons (or, even worse, daughters) for a day out at the cricket and who had found themselves in the middle of the boisterous rabble in the crowd from hell.

This chronology suggests that, from my perspective as an annual visitor to the Headingley test match, the marked decline in spectator behaviour on the Western Terrace took place in the period between 1986 (the fairly innocuous Mexican wave) and 1989 (widespread drunken rowdiness). However, a broader overview suggests that this was effectively a continuation of the more pervasive trends at test match cricket grounds that had been established well before that, ranging from the increased incidence of pitch invasions by exuberant or drunken spectators through to fighting between rival supporters. In *The Art of Captaincy*, Mike Brearley refers to an example of the latter – at the England versus Pakistan World Cup cricket match at Headingley in 1979 (at which I was not present) – in the context of a much more widespread deterioration in standards: "Cricket crowds are getting more unpleasant... Vocal violence is also worse. Jeering, exultation and abuse have all increased, while humour has decreased. Mindless chanting is commonplace. Crowds... demand instant satisfaction; their criticisms are crudely sexual. A cricket match is often, now, an outlet for a vicious streak". Brearley's book was first published in 1985.

In 1989, Dad and I watched Australia rattle up a total in excess of 600, as Steve Waugh, on his first tour of England, made a big hundred. He was given some improbable support from the fast bowler, Merv Hughes – hitherto known more for his moustache than his batting – who made a half century as the England bowling went to pieces. I watched Waugh carefully as he waited for the short balls outside the off stump that he could cut for four or the overpitched balls on or outside the off stump that he could drive for four. It looked ridiculously easy. It was rather like seeing the new Australian rugby league players in 1982: I knew that I was watching a batsman, with an immaculate and efficient technique and the ability to bat for long periods, who would be a thorn in the England flesh for a long time to come.

When England saved the follow on, there was a collective sigh of relief around the ground – and probably in the England changing room as well – in the expectation that the test match would be saved and that the backfired gamble of bowling first would not be costly. But it made no difference. Australia rattled up some quick second innings runs and then

Terry Alderman bowled England out on the last afternoon. Australia took a 1–0 lead in the series and, in terms of the Ashes, established a supremacy that would not be reversed until 2005. By the time that they had sealed the Headingley win, I was back at work at the economic consultancy in London, where a different set of pressures was beginning to build.

The routine that Dad and I entered into for each year's Headingley test match was to attend on the second and third days. Accordingly, I would apply for tickets for the lower tier of the Main Stand for the Friday and the balcony of the same stand for the Saturday. This arrangement worked well, apart from in 1991 against the West Indies, when we found ourselves at the back of the lower tier and behind the solitary pillar in that part of the ground. When I discovered where we had been placed, I looked at the seats with a mixture of anger and incredulity: it was simply astonishing that Yorkshire CCC had thought it at all reasonable to sell those particular places. Fortunately, the places to one side were not taken up, and we were able to move along the row, so that a serious diplomatic incident with the secretary of the club was narrowly avoided. The lesson was learned for subsequent years, however. When applying for tickets for test matches, I would write "not behind the pillar" boldly on the form which accompanied my cheque, no doubt to the annual bafflement of the administrative assistant in the Yorkshire CCC offices. (Note for future reference: avoid the Lower Tier, Block B2, Row Q, Seats 8 and 9).

1991 was Graham Gooch's match. He batted for over seven hours through bitterly cold weather and interruptions for squally rain to make 154 in the England second innings: a phenomenal effort, given that the next highest score in the innings was 27. Gooch was majestic, as he played the full range of shots – cuts, pulls, on and off drives – all around the wicket. The debutant Mark Ramprakash also made his mark with a spectacular one-handed diving catch at mid wicket to dismiss Phil Simmons. It was a fine effort, which helped to spur an efficient England fielding performance, although I also thought, rather uncharitably perhaps, that there was an element of style over substance. The ball was in the air for some time and it came to the fielder at a reasonably height: it was precisely the sort of chance that an international cricketer should be taking although, admittedly, not all the England fielders of that time would have done so.

It was in this game that the England medium fast bowler, Derek Pringle, received what the *Yorkshire Post* later described as "ironic hero worship" from the section of the crowd that straddled the junction of the Western Terrace and Main Stand. This continued for several overs in the course of which Pringle took the wicket of the late order West Indian batsman, Malcolm Marshall. It was a cricket crowd's equivalent of post-ironic humour, to which my father and I subscribed without hesitation. Pringle was a good enough cricketer to play in 30 test matches for England but, in the local parlance, he was never going to break any bottles: a test match career batting average of 15 and 70 wickets at an expensive 36 runs apiece attest to that. Nonetheless, for several years afterwards, when Dad and I went to the Headingley test, one or other of us would ask if the other remembered "Pringle's Test", each time with a cod-nostalgic emphasis, as if we were two retired brigadiers recalling an Eton-Harrow encounter from the 1920s.

Graham Gooch scored heavily again for England in the following summer's Headingley test match, this time against Pakistan. The opposition's bowling attack was again formidable – Wasim Akram, Waqar Younis, Mushtaq Ahmed – but Gooch rattled up 135 and shared in an opening partnership of 168 with Mike Atherton, which took England to within 30 runs of Pakistan's first innings total. Gooch was an imposing figure at the crease, with his upright stance and an impressive array of strokes that reflected his effective combination of power and timing. On this occasion, his striking physical appearance was established by a bright white batting helmet that was matched by the long billowing sleeves and counterpointed by the darkness of his unshaven beard.[39]

The Pakistanis looked to be disarray, as exemplified when a throw from Wasim Akram from (if memory is correct) the fine leg boundary slipped out of his hand and ended up at the far side of the ground at third man. But one of the great virtues of test match cricket is how quickly one side can wrestle back the upper hand from the other. Waqar Younis and Mushtaq Ahmed led a determined fightback on the Saturday, when England collapsed from 270 for 1 to 320 all out and the last six England batsmen registered exactly two runs off the bat. England held their nerve, however – the demon Pringle took three wickets in Pakistan's second innings in support of the debutant Neil Mallender's five – and duly won the match on the fourth day.

Alec Stewart writes interestingly about this type of batting collapse in *Playing for Keeps*, noting that England succumbed to it on more than one occasion during this 1992 series against Pakistan. He gives the credit to the bowlers – Wasim Akram and Waqar Younis – rather than deficiencies in the batting, noting that it was usually easier to score runs at the top of the batting order when the ball was still shiny, as Gooch and Atherton had done, rather than later in the innings when the "reverse" swing could be effected: "It takes a huge talent to master reverse swing and they were whizzbang bowlers... making the old ball go round corners at speed... the ultimate test for any batsman around that period".

Stewart also notes the degeneration in the atmosphere between the two sides that had occurred by the middle of the series – Headingley was the fourth test match – referring in particular to England's suspicions of ball-tampering by the Pakistanis and Pakistan's dissatisfaction with the home umpires. The same two issues – ball-tampering and umpiring – were to dominate the final stages of the corresponding series in 2006, when the Pakistanis refused to take the field after tea on one of the days at the Oval, thereby forfeiting the match. This occurred despite the fact that "neutral" umpires were now the standard at test match level and that the relationship between the two sides was generally more respectful than it had been 14 years earlier.

The Yorkshire side flattered to deceive in the 1980s, often beginning the season quite promisingly but running out of steam well before the end of the year. They won the John Player Sunday League in 1983, captained by the returning and 51-year-old Ray Illingworth, and beat Northamptonshire in the final of the 1987 Benson and Hedges Cup at Lord's, but that was all. And, even in 1983, the one day success was accompanied by finishing bottom of the county championship, the first time this had occurred in the club's long and proud history. The local reporting of the catalogue of disappointed ambitions was regularly sent on to me by my father. In February 1991, for example, the introduction to a series of articles under the "Yorkshire Cricket in Crisis" banner in the *Yorkshire Post* stated that: "Yorkshire have become a laughing stock with their internal disputes, splinter groups, acrimonious hirings and firings and failure to halt a slide into perhaps terminal decline". This was not journalistic sensationalism. The newspaper's cricket correspondent, the late Robert Mills, was a highly respected chronicler of the county side's fortunes and the description seemed accurate enough from my distant perspective in London. Nonetheless, it made for sad reading, as I thought back to my introduction to the Yorkshire side in the mid 1960s and their successive championship-winning seasons.

In the one-day cup competitions, I watched Yorkshire stumble to two painful semi final defeats in matches against Warwickshire. In 1982, Andrew Carter and I went to the Nat West Trophy match at Edgbaston. Yorkshire battled bravely against Bob Willis's new ball attack, but that they had not registered a big enough total became evident once Warwickshire replied and their openers put on a century opening stand without a great deal of difficulty. When Yorkshire did make the breakthrough, this only brought the West Indian batsman, Alvin Kallicharran, to the crease. He promptly swept his first ball high into the air towards the deep square leg fielder on the boundary to our left. The fielder was Geoff Boycott. Notwithstanding

Boycott's 20 years in the professional game, I promptly decided that he needed some advice and so I stood up from my seat and shouted: "Catch it, Geoff". Geoff did indeed catch the ball, but it was to no avail in the grand scheme of things as Warwickshire ran out easy winners.

Two years, the same sides met in the Benson and Hedges Cup semi final at Headingley. This time, when Warwickshire batted first, Yorkshire did not get Kallicharran out so cheaply. He stroked the ball around the ground, apparently effortlessly, and reached 85 without appearing to exert himself at all. It was just skilful batting – timing and placement – and I had little alternative but to sit back and watch in admiration. Then, Kallicharran risked a second run to an alert Phil Carrick, fielding on the boundary, and ran himself out. Yorkshire made a valiant effort to match Warwickshire's sizeable total, thanks to an elegant innings from Martyn Moxon and a typically belligerent one from David Bairstow. (At this time, I was still playing club cricket, in Surrey, and I decided that I would make a determined effort to add a replication of Moxon's skilful on-drive to my limited repertoire of strokes). Bairstow took his side to the brink of victory before slashing a short ball and being brilliantly caught by Paul Smith on the cover boundary. Yorkshire fell three runs short. For me, the disappointment at their narrow failure was compounded by the fact that the decisive blow had been struck by Smith. I knew that he was a useful cricketer, but – with his long hair, loose billowing shirt and invariably grass-stained flannels – he was also undoubtedly the scruffiest player in the first class game.

For his part, Smith had little reason for any reciprocal affection for Headingley and its spectators. In *Wasted ?,* he describes how "[Bairstow] smashed it as hard as you'll see. Luckily, my young eyes picked the ball out of a backdrop of thousands of coloured t-shirts and I was able to dive forward and the ball stuck in my right palm. It turned the game". Smith then reports how, shortly afterwards, a full can of beer flew past his face as he ran along the boundary to field the ball and later, as he sprinted from the field at the end of the game, several Yorkshire supporters tried to hit him and wrestle him to the ground. Not guilty, I hasten to add, in case more is read into my disappointment at the result than is intended.[40]

The England team also had only modest success in the years between the Ashes winning series of 1981 and 1985. The lack of variation in their bowling was evident against Pakistan at Lord's in 1982, when an attack comprising four similar seam bowlers – Botham, Jackman, Pringle and (Ian) Greig – together with the flat off spin of Eddie Hemmings was despatched for 428 for 8 declared in the visitors' first innings. By contrast, with Imran Khan leading from the front with his aggressive fast bowling, Pakistan had much more zip and menace at their disposal. Robert Gausden and I watched from our seats in the Grandstand as the leg spinner Abdul Qadir proved far too skilful for the England middle order – Botham, Pringle and Greig again, plus the wicket-keeper Bob Taylor. Qadir was a marvellously exciting bowler to watch: mysterious and confident, ripping the ball through his fingers as he waited at the end of his run-up and then bounding up to the wicket and delivering the ball with his high arm action. He was the bowler who flew the flag for match-winning leg spin bowling at test match level – in advance of Mushtaq Ahmed, Anil Kumble and Shane Warne – and, for that, the cricket world is in his lasting debt.

Dad and I made two visits to Lord's Cricket Ground. The first was in June 1986 for a John Player Sunday League match. Yorkshire scraped together an inadequate total, their tail end batsmen unable to resist the temptation to indulge in some fairly ungainly and thoroughly unsuccessful slogging at the experienced Middlesex spinners, John Emburey and Phil Edmonds – the same Phillippe Henri whom I had seen take five Australian wickets on his test debut 11 years earlier – losing their wickets in the process. In bright sunshine, we watched from the Nursery End as the innings disintegrated. Yorkshire lost their last 6 wickets for 11 runs, with Emburey taking four wickets in the last over. Dad looked on in dismay: "This is just embarrassing". At the interval, we walked round to the front of the pavilion and I asked the official at the door whether we could go in. I knew the answer: I could, because I was a Yorkshire member and there was a reciprocal arrangement with other counties that enabled me to visit the pavilion at away fixtures; but Dad couldn't, because he was not a member. As I had been inside the Lord's pavilion before, I said that Dad should take my ticket and have a look around himself, and I would wait outside. Oh no, said the man: that wouldn't be possible because it wasn't dad's ticket. I said that my father had come all the way from Leeds and that it would be a shame if he couldn't go in, because he had always wanted to see the Lord's pavilion. The jobsworth said that Leeds wasn't really that far away. I told him to forget it then, and I ushered Dad away from the entrance as if to go back to the far end of the ground. The plan worked. The officious tosser on the door said that we could go into the pavilion if we were quick about it and didn't tell anyone.

Dad and I were standing in the Long Room, admiring the famous paintings and the other cricketing memorabilia, when the Yorkshire team wandered through on their way out on to the field, leaving their stud marks amongst the thousands of others in the covering on the floor. When the Middlesex batsmen appeared, I noticed the intense look of concentration in the eyes of Wilf Slack. He stared ahead, clearly unaware of the people milling around him in the room as he left to go out to bat. He walked past me without knowing that I was there, absolutely focused on the job in hand.[41] And it worked: Slack reached an unbeaten century as Middlesex easily knocked off the runs to win by nine wickets. Having ignored the doorman's request to make a quick visit, Dad and I were still in the Long Room when Slack was applauded through on his return by the Middlesex and MCC members. We clapped too, recognising a good cricketer who had performed in a highly professional way. Less than three years later, as I was walking to Blackfriars station on my way home from work one winter's evening, I noticed the striking headline on the billboard for that day's *Evening Standard*. I purchased the newspaper and read that Wilf Slack had collapsed and died at the age of 34.

Our second visit to Lord's was for the Benson and Hedges Cup final of 1987: Yorkshire versus Northamptonshire. Just over three months after the Yorkshire rugby union side had defeated Middlesex at Twickenham to win their county championship, the cricketers had reached their first Lord's final for a one-day competition since 1972. It was a warm day and Dad and I took our places in the packed Mound Stand, two rows back from the boundary edge.

Yorkshire started well. Paul Jarvis was too quick for the Northamptonshire captain, Geoff Cook, who spooned a catch to short leg. Jarvis also accounted for the dangerous Allan Lamb, who edged a wide delivery through to David Bairstow behind the stumps: Dad was impressed that Lamb walked off without waiting for the umpire to raise his finger. Then, the equally dangerous Wayne Larkins mistimed a shot and sent the ball high into the air in our direction. The Yorkshire captain, Phil Carrick, took a smart catch running back towards us from his mid off position. It was not an easy dismissal to make, but Carrick, usually not the most athletic of fielders, judged it perfectly: it was if he was back in the Bradford League at Farsley or Pudsey St. Lawrence. After he claimed the ball, he gave a little punch of success towards the Yorkshire supporters in our section of the ground and smiled widely. We roared back in appreciation. Afterwards came the Northamptonshire fightback, cheered equally by their band of supporters on the far side of the ground and led by the determined David Capel, who scored 97 out of the 244 for 7 that his side had made when the innings closed.

The Yorkshire openers were Martyn Moxon and Ashley Metcalfe, both talented players. After a short time, Yorkshire had reached 18 for no wicket and Moxon had scored all 18. A broad Yorkshire accent, located somewhere behind me, asked a couple of general questions: "What's up with Ashley? Isn't he bothering today?" Metcalfe might have heard him. In no time at all, he had caught Moxon up, and the pair advanced the

Yorkshire score towards the 100 mark. Then, Nick Cook bowled Moxon with the perfect left arm spin delivery, beating the outside edge of his bat, before calmly receiving the congratulations of one of his team mates with a low-key shake of the hand. When Metcalfe was out shortly afterwards and the succeeding top order batsmen were also dismissed relatively cheaply, it appeared that the game might be slipping away. Enter Jim Love – formerly of the Leeds Schools Under 14 XI and the England one-day international side – who proceeded to play his most significant innings for the county in a career of over a decade. By the time the final delivery was due to be bowled, the scores were level, but Yorkshire were ahead on points as they had only lost six wickets to Northamptonshire's seven. Northamptonshire's West Indian fast bowler Winston Davis steamed in and bowled a good length delivery on Love's middle stump. He blocked it with a hurried defensive stroke and, with both arms, raised his bat in the air in triumph. Yorkshire had won by virtue of losing fewer wickets when the final scores were level.

As Phil Carrick received the trophy on the pavilion balcony, the chant of "Yorkshire, Yorkshire" rose up from the hundreds of success-starved supporters who had gathered on the outfield below. Dad and I were amongst them. It was a rare occasion for us to be so heavily involved as part of the massed ranks of the partisans, rather than objectively viewing the winning side's triumphal celebrations as interested neutrals. I thought back to the scene at Headingley 10 years earlier, when Geoff Boycott had appeared on the Headingley balcony after having scored his hundredth century in the 1977 test match against Australia and the same chant had rung around the ground.

The euphoria surrounding Yorkshire's long-awaited success was still evident the following month, when the side played Lancashire in a Sunday match in what was then called the Refuge Assurance League, the John Player sponsorship having finished the previous year. This was a family outing to Scarborough for my parents and me and my fiancée, Angela.

The ground was full on a warm afternoon. But it was a strange day, and not entirely a pleasant experience. We took our places on the pavilion side of the ground and to the right of the sightscreen. Somewhere behind us, within unfortunate earshot, was a small group of young men – late teens and early twenties, probably – who were clearly of the Western Terrace tendency on test match days. They were not large in numbers but, as the combination of sun and beer took hold, their interventions became louder and courser. I sensed that they were looking for trouble, and not only with any of their Roses counterparts who might have been encountered. At one point, they were arguing with a soft faced youth, who announced, to jeering from the group, that he came from Driffield in East Yorkshire. Some time later, I saw the same youth standing by himself, some distance away to my right, with blood trickling from his nose.

My other memories of the day are also principally of other non-playing incidents. Before the match, the Lancashire side gathered in the outfield near to us to undertake some loosening and stretching exercises. One of them was the 46 year-old Jack Simmons – nicknamed "Flat Jack" because of his flightless (and generally parsimonious) style of off-spin bowling – who had been a fairly rotund player even when he was younger and fitter, but who was now clearly not impressed with his coach's exhortations to lean over and touch his toes. The spectators near us saw what was happening and began to give the player some ironic encouragement. My father looked across at Simmons's efforts and remarked, with a wry amusement, on his less than full commitment to his side's fitness regime. But I admired Simmons's longevity. After entering county cricket at a relatively advanced age, in his late twenties, he had been a key figure in Lancashire's consistent one day success for the better part of two decades, and Lancashire were using him wisely as a mentor as another generation of their younger players came through into the first eleven.

Later, when Yorkshire were batting, one of Simmons's colleagues took up a fielding position on the boundary near to us. At one point, the fielder decided to discard one of his sweaters, which he left draping across a small boundary board on which some instruction to the crowd was given: that we should not walk behind the bowler's arm, or run on to the outfield, or such like. He resumed his position facing the play in the expectation – I assume – that the Lancashire twelfth man would come round the boundary and take the sweater back inside the pavilion. However, I noticed that the sweater remained on the board for some time. Then, one of the Yorkshire batsmen hit a huge six into the crowd on the far side of the ground. The supporters around us cheered as we followed the ball against the background of skyline and buildings until it landed safely in the crowd on the terracing near to the entrance to the ground. When the fielder returned to his position on the boundary edge near to us, he realised that something was wrong. His sweater was not there, and nor had the twelfth man been to collect it. I could see his anxiety at the wrath that he knew he would incur from his senior colleagues and management: the county cricket sweater is a valued item, not to be carelessly lost. I also reluctantly recognised the *chutzpah* of the opportunist thief, whoever it was, who had picked his (or her) moment to perfection: that is, precisely when everyone's gaze (including the fielder's) was on the cricket ball's flight over to the far side of the field.

Lancashire won a high-scoring match, the winning boundary being struck with two balls to spare. The average scoring rate during the afternoon was over six runs per over, as the batsmen on both sides took advantage of a perfect pitch and a fast outfield. The one bowler to shine was Simmons, who delivered his full complement of eight overs to take 3 wickets for 28 runs. Flat Jack: experienced, efficient and professional and – on this occasion – the difference between the two sides.

For Angela, it was all a rather strange experience. She had never been to a county cricket match before and, not surprisingly, was disconcerted by the behaviour of the local beer drinkers. More than that, however, she found it frustratingly difficult to follow the path of the ball. It made me realise how much I took for granted in terms of seeing the ball go where I expected it to go. In the vast majority of cases, when a batsman played a particular shot, I could tell whereabouts in the ground the ball would be likely to go – in which direction and how far – by the nature of the shot, especially the positioning of the batsman's feet and of his arms and body, and by my assessment of whether the ball had been "middled". Angela did not have that knowledge base and her enjoyment of the game was severely curtailed by her only rarely seeing where the ball had been hit.

In contrast to the one day matches, there was no rowdyism for the county championship games. My visits to these were rare, although I did accompany Dad to see a strong Middlesex side in 1990, with the West Indian test player Desmond Haynes having scored a century, take control of a game at Headingley. When Yorkshire were batting, most of the noise seemed to be on the pitch, with several Middlesex fielders showing their approval every time the spinner, Phil Tuffnell, landed a ball on a length by applauding loudly and shouting encouragement. "Well bowled, Cat". "Great bowling, Cat". "I like it, Cat". Their voices carried across from the middle of square over to the scattering of spectators around us. And they did so after virtually every delivery. "Great bowling, Cat". "Well bowled, Cat". I had no idea what all this was doing for the concentration of the Yorkshire batsmen, but it certainly annoyed us. "Why don't they shut up?", my dad asked. I replied that I assumed that was how the first class game was played these days. Perhaps it had always been played like that, and I had never noticed.

One of the Yorkshire bowlers was new to me, though I had seen his name in the papers after he had made his county debut at the end of the previous season. He charged up to bowl as quickly as he could, aided by an energetic action and the enthusiasm of youth. And he did this for a long period, notwithstanding the stranglehold that the Middlesex batsmen had taken on the match. After he had delivered the ball, the bowler strode purposefully back to his mark, at the end of a straight run, and charged up to the wicket to try again. He was rewarded with four wickets.

My father was a far more frequent visitor to Headingley than I was at this time. After the trauma of his early retirement – and the shattering blow to his confidence that his bullying employer had given – my mother had ensured that he did not remain in the house all day, but that he had gone out to watch his sport: rugby in the winter, cricket in the summer. Watching Yorkshire play at Headingley was part of that recuperative process, and I was grateful that these regular opportunities presented themselves. My father attended the matches whenever he could, particularly at the beginning of the cricket season when the Headingley fixtures came one after another, dutifully collecting the scorecards and match programmes to add to the collection in the large cardboard box in my old bedroom at home. He had seen this new player before, of course. "He's a promising lad, that Darren Gough."

The Fifth Age

The Detached Traditionalist

Relocation to a new city (and country) provides a fresh set of local sporting cultures to explore, although the (now) traditional highlights of the spectating year also remain on the schedule. The conservatism of middle age is revealed, as I note the changing nature of the sports themselves.

Chapter 18

Murrayfield

In April 1992, I became a civil servant and took up a post in the Scottish Office, the pre-devolution department of the UK Government in Scotland. This move was not without its risks: I was in my late thirties and had no real connection with Scotland, apart from a long deceased grandmother, Catherine Kerr McBride from Lanarkshire. Although most of the Office's staff were located in Edinburgh, with many later moving down to Leith, I was based in Glasgow. Angela and I – by now married with a young son and with another child due in the autumn – moved to Milngavie, seven miles to the north of the city centre. I remained in Glasgow after the establishment of the Scottish Executive as the devolved system of government in 1999.

My career change enabled me to play a (very) small part in the historic shift in the governance of Scotland which devolution has represented, initially with the Labour-Liberal Democrat coalition and then, from 2007, with the minority Scottish National Party administration, until my early retirement in 2011. As a civil servant, I was within the system: a component of the new arrangements. At the same time, as an Englishman in Scotland, I have also been able to undertake my favoured role as detached observer. In the narrow terms of the Scottish Office and Scottish Executive/Scottish Government, it would probably be more accurate to describe the latter function as a semi-detached one, as I have been able to see and reflect on the progress and the mistakes that Ministers and administrators have made in the new governmental arrangements. However, more broadly, I have also played the part of the foreigner in a strange land, as I attempted to identify those aspects of Scottish life which were no different to those that I had experienced in Yorkshire or Cambridge or London and to separate these from the differences in lifestyle and culture that can be attributed to the history or religion (or both) of Scotland. The latter is a fascinating area of analysis which, of course, extends far beyond the terms of reference I have set myself in this volume: a good reference point is Murray Watson's *Being English in Scotland*, published in 2003.

Milngavie is the home of the West of Scotland Football Club. The name is instructive. It is a rugby union club, of course, but its formation dates from 1865: that is, before the establishment of the Scottish Rugby Union.[42] It is a proud club and a long list of international players have worn its colours. For my generation, the fact that the list includes Sandy Carmichael and Gordon Brown of Scotland and the British Lions – distinguished warriors in New Zealand and South Africa in the 1970s – is of some significance. I immediately felt at home at the ground itself, at Burnbrae, which was surrounded by open space in the form of the other pitches, the large car park behind the wooden stand and, behind the row of trees along one touchline, the local suburban railway track with its half hourly service into Glasgow. The ground sloped down away from the stand, from one touchline to the other, and, in that respect, reminded me of the Roundhay club's ground in Leeds.

Just down the road from the West of Scotland clubhouse, near a roundabout and opposite a large DIY store, is a short section of the restored Antonine Wall. This was the defensive line, stretching 37 miles across central Scotland, begun in AD 142 during the reign of the Roman emperor Antonius Pius. The wall protected a military road which ran behind it to the Roman fort in nearby Bearsden. The Antonine Wall did not function for long, being abandoned after twenty years, when the Romans withdrew from Scotland and pulled the frontier back down to the more substantial barrier of Hadrian's Wall. But the Wall's place in British history is guaranteed. I was – and remain – immensely attracted to the idea that, in addition to having a famous rugby club located within a short walk of our new home, we were resident in a place that had been the northernmost frontier of the Roman Empire. Put simply and in a modern context, the Romans got as far as HomeBase.

West of Scotland had a good fixture list including, as might have been expected, the clubs that constituted the traditional core of Scottish rugby – that is, the sides that had initially been the old boys' clubs of the major public schools (Heriot's FP, Watsonians, Stewart's Melville FP) and the hard-edged sides from the Borders towns (Gala, Hawick, Jed-Forest) – as well as rivals in the west looking at the next fixture as the opportunity to secure local bragging rights (Glasgow Academicals, Glasgow High-Kelvinside, Clarkston). For me, these were (mostly) glamorous names and, after an initial outing to see West beat Dundee HSFP (who included the young Andy Nicol, a later captain of Scotland, at scrum half) 22–12 at the beginning of the 1992–93 season, I looked forward to the fortnightly visits of these teams to Burnbrae. It was immediately clear that although, in between the division two fixtures in the McEwan's League, many of these games had a "friendly" status, there was no shortage of aggression on the pitch. In that first season, whilst watching West play Stewart's Melville FP from the lower touchline, I saw the former British Lions captain, Finlay Calder, take exception to something done after a kick off to one of his teammates on the far side of the ground, causing him to attack the West hooker Steve Blair with some venom. It took a considerable effort on the part of both colleagues and opponents to separate Calder from his target.

Blair was one of a group of experienced club – and, in some cases, district – players whom West of Scotland could call on, including Dave Barrett at stand off and John Lonerghan in the back row. The tradition at West seemed to be to supplement these players with a regular supply of younger players recruited from the rugby playing schools in the west as well as with some imports from outside the area (and, indeed, outside the country). After the club had duly been promoted in my first season, Blair himself was to lose his first team place at the beginning of the 1994–95, in his case to a promising teenager hooker. The latter impressed more or less from the outset, apparently able to handle the physical challenges of the front row and possessing an impressive turn of speed, and West's tactic of launching their new tyro from a line out peel to run at the opposing stand off began to bear fruit very quickly. Gordon Bulloch dutifully served his apprenticeship at the West of Scotland club, playing for four seasons before graduating to the newly formed professional Glasgow team and then going on to represent Scotland and the British Lions. His younger brother Alan was not a bad player either: a strong centre with excellent basic skills, he also became a Scottish international.

By the 1997–98 season, West of Scotland were close to being the leading club side in Scotland alongside the formidable Melrose and Watsonians. However, within a very short period of time, the bulk of this team had moved elsewhere, as the newly established professional era saw several players hoovered up by the Glasgow district side or go on to other clubs. When I took my father to Burnbrae in October 1998 to watch the ambitious Glasgow Hawks club, the visitors swept West of Scotland away by 50 points. The following season, in which the glossy match programme was replaced by a much less impressive paper version – an indicator which I have often found to be a useful proxy for a club's fortunes on the pitch – West of Scotland were relegated back down into the second division. The club was a first class example, therefore, of a casualty of the professional era in Scottish rugby. It was unable (or unwilling) to sustain a top class side, with the result that the level of success on the field rapidly declined and, within the Premiership framework of Scottish club rugby, the club swiftly fell through the ranks. The good young players such as Andrew Henderson – a brave and skilful centre, later also to represent Scotland – served far shorter apprenticeships than had the Bullochs before moving on to a higher grade. At the end of the 2001–02 season, the club was relegated to the third division, where it remained at the end of 2005–06.

By that time, my support had ebbed away. This was only partly because of the deterioration in West of Scotland's performances and results. The reduction in my interest was probably also the reflection of a more general malaise affecting the diminished status of club rugby in Scotland, which had meant, critically, that the top level players were no longer engaged at Burnbrae. In the early years, Finlay Calder had been followed, at various times, by such as Gavin Hastings, Scott Hastings, John Jeffrey, Sean Lineen, Craig Chalmers, Brian Redpath and the young Scott Murray and Simon Taylor. With the professional era, a Saturday afternoon at Burnbrae no longer had the attraction that it once had had. I was genuinely sorry about that – and I hoped that, in time, the position would be reversed – but, in essence, along with thousands of other followers of Scottish club rugby, I voted with my feet. That we did not all move across to follow the district/professional sides in the same numbers has been a longstanding issue that the Scottish Rugby Union has not resolved.

In the meantime, at Burnbrae, the old wooden stand first of all began to fall down and then was burned down, being replaced by a new modern stand giving an excellent and uninterrupted view across the whole pitch. Unfortunately for the West of Scotland stalwarts, who had raised the finances and overseen its construction, the view from the stand was of third division Scottish club rugby. The doldrums would not last for ever, fortunately.

Of all the sports spectating experiences I have had in Scotland, the most revealing was the rugby union World Cup Sevens tournament held at Murrayfield in April 1993. My parents were visiting us for the weekend, and Dad and I attended the finals of the three-day competition on a wet Sunday.

I had followed the preparations for the tournament fairly half-heartedly in the newspapers. The general consensus was that England had not particularly given the competition much thought either and that this had been reflected in the squad they had chosen. Even allowing for the absence of the British Lions contingent about to head off to New Zealand, the squad contained very little international experience. The captain was the Harlequins winger, Andrew Harriman, who had played one international against Australia five years earlier, but was – so the reports implied – essentially a good club player. He was supported by some promising younger talent. But it was a makeshift squad, as reflected in the inclusion of one of the second XV players from the Wasps club.

The reality was somewhat different. Harriman was an outstanding sevens player, with an electrifying turn of pace. In the forwards, Chris Sheasby was also highly adapt at the particular skills and techniques that the abbreviated form of the game requires. The younger players included Tim Rodber and Nick Beal, both future British Lions. And the junior player from Wasps was the 21 year-old Lawrence Dallaglio.

England won the tournament, after playing New Zealand, South Africa and Australia at the quarter final group stage and then defeating Fiji and Australia, respectively, in the semi-final and final. Against Fiji, the match turned on an incredibly brave tackle by the Wakefield scrum half, Dave Scully, on one of rampaging opposition forwards, Mesake Rasari, which freed up the ball and allowed a try to be created for Harriman. The saddest sight in that match was the pathetic attempt – a failure, fortunately – by one of the Fijians to trip up Dallaglio from behind as he sprinted away down the touchline to set up another try for Harriman. In the final, the tone was set in the first minute when, under considerable pressure, England skilfully worked the ball away from a dangerous position inside their own 22 and moved it along the line to allow Harriman an early opportunity to take on David Campese on the outside; Campese was left standing, as Harriman rounded him with ease and sprinted away into the distance. England pulled away to 21–0, with tries from the hugely impressive Dallaglio and Rodber, the former after a galloping run from Sheasby and the latter after Beal had created space in the middle of the field and released Rodber to charge in from the half-way line. Australia came back with three tries of their own, their cause aided by a series of penalty decisions in their favour, but England held on to win 21–17. For the record, the England coach was Les Cusworth – ex Normanton Grammar School, against whom I had played for the Roundhay School first XV in 1971 – who had been a renowned sevens player in his schooldays and who had subsequently progressed via the Wakefield club to Leicester and England.

My father and I were thrilled at the England win. It just seemed so typically English. The squad had apparently been under-resourced and inadequate; they had turned up at Murrayfield to do their best, subject to the normal constraints faced by the gifted amateur, who does not wish to be seen to be trying too hard and is apparently indifferent to the outcome; and they had won the tournament. I wondered afterwards if, perhaps, the press reports had been part of a grand conspiracy designed to take their rivals' eyes off the ball, but I quickly ruled this out. The truth was that England knew exactly what they were doing. They were well led, both on and off the pitch. Their players were confident and ambitious, with the ideal combination of pace, power and skill for this demanding version of the game. And, as exemplified by Scully's tackle, they had the courage and mutual support to produce the overall victory.

The finals of the tournament were interesting, however, not only for the events on the pitch – hugely enjoyable though these were – but for the experience that Dad and I had over the course of the day, as we looked around the stadium from our seats in the middle of the South Stand. Looked and listened. Whilst there was a sizeable minority of England supporters, the majority of the crowd had come to support the other sides taking part on the day and, of these supporters, the majority in turn was obviously Scottish. The stance that most of this element of the crowd decided to take was, unequivocally, to support whichever side England was playing. As Dad and I attempted to read the signals behind all this, I realised that this was not just a friendly attempt to wind up the England supporters or the England team. Simple observation of the behaviour and reactions of many in the crowd around us confirmed that it was a genuine – and, in some cases, passionate – desire to see England beaten. New Zealand, South Africa, Fiji, Australia: it did not matter which side it was; they were simply the conduit through which the Scottish supporters wished to see the England colours lowered.

By the time the tournament was being played, I had lived in Scotland for a year and I more or less knew what to expect. It was an experience that was to be regularly repeated in later years. I watched England play Italy in the final qualifying match for the 1998 soccer World Cup finals in a pub in Milngavie, in which the whole of the crowded bar was cheering for Italy, apart from a small knot of Rangers supporters situated in one corner. By the time of the 2002 World Cup, many of the citizens of Glasgow had graduated to wearing Argentine shirts or flying the Argentine flag from the windows of their homes in order to demonstrate where their preference for the winner in a vital group quantifying match might lie. In advance of the next tournament, four years later, no less a public figure than the First Minister of Scotland, Jack McConnell, stated that he would be supporting Trinidad and Tobago, rather than England, in the group stage on the grounds that a number of their players turned out for Scottish clubs.[43] I judged that McConnell's intervention was some sort of attempt to outflank the Scottish National Party but, frankly, it came across to me as simply mean-spirited.

I also thought that it was politically ill-advised, given that about 9 per cent of the population of Scotland – and, presumably, a similar proportion of the electorate – is English. If the First Minister's preference was interpreted as "Anyone but England" to win the World Cup in 2006, he could not have been surprised when, in the election for the Scottish Parliament in 2007, at least part of the electorate voted on the basis of "Anyone but Jack".

At the time of the World Cup Sevens in 1993, however, my father was undoubtedly shocked by the reaction of the Murrayfield crowd. This was not what he had expected. His late mother had been Scottish and, whenever the rugby internationals had been on television, he had always supported the Scottish side in whichever match they were playing, if the opponents were not England. I can distinctly remember one occasion, when I was a boy and the Camberabero brothers were playing for France against Scotland in a match we were watching on our black and white set, he chastised me firmly for saying that I wanted France to win.

It is a free country, of course. The Scottish rugby supporter – and the First Minister for that matter – can cheer on any side he or she wishes. And I will not attempt to explain the psychology of the crowd's shifting allegiances at Murrayfield that day. History and politics are not a bad place to start, however. At the time of the 1993 tournament, Mrs Thatcher was no longer Prime Minister, but the Conservatives were still in office at Westminster, and the devolution of government to a Scottish Parliament – let alone full independence – seemed a long way away. Not that I think having a devolved system at that stage would have made any difference to the collective mindset of that part of the Murrayfield crowd.

The distinguished Scottish politician Jim Sillars – formerly of Labour, before joining the Scottish National Party – has famously referred to a high proportion of his countrymen as being "ninety minute nationalists". I think there was a great deal of that perspective of the world present at Murrayfield on this occasion: the view that anything representing England was to be despised and put down, whilst knowing that the cross on the ballot paper at the next election would still safely find its way against the name of one of the unionist party candidates. But I also thought it was pathetic. Not pathetic in the way that the Fijian's vain attempt to trip the disappearing Dallaglio had been, but pathetic in the sense that the inhabitants of a great and proud country should feel obliged to demonstrate their feelings of inferiority – for it is difficult to see what else they could have been – in such a way.

Nearly two decades on – and with the Scottish Parliament now firmly and irrevocably established – the underlying mindset of the Scottish towards the sporting fortunes of their southern neighbour does not seem to have changed a great deal. Of course, I fully recognise that, in many respects, the

English do not do themselves any favours. In particular, the Scottish sports follower has a noticeably paranoid perspective on the repeated references by the English media to the 1966 World Cup win, whenever England either qualify or make progress in the finals of a major soccer competition. I am led to believe that, when John Motson was commentating on an England international football match, there was an active market in spread betting on how long it would take him to refer to the famous Wembley victory; in one of the Euro 2004 matches, it was less than two minutes before he had mentioned that England were wearing red shirts, the same as Bobby Moore and his team had worn on that historic occasion. The usual form of retaliation for the Scottish is to refer to their side's victory over England in the Home International championship in April 1967, with its stock footage of the late Jim Baxter playing "keepy uppy". For some reason, the fact that England, in those pre-substitute days, ended up with nine fit players, with Jack Charlton hobbling around at centre forward and Geoff Hurst playing as a makeshift centre half, is curiously overlooked.

All that is relatively harmless. I was more concerned about the front page of a *Herald* sports section on the Monday after one of the Six Nations weekends in the 2005 competition. Scotland had suffered a heavy defeat at home to Ireland and the banner headline read: "Heaven help us.... quickly". There was the customary hand-ringing by the now familiar (to me) rugby correspondents about the side's deficiencies in the match ("a hopeless Scottish performance"), the future of the coaching staff and the general state of Scottish rugby. England also lost that weekend, 17–18 to France. On the right hand side of the page, therefore, was a summary of the latter game under the heading: "But it's not all bad news". No doubt, the editorial staff of the Glasgow-based newspaper, which claims to provide a serious record and analysis of contemporary affairs, thought this was a clever way to make a joke for its readership (or, at least, the non-English part of it). When I saw the headline, however, I immediately thought back to the World Cup Sevens afternoon at Murrayfield almost 12 years earlier. I thought it was pathetic, again, and continued evidence that the so-called "Scottish cringe" remained alive and kicking. In this context, the First Minister's comments in advance of the 2006 football World Cup were not really a surprise.

Apart from one game against England, my attendance at Murrayfield for the rugby union internationals at fifteen a side has been from the objective perspective of the neutral observer. In 1993, my college friend, Llyr James, came up from Wales with a large group of his friends and acquaintances to watch their side lose 20–0. We again sat in the South Stand, where it was probably the coldest I have ever been at a major sports stadium. Murrayfield was in the process of being rebuilt, and the gaps in the construction allowed the strong gusts of the northerly winds to surge around about us. To make matters worse for Llyr, Wales were lucky to get nil. They were outplayed and out-thought by Scotland, for whom Craig Chalmers, playing at stand off, gave an immaculate display of kicking to repeatedly drive his forwards huge distances down the field; by contrast, his opposite number, Neil Jenkins, struggled to master the blustery conditions.

In the same season, Scotland also defeated a disappointing Ireland side at Murrayfield, again viewed by me from my usual vantage point in the South Stand. After that, until 2006, it was a question of Scotland being regularly beaten – in many cases, heavily beaten – by a series of superior visiting teams. In November 1994, it was South Africa, for whom the speed and strength of Jost Van der Westhuizen at scrum half was a dominant feature, as he scored two of the tourist's five tries. The wisdom of hindsight confirms that South Africa were carefully building the platform – based around the excellence of Van der Westhuizen, Mark Andrews in the second row and Francois Pienaar as captain – that would take them to World Cup success the following year. (After the Scotland-South Africa match, I caught a train down to Leeds to watch the following day's Great Britain versus Australia rugby league international: another victory for the touring side).

In 1998, it was both France and England in the Five Nations Championship. France were an excellent side, noticeably quick at clearing the ball away from the rucks through their excellent half backs Philippe Carbonneau and Thomas Castaignede and creating the space for Olivier Magne and the Livremont brothers in the back row to run at the outside backs in the Scottish defensive line. Magne, in particular, would not have looked out of place on the rugby league pitch, fulfilling this role in the way that modern second row forwards often do in the league code.

England were also impressive, apart from in the last five minutes when, with a commanding lead, they took their foot off the gas and allowed a couple of consolation Scottish tries. For this match, their captain was Lawrence Dallaglio, who had progressed from the Wasps second XV to the leadership of his country and whose entry on to the Murrayfield pitch before the start of the match – a majestic sprint at full speed, closely followed by the rest of his team – signalled England's intentions for the afternoon. Paul Grayson played a cool and controlled game at stand off, marshalling his attacking colleagues and kicking his goals. The effect of those two late tries was curious, however. It enabled the Scottish team to leave the field on a relative high, having been emphatically behind on the scoreboard beforehand, and it certainly raised the spirits of the Scottish supporters. By contrast, I was left with a feeling of anti-climax – yet again, after watching an England rugby union performance – and, looking at the cheery faces around me, I had to remind myself which side had actually won the game by 34–20.

And so on for Scotland's games against the other major rugby nations. My father and I saw a valiant display against South Africa in one of the group matches of the 1999 rugby union World Cup: a Scottish effort that was badly disrupted when the newly imported centre, John Leslie, had to leave the field through injury. Although losing this match, Scotland did qualify for the quarter finals of the competition, at which point they were beaten, though not disgraced, by New Zealand on a foul Edinburgh afternoon. I was grateful that I watched this game in the warmth and comfort of my living room. New Zealand opened up a lead in the first half, which they were never in any real danger of losing, although Scotland had marginally the better of the scores after half time. Unfortunately, this prompted one of those rugby clichés that I really detest: the claim by a Scottish player that, although they had been beaten overall, they had "won the second half". I have always thought this line to be risible. The idea is to score the most points over minutes 1–80, not just minutes 41–80.

By the end of 2004, the danger signs for the Scottish international side were clear. A friend in Milngavie, Tim Black, invited me to the match against Australia, which was played at Hampden Park. It was my first visit to the famous stadium, which is much changed of course from the days when it accommodated crowds of over 130,000 for the major soccer matches. However, although its capacity has now been considerably reduced – 52,000 – there were swathes of empty seats all around the ground. The attendance figure was not helped by the fact that Celtic were playing Rangers on the same day, with a lunchtime kick off, a few miles across the city, although I did doubt whether many spectators at either match would also have attended the other event had they been able to do so. Tim, a Celtic follower, did not enter Hampden in the best of spirits, as his side were 0–2 down and had had two men sent off by the time the rugby kicked off.

Australia won comfortably enough, although there was a decisive moment just before half time, when the flanker George Smith made a break down the middle of the field and was tackled from behind. The ball seemed to go yards forward as he attempted to pass, but the referee did not stop play and, moments later, Australia crossed the line for a try. The later explanation given by the referee, the Irishman Alan Lewis, was that Smith had attempted to pass the ball backwards and it had rebounded forwards off his shoulder and was therefore not an infringement, and the action replays on the television suggested that this might well have been the case. Lewis's problems were twofold. First, this is a poor law and analogous to that which prevailed briefly in the 1970s, when play was allowed to continue after a tackled player had dropped the ball and it had gone forward. In addition, I suspect that very few people in the crowd were aware of it in the first place: I know that I wasn't. As a result, not surprisingly, the referee was given a widespread and vociferous condemnation as he left the pitch at half time. My own particular grievance came just after this, when it took 20 minutes for me to be served with two coffees at the food and drink counter in the main stand. The urgent need for Tim and me to satisfy our needs for a caffeine intake, combined with the pedestrian service, caused me to miss the start of the second half. All this was placed in its proper context at the end of the match, however, when the referee came off the pitch and was told by an official that his father had died. As ever, some things are more important than others.

Living in Glasgow gave me ready access to the matches played by the district side and other representative rugby teams, initially in the last years of amateurism and then in the new professional era, which the Scottish Rugby Union authorities entered with apparent reluctance. The Glasgow High School ground at Anniesland was the venue for a Scotland "A" fixture against New Zealand in November 1993 and a Combined Districts match against South Africa a year later. On both occasions, the Scots fought bravely, but were ultimately outclassed. In the first game, the formidable Va'aiga Tuigamala exposed Kenny Logan's faulty defensive technique by running through him in the build up to a New Zealand try though, to be fair to Logan, Tuigamala would test sounder defences than his in his All Black days and in his later period in rugby league with Wigan. In the South Africa game, one of the visiting centres – Pieter Muller, I think – finished off a sweeping move to dive over for a try, only for one of the Scottish wingers to come rushing in and land on top of him, leading with his knees. This was something that seemed to be becoming increasingly common and it always surprised me that referees – or, indeed, the try-scoring players – did not take a harder line on it. In a later press report, I read that the well-known novelist and peer and rugby expert, Jeffrey Archer, had formed a similar view on seeing this particular incident and had offered the opinion that the player should have been ordered from the field. I'm not sure that I would have gone that far, but it was a disconcerting experience to realise that, on this issue at least, Archer and I were on vaguely the same wavelength.

The Scottish Rugby Union was slow to recognise the changes that the professional status would bring to the game and the Glasgow district side has often found it difficult to match the opposition in the new competitive frameworks that were established. It has not been helped by having a fairly nomadic existence, playing its major matches at the Scotstoun Stadium, the Partick Thistle football ground at Firhill and at Hughendon on the Great Western Road: all perfectly adequate venues but, given this turnover in location, not providing the established continuity that the side has needed to build up its local identity and supporter base. The branding of the side has also gone through several phases: Glasgow followed by Glasgow Caledonians followed by Glasgow Rugby. For the 2005–06 season, the side was re-christened, yet again, as the Glasgow Warriors.

It was clear to me that, in the first couple of years of the Heineken European Cup competition, some of the visitors were simply too streetwise for the local side. Wasps and Pontypridd certainly came into this category in matches where the presence of Lawrence Dallaglio and Neil Jenkins in their respective sides was symptomatic of the experienced authority that Glasgow were attempting to deal with. On the other hand, over the same period, Glasgow also secured some good wins over notable opposition, including Swansea and Ulster. Since then, there has been an intermittent progress. At Hughendon in December 2004, the visiting Llanelli Scarlets side – cleverly prompted by Dwayne Peel at scrum half and superbly marshalled in the forwards by Chris Wyatt – controlled most of the match and yet would have lost had the Glasgow winger Gareth MacLure held on to a crossfield kick in the last minute of the match as he jumped for the ball and landed over the try line. I enjoyed watching Wyatt, with his combination of hard forward graft and imaginative positional play. He also had outstanding ball handling skills and, in another era, would have been a prime target for the scouts of the principal rugby league sides.

I reflected on the Glasgow-Llanelli game for some time afterwards. I watched it from a low bank of terracing behind the dead ball line at the Hughendon Road end of the ground. In the normal way, I was interested in the players in front of me in their roles as active participants in the contest: who were the playmakers? who was relishing the physical challenge? whose skills let them down under pressure, and so on. In addition, however, as also always the case, I was interested in the players as individual people who had reached this particular point of their lives on this particular day. This is a perspective that has fascinated me through my spectating career – I can recall that the same thoughts would occur to me regularly on the touchline at Parkside or near the boundary rope at Bradford Park Avenue cricket ground, for example – and it seems to take hold when I am physically close to the action, so that I can focus on the immediate and detailed identification of specific players. On this occasion, I watched the Llanelli replacements as they did some routine warming up in the dead ball area in front of me. My expectation was that these were players who might get on to the field if one of their colleagues were injured or, if not, as a token substitute in the closing minutes of the match. There was a strong possibility that they would not participate at all. They had come all the way from south Wales to Glasgow, but they were not in the Llanelli starting line-up and they might not get a game. I wondered what Arwel Thomas – a talented fly half who had once been the first choice for Wales – thought about that.

I realised that the extensive demands on professional rugby clubs, as with their soccer counterparts, meant that they were required to run a squad system, if they were to sustain their competitiveness over the course of a season. In addition to Thomas, his side's replacements bench included three other Welsh internationals (and there were also two of their Scottish counterparts on the Glasgow bench). But I stuck with Thomas, in his distinctive Llanelli tracksuit, as he jogged up and down the dead ball area and gently honed his passing and kicking skills. His job of work had brought him to Glasgow, where his teammates would have the first crack at taking on the opposition. Perhaps, ultimately, that is all it amounted to: I was observing someone going about their job of work, albeit not very actively in this instance. But I sensed there was something more: I was also observing someone whose career path – with its triumphs and disappointments – had brought him to this particular location (the dead ball area of the Hughendon rugby ground) at this particular time (a bright Sunday afternoon in December). I wondered whether he was content with this state of affairs, or would rather be somewhere else.

On other occasions, Glasgow were simply overwhelmed. A quarter final play-off defeat in the first year of the Heineken Cup, in which they conceded 90 points at Leicester, illustrated the vast gulf that had opened up when measured against the leading English club sides. In November 1998, I watched Glasgow Caledonians fulfil the role of practice fodder for the touring South Africa side in a match played at Firhill. The tourists, it has to be said, were hugely impressive. They had a mastery of the technical skills, played as a team, congratulated each other warmly as the try count racked up, and were superbly led by the young captain, Bobby Skinstad, whom I watched closely. He was continually encouraging his players and clearly working hard to develop a powerful team spirit. It surprised me later that he did not retain the South African captaincy for much longer. The tourists also relished the physical challenges. This was no surprise, of course, given the central role of such confrontation in the ethos of South African rugby, but it applied to every member of the side. On one occasion, the heavily built Glasgow back row forward Gordon Mackay ran with the ball and identified the South African winger, Breyton Paulse, as the player to attempt to run through: 6 feet 4 inches and 17 stones versus 5 feet 10 inches and 12 stones 7 pounds. Paulse promptly executed a text book tackle on the oncoming player, using Mackay's momentum to his advantage by lifting him up and dumping him unceremoniously on to his back.

The only consolation for Glasgow on a long evening under the South African cosh was the impressive performance of the centre, John Leslie, the son of a New Zealand test rugby player and with a Scottish grandparent in his family tree. He had arrived in the country only a few days before and, after this performance, he was fast-tracked into the national team. He was not the only one to take this route: in recent years, the Scottish granny or granddad has come to the service of several rugby players born in the southern hemisphere who judged that they would be unable to break into their domestic national sides. From my detached perspective, I was not convinced that this was the right strategy, as not all of these players – Leslie included – played their club rugby in Scotland and relatively few stayed in the country after their international careers came to an end. It is not easy to see what their lasting legacy has been, apart from Scotland winning the Five Nations tournament in 1999, after England's complacency against Wales at Wembley cost them the match and the title. For what it is worth, I do not like the grandparent rule in the first place: I would restrict eligibility to the birthplaces of the parental generation.

Chapter 19

Troon

A central component of Scottish culture in the west of the country – and one that clearly captures both the legacy of history and the impact of religion – is football. It was inevitable that I would be drawn to the stadiums of both Celtic FC and Rangers FC – Celtic Park and Ibrox – before very long, and so it proved. Within a fortnight of moving up to Scotland in 1992, I was standing behind the goal watching Celtic play an end-of-season fixture against a weak Dunfermline side that had already been relegated from the Scottish Premier League. I had taken the train from Milngavie a couple of stops beyond my daily departure point of Central Station and got out at Bridgeton and then walked the short distance down the London Road to the stadium. The reputation of the east end of Glasgow as a dangerous location in which to venture as an obvious outsider was difficult to shift during the latter part of my journey. I attempted to look ordinary and not to say anything and to avoid any eye contact that might be misinterpreted. The terracing was basic, if not dilapidated, and the crowd was relatively meagre. The ground and the club had clearly seen better times. To my right, I looked across to the feared "Jungle" of home support, about which I had already heard much and where, I was told, the local hardcases congregated. Needless to say, the game and my journey to and from the ground passed without incident.

I bought my match programme and looked through the names on the teamsheets. Some of the home players were known to me from their time with English teams, as seen on television down south – Tony Mowbray, Tommy Boyd, Gary Gillespie – but the Dunfermline line-up was of complete strangers, including the defender Davie Moyes, an ex-Celt whom the programme described as having been an excellent buy for the club following his £42,500 move from Shrewsbury Town. A dozen years later,

David Moyes, as manager of Everton, had unexpectedly but deservedly led his side into the qualifying matches for the 2005–06 European Champions League. Celtic won comfortably. Throughout the match, a man behind me shouted "Come on, Slippers" every time Charlie Nicholas got the ball. "Come on, Slippers. Show us what you can do, Slippers. Come on, Slippers". I was keen to ask him the obvious question, but I didn't.

The visit to Ibrox to see Rangers took place at the beginning of the following season, when the home side drew Leeds United, of all teams, in a two-legged tie in the early stages of the European Cup. Some time before the match, Rangers announced that a limited number of tickets would be available to non-season ticket holders, who were willing to queue at the ground early one Saturday morning. It was also announced that Leeds United supporters would not be allowed to attend the fixture, just as the Rangers support would not be admitted to the return fixture at Elland Road. I duly turned up at Ibrox on the appointed day and joined a long queue. After we had waited around for a couple of hours, and made very little progress, a steward came down the line asking if anyone wished to pay using cheques which had already been made out, supported by a completed stamped addressed envelope. I had all this to hand and so I handed it over and headed home. I never heard anything more about the application.

My ticket was obtained courtesy of one of my new work colleagues, who somehow acquired the half dozen tickets that enabled a group of us from the office to attend the match together. This was one of those occasions when, living away from Leeds, I was identified as an obvious Leeds United supporter on account of the fact that I had been born and brought up in the city. On this occasion, my usual protestations of "I'm more a rugby follower, really" was either ignored by colleagues or, more probably, uttered at a fairly low volume, given that the opportunity to go to the game had presented itself. It was impossible to resist: the so-called "Battle of Britain" between a powerful Rangers side and the previous season's surprise champions in England, who had pipped Manchester United to the title on the last day of the season.

It was obvious that, at that stage, the Rangers club was in a far healthier state than Celtic. Off the pitch, the club was benefiting from the significant investment that the chairman, David Murray, had driven forward in stadium improvements. On the pitch, more relevantly for the supporters of both clubs, Rangers were in the middle of the nine-in-a-row sequence of championship successes that was to match the Celtic record of the late 1960s and early 1970s. It is difficult to overstate how emphatically the Celtic achievement had cast a shadow over the clubs' rivalry and the importance to the Rangers club and its supporters of re-establishing historical parity. (I judged it prudent not to suggest to any of my new colleagues that even Celtic's record lagged behind the 11-in-a-row run of championship wins achieved by the St George rugby league club in Sydney up to and including 1966). This was brought home to me shortly after I had arrived in Scotland, when Rangers were on the brink of winning the fourth title in this run. It was at this point that I was given an immediate lesson about the challenge that the Celtic feat presented. Late one evening, I suggested to a taxi driver, who had revealed himself as a Rangers supporter, that he must be fairly pleased that the league championship was about to be retained. He brusquely replied that he would only be satisfied when they had matched the Celtic achievement of nine consecutive title victories. There was no emotion or threat in his voice when he said this: it was a matter-of-fact statement and an early reminder for me to treat any conversations in this city on the subject of football with due caution.

My office colleagues and I sat in the Govan Stand with its excellent view across the pitch. In the minutes leading up the kick-off, with the ground full and no away support to disturb the proceedings, the intensity of the crowd's expectations reached a fever pitch. This seemed to be the result of the combination of the importance of the fixture itself and, irrespective of the game, the fact that 45,000 Rangers supporters were gathered at the one place. The roar was deafening – one of the loudest I have ever heard at a sports stadium. "Hello, hello..." *The Sash*, complete with reference to wading through Fenian blood, rang out around the ground.

Within a minute of the kick off, there had occurred one of the nano-dramas that I have specifically recorded from across the spectrum of my sports spectating. On their first attack, Leeds United won a corner on their right. The ball came into the Rangers penalty area and was headed out to the Leeds midfielder, Gary McAllister, who was lurking at the angle of the penalty area, also on the right hand side. In a textbook demonstration of the skill – angling his body, taking his weight on his non-striking leg and keeping his head over the ball – McAllister volleyed the ball into the top far corner of the Rangers net. In its own right, it was undoubtedly one of the best goals I had ever seen. However, in the context of the match, and of the occasion, it was absolutely – indeed literally – breathtaking. The Leeds United players mobbed McAllister to the sound of absolutely silence around the ground. The proverbial pin was dropping. Or, at least, it would have been, had not the goal elicited a joyful response from a small knot of Leeds United supporters – probably no more than a dozen altogether – further down the stand on my right hand side. This only added to the home supporters' grief. Not only had their side fallen behind before the opening skirmishes had been properly engaged – and conceded a precious away goal into the bargain – but the sanctity of the ground had been invaded by those who were not welcome. There was an ominous murmuring of hostility towards the Leeds supporters, who, after obviously concealing their identity in order to gain entrance to the ground, were now completely open in their allegiance. My response to the goal was more muted, and considerably safer: "Bloody hell".

I had been here before. In 1970, Leeds United had played Celtic in the semi-final of the European Cup, another "Battle of Britain". The first leg had been played at Elland Road and, after I had settled down to watch the highlights on television that evening – without knowing the score, of course, as was my usual preference – I had been astounded when George Connelly scored for Celtic in the first minute. My reaction had been exactly the same: "Bloody hell". My parents, who had been in the room at the time, were themselves taken aback by the profanity uttered by their supposedly mild-mannered son. Celtic went on to win that fixture 1–0 and then defeat Leeds again in the second leg in Glasgow in front of an official attendance of 136,500.

The outcome was different this time, however, as the early scorers did not take advantage of their flying start to secure the overall victory. To their credit, Rangers kept their composure and recovered well, scoring twice to win 2–1. They had a fair sprinkling of big match players – Ally McCoist, Mark Hateley, Trevor Steven – who, after the early setback, did not panic, but set about trying to turn things around in a professional manner. Here was another echo from the past: Mark Hateley, the teenage centre forward whom Dad and I had seen playing for Coventry City in the FA Cup tie against Leeds United at Elland Road in 1981, was now resident in this half of Glasgow and relishing the weekly confrontation and the physical challenges of the Scottish Premier League. However, I thought the best player on the pitch was Ian Durrant in the Rangers midfield. He shaded his duel with the aggressive David Batty and, most noticeably, used the possession that came his way in a consistently intelligent and efficient manner. It was like watching John Robertson on that day at Portman Road playing for Nottingham Forest against Ipswich Town: Durrant did not waste a pass. In the event, Rangers progressed into the next stage of the competition with something to spare. Hateley scored an early goal from long range in the second leg and later laid on another for McCoist, leaving Leeds well beaten. The next day, back in the office, I took it like a man. My familiar protestations – "I'm more a rugby follower, really" – cut no ice at all with the McCoist and Durrant supporters. Meanwhile, the Celtic contingent amongst my colleagues kept their counsel whilst, I sensed, at the same time being seriously aggrieved that Leeds had not done them the obvious favour.

My two other visits to Ibrox were for international matches that were played there whilst the national stadium at Hampden Park was being re-developed: a Scotland versus Italy World Cup qualifying game in November 1992 and an "international challenge" match against Germany the following March. Neither game particularly sticks in the mind and even the World Cup match did not have the intense and passionate atmosphere of the Rangers versus Leeds United confrontation of the previous month.

Scotland had a reasonable side. They had played with distinction and spirit in the European Championships in the summer of 1992 and the squad for the qualifying game had some talented Old Firm players (Andy Goram, Paul McStay, Ian Durrant, Ally McCoist) supplemented by English-based players such as Gary McAllister and Gordon Durie, the latter later to transfer to Rangers. However, the player who really caught the eye was the 21 year-old Alan McLaren, who was deputed to mark the dangerous Italian forward Roberto Baggio. He gave an immaculate performance, demonstrating a fine positional sense and a calm authority in only his fourth international match. One commentator in the match programme for the later Germany game described him as a future Scotland captain in the making. Unfortunately, it was not to be. Although McLaren later secured the transfer from Hearts to Rangers that would have given him the opportunity to play in a successful side that was regularly accessing European competition, he succumbed to serious injury and his career was effectively over by his mid 20s. By this time, the attention of most of the spectators at a Rangers match or a Scottish international would have been on his successor and his colleagues, with McLaren already having taken on the status of a name from the past. It was an unfortunate reminder that, for any particular star at any particular time, the place in the spotlight might turn out to be short-lived.

For many years after moving to Scotland, my only other Glasgow-based spectating of a soccer-related activity was off the pitch. The Christie's offices in Bath Street had occasional auctions of football memorabilia and, in October 1994, I took a morning off work to observe one such event. As one would expect, it was organised in a highly professional manner. The catalogue for the auction was handsomely produced with detailed descriptions of the wide range of lots on offer: medals, caps, programmes, footballs, shirts, and so on. The lots themselves varied enormously: lot 70F was a nine carat gold medal awarded to HH Lees of Wolverhampton Wanderers FC for winning the Football League Division 3 Championship, Northern Section, in 1923–24; the expected price was £250–£300. By contrast, lots 151–207 – "the property of a collector" – comprised over 6,000 match programmes from the full spectrum of British club and international teams; I was a little surprised that the total expected price of this collection was only in the range £4,300–£6,400.

Some of the lots were based around the collections of medals and other memorabilia won by individual players. There were 6 lots associated with Arthur Rowley, including the football with which he broke the British league goalscoring record with his 411th goal in 1962 (estimated price £100–£150); the FA Cup winners medal Harry Makepeace won with Everton in 1906 had an estimated price of £2,000–£3,000; the league championship medals won by Dennis Viollet, a later survivor of the Munich air crash, with Manchester United in 1956 and 1957 were expected to reach £1,500–£2,000 each. Other players who were selling material were of a more recent vintage, including Terry Curran and Frank Gray, who were almost my exact contemporaries.

The prime lots – and those that had probably encouraged the appearance of the television news crews – belonged to Tommy Gemmell, one of the "Lisbon Lions" who won the European Cup for Celtic in 1967. I had learned very quickly on arriving in Glasgow that the fascination (of one half of the city at least) with this side, and the awe in which it is held, remained very powerful, and this emphatically is still the case to this day. Gemmell had 31 lots on offer, including the medal from that match (estimated price £8,000–£12,000). However, during the auction itself, events took an interesting turn. Although the bidding was keen, it soon became apparent that the same bidder was determinedly seeing off the competition for every single lot. When I heard later that the successful bidder was associated with Celtic FC, I thought this was an admirable move by the club. It kept Gemmell's collection in one piece, and it kept it in the Celtic family.

Years later, I checked up on the details of the auction in the autobiographical *Tommy Gemmell: Lion Heart*. Gemmell reports that the Glasgow-based entrepreneur, Willie Haughey, spent £33,000 on the collection, which was subsequently mounted and displayed in the Celtic boardroom. As Gemmell himself notes, this is a far more appropriate resting place than the polythene bag at the bottom of his bedroom wardrobe. And it remains an admirable outcome.

And what else in Scotland, apart from the rugby union and the football? Well, rugby league and cricket, obviously. Scotland played Ireland at Firhill in August 1996, the first time that international rugby league had been played in the country since 1911. The two sides drew heavily from the professional clubs of the north of England and, as a result, the plethora of Lancashire and Yorkshire accents heard on the pitch suggested that the grandparent rule was being adopted even more liberally here (for both teams) than for the Scottish rugby union equivalent. There was one brilliant moment, when the Ireland right winger ran down the touchline, close to my position in the main stand, and hared for the corner. The Scotland full back was Alan Tait who, covering across at pace, completed an absolutely textbook try-saving tackle just in front of the corner flag. The tackle could not have been bettered for any instructional video. It was an exemplary piece of skill from a player who graced both codes with some distinction.

In October 2000, the Scotland side, now supplemented by some antipodean as well as northern England accents, were back at Firhill for that year's Rugby League World Cup group match against Aotearoa Maori. By a remarkable coincidence, my father was visiting us that weekend. It was a good hard-fought game, in which the Maori's physical strength and skill were too much for the hosts in the end. The captain, Tawera Nikau, revelled in both aspects of the play and led his team from the front. This was a player who gave much to the game in Britain, Australia and New Zealand; Dave Hadfield's account, in *Up and Over: A Trek Through Rugby League Land*, of the subsequent tragedies to befall him makes extremely sad reading.

The amateur side of the game was demonstrated in the two Scottish Grand Final matches I witnessed at the West of Scotland rugby ground at Burnbrae in 2000 and 2001. Both featured the Glasgow Bulls versus the Edinburgh Eagles, with each side winning once. I recognised some of the players from matches involving West of Scotland – for example, the Glasgow captain, David Jamieson, who had propped for the local rugby union side a few seasons earlier – and I thought there was something admirable in the players' efforts to adhere to the skills and disciplines of the different code. The best player on show on both occasions was an Australian called Howard Cameron, who was in the Glasgow team. I was impressed, also, that the referee for the 2000 match was Steve Ganson, one of the best in the professional league, who had been the reserve referee for the Challenge Cup final between the Bradford Bulls and the Leeds Rhinos at Murrayfield earlier in the summer.

The general interest in cricket in Scotland took me by surprise. A keenly contested national league club competition thrives, supplemented by professional players from at home and overseas, notwithstanding the weather, especially in the west, where it is generally wetter than to the east or in England. In May 1995, I took the opportunity to watch the Scotland side play Yorkshire in the group match in the Benson and Hedges Cup. The match was played at the West of Scotland cricket club, which is located not at Burnbrae but in Hamilton Crescent in Partick. (That more is not made of the fact that this was the location for the first ever soccer international – a goalless draw between Scotland and England in 1872 – is something of a minor mystery to me). The overseas professional recruited by Scotland that summer was Malcolm Marshall, a frequent terroriser of England batting line ups in the previous decade, whom Dad and I had seen bowl the West Indies to victory at Headingley in 1984 with the lower part of his left arm in plaster. And the Scotland captain – and director of cricket – was none other than Jim Love, formerly (still) of the Leeds Schools Under 14 XI (1969), Yorkshire Cricket Federation XI (captain, 1974), Yorkshire first XI and England one-day international XI. Unfortunately, Scotland were not up to the mark. Only Love himself, with an aggressive half century, put the Yorkshire bowling under any pressure. Marshall was dismissed cheaply and did not take a wicket, casting a fairly forlorn figure in his new and temporary environment. The modest Scotland total was knocked off by Yorkshire without the loss of a wicket, thanks to the captain Martyn Moxon and a promising young player called Michael Vaughan.

Scotland fared little better three years later, when the attractive ground of the Grange cricket club in Edinburgh staged one of the group matches in the 1999 Cricket World Cup. The opponents were New Zealand. It was the familiar story, which I have previously observed in much of the rugby union context. New Zealand were too streetwise and professional and, quite clearly, more skilful. Scotland batted first and made a modest total, and New Zealand easily reached the target by mid afternoon. It was a pleasant half day in the sunshine in the company of a couple of friends from Milngavie, but the result was never in doubt and, by tea time, we were in one of the pubs near Haymarket station watching the soccer play off match from Wembley between Watford and Bolton Wanderers, from which the former emerged to take that season's final promotion place into the Premiership.

To supplement the rugby league and cricket, my experience of sports spectating in Scotland has also incorporated Highland Games and golf. The former was not witnessed in the Highlands, I should hasten to add, but rather closer to home: in Milngavie, to be precise. The Bearsden and Milngavie Highland Games has been an annual event since 1973, usually held on the second Saturday in June. In the years that I have attended – intermittently from 1994 – it has been held in the extensive grounds of the West of Scotland rugby club. For the English observer, it is an interesting day. The games include the traditional Highland sports and activities – athletics (with the competitors handicapped according to previous performances), tug of war, Highland dancing, tossing the caber, bagpipes competitions, wrestling, tossing the haggis (though how traditional this is, I'm not sure) – as well as modern interlopers such as five-a-side football and police dog demonstrations. Each year, there is a chieftain to open the games and present the prizes, usually a local or regional celebrity (loosely defined). In the Games we have attended, these have included Toby Anstis (BBC Children's Television), Alison Sheppard (Olympic swimmer), Diane Youdale ("Jet" from *Gladiators*), Dominic Wood and Richard McCourt (Children's BBC Television), Annette Crosbie (actress), Craig Phillips (a winner of *Big Brother*), and John Lambie (manager of Partick Thistle). In 2005, the chieftain was Taylor Ferguson, a well-known local hairdresser, who thus followed in the tradition of belonging to a somewhat eclectic list which, prior to our arrival in Scotland, had also included Red Rum and Rod Hull and Emu.

All this is fine and, as the family and I have wandered around the Games, I have usually thought that the event was both touching and impressive – a valiant attempt by the local worthies of Bearsden and Milngavie to provide a good day's entertainment in the name of the districts – though I have never underestimated the serious nature of the actual competition in the various sports and activities. The downside to the event is the tacky funfair that takes place elsewhere in the grounds and at which my children, not surprisingly, were consistently keen for me to spend hard-earned money on their behalf. It takes only one dart to bounce straight off the target picture on a dartboard for the thrower to realise that he is being taken for a ride.

Back at the Games – in which, to their credit, the children also showed some interest – I think that it is the study of the individual competitor that is the most revealing: the sprinter in the handicapped race in front of the main rugby stand, the Highland dancer in her immaculate costume and sternly swept back hair, the drummer in one of the pipe bands concentrating on the maintaining the correct beat. One year, when my children and I had taken our places at the back of the stand to eat our sandwiches, I watched as one of the runners for a long distance race prepared himself for the event by lapping the track: he did this for a good 45 minutes and must have done something like twelve to fifteen circuits. When his event came, he nodded and chatted briefly to those of his competitors whom he obviously knew, and then took his place half way round the track and with a considerable handicapped advantage over them. The other runners overtook him long before the end of the race and he trailed in last. He then shook the hands of the other athletes before moving over to pick up his track suit and head back to the changing rooms. I hope that I did not feel sorry for him, because that would have been patronising and ill deserved. I admired him for his effort. It was him out there and not me.

The golf was at the highest level: the Saturday of the Open Championship at Troon in 1997. I went for the same reason that I had attended the Ryder Cup at Walton Heath in 1981: the tournament was in the vicinity and there was really no excuse not to go. The authorities in charge of the event could not have made it any easier. A ticket bought at Central Station in Glasgow covered the return train fare to Troon, the bus connection between the railway station and the golf course, and entry to the course. I forget exactly how much it cost, but I remember thinking it was a bargain. Once I had entered the course, I then invested a further £20 on an Open Championship golf visor: a more questionable purchase in terms of value for money, but then I have always thought that it is useful to get the acquisition of souvenirs out of the way as quickly and efficiently as possible.

It was an absolutely spellbinding day. I began by finding an excellent niche near the first green and watched there for over two hours as the stream of well-known players came through: Jack Nicklaus, Vijay Singh, Bernhard Langer, Tiger Woods, Colin Montgomerie. Often, the crowd around me would swell significantly as the constant members of the gallery around the green, of whom I was one, were joined by each player's supporters as they followed him around the course. But I was happy where I was. I had a good view down the course and so could see both the approach shot and the action on the green, as each player made his attempt for birdie and par. There were relatively few of the former. Tiger was short of the green with his second shot, but played a slow and elegant pitch up to close to the hole, the ball seeming to travel in a high and graceful parabola. As we waited for a pair to come through, I struck up a conversation with the man next to me at the side of the green. He had driven up the motorway that morning from Lancashire. His enthusiastic description of his departure in the middle of the night and of his long drive back later on at the close of play merely confirmed to me how pathetic it would have been if I had not been bothered to make the journey from Milngavie.

After the first hole, I wandered down the course, stopping occasionally when a decent vantage point was offered, though these were not easy to find by the middle of the afternoon, when the size of the gallery was at its peak. I stopped by the 15th green and then walked on to the 13th green, where the same order of players naturally came through again – Nicklaus, Singh, Langer, Woods (on his way to registering a round of 64), Montgomerie – their spirits having been either raised or dampened by their intervening successes or failures. It was a hot day, and I was grateful for the bottled water that I had made sure to bring, especially when I had reached the far corner of the course next to the railway line. At one hole, I watched from close to Montgomery as he played uphill and out of the short rough; on another, Padraig Harrington boomed a long second shot into the centre of the green.

Darren Clarke had been the overnight leader after the first two rounds – two strokes ahead of his playing partner, Justin Leonard – and I stood behind the 10th green for another two hours as the last ten pairs on the course – including Greg Norman, Tom Watson and Fred Couples and concluding with Leonard and Clarke – attempted to maintain or improve their position. Later, I stood behind Jim Furyk on the 17th tee, as he went through his ugly practice swings, and watched him send his drive down the middle of the fairway. Leonard was a new name to me, but he looked well organised and composed. The following day, he won the 126th Open Championship.

But the highlight of the day came before I had seen a competitive shot played in anger. It occurred almost immediately after I had entered the course and I have allocated it a place amongst the nano-dramas of sporting activity that I have featured throughout this volume. A group of players was on the practice range. One of them was Payne Stewart, a tall and imposing figure, characteristically attired in his usual flamboyant plus-fours. He was putting the final touches to his preparation for that day's round, thereby adding to the thousands of hours of practice and yet more practice that had brought him to Troon on that particular morning. In the world of golf, there has been no more apposite comment than Gary Player's response to a journalist who described him as a "lucky" golfer. "It's funny", said Player, "The harder I practise, the luckier I get".

The first practice stroke I saw Stewart play was a routine iron down the range and, from my perspective, over to my right. It was a stroke of poetic beauty: smooth, unhurried, crisp and effortless. And it was the outcome of those thousands of hours. Stewart's practice shot was, no doubt, no more impressive than the dozens of others he would have played in his warm up or, indeed, the practice strokes made by many of the other players on the range that morning. And, no doubt, there were countless extraordinary golf shots played on the course that day, from seemingly impossible positions and with miraculous results. I had seen Stewart play many times on television. But this was the real thing, and my response was analogous to those that had followed my seeing other professional sportsmen at the top of their games: Alan Old, John Robertson, Geoff Boycott, Ellery Hanley. This time, the setting was on a bright sunny day against the background of a clear blue sky. I watched a practice shot by Payne Stewart. And it took the breath away.

Chapter 20

Stade de France

After I moved with my family to Scotland in 1992, the frequency of my attendance at the major rugby league games in Leeds declined, although the visits were not eliminated completely. On a dank and drizzly day at Headingley in November 1993, from my seat in the main stand, I anticipated the inside pass that one of the New Zealand players attempted in the third test, as his side attacked the Great Britain left hand flank near the home side's try line. More relevantly, so did Jonathan Davies, who intercepted the pass in more or less full stride and sprinted, uncatchably, the 85 yards or so to the New Zealand try line. He was roared all the way home by the crowd around me – including, with great enthusiasm, by my father – although, to me, it was clear that, once he had taken the ball, Davies would convincingly make the distance.

Great Britain had won the first two tests with something to spare and did so again on this occasion, though not before one of the substitute players, Sonny Nickle – now of St Helens, but whom I had last seen being sent off whilst playing as a teenager for Hunslet against Castleford – maintained this tradition by being dismissed for an off-the-ball foul on one of his opponents. My father was quick to point out that Nickel was one of three former Hunslet forwards – with Kelvin Skerrett and Michael Jackson – in the Great Britain line-up. However, it was another of the home side's forwards who particularly impressed with his speed and power: Andy Farrell, making his international debut at the age of 18. I watched him (and the rest of the players on the pitch) and realised, not for the first or last time, that my life was inexorably moving on: I was over 20 years older than Farrell.

Defeating New Zealand was one thing; beating Australia in a three match test series remained something else. The following autumn, at Elland

Road, with the series standing at 1–1, my father and I saw Great Britain again come up short in the third game. The margin of defeat was not quite as heavy as those we had witnessed in the 1980s, but the tourists were still too strong. I watched the Australian half backs – Laurie Daley and Ricky Stuart – with particular admiration. Their passing was immaculate: Stuart's, reflecting his rugby union background, arrow-like from the ground at the scrum or the play-the-ball and Daley's in open play, the flick of his wrists directing the ball with speed and precision to his intended target.

In his autobiographical *Made for Rugby*, the Great Britain prop forward Barrie McDermott describes how the home side pounded the Australian line in the third quarter, having trailed only 7–2 at half-time, but were unable to score. The Australians subsequently pulled away to win 23–4 and retain the Ashes. McDermott also reports on the bizarre – and unsuccessful – plan for his side to make an additional (and illicit) substitution by arranging for his fellow prop forward Karl Harrison to nick his ear with a razor at half-time, so that he (McDermott) could play as a blood replacement for Harrison before his duly repaired colleague took the field again for the last 15–20 minutes: "The blood was gushing out of Karl's ear in the changing room, but as soon as he went out for the start of the second half… the bleeding stopped. No matter how much he pulled at his ear, he couldn't get it to start again, so I didn't get back on". As ever, I found that the post-match feeling after these autumn internationals was one of anti-climax, with the eager anticipation of the contest now fully spent, the game over and, as we journeyed cautiously home in dad's Chrysler Sunbeam, the darkness of the early winter's evening having already fallen.

The visits back to Leeds for Christmas and Easter gave me the opportunity to accompany Dad to watch Hunslet in their final years at Elland Road and then at their new ground at the South Leeds Stadium, of which more later. But the club was at a low ebb in the early 1990s: the defeat I saw against Bramley in December 1993 was part of the sequence of twelve months' home league fixtures without a win. My father remained loyal, of course, dutifully collecting the match programmes and storing them safely away in my old bedroom in the house in Moortown. However, as Angela and I now had two small children in tow, there were other priorities to be satisfied on these visits home, as my parents spent time with their grandchildren.

It was a short time later – in the mid 1990s – that my mother adopted the curious habit of surreptitiously turning off the immersion heater in my parents' house whenever someone else had put it on to heat the water. At the time, I did not know it was her, so my reaction tended to be the self-pitying cry of "Who's turned off the hot water again?" when I realised that there was none available. I was more disconcerted when, on one occasion, after I had asked her where the red three-volumed *The Reader's Digest Great Encyclopaedic Dictionary* was, my mother claimed that we did not possess a set. The reason for my disquiet was that completing the general knowledge crossword in the *Sunday Express* had been a weekly exercise that she had attempted for as long as I could remember using the same reference book. Some time afterwards, my sister informed me that Dad had later found some of the smaller Christmas presents, unwrapped, squirreled away behind the living room sofa.

Notwithstanding my departure to Scotland, the annual tradition for my father, Vic and me to attend the rugby league Challenge Cup final was emphatically maintained. Indeed, it was expanded. The day trip to the match was enhanced into a fixed routine for the whole of the cup final weekend. We quickly established the tradition of staying in a hotel at King's Cross – either the Great Northern or the Royal Scot – for the Friday and Saturday nights. Friday evening would entail a fish and chip supper in the Royal Scot, followed by a few drinks in whichever hotel we were staying. Following the cooked breakfast on the Saturday morning, we took the Underground to Wembley so that we arrived, as before, just as the curtain-raisers were in full swing. Afterwards, irrespective of how late we left the stadium, there was always the long queue in Wembley Way as we headed back towards the Underground station. We would have dinner in the hotel, with a few more drinks in the bar, before going our separate ways after breakfast on the Sunday. It was a routine that quickly became a ritual: unchanged each year, much loved and anticipated and, it seemed, increasingly quick to come around again as the years passed. Presented this way, it appears to have been an exercise in continual eating and drinking – though neither to excess – the timetable for which was determined by the rugby match. It was also, in microcosm, an example of the traditions maintained by many rugby league supporters from the north of England, for whom the trip to the Wembley cup final was a greatly anticipated event each year, irrespective of which teams were playing and notwithstanding that the improved communications by road and rail made a visit to London much more easily undertaken than it had been for their parents' and grandparents' generations.

For my father and me, the unspoken part of the routine was that he would pay for our Wembley tickets, and, as the corollary, I would fund the two days' play at the Headingley test match (of which also more below). As a result, he was always nervous beforehand about the quality of the seats he had purchased. In most years, we were in the upper tiers and he was able to breathe a sigh of relief as we climbed the wide steps within the ground and headed upwards towards a good view. In some other years, he was disappointed, for example in 1993, when we were seated in the lower tier to watch Wigan extend their run of consecutive wins, this time against Widnes. The seats at this level never seemed to me to be satisfactory anywhere around the Wembley bowl: the gradient of the seating was too shallow and, when one person anywhere in front stood up to watch the action, everyone behind them had to follow suit.

By the time of the 1993 match, Martin Offiah had been transferred from Widnes to Wigan, and it was patently clear that there was no love lost between him and some of his former team-mates. When Offiah fell on to one particular loose ball, the former Welsh rugby union international John Devereux clattered into him with unconstrained ferocity. Unfortunately, the Widnes forward Richie Eyres overstepped the mark, even by the uncompromising standards that operated at this level. He was judged to have elbowed Offiah as he was running past him and, following a consultation between referee and touch judge, was summarily sent from the field. Eyres again: the same player whose dismissal against St Helens in the 1989 semi final had probably cost Widnes their place at Wembley that year. Later in the game, I watched one of the players who had gone in the opposite direction to Offiah: Bobbie Goulding, formerly of Wigan, but now playing at scrum half or hooker for Widnes. It was clear that, by that time in the match, his temper and competitiveness had got the better of him: indeed, he seemed to have lost the plot completely, as he ran into or tackled his opponents with a wild-eyed violence. Jason Robinson, who played in this match for Wigan as an 18 year-old, recalled in *Finding my Feet: My Autobiography* that "near the end Bobbie Goulding caught me round the head with a late tackle and there was a brief, but ugly, brawl". He then goes on to describe, with a painful honesty, the celebratory drinking culture at Wigan, of which he readily became part.

In the following year's final, Wigan played Leeds, as they would also do the year after that. Accordingly, analysts of the sport probably regard 1994 as the year in which the nature of the competition at the top of the rugby league hierarchy in Britain became firmly established for the next decade and beyond. Wigan, Leeds, Bradford, St Helens: of the 36 places at stake in the 18 Challenge Cup finals between 1994 and 2011, these clubs took 27 of them, exactly three-quarters. When allowance is made for the occasions in which these teams were drawn against each other in the earlier rounds of the various years' tournaments, this represents a fairly tight control over the distribution of the honours. Indeed, following the 1986 Challenge Cup final (Castleford versus Hull KR), it was not until 2009

(Huddersfield Giants versus Warrington Wolves) that at least one of these clubs did not feature. The same four clubs are also the only ones to have won the Grand Final of the Super League since its establishment in 1995.[44]

My college friend, Llyr James, went to the 1994 final with some of his friends from Wales. He told me later that the roar when Garry Schofield scored a try for Leeds at his end of the ground was the loudest he had ever heard at a rugby match. However, Schofield's effort was in vain, as Leeds failed to halt their run of lack of success. Martin Offiah was the game's dominant player, winning the Lance Todd Trophy as man of the match for the second time. From my specific perspective, he is also responsible for the next of the nano-dramas which I report in this volume. The incident is a classic example of its type because it was one of those in which I realised in advance – and, I suspect, earlier than 99.9 per cent of the people in the stadium – what was going to happen.

Although playing on the left wing, Offiah took a pass as first receiver, running to his right, when Wigan were under severe pressure close to their own line early in the game. Once he had broken the initial tackle, I knew instantly that he would score in the corner at the other end of the field. It was as if my mind had time-shifted forward. Having evaded the first line of defence, Offiah was obviously going to run clear of the covering tacklers. That left him in open field with only the Leeds full back, Alan Tait, to beat. For most wingers in this position, this would be a difficult challenge, given Tait's renowned defensive qualities. Tait's problem, however, was that he was in the middle of the pitch and could not use his invisible ally – the touch line – to his advantage, in the way that he would later do when he played for Scotland against Ireland at Firhill in 1996 and, no doubt, also on countless other occasions. Offiah's basic speed – which could conservatively be described as blistering – was too much for Tait and the winger ran around him on the wide outside and touched down near the corner flag. It was exactly as I had envisaged less than ten seconds earlier. After Offiah had placed the ball on the ground and was about to begin his celebrations, Tait caught up with him and – as a mark of respect, I thought – patted him gently on the back.

And so the routine continued for the rest of the decade. Wigan beat Leeds again in 1995, thanks to two tries from Jason Robinson, the second of which was a typically scooting effort from a play-the-ball. Although I cannot be certain, I think that my father pointed out, as Robinson walked back to his mark, that he was a product of the Hunslet Boys rugby league club Under 10s team. Robbie Paul scored a brilliant hat trick for the Bradford Bulls in 1996 and still ended up on the losing side, after St Helens had mercilessly exposed the vulnerability of the Bradford full back,

Nathan Graham, to the high kick. St Helens's tactical leadership was provided by their captain, Bobbie Goulding, who thus enjoyed a considerably happier afternoon than he had done playing for Widnes against Wigan three years earlier. In 1998, Sheffield Eagles defeated the mighty – and, probably that day, fatally complacent – Wigan, thereby recording a shock victory to rank alongside the Featherstone Rovers triumph over Hull FC in 1983.

In the 1997 final, St Helens repeated their victory of the previous year over Bradford by winning another high-scoring match 32–22. In this particular season, however, there was also a Plate competition for those sides that had been defeated in the fourth round (i.e. the first round in which the clubs from the Super League had entered). As Hunslet had played Bradford in the fourth round (and lost by 10–62), they had qualified – if that is the right word – for the Plate. Subsequently, and rather improbably, Hunslet had then beaten Huddersfield, Workington and Widnes – all sides in the division above them – to reach the final against Hull Kingston Rovers. As the Plate final was played as a curtain-raiser to the main event, the Hunslet club therefore took part in a Wembley final for the first time since the classic match with Wigan in 1965.

The fairytale ended rather abruptly. Hull KR were also in the first division – one above Hunslet – and were far too fast and skilful, racking up a half century of points and winning comfortably. From my perspective – as an infrequent observer of the side – it was clear that Hunslet had several good players and two or three others who were not in the same league as their opponents, and Hull KR exploited the weaknesses with ruthless efficiency. I think that my father was a little embarrassed by the final score – 14–60 – but he recognised that his side had done well to get their place in the sun.

More generally, I did wonder about the validity of the Plate concept. I recognised it from the days of schools' rugby sevens tournaments, but that struck me as different (and legitimate), given that a school side would welcome at least one more game if they had travelled some distance to a tournament and been beaten in the first round. But the rugby league authorities' idea seemed flawed, given that both Hunslet and Hull KR had failed in the competition proper. Had Hunslet pulled off a minor miracle and beaten Bradford, and then lost in the next round, they would not have played in the Plate. It would appear that the authorities quickly thought along the same lines, as the Plate competition was not repeated in the following season.

There was much about Wembley that I did not like – the views from the lower seating, the crampedness of the seats, the inane chatter of the ground's master of ceremonies that became a regular feature in the later years – but I always enjoyed the occasion. Attending as a neutral, I looked with interest on the games' allocations of triumph and despair and on the responses of those so affected. After one of Wigan's successful games, it was impossible not to be swept up in the euphoria of their supporters – the better part of half the stadium bedecked in cherry and white – as Tina Turner's *Simply the Best* roared out into the early summer sunshine. Most important though, the Challenge Cup final was an annual fixed point in the lives of the three of us – my father, Vic and me – who attended together. As the years passed, it provided reassurance and continuity. I knew that dad, in particular, needed that, as the extent of his caring responsibilities at home began to increase. His trip to London for the Sheffield Eagles-Wigan final of 1998 was characterised by more than the usual number of telephone calls back to my mother at home in Leeds. He wanted to make sure that she had locked the doors properly and had not inadvertently left a gas tap switched on in the kitchen.

The Leeds Rhinos (as they had now become) ended their Challenge Cup drought in 1999, when they beat London Broncos in the last of the finals to be played at Wembley before the stadium was demolished for redevelopment. Although Leeds won comfortably in the end – 52 points to 16 – it was London that had taken a 10–0 lead early in the game and they held the lead again at the beginning of the second half. But Leeds ran riot in the last 20 minutes, when the unheralded winger, Leroy Rivett, completed the unprecedented feat of scoring four tries in a Wembley final.

Leeds deserved their triumph. They had defeated Wigan, St Helens and Bradford to reach the final – the hardest possible route – and they were simply too strong and powerful for their opponents. By now, they had some proper steel in their pack – Adrian Morley, Barrie McDermott, Anthony Farrell – and were no longer to be bullied out of any forward battles. The sight of Morley taking a perfectly timed short pass at full speed and flashing down the left hand channel on the far side of the ground typified his side's devastating attacking potency in the latter stages of the game. The brave try-saving tackle on Morley by Tulsen Tollett only delayed the inevitable, as Leeds recycled the ball quickly from the play-the-ball and scored shortly afterwards. Later, as Iestyn Harris ran in another try by the posts to take the Leeds score closer to the half century mark, I looked across to see Vic give a silent clench of his fist in celebration. The long years of under-achievement were over for him as well.

The 1999 match was the last that my father, Vic and I attended together, as our routine of Challenge Cup final weekends came to an end. With the Wembley re-development now in (slow) progress, the event went on its travels and, for Vic, the prospect of the long journey from Hampshire to Edinburgh, where the 2000 match was played, was too much. My father and I went to the games at Murrayfield (Bradford versus Leeds in 2000 and St Helens versus Wigan in 2002) and Twickenham (Bradford versus St Helens in 2001), the last of these in the rare company of my sister, Rosemary, who was attending her first rugby league match.

Unfortunately, she chose the least attractive of these three fixtures. The 2001 final was played on a wet afternoon, on which the two sides struggled to come to terms with the conditions, although there was much to admire in the brilliant tactical kicking of the St Helens half backs, Sean Long and Tommy Martyn, which Bradford found difficult to cope with near their own line. It was little consolation that the conditions were even more troublesome for the half-time entertainment – the manufactured pop band, Hear'Say – who found that the surface water on their small temporary stage made their rehearsed choreography almost impossible to perform. They struggled around like novice ice skaters on a municipal rink, with one of them falling over completely at one point. To round off the afternoon, it seemed that no-one had informed the railway authorities that, after the game, there would be a significant demand for transport back into London from Twickenham station. We joined the long queue of wet – and remarkable patient – travellers waiting for what appeared to be the normal Saturday afternoon suburban service.

The two finals at Murrayfield were much more enjoyable. The 2000 final was the first at which the video referee was called upon to adjudicate on marginal try-scoring decisions, and I was struck by how the moments of anticipation in waiting for his decision added to the general excitement and tension of the occasion. The fourth official was not needed for the try of the match, however, when the Bradford centre, Nathan McAvoy, broke through the Leeds defence and, without breaking stride, chipped the ball over the covering full-back and caught it again before it bounced to cross the try line near the posts. Two years later, the Wigan victory was something of a surprise, given the way that St Helens had put Leeds to the sword in the semi final. In this game, one piece of particularly clever play caught my eye. The Wigan captain, Andy Farrell, was tackled just short of the St Helens line and, with one tackle remaining in their set, it was obvious that Wigan would attempt a drop goal. After Farrell got up from the ground, he made as if to play the ball, but then hesitated and drew the referee's attention to the fact that the St Helens players needed to be behind their line, rather than gaining an unfair advantage by charging up on their opponents earlier than they were allowed. Farrell would have known that the referee would ignore him. But his action had the vital effect of halting the St Helens defenders and putting them on the back foot, and he duly created the extra split second in which the drop goal attempt could successfully be made by Adrian Lam.

I was a mature rugby league spectator by now, of course. I knew what I was looking for. Needless to say, I enjoyed the overall confrontation between two evenly matched teams, which was provided in all three of these post-Wembley finals. At its most fundamental level, this involved the engagement of the heavy battalions on both sides, as they sought to bring their opponents to a collective exhaustion. But I also took pleasure in the fine detail: the precise tactical kicking of Long and Martyn, the skill and confidence of McAvoy, the streetwise professionalism of Farrell. These were the touches of cool-headed class that stood out from the chaos of the general conflict. And they were the differences, on their respective days, between their sides winning and losing.

The Murrayfield finals were enthusiastically presented and reflected considerable credit on the Scottish Rugby Union and the other organising authorities. For both games, Dad and I had excellent seats opposite the main stand although, from my several visits to Murrayfield, it seems that the view of the pitch is guaranteed to be very good wherever one is situated. My only gripes were twofold. First, that the SRU had a policy of littering the playing area with loose paper as part of the immediate pre-match fireworks display. It has never been clear to me why a top class rugby match – whether rugby league final or rugby union international – should look as if it is being played in a council rubbish tip. Second, as their contribution to the 2002 pre-match entertainment, that year's flavour of the month – Atomic Kitten – performed their whole set, albeit a short one, facing the main stand and with their backs entirely to us on the opposite side of the ground, apart from one half-turn by one of the singers right at the end. I put this down to the likelihood that this was how they normally performed, whether to a concert audience or, more likely, for a video promotion. However – and I acknowledge that this is probably my pedantic side coming out again – it would have been better for the performers to have recognised that they were being viewed from all sides. For completeness, I should record that Tony Hadley (formerly Spandau Ballet) was much more audience-friendly in 2000, although, in my view, the top marks for the supporting cabaret at the Challenge Cup final would be narrowly won by Bonnie Tyler at the Leeds-Wigan final at Wembley in 1994.

As with the rugby league, so with the cricket. After I took up residence in Scotland, there was the occasional visit to Headingley to watch a Yorkshire game, but these became increasingly rare. My father and I saw the rain-interrupted first day of a Nat West Trophy match against Warwickshire in 1993. Allan Donald was far too quick for the early order Yorkshire batsmen and, from our view on the Western Terrace at the angle of square leg, we watched as he gave Paul Grayson a torrid time. Grayson was repeatedly beaten outside his off stump before, with his feet hardly moving at all, he was comprehensively bowled out. The following year, in a Equity and Law league game on a Sunday afternoon, Paul Hartley opened the Yorkshire bowling with two leg stump half volleys which the Hampshire batsman, Robin Smith, despatched effortlessly to the mid wicket boundary. I remarked to Dad that it was a good job Smith was such a slow starter. The Yorkshire response was spearheaded by their overseas player, Sachin Tendulkar, but he found it difficult to raise his scoring rate and the home side was always behind the required rate. In the end, Hampshire won by eight runs, Smith's two opening strokes – or Hartley's two opening looseners, depending on one's perspective – effectively representing the difference between the two sides. In 1998, we watched the second day of a county championship match against Surrey, in which the visitors' strong batting line up – Mark Butcher, Alec Stewart, the Hollioake brothers – was dismissed cheaply by Craig Hamilton and the young Matthew Hoggard. Craig White, opening the Yorkshire second innings, then played a series of classical cover drives to set him on the way to the century that would provide Yorkshire with the opportunity to set an unreachable target on the following day. It was the first time I had seen Hoggard: strong, powerful and accurate. As with Darren Gough on the occasion that I had watched him against Middlesex several years earlier, there was something about his approach – in this case, determined and persevering, with a neat shape to his stock outswinging delivery – that suggested the promise of much more to come.

As with the Challenge Cup final weekend, the tradition for Dad and me to attend the Headingley test match was also maintained during my exile in Scotland, almost always for the play on the Friday and Saturday (the second and third days). However, after Graham Gooch has led his side to victories against the West Indies in 1991 and Pakistan in 1992, it took some time before we were able to see any part of another England win. In 1993, Australia compiled another huge first innings total – 653 for 4 declared, with centuries from Steve Waugh again and David Boon and a double century from Allan Border. Paul Reiffel – not dissimilar, in retrospect, to Hoggard in his speed and accuracy and the generally rustic approach to his business – took eight wickets in the match to secure a comprehensive innings victory for the tourists. In his *Out of My Comfort Zone: The Autobiography*, Waugh provides a revealing insight on the tough approach being adopted by his captain during their massive partnership of 332. At one stage, Border's instruction was: "Don't relax, let's keep the mental and physical degeneration going".

Four years later, in 1997, Australia managed a mere 501 for 9 declared after Matthew Elliott – who, several years later, was to win a Lord's one-day final for Yorkshire – was dismissed on 199 and Ricky Ponting registered his first test century. This was after England had been bowled out for a low total in their first innings, their batsmen unable to cope with the Australian seamers on what appeared, at that stage, to be a pitch of variable bounce. The false promise of the England batting seemed to be captured, in microcosm, by the lower order entry of Darren Gough, whose purposeful march to the wicket was loudly cheered by his raucous admirers on the Western Terrace. He was dismissed second ball.[45]

The key incident in the match occurred after Gough had gallantly responded with a couple of quick wickets and Australia had progressed unconvincingly to 50 for 3, when Elliott was dropped by Graham Thorpe at slip off the bowling of Mike Smith. Smith, Yorkshire-born, had had considerable success with Gloucestershire over the years with his accurate left-arm seam bowling, notwithstanding a curious delivery stride, in which he seemed to slow down and lose significant momentum before letting go of the ball. On this occasion, however, his confidence seemed to drain away after Thorpe's error and he did not take a wicket in what turned out to be his only test match. Elliott's partnership with Ponting of over 250 took the match far out of England's reach and, by the end of the truncated third day, it was clear that the home side was again being seriously outplayed.

Another fascinating insider's perspective on these matches is provided by Alec Stewart in *Playing for Keeps*. In the 1993 Ashes match, England fielded four pace bowlers with a combined test experience of five matches. The side also included Mark Lathwell of Somerset – "a great natural talent", according to Stewart – who was "the one England player of [Stewart's] era who I believe just didn't want to be there… Despite all our efforts to involve him in conversations, we couldn't drag anything out of him". For Stewart, Lathwell was simply overawed by the whole test match scene. The England captain, Michael Atherton, made the same point in his *Opening Up: My Autobiography:* "I said to him 'Good luck, the crowd are rooting for you' 'They won't be in a minute when I'm on my way back' he replied". I thought that Lathwell looked inhibited in his footwork, especially against Shane Warne. On the 1997 match, Stewart reports that Atherton was furious that the England selectors (of whom he was not one) had preferred Smith to Andrew Caddick. Stewart sided with his captain on this one: "our selectors played right into [the Australians'] hands by picking the wrong bowling line up". Reading Stewart's candid account, it is not difficult to see how the Australians' superiority on the field of play was based on the psychological domination that they had established over the England changing room.

Allan Border's instruction to Steve Waugh of four years earlier was paying rich dividends for his successor as Australian captain, Mark Taylor.

The 1994 test match against South Africa was the first that Headingley had staged against these opponents since 1955. The batsmen were generally in control on a slow pitch, apart from in the South African first innings, when the captain Hansie Cronje faced up to his first ball from Phillip DeFreitas, who had just taken his first wicket. Cronje played an immaculate forward defensive stroke, only to hear the death rattle of his stumps being shattered behind him. He retained the pose for several seconds as the crowd cheered jubilantly around the ground, before turning around slowly and trudging back to the pavilion. With what we have learned about Cronje since, the obvious question to ask in retrospect is whether this was a genuine victory on DeFreitas's part. He no doubt thought so at the time, as did we, and I hope this interpretation remains the correct one. The fact that the issue is raised at all – and that any doubt might exist about the legitimacy of the sporting action that thousands of spectators paid to see – is only one of the unpleasant aftertastes that remains, following the revealed corruption in international cricket at this time.

My father and I maintained the routine of watching the Friday's play from the main part of the Football Stand and then transferring on the Saturday to the upper balcony. Both gave good perspectives on the whole ground, though we had a marginal preference for the latter, given its higher elevation. This is not to say that the neurotic in me did not manage to find some fault in the seating arrangements. The most obvious fault was that the seats were cramped, especially in the balcony; for a members' section at a test match cricket ground, the level of comfort was poor, to say the least. In 1994, in addition, we were placed right next to the radio commentators' section in the middle of the balcony. Quite apart from the generous privilege of being able to watch the champagne bottles regularly enter the Test Match Special booth, and of seeing the later effects of their contents on the eyelids on one or two of the distinguished summarisers located there, it meant that we were right next to the small posse of independent radio reporters, whose regular broadcasts to their listeners – repetitive and loud – were not screened off within a separate studio. On other occasions, spectators in the balcony – not us, fortunately – were subject to consistent, though independent, attacks by wasps and by pigeons. One year, one of the latter took particular exception to an unfortunate man situated a couple of rows in front of us and to our left, who twice received direct bombing hits.

However, these distractions were as nothing, compared with the delights to which Dad and I were subjected in the balcony on the third day of the West Indies test match of 1995. It is the case, of course, that one of the great unknowns about watching any sporting event is the inevitable uncertainty about who one's immediate neighbours will be. In most instances, this does not matter. On an open terrace, there is an opportunity to move to somewhere else. At a rugby or football match, or at the boxing or horse racing come to that, the noise and exuberance of the occasion are usually more than sufficient to drown out the individual inanities that may be muttered in the near vicinity. But it is different at a cricket test match. My view is that, whilst it is recognised that there will be comments and cheers and groans from the neighbours – and, indeed, that these should be an essential constituent of the occasion – there should also be opportunities for the individual spectator to enjoy some quiet reflection on the unfolding course of the events on the field. Does this seem reasonable, or am I reverting back to my retired brigadier persona?

On this particular occasion, my father and I enjoyed – if that is the word – the company in the balcony row behind us of a group, whose purpose in coming to the cricket had clearly been to catch up on the social gossip of the middle class Home Counties. It did not take long to learn that their names were Lawrence, Jonathan, Jocelyn, Vanessa and one other. Jonathan (or it might have been Jocelyn) was married to Vanessa; they had come up from London the previous day and stayed overnight at the Queens Hotel. At least two of the group were solicitors; another worked for the BBC. One had been in the Coopers and Lybrand hospitality suite at a previous Headingley test match.

Before going any further, I should report that I have nothing against the middle classes of the Home Counties; indeed, for many years, I would have counted as one of these myself. Whatever snobbery might have be linked to my homicidal perspective on the group, it was not the inverse type associated with class warfare. The basic problem was that the group did not stop talking for the whole of the pre-lunch session.

They started more or less as the West Indies resumed their innings at 11 o'clock on a cloudy, thick-sweater day. Phillip DeFreitas and Peter Martin were bowling tightly to Keith Arthurton and Junior Murray. The group had obviously not met for some time. The conversation started with the vital things in life, such as the difficulty in finding a good au pair. Jocelyn (or it might have been Jonathan) had employed eight or nine over the years, but had decided that that was enough for now. Next, the tennis club. J (or it might have been J) explained to the group how Vanessa's efforts as treasurer and secretary had resurrected the club's fortunes. Vanessa modestly rejected the accolade. The tone for the day was established.

On the field, the events of the test match were unfolding: DeFreitas trapped Murray into driving a catch to a perfectly positioned fielder at short extra cover; Ian Bishop and Curtley Ambrose found themselves at the same end of the pitch and the former was run out by 22 yards; a wild delivery from Devon Malcolm exploded out of footmark and flew over the boundary, first bounce, for four byes. From behind me, more information was provided. The couple's children – "the brutes" – were able to attend a good school in their catchment area: to have attended it from outside would have cost at least £2,000 per term. On the work front, one of the solicitor's business was brisk; he was clearing £150,000 a year gross.

The cricket continued with England taking their turn to bat – and not without comment. "Good shot", Lawrence pronounced knowledgeably, as Hick pulled a short ball from Bishop to the boundary. "He's a class player", suggested Jocelyn, as he repeated the shot to the next delivery. "Wonderful shot", roared Jonathan, as Hick connected powerfully again, only to see Courtney Walsh pouch the catch on the long leg boundary. Graeme Hick was not the only one to fall for Ian Bishop's three card trick.

The group was not discouraged. A lengthy discussion about golf courses in the suburbs of London was followed by a seminar on the heating requirements of Jonathan's cottage in Cornwall. Was central heating really necessary, as the weather was undoubtedly warmer down there? While we pondered on this, the West Indian fast bowlers, scenting the kill in England's second innings, roared in with their customary skill and menace. Their progress was halted by Thorpe's brave resistance and Dickie Bird's lightmeter. Jocelyn wondered why Thorpe's test match batting average was so low. (He meant Ramprakash's, presumably).

And still they did not stop. Indeed, having swapped their seats at one of the breaks in play, they were in the happy position of having to recount their tales again. Vanessa stated how lucky they were with the school in their catchment area and how well the brutes were doing; one of the solicitors was clearing £150,000 per year; J said that he and Vanessa had come up the previous day and were staying at the Queens Hotel; on a previous occasion, hospitality had been provided in the Coopers and Lybrand suite; the tennis club had been saved.

I reflected on the experience of that occasion in the balcony at Headingley for quite a long time afterwards. Before the day's play, I had expected that I could view the clowns and jokers on the Western Terrace providing the background entertainment at a respectful distance. I would be away from the Mexican waves, the flying beer and the laddish excesses. I would be amongst those whose principal aim would be to watch the cricket.

Instead, I found myself asking three questions, which – given that the experience of watching sport is the subject of this volume – are worth repeating here. First, did I feel intrusive – nosey even – as I learned more about the group? Of course, it was none of my business where they lived (Yorkshire and London), how old they were (40s), where they went to university (Durham and Bristol), what jobs they did, what level of conveyancing fees they charged, what sports they played, how old Vanessa's children were (10 and 12), on which days Lawrence was going to be entertained at the next test match at Lord's (Thursday and Friday), how much food and wine they had brought ("stacks"), where they had bought their sandwiches that morning (Marks and Spencer). The point was: I didn't want to know. I was not listening; I was hearing.

Moreover – a key point, I think – they wanted me to hear. It was not only the unbroken conversation, or its tedium, or its accent (a sort of poor man's Henry Blofeld, but without the Etonian pedigree). It was its subtle volume, loud enough to be easily audible for two or three rows in front. The group was, in other words, "lording it": an unpleasant habit at the best of times and, I would beg to argue m'lud, a capital offence in the members' enclosure on the third day of a Headingley test match. A less tolerant person than I might have checked the weight-bearing capabilities of the steel rafters at the top of the stand, in case a spare noose became available.

The second question was also self-directed. Was it actually me who was being unreasonable? Or neurotic, even? If a group of old acquaintants wished to chew the fat, who was I to deny them? Besides, compared with the troubles that other people have from their neighbours – at the time, I remember thinking about an unruly council estate, or a desperate Bosnian enclave – what right did I have to complain about a temporary inconvenience? My uncertainty on this point did not last long.

The final question was: could they be stopped? Not easily. An obvious ploy might have been to threaten some sort of physical violence. However, striking a solicitor is a risky business at the best of times and not to be undertaken without careful consideration, particularly when another solicitor is present. The more considered approach – and the one that was eventually adopted – was to ask politely that the group refrain from continuous chattering and allow those of us who had come to watch the cricket to do so. After I had done this, I happened to glance at the man seated a couple of places away to my left, who immediately responded with a short nod of approval. The result from behind was sadly predictable, however, as the muttered responses came back – "unbelievable" – interspersed with references to the noise from the Western Terrace. That said it all, of course. As far as Jonathan, Jocelyn and company were concerned, they were behaving reasonably. They were not drunk or throwing beer; they were not Mexican waving; they were not taunting stewards or police. They were, however, missing the point completely.

England eventually won a Headingley test match in 1998, when Darren Gough took Makhaya Ntini's wicket on the last morning to secure a victory over South Africa by 23 runs. Gough gained the benefit of a borderline lbw decision, given in his favour by the Pakistani umpire, Javed Akhtar. In *Playing for Keeps*, Alec Stewart notes that Akhtar had a poor match, though he is quick to point out that the umpire's decisions did not favour one side in particular and that, from his perspective, the Ntini verdict looked the correct one: "stone dead". Interestingly, in his impressive *Opening Up*, Michael Atherton states that this was "...the nastiest, most ill-tempered match that I have ever played in and throughout it was clear that neither side had much regard for the other".

Earlier in the match, on the Friday, we saw Hansie Cronje improve on his brief appearance – his first ball dismissal by Phil DeFreitas in 1994 – with a resolute and skilful half century and Mark Ramprakash provide a repeat of the diving mid-wicket catch with which we had seen him dismiss Phil Simmons of the West Indies in 1991, this time to remove Jacques Kallis. Then, on the Saturday, after Atherton was given out to the first ball of the day – "I got a huge inside-edge on to my pads, only to be given out leg before by umpire Javed Akhtar" – we watched Nasser Hussein grind through the rest of the day to score 80 against the formidable South African new ball attack of Allan Donald and Shaun Pollock and the support bowling of Ntini, Kallis and Brian McMillan. Hussein's was something of an old-fashioned test match innings, determinedly appropriate for his side's requirements at the time, though with some crisp drives and pulls. We noted the calmness that both he and Mark Butcher showed under the regular verbal assault that, even from our position in the balcony of the Football Stand, we could see they were receiving between deliveries from McMillan. I enjoyed watching Donald, a consistently excellent bowler over many years, with his smooth run up to the wicket characterised by the high lift of the backs of his heels; in that respect, he reminded me of the Australian bowler, Jeff Thomson, although any mirroring of their actions was lost once the delivery stride was reached. By contrast, I always thought that Pollock's action was more rigid and ungainly, as if he was struggling to loosen the constraints imposed by some invisible corset: he was an impressive cricketer, nonetheless.

The South Africans were back at Headingley the following summer, this time for a decisive match in the second round of group matches – the so-called Super Six competition – that would determine which sides would reach the semi-finals of the 1999 Cricket World Cup. Their opponents were Australia and the bare fact of the situation for this match was that, if South Africa won, Australia would be out of the tournament, their earlier defeats against Pakistan and New Zealand also counting against them in this round.

My father and I eschewed our usual positions in the Football Stand to watch the game from the small open stand at the top of the winter cricket nets. I had seen Yorkshire matches from there before with some ambivalence. The view of the overall arena was very good, but there was a feeling of distance from the action and from the rest of the spectators, and it could be an exposed location if the weather was at all inclement. On this particular day, however, it was a good vantage point, and it was from there that I viewed the next of the nano-dramas that I have been reporting throughout this volume.

South Africa made a sizeable total, though it would have been even larger had the middle order acceleration not been limited by some impressively tight and controlled bowling from Shane Warne. In response, chasing 271 to win, Australia lost three wickets before they had reached 50. Much depended on the captain Steve Waugh being able to repeat his longstanding test match success at Headingley within this one day environment. After a promising start, it seemed that he would not. He played an uncharacteristically lame chip shot on to the leg side and appeared to have been caught by Herschelle Gibbs. The ball spooned from Waugh's bat into a gentle loop and Gibbs ambled across to take the catch. I thought that Waugh was out and, judging by the immediate collective reaction of the crowd around me, so did everybody else. Then, unbelievably, we saw the ball rolling along the ground and Gibbs running to re-gather it. The archetypal "dolly" catch had been spilled. The moment of nano-drama is at that point. I had seen Waugh give the catch and Gibbs apparently take it; the captain was out; this key player was to play no further part in the game; Australia were a considerable step closer to elimination from the World Cup. Not so. There was a gradual realisation throughout the watching crowd – shock, mixed with an element of horror on Gibbs's behalf – that the catch had been spilled and that Waugh would be continuing his innings.

A couple of hours later, Waugh was still batting when, in the last available over and with a century to his name, he scrambled through for the run that brought the scores level and, with fewer Australian wickets having fallen, guaranteed his side's passage into the semi-finals. He ran several yards past the stumps towards us and pumped his clenched fist towards the ground in celebration. Australia were still in the competition. In the following morning's *Yorkshire Post*, the cricket correspondent, Robert Mills, described Waugh's innings as the finest one-day innings ever seen at Headingley. Waugh himself, in *Out of My Comfort Zone: The Autobiography*, states that one particular shot played in the 90s – a slog-sweep for six off the opening bowler, Steve Elsworthy – was the greatest shot of his career. A week later, having narrowly beaten South Africa again in the semi-final, Australia convincingly won the tournament with an easy victory over Pakistan at Lord's.[46]

The perspective of time only adds to the complications surrounding the Gibbs incident, as he was one of those heavily implicated in the Cronje scandal. However, whilst the result of at least one other fixture in the 1999 Cricket World Cup has been tarnished by subsequent corruption revelations, I am not aware that this particular Headingley match has been similarly tainted. The explanation given at the time, which I have always thought entirely reasonable, was that Gibbs jarred the ball against his right hip in the act of tossing the ball into the air. In his autobiography, Waugh describes Gibbs's blunder as "a miraculous event" which served to prolong his one-day international career, as he suspected defeat for Australia would have meant he would not have been selected again. Waugh also states, astonishingly, that, prior to the match, Shane Warne had alerted his colleagues to Gibbs's susceptibility to this type of error. Waugh reports that he consoled Gibbs by informing him that he had just cost his team the match: undoubtedly one of the more prescient examples of sledging to have occurred on the international cricket field.

In 2000, the Glasgow Women's Half Marathon was held on a Sunday. The relevance of the timing of this event in the athletics calendar was that the family and I arranged, in advance, to travel back from Leeds to Glasgow on the Saturday of the Headingley test match so that my wife, Angela, could participate in the run on the following day. This would leave the first two days – Thursday and Friday – for my father and me to go to the cricket. It was a break with our existing tradition of attending on the Friday and Saturday of the test match, but it was obviously the best way of meeting the various family interests.

As it happened, the test match, against the West Indies, was completed before the end of the second day's play. In the respective first innings, whilst not unplayable, the pitch gave some assistance to the bowlers, notably Craig White and Curtley Ambrose, and the West Indies began their second innings on the Friday afternoon in arrears by exactly 100 runs. They were subsequently bowled out for 61 – the lowest ever completed test match innings at Headingley – the top order batsmen unable to cope with Darren Gough's speedy swing bowling, which accounted for the first four wickets. There was a frenzied excitement as the Yorkshire crowd roared Gough to the crease for his attempted hat-trick ball to Brian Lara, another full-length swinging delivery which the batsmen only negotiated with some urgency and considerable skill. Dad and I then looked at each other in astonishment as Lara surrendered his wicket for the second time in the match by padding up and being given out leg before wicket to a straight delivery. The end was swift. Andrew Caddick completed the rout by taking four wickets in an over.

It was therefore with some irony – although, in my view, it was entirely the correct decision – that the man-of-the-match award should go to a batsman, Michael Vaughan, who made a fine half century in difficult circumstances. Vaughan displayed a judicious shot selection and – during the decisive partnership with Graeme Hick – led some aggressive running between the wickets. The latter feature of Vaughan's approach was particularly noticeable: it was as if he had deliberately decided to change the tempo of the England innings, not through any extravagant shot-making *a la Botham*, but by disturbing the psychological comfort of the bowlers and fielders. It struck me at the time as an impressively mature innings from someone who had only played half a dozen test matches and I was intrigued that, notwithstanding his inexperience, Vaughan was playing the lead role in the partnership with a batsman who was playing for England for the 60th time. At the end of the match, by the time that Viv Richards came to announce who the recipient of the award would be, the euphoric crowd that had gathered in front of the Football Stand was making so much noise that his short speech could not be heard. Instead, we looked across to the large screen on the far side of the ground. When the camera picked out the England players and Vaughan started to walk forward, there was another huge roar from the assembled masses.

Nearly a decade later, I looked up Vaughan's reflections on this innings in *Time to Declare: My Autobiography* and noted with a smug satisfaction that the characteristics I had identified on that particular day were also those that he had chosen to describe: "There was something about him [Hick] that made me feel that I was the senior partner when we were out there together, despite it being only my 7th test... I said... that we should try and run them ragged and so the first opportunity we got, with the ball trickling to third man, I hared it back for a second, and that set the tone".

England were successful again in 2001, thanks to a misjudged declaration by Adam Gilchrist, the captain of Australia in Waugh's absence through injury, and the best innings of his test career by Mark Butcher, whose 173 not out took England to an improbable victory on the final day. Dad and I watched Alec Stewart make the top score in England's first innings, thereby following Bill Athey as a contributor to the household funds at the expense of the on-ground bookmaker, by playing a series of uninhibited one day strokes in response to the fall of wickets at the other end. *Wisden* subsequently explained this as due to Stewart being unhappy about his demotion to number seven in the batting order, so that he "responded with a bizarre innings of 76 not out, throwing the bat with daredevil irresponsibility".

However, my main memory of the match is of the end of the lunch break on the Saturday. As usual, Dad and I had taken our sandwiches and coffee through to the stand overlooking the rugby ground on the other side of the Football Stand, where it was possible to spread out a little on the available seating. We returned to our seats just as the Australians were taking the field for the afternoon session. They did so through a guard of honour made at the boundary edge by a group of disabled cricketers, dressed in their whites, who had given a demonstration of their skills on the outfield during the break. This was a courageous group – including some blind and some with missing limbs – and they formed two lines to welcome the Australians as Gilchrist led his team on to the ground. Most of the Australians jogged or walked straight through the disabled players' tunnel, clearly focusing on their immediate tasks when play resumed, though Gilchrist held out a large wicketkeeping glove to the player at the end of one of the lines. The last player out was Shane Warne, who stopped and went slowly along one of the lines, shaking hands with everyone in it. I found this incredibly moving. Good on you, mate, I thought.

The 2002 test match at Headingley was the first involving India since the Mexican wave accounted for the wicket of Mohammed Azharuddin in 1986. The tourists produced a batting masterclass, particularly Rahul Dravid, whose innings began when the pitch was at its liveliest on the first day, but whose unflappable temperament and immaculate technique took him to 148. Sachin Tendulkar batted with equal skill and panache to make 193, accelerating rapidly towards the end of his innings, when one of his sixes – off Andrew Caddick – was deposited several rows back into the members' seating in front of the old bowling green. The Indian captain, Sourav Ganguly, came in to rub salt into the tired England bowlers' wounds. He also reached a century, violently opening his shoulders to Ashley Giles in the gathering gloom on the Friday evening to strike some massive blows over and around the old pavilion. During the Tendulkar-Ganguly partnership, the lights on the scoreboard came on – one, then two, then three – to signify that the light was deteriorating; in the meantime, somewhat surreally, the ball kept disappearing across or over the boundary rope, as India eventually amassed 628 for 8 wickets. I don't think Dad or I really minded. We would have wanted England to win, of course, rather than watching them toil as we did, but, as throughout our spectating experiences together, we were also keen to see the best exponents in their particular sports performing at the top of their games. The Indian batsmen certainly fell into that category.

The India test match of 2002 was the last that I attended with my father at Headingley. After belatedly establishing the routine after his retirement in the early 1980s – and beginning with the West Indies test match of 1984, when we had watched Malcolm Marshall demolish the England second innings with his left wrist and thumb in plaster – we attended a total of 15 tests over this period and watched the continual evolution of the England team from Ian Botham and David Gower through to Andrew Flintoff and Matthew Hoggard. (In an exercise of anorakian proportions, I later calculated that we had seen 69 different cricketers play for England, of whom over half – 36 – we viewed only once. Michael Atherton and Alec Stewart were the most frequently observed players, both with 10 appearances[47]).

For my father and me, the Headingley test match therefore played an analogous role to that of the rugby league Challenge Cup final at Wembley. Although the timing of the match varied each summer – from early June to mid August – it was still a fixed point in the annual calendar. Every year, Dad and I went through our established routines: parking the car in the same spot at the corner of two of the neighbouring streets, walking down the hill past the terraced houses to reach Kirkstall Lane, leaving our bags on our allocated seats, watching the players go through their pre-match warm-up routines, going for a coffee in the bar under the Football Stand with its photographs of past Leeds rugby league players on the walls, retreating to the seats in the rugby ground to eat our sandwiches at lunchtime, staying on after the play had finished to watch the ground clear. A great deal of what we experienced at the test match changed from year to year, of course: the cast of players, the detail of the Headingley ground, the prevailing weather. And, there were the bigger issues, outside of watching the cricket, that affected our everyday lives, not least the health and wellbeing of our families and friends. But, notwithstanding all this, the Headingley test match was an event that remained constant. It provided us with reassurance and familiarity and, not least, the unspoken pleasure of our shared participation in the event itself.

Apart from the occasional visits to the Bearsden and Milngavie Highland Games, I have not engaged my own family in the science of sports spectating. Their interests lie elsewhere. The closest I have come – so far – was during a holiday in Paris in 2000, when I persuaded them that we should take the guided tour of the Stade de France. And very good it was too, we all agreed, as we saw the full vastness of the stadium, with its movable blocks of seating, which can be rearranged according to the type of event taking place – rugby or soccer international, pop concert, and so on – and walked along the edge of the pitch. The highlight was our visit to the changing rooms, in which the individual places were labelled with the names of the players who had contested the soccer World Cup final between France and Brazil of two years earlier, which of course had been played at the venue. My wife dutifully photographed her husband, his arms around his two children, as he sat in the places respectively allocated to Ronaldo and Zinedine Zidane.

The Sixth Age

The Affluent Reflective

The affluence of a comfortable middle class lifestyle enables me to move up the price range for some of the sports events I attend. Although more selective, these continue to encompass both the local and the international. Changing family circumstances lead to reflection on the passage of time.

Chapter 21

FedEx Field

In February 2005, 30 years to the month after my first visit to Cardiff to see a Wales versus England rugby union international, I went to the Millennium Stadium to see the corresponding fixture. I had heard a great deal about the stadium, of course – in particular, about how the volume of noise is exacerbated when the stadium is full and the retractable roof is closed – but, nonetheless, I was still taken aback by the passion of the occasion and the magnificence of the venue.

The fixture was played on the first weekend of the 2005 Six Nations Championship and, perhaps because Wales sensed their opportunity to beat England at Cardiff for the first time in 12 years, there was a huge amount of expectation and media hype in the build up to the game. From the English perspective, I shared the feeling of foreboding. Wales had run both South Africa and New Zealand very close in the autumn internationals. Moreover, there was no doubt that the England team had peaked in 2003 and, even then in my view, they had reached their zenith, not in the rugby union World Cup itself during the autumn, but in the preceding months, when they had demolished Ireland at Lansdowne Road to win the Grand Slam and then gone on to defeat both Australia and New Zealand away from home on their summer tour. The England XV that took the field against Wales included only five of the players who had started the World Cup final against Australia.

The centre of Cardiff was a sea of red from lunchtime onwards – to gain entry to some of the pubs, there appeared to be queues to join the queues – and I could sense the tension increasing as the time for the early evening kick off approached. As the players took the field, I nodded in the direction of the England captain, as he led his side out, in recognition of the fact that he was the former player with the Hunslet Boys rugby league club,

Jason Robinson, who had followed his successful career with Wigan by reaching the pinnacle of the union code. I thought of my father, who would have had something to say about that.[48]

England started poorly, overthrowing at their first line out, thereby presenting Martyn Williams with the opportunity to gain possession and allowing Stephen Jones to find a long touch deep into England's half. The Welsh players and their supporters gained an immediate psychological boost. Thereafter, in truth, both sides made a series of errors as the players seemed to be undermined by the tension of the occasion and the closeness of the score. Although England were on the back foot for much of the game, they should have won the match. By the time that the game entered its final minutes, England had edged ahead by 9 points to 8, having registered three penalty goals to a Wales penalty and an excellent try rounded off by Shane Williams after a long cut-out pass by the impressive Michael Owen.

It was then that a key difference between the England World Cup winning side and the successor XV was revealed. With the minutes ticking away – and instead of running the clock down and playing for position – England attempted an ambitious passing move against the pressing Welsh defence. A long pass to one of the back row forwards was spilled and went to ground. I groaned audibly. Why had they attempted that particular move at that particular time? I am certain that, had the streetwise professionalism of Martin Johnson or Richard Hill or Neil Back been at hand, Wales would not have had the chance to re-gather possession. Instead, they were awarded a scrum, from which the scrum half Gareth Cooper made a useful half-break and put in a teasing grubber kick into the England half which Robinson, advancing from full back, fell on bravely only for an England player to be penalised for not staying on his feet at the ruck.

This was the cue for every Welsh supporter in the ground to call for their flamboyant centre, Gavin Henson, to be given the chance to kick the winning penalty goal. Henson had already played a strong match, kicking superbly out of hand and delivering a couple of his heavy tackles on the young England centre, Matthew Tait, which noticeably lifted his side and its supporters. The tension level rose another few notches.

Llyr James and I had the perfect view of the penalty kick. It was wide out on the right hand side of the field and about 45 yards from the posts and, from our vantage point, we had a clear perspective of the line that Henson would have to take. I had been in this position before, of course – watching the late efforts of Dusty Hare for England against Wales in 1980, Hare again against Wales in 1981, Lee Crooks for Great Britain against New Zealand in 1985, amongst others. The difference here was that it was a player from the side I was not supporting who would be taking the kick.

Henson never looked like missing. Whatever nerves he might have been feeling, he did not reveal in the slightest. Instead, like Hare at Twickenham and Crooks at Elland Road, he made the perfect contact with the ball. As soon as he struck the kick, it was clear to Llyr and to me that the direction was perfect. All that mattered now was whether there was sufficient weight in the stroke and that, also, was almost immediately apparent. The ball had not travelled more than a few yards before Llyr said quietly, "Oh, yes". I knew, from the tone of his voice – and the character of the man – that this was not a triumphalist exclamation of victory, but a matter-of-fact recognition of the impending reality. It was a statement, on both our behalves, that anticipated the pandemonium of the following seconds and minutes.

The cacophony of noise as the touch judges' flags confirmed that the kick had been successful presented a violent assault on the eardrums. My immediate thought, however, as I watched the unfettered scenes of jubilation around me – and as irrational as it might therefore have seemed – was that England had not yet lost the match. There were still a couple of minutes to be played. The kick-off, if carefully placed and vigorously chased, could yet induce a Welsh infringement and the chance of a final England penalty kick. "Keep cool", I shouted at the England team, albeit silently. If they could manage to get this final test of the basics right, there still might be a opportunity to steal the match. It was not to be, of course. England failed this last examination of their professional ruthlessness. The kick off was too long, Wales gathered the ball comfortably and cleared their lines with ease. When the referee signalled the end of the match, it was time for the party in Cardiff to begin.

The following day, the *Wales on Sunday* newspaper allocated 17 pages to the match. 6 weeks later, after Wales had defeated Ireland 32–20, also at the Millennium Stadium, to win their first Grand Slam since 1978, the corresponding allocation within the newspaper was a mere 30 pages.

Gavin Henson's kick constitutes the final nano-drama described in this book. At one level – and, of itself, this is obviously not be understated – it was the match-winning score, played out against a background of fervent passion and desire. But, as described, I had seen similar scores on other occasions in the past. What raises this particular kick even further – as shown by Llyr's reflective reaction – is that it was an example of how a critical component of the excitement of watching a sports event is in the anticipation of the outcome of a given action, including that anticipation which has a life span of only a few seconds. When the ball was in the air and travelling towards its destination, Llyr and I knew what was coming next and, in our different ways, we could enjoy that moment of clear-sighted prediction.

Henson's is the eleventh such sporting nano-drama identified here – a "First XI" – and I list them below for completeness in chronological order. It should perhaps be noted that the distribution between the sports – 4 rugby league, 4 cricket, 1 rugby union, 1 football, 1 golf – has not been pre-determined through some sort of artificial quota system, but is the straightforward outcome of the items that have been identified as the narrative has progressed. As it happens, the distribution probably does also represent a complementary reflection of the respective emphases between rugby, cricket and other sports in the chapters of this volume. The selection of the First XI is a personal choice, of course, based on the necessary condition that they were all witnessed by me. Somebody else's choice would be different. That, of course, is the key point.

A "First XI" of Sporting Nano-dramas		
1	April 1965	Rugby league
	Alan Preece seizes on to a loose pass near the Wakefield Trinity try line and runs under the posts to score Hunslet's first try in the Challenge Cup semi final at Headingley.	
2	September 1965	Rugby league
	The crowd's sense of excited anticipation as the ball is swept across the Castleford back division to the teenage Roger Millward, playing on the right wing against Hunslet in the Yorkshire Cup semi final at Parkside.	
3	August 1977	Cricket
	The moment that Geoff Boycott, playing for England against Australia at Headingley, connects with his on drive, off the bowling of Greg Chappell, to take him to his hundredth first class century.	
4	August 1977	Cricket
	Derek Randall's piece of mesmeric fielding to run out Rick McCosker in the same test match.	
5	May 1980.	Rugby league.
	Brian Lockwood's sublime pass to set up Steve Hubbard for a try for Hull Kingston Rovers against Hull FC in the Challenge Cup final at Wembley.	
6	July 1981	Cricket
	The first delivery received by Geoff Boycott on the Saturday morning of the Headingley test match, bowled by Dennis Lillee of Australia, against a background of absolute silence across the ground from the capacity crowd.	
7	October 1992	Football
	Gary McAllister's volleyed goal for Leeds United in the opening minutes of the European Cup tie against Rangers at Ibrox Stadium.	

8	April 1994	Rugby league
	Martin Offiah breaking the first line of the Leeds defence, thereby opening up the opportunity for him to score a spectacular long range try for Wigan in the Challenge Cup final.	
9	July 1997	Golf
	The smooth beauty of Payne Stewart's swing, as seen on the practice tee, before his round on the Saturday of the Open Championship at Troon.	
10	June 1999	Cricket
	Herschelle Gibbs of South Africa dropping the easiest of catches offered by Steve Waugh, when Australia were struggling in the match and on the brink of being eliminated from the World Cup.	
11	February 2005	Rugby union
	Gavin Henson's penalty kick, as seen in flight, to win the Six Nations match for Wales against England at the Millennium Stadium.	

The Millennium Stadium was the first of three major sporting arenas that I visited in 2005. The year ended at Murrayfield for a Scotland versus New Zealand rugby union international, described later, but before that was the small matter of the Olympic Stadium in Barcelona, during the course of a long weekend with the family in the Catalan capital in October. On a visit to the main tourist information centre in Placa de Catalunya, I happened to notice that tickets were available for the match between Espanyol and Cadiz in the *primera divisio* of the Campionat de Lliga on the Sunday evening. The prices of the tickets varied from 20 to 40 euros and I went for the top of the range.

The stadium was a couple of miles across town from our hotel, but my journey there was straightforward. The Olympic complex was one of the stops on one of the impressive city bus tours that the tourist office organises and, as I had a two-day open-ended ticket, I simply repeated half of the tour that we had undertaken earlier in the day in order to arrive at the right place. It was about 5.30pm, an hour and a half before the kick off, and I used the time to wander around the outside of the Lluis Companys Stadium a couple of times in the bright early evening sunshine.[49] The rival supporters began to gather in the environs of the stadium – the home side's in their colours of broad blue and white vertical stripes and Cadiz's in a bright yellow – the latter much smaller in numbers, of course, but loud and surprisingly confident for a side near the foot of the league table. I watched the interchanges of chanting and singing and was pleasantly struck by the lack of any aggression or confrontation.

The stadium had been built in 1929 and, although enlarged and overhauled for the 1992 Olympic Games, seemed to have retained much of its original character and structure. The latter reminded me of the (pre-demolished) Wembley, with the steps leading up to the entrance gates, the refreshment areas on the wide circuit inside the stadium and the solid staircases, one of which led up to my seat on the second tier. The lush playing surface of the pitch lay on the far side of the athletics track (which was not a feature of Wembley, of course). My seat in the main stand – the only part of the ground to be covered – was opposite the finishing line of the track: the exact place at which Sally Gunnell had won her gold medal in the 400 metres hurdles in 1992. As the daylight quickly faded, I watched the moon rising in the sky above the open stand on the opposite side of the pitch, the wooded hill of Montjuic over to the right.

I think the football commentators would describe the match as a game of two halves. In the first half, both sides illustrated why they were in the lower half of the division. There was plenty of energy and some trickery, but too many passes went astray and neither side was able to build a concerted attack; in the first 45 minutes, there was not a single shot on target at either end. In the second half, it was a different story: two goals, three bookings and a sending off.

Both goals were scored by Cadiz. As the game progressed, they seemed to realise that, with their solid defence in firm control of the Espanyol attacking threat, there was scope for a more rewarding evening. The centre half De Quintana and the left back Raul Lopez, in particular, provided a dominant physical presence that, apart from one early misunderstanding with their goalkeeper, confirmed Cadiz's reputation for defensive frugality. And so it was that, from the two main opportunities that were presented to their side in the last quarter of the game, Pavoni and Jonathan Sesma scored the decisive goals. Each was greeted with unbridled delight by the few hundred Cadiz supporters who had gathered together in an isolated group in the upper tier of the stand over to my right.

Espanyol became less threatening as the game progressed and their supporters in the main stand behind me and to my left made their displeasure evident. They looked like a team in need of a boost to their confidence. The sight of the midfield player, Juanfran, slowly and reluctantly (and, I thought, petulantly) trudging off the pitch straight to the changing room after being substituted appeared to be symptomatic of a general lack of team spirit. Just before the end, the right back Armando Sa, who had started the game brightly but whose performance had deteriorated over the course of the evening, was caught by the referee lashing out at an opponent in a late tackle. The following day's *La Vanguardia* reported that the colour of his *tarjeta* was *roja*: a straight red.

I enjoyed the evening. Although the stadium was only about a quarter full – the newspaper reported that there were 21,950 *espectadores* – the effect was mitigated by the use of half a dozen huge brightly coloured advertising banners over the blocks of seats on the lower level behind each goal. As Espanyol struggled, the agitated shouts – incomprehensible to me, of course – of some of the spectators behind me rang out into the evening air. I looked around the stadium and attempted to make a permanent mental picture: as ever, the finger nails drove into the palm of my left hand.

It had turned out that our weekend visit to Barcelona had coincided with an away fixture for the city's principal team – Barcelona had played at Deportivo la Corunna on the previous evening – so I was aware that my visit to the Nou Camp would have to wait for another occasion. But I did not mind. If I had seen be able to see Barcelona, I would not have watched a game in the Olympic Stadium. As the referee blew the final whistle, and the Cadiz players ran across to salute their ecstatic supporters to my right, I thought back to the match that I had seen in the corresponding venue in Munich in 1975, when the away side (on that occasion, Dynamo Kiev) had also prevailed against the home favourites.

It was inevitable that, on returning home from Barcelona, I would track the fortunes of Espanyol and Cadiz over the remainder of the 2005–06 season. However, their respective fates were not what I would have predicted on the basis of their encounter on that October evening. Although Espanyol hovered close to the relegation zone for most of the season, they managed to avoid the drop after scoring a last minute goal in their final match of the campaign against Real Sociedad. Even more surprisingly, they won the Spanish Cup – the Copa del Reys – beating Real Zaragoza in the final in April. For Cadiz, the season was less successful: they finished third from bottom of the league and were relegated.[50]

And so, in August 2006, to Headingley for the clash between Leeds and Wigan – or, in the modern-speak of Super League, to the Headingley Carnegie Stadium for the Leeds Rhinos versus Wigan Warriors. This was my first visit to the ground for a rugby league match since 1994 and, indeed, my first Super League game. Reading the following day's papers – *Yorkshire Post* and *Yorkshire Evening Post* – one might have thought that this had turned out to be a routine match between two sides that had seen better days. Leeds's defeat was their fifth in a row – including a dismal Challenge Cup semi-final performance against the Huddersfield Giants two weeks earlier – thereby equalling their worst sequence of results since 1996. For Wigan, the victory marked the latest stage in a revival that had seen them progress from apparent relegation certainties half way through the season to maintaining a place in the cluster of teams that was seeking to avoid the drop within the handful of matches left to play. (The side that eventually missed out was Castleford, with Wigan avoiding relegation by three league points). For my part, I thought it was an absolutely pulsating encounter, partly through the spirited nature of the Wigan fightback from 6–14 down to 20–18 winners, but also because of the unremitting ferocity with which the two sides attacked each other, the speed they brought to their handling movements and the consistent demonstration of individual skills under the most severe pressure.

Not all the skills were appreciated by the solid Leeds support around me in the main stand. There was a near silence when the quick feet of the Wigan centre, David Vaealiki, allowed him to evade a couple of tacklers and send the impressive young full-back, Chris Ashton, over the line for a try. I was relieved that my comment of "What a good try" was muttered sufficiently quietly as to be inaudible to those in the nearby seats. I was also hugely impressed by the sustained effort of the Wigan prop forward, Stuart Fielden – recently acquired from Bradford Bulls in the most expensive transfer in rugby league history – and his unquenchable appetite for physical confrontation with the opposite front row forwards, including his former Bradford team-mate Jamie Peacock. At half-back, I admired the organisational skills of the Australian, Michael Dobson, who, notwithstanding the repeated efforts by the Leeds chasers to pressurise his kicking game on the last tackle, consistently pinned the Leeds full back and wingers back into deep defence. Dobson reminded me of Shaun Edwards – albeit a slightly taller version – in his composure and leadership, which were hugely impressive for a 20 year-old. On the other side, I joined in the general celebration when Leeds's massive second row forward Ali Lauitiiti gathered a bouncing ball facing his own line and then, from thirty yards out, showed pace and power to force his way over by the corner flag. In the second half, when Leeds had only the hint of an overlap on the right hand side of Wigan's defence, it was the slight delay in Lauitiiti's pass to Keith Senior that drew in the extra defender and allowed the Leeds centre to send Ashley Gibson in for another try in the corner. If anything, this was even more impressive than Lauitiiti's solo try. He and Senior had virtually no room in which to move and yet their combined skill and instinct created the scoring opportunity. Skills, instinct and – like the late Payne Stewart in an earlier context – thousands of hours of practice over their respective careers.

The most dramatic moment of the match came a quarter of an hour from the end when Wigan took their final and decisive lead. Leeds lost possession deep in the Wigan half and the visitors swept upfield in a movement of pace and precision. Although the winger Mark Calderwood was halted in a covering tackle, the Leeds defence did not re-group in time and Ashton took advantage of their disarray to make further ground before passing to the supporting Calderwood, whose basic speed took him over the line. The sizeable gathering of Wigan supporters behind the posts roared their approval at the course that the game had taken thanks to Ashton and Calderwood's thrilling intervention. For the Leeds supporters around me, the irony was not lost. Calderwood had been a home favourite for several years up to the end of the previous season, having scored over 100 tries during his time at the Headingley club.

I was already aware, of course, that the presentation of top-flight rugby league had changed a great deal since my last visit to Headingley. Some of it worked; some of it didn't. I sensed a general weariness in the crowd to the determined efforts of the exuberant match-day announcer to stoke up the fires of enthusiasm in his pre-match team announcements and his periodic updates of the score. It might also have been the case that, after more than a decade of Super League, the routine presence of the loud pre-match music, the team mascots and the young cheerleaders also seemed rather tired. I remain a fan of the large screen, however, with the second-by-second countdown of the playing time and the additional drama it brings to the third referee's call on the marginal decisions. On this occasion, I would also credit the Leeds club for their invitation, both before the game and at half-time, for a mid-pitch performance by an Elvis Presley impersonator. The announcer informed us that the performer was someone with a regular presence on the West End stage by the name of John E Prescott. How close, I thought – that single initial – to a story that would have been really sensational. Other things remained the same. Before the game, as I sat in one of the seats in the members' enclosure of the adjoining cricket ground, reading the match programme and generally watching the world go by, I was struck by the relaxed way in which the two sets of supporters made their way to their respective parts of the ground. There was no hint of trouble or any sort of antagonism; it was the reassuring maintenance of a noble tradition of respectful support amongst the followers of this particular sport.

The pre-match warm-up on the pitch is something else that did not exist before the Super League era. As the Wigan team was at my end of the ground, I watched them go through their paces with some interest. The routine was extremely well organised. The players were not simply jogging up and down but, at different times, practising their passing (and missed passing) skills and rehearsing their running lines as well as simulating a series of defensive line-ups. One thing struck me above everything else, however: the body shapes. When Wigan ran on to the pitch, they looked

– almost to a man – tall and sleek. They were aided, as most teams seem to be these days, by the tight-fitting design of their shirts, which no longer have any spare bits of collar or other material around the sleeves or midriff, which a desperate opponent might seek to grab hold of when making a tackle. But even so, as they took their positions, the Wigan side looked exactly what they were: a set of professional athletes at the peak of physical fitness and governed by a full-time regime of training, diet and controlled preparation. I studied Stuart Fielden closely: six feet two inches, 17 stones 11 pounds and not an ounce of fat to be seen.

A couple of months after the Leeds-Wigan encounter – in October 2006 – a family holiday in Washington DC brought me to the Washington Redskins versus Tennessee Titans game in week 6 of the regular season of the National Football League. Somewhat to my surprise – I had anticipated that all the tickets would have been taken by season ticket holders – a speculative telephone call to the Redskins' ticket office produced a positive result for (to me) the bargain price of $63, including commission and local taxes.

The Redskins play at FedEx Field in Landover, Maryland – easily reached from our hotel on 9th Street by the subway (modern, clean and swift) and then shuttle bus ($3.70 and $5 return, respectively) – and I set off in good time for the 1.00pm kick off. The Redskins colours – burgundy, white and gold – were widely evident on the jackets, shirts and caps of most of my fellow travellers: I felt much more at home when I had purchased my distinctive cap ($21, made in Macao) from a stall outside the stadium. With time on my side, I followed my usual routine of two laps of the stadium, one outside with the long views over the Maryland commuter belt and the other, having passed through the turnstile, on the loud and busy inner circle. Not surprisingly, there was no shortage of retailing opportunities – food and drink, clothing, flags and other souvenirs – but I restricted myself to the cap and a bottle of water ($5), the latter retrieved for me by a large woman from a huge ice bucket. As with my visit to the Madison Square Garden for the basketball game many years earlier, I was interested to see that the purchase of beer – including within the seating areas of the stadium – remained one of the options open to me.

The FedEx Field stadium itself is a huge open bowl – all-seated, of course – with four distinct and sweeping tiers, again in the team colours. It turned out that my seat was even more of a bargain than I had expected: a prime location on the back row of the first tier, behind one of the corner flags, with an uninterrupted view of the whole pitch. I took my place with the stadium clock counting down to the kick-off – 40 minutes to go – and cast my eyes over the pitch, which was already crowded with players and coaches conducting their final routines. Loud driving music blasted through the stadium's loudspeakers. It was a warm and sunny Sunday afternoon under a cloudless sky. And it was fantastic.

When the game started, I sat in my seat and watched the action on the pitch and then watched again as the selected replays were shown on the big screen at the far end of the stadium. I listened to the comments of the Redskins supporters in the seats around me and looked around at the vast expanse of the stadium itself. I have had a soft spot for the Redskins since the Channel 4 coverage of American Football in the 1980s, when they had been Super Bowl champions three times under the tutelage of the head coach Joe Gibbs and spearheaded by the quarterback Joe Theismann and a fearsome running back (and my near namesake) called John Riggins. Around the stadium, circling one of the upper tiers, were the names of many of the players of that generation – Joe Jacoby, Dave Butz, Dexter Manley, Art Monk *et al* – together with other prominent past Redskins. I was aware that I would not be able to recognise any of these players by sight today – and I doubt if, with the exception of Theismann, I would even have done so at the time – but their names were still familiar in the tone and accent of the American commentators of the time. On leaving the stadium, I saw an advertisement for the John Riggins show on ESPN Radio ("The Home of the Redskins"); the following day, on television back at the hotel, Theismann was explaining what the Chicago Bears had to do to overturn a 20 point half time deficit against the Arizona Cardinals (which they did).

Washington went into the game having won 2 of their 5 previous matches: I picked up that they were "2 and 3". Tennessee were "winless" – 0 and 5 – so it was logical that the previous day's *Washington Post* should report that the Redskins were favourites to win by 10 points. However, on receiving the kick-off, the Titans began confidently and, ominously for the home side's defence (or "defense"), they took the ball down the pitch for 11 plays in their opening drive before Rob Bironas kicked a 32-yard field goal. Thereafter, Washington looked to be taking control and, when they scored a second touchdown in the opening play of the second quarter to take a 14–3 lead, it seemed as if the predicted 10 point margin might be a considerable underestimate. The crowd shouted its approval, orchestrated on the pitch by the hyperactive and appropriately named Marcus Washington and with the touchdowns celebrated by the appearance of three men sprinting across each of the end-zones carrying huge Redskins flags.

But the Titans did not give up. Prompted by their young quarterback, Vince Young, they came back with another field goal, two touchdowns and a safety (when the Redskins punter had his kick charged down and the ball ran out of play over the deadball line) to lead 22–14 by the end of the third quarter: 19 unanswered points. Meanwhile, as the Redskins began to make more errors – incomplete passes, fumbles, missed tackles, a dropped interception (Marcus W) and some costly penalties (including 15 yards against MW for roughing the passer) – their supporters let their feelings known with some prolonged and repeated howls of booing. I wondered if this was a standard reaction by this particular home crowd when things were not going well, as it appeared to have been at the Olympic Stadium in Barcelona, for example, when Espanyol were being beaten by the lowly Cadiz: I learned later that it was highly unusual for the Redskins.

We were now into the fourth quarter and it was the Redskins' turn to fight back. The quarterback, Mark Brunell, threw a long pass to one of his wide receivers and, shortly afterwards, the scores were level at 22–22 following a touchdown and a two-point conversion. The crowd changed gear. After the Redskins (as the scoring side) had kicked off again, the Titans took possession of the ball deep in their own half. It was at this point – as Young stood behind the centre in his offensive line to begin the attempt to move the ball down the field – that the roar from the crowd was probably the loudest I have ever heard at a sporting event. Around me, the sense of excitement and tension reached a crescendo, as the game's decisive actions were about to unfold. The supporters were indeed the Redskins' "12th man" – as the stadium announcer had urged them to be before the game started – seeking to intimidate and/or bewilder the quarterback into a game-deciding error. Everyone was on their feet with many fans waving their Redskins caps in the air, as if exhorting their comrades in battle to shout even louder. It was clear that Young was struggling to impart his instructions to his beleaguered team-mates. However, the Titans did not panic. The balance of territory shifted again as the visitors progressed down the field and, with the stadium clock showing that there were 5 minutes 11 seconds to go, Rob Bironas kicked the winning field goal for the Tennessee Titans from 30 yards. When a Brunell pass was intercepted with 54 seconds remaining, the vast majority of the crowd – 88,550 in total – knew that the game was effectively over and started to make for the exits.

The inquests had started amongst the season ticket holders around me well before the final whistle. One young black man wearing a replica Clinton Portis shirt bewailed the Redskins' lack of threat on offense: "We ain't got nothing, man". (This was slightly unfair on Portis, who had rushed for two touchdowns). Later: "I don't know who he was throwing to", as another Brunell throw went astray. One of his neighbours was more critical of the defense: "He's not big and he's not fast, so why is he running over us". This was a reference to the Titans' elusive running back, Travis Henry, who rushed for a total of 178 yards and a touchdown, including some hard yardage made late in the game when the shadow of the stadium was lengthening across the pitch and the Titans were under pressure. Needless to say, all of Henry's yards were bravely made in light of the severe physical threat posed by the Washington defensive line. I listened to the comments around me with interest, just as I observed who was making them. They were all experts or touchline coaches, and they were entitled to be, having paid their dollars to support their team.

What was most striking, however, was composition of those in the seats around me – male and female, young and old, black and white. I took pleasure in seeing this. The couple next to me were a middle-aged woman and her mother; it was the latter who was the fervent Redskins supporter offering me the high-fives when the touchdowns were scored by the home side. It was also her granddaughter, who was one of the Redskins cheerleaders. "She's got blond hair", she proudly pointed out, though this only reduced the number of candidates by about a third. (The half-time show was a routine by about 100 former Redskins cheerleaders from the 1960s through to recent seasons – "the alumni" – all of whom were uniformly attired in black tops and slacks and carrying two large burgundy and yellow pom-poms. Theirs was no mean performance in the mid-afternoon heat).

I have reported earlier on the two American Football games I saw at Wembley in the 1980s. I had enjoyed both of those occasions, but I had recognised at the time that they had been pre-season warm-up matches. This was the real thing. The contacts on FedEx Field were violent and I winced at some of the tackles, especially when a running back was stopped by the legs and another tackler came in to hit him on the upper body. I was impressed by the fleet-footed running of the kick-off receivers and by the heights and distances achieved when the ball was punted downfield. And, even from my place in the stand and allowing for the armoury of body protection that the players wore, I could register the sheer size of some of the proponents. The three players in the middle of the Redskins offensive line – the centre and the right and left guards – averaged 6 feet 5 inches and 317 pounds (22 and a half stone).

Off the field, there was also much to admire. I have already remarked on the cosmopolitan nature of the crowd. For the British visitor, the roughly equal balance of black and white supporters is an unusual sight at a major sporting event. The Redskins supporters, whilst passionate and vociferous, were also fair. When Vince Young received a heavy tackle, resulting in him receiving attention and then hobbling from the field, there was a sporting round of applause, notwithstanding the tight scoreline. In addition, throughout the game, I should report that I did not hear any swearing or foul language from anyone around me, even when the referees dramatically threw down their yellow flags and a couple of disputed calls were made against the home team. The contrast with a major soccer match in England or Scotland is so stark as to be incredible. I also liked the brashness of the occasion: the dramatic entry of the flag-carriers and then of the coaches and players themselves before the game, the fireworks, the cheerleaders, and the marching band playing "Hail to the Redskins". I smiled at the requests on the giant scoreboard whenever the Redskins (rather than their opponents) prepared for an offensive play: "Quiet, please. Offense working". (It was hardly the scoreboard operator's fault that, unfortunately, it wasn't). The in-game commentary, in which the outcome of each play was relayed through the stadium's loudspeakers, was excellent.

More generally, as ever, I was also interested in what the behaviour of those around me and the presentation of the match itself said about the background circumstances – in this case, about the country – in which it was being played. At the individual level, I could not help but observe the ruthless efficiency with which a man seated a couple of places in front of me finished off a bucket of popcorn. At the corporate level, I noted the heavy presence of some of the economy's major institutions: the main sponsors on the scoreboard were FedEx, Ernst and Young, Budweiser and the Bank of America. It was not a surprise that the focal point of the pre-match activities was the singing of the American national anthem (rather well, indeed, by a male opera singer whose name I unfortunately did not catch). But it was also revealing, I think, that the coin toss was conducted in the presence of a 4-star general. Moreover, this was not the only military theme. During the breaks in the match itself, some of the advertising time was taken up with recorded messages from individual US troops on duty in Iraq and Afghanistan; they were always greeted by rounds of applause. Another advertisement offered invitations to text the troops to tell them what a great job they were doing.

And so, at the end of the game, the Washington Redskins season's record stood at 2 and 4, whilst the Tennessee Titans had advanced to 1 and 5. For the Redskins' head coach and his 20 assistant coaches (as listed in the match programme), the odds on reaching the Super Bowl play-offs at the end of the regular season had become somewhat longer. One of the columnists in the following day's *Washington Post* offered the view that the Redskins were "utterly without a coherent sense of who they are" as well as "hopeless" before concluding, perhaps most damningly, "it's possible they just are not very good". The head coach, appointed for his second stint in 2005, was the mastermind behind the Redskins' successes of the

1980s: Joe Gibbs. He looked to have a hard task in front of him.

I repeated the nature of this excursion a year later, in October 2007, when another family holiday brought me to Chicago. This time, it was the Chicago Bears versus the Minnesota Vikings and I had prepared in advance, having purchased my ticket from an official website used by Bears season ticket holders to recycle tickets not required for a particular game. And so it was that, less than a month after spending £85 for my ticket for the Scotland-New Zealand Rugby World Cup fixture, I signed up to pay $217 (plus $33 tax) for a seat in the first row of the third tier, exactly behind the goalposts. Even with an exchange rate of two dollars to the pound, this sum comfortably exceeded my record expenditure to indulge in sports spectating.

A 40 minutes walk from the Palmer House Hilton through the early Sunday afternoon drizzle brought me to Soldier Field (not to be confused with Soldiers' Field in Roundhay, Leeds, where my father had taught me how to catch a rugby ball and had honed my forward defensive stroke over 40 years earlier). By the time that the game started, the drizzle had turned into a steady downpour and, as I sat in the open stadium, I did attempt to recall the last time I had received such a thorough drenching when watching a sporting event. The stewards at the stadium entrance had done a steady trade in confiscating brollies on the unpersuasive grounds that their use would either constitute a health and safety risk to those sitting nearby or would inhibit the views of other spectators (or possibly both together). I had decided to hide my brolly in the grounds of the nearly Field Museum, though there was no sign of it when I went to retrieve it afterwards.

Apart from the weather, there were several parallels with the Washington-Tennessee match: the efficiency of the fast food vendors, whose shouts of "No line, no line" proclaimed their immediate availability for business; the widespread consumption of beer by a couple of fans in the tier immediate below me, their replenished stocks being summonsed by the shout of "Here... Miller" to the young salesman patrolling this particular beat; my inability to resist the overpriced merchandise in the souvenir store (where I paid $25 for a scrawny Bears cap); and, inside the stadium, the apparent absence of any spare seats once the game had started, notwithstanding the dismal weather. As before, I was also struck by the excellence of the in-game match commentary over the public address system, the immense physicality of some of the tackles and, not least, the plethora of Bears coaches in the crowd around me, as the Vikings appeared to take control of the match.

The game was evenly poised at half-time – 14–14 – the highlight of the first half being an 89-yard punt return by Devin Hester, the Bears star player, whose amazing dexterity and speed off the mark to avoid tackles after the initial catch was too much for the hulking Vikings chasers to cope with. At the moment that Hester ran into the Vikings end-zone, I realised that I was probably the only person in the ground who was reflecting on the clear parallel with another dazzling runner with rapid footspeed and an unpredictable change of direction. In both his particular skills and general excellence, Devin Hester presented an uncanny resemblance to Jason Robinson.

In the second half, the lead for the Minnesota Vikings was given by Adrian Peterson, their rookie running back, who completed three touchdowns, including two from 73 and 67 yards, and who ran for 224 yards plus another 128 yards in kick-off returns. (I learned in the 13 page coverage in the following day's *Chicago Sun-Times* that this yardage represented the most ever by a Bears opponent). Peterson's third touchdown, with just over 4 minutes left, signalled the start of a fans' exodus, which picked up speed with the next Vikings interception; I judged that perhaps a quarter of the crowd departed at that point. However, unlike the reaction of the Washington fans, there was no booing, just a resigned silence.

The inevitable happened, of course. The Bears immediately sprung into action and, to widespread joy amongst the remaining fans, scored two converted touchdowns to level the scores at 31–31. But the Vikings were not finished. After the second touchdown, the Bears kick-off was returned 53 yards by Peterson and then, with exactly one second left on the clock, Ryan Longwell kicked a career-best 55 yard field goal to secure the win for the visitors. I had the perfect view of this from my seat right in the middle of the goal, as Longwell kicked towards the far end of the ground. I could tell instantly that his aim was straight enough and that all that mattered was the length of his kick. If Devin Hester was the near replica of Jason Robinson, then Ryan Longwell's achievement echoed that of Gavin Henson, albeit with a slightly smaller ball and over a longer distance.

Here, on a wet Sunday afternoon, was a microcosm of sport's theatre and drama: the punctuation of joy and delight. It cost me $250, including taxes, and it was worth every cent.

And so, where else in the world, apart from Stade de France in Paris and the Millennium Stadium in Cardiff and FedEx Field in Maryland and Soldier Field in Chicago? Well, Ostersund in Sweden, obviously: that country's leading stadium for Alpine Biathlon.

In December 2009, my civil service responsibilities in what the minority Scottish National Party administration now called the Scottish

Government (as opposed to Scottish Executive) took me to a conference in the small town of Are in the Norrland region of Sweden, more or less in the middle of the country. During the brief hours of daylight, it was bright and clear and cold; at night, there was an icy snowfall and the temperature fell to minus 15 degrees Centigrade. Needless to say, the Swedes did not make a big deal of this. They put the proper tyres on their cars and wore the proper clothing (if they ventured outside) and made sure that their buildings (in my case, the hotel) were properly built, and they just got on with life.

Ostersund – about 50 miles from Are – is the region's largest town and the site of the regional airport. More relevantly for my visit, its winter sports stadium was the venue chosen for our final morning's study visit on the use of EU Structural Funds. By a neat coincidence, the day we were there happened to be a practice day for competitors in the Ostersund leg of the International Biathlon Union World Cup (or "Skidskytte"). Biathlon involves cross-country skiing whilst carrying on the back a rifle that is periodically used, from either a prone or standing position, for shooting at a fixed target. The shooting is done inside the stadium (though facing away from the other skiers and the spectators' terraces), the competitors having returned from their ski over several kilometres of the local countryside.

At this point, I should acknowledge that I have inherited an endearing characteristic of my father, which was that, from the shortest period of observation – say 10 minutes watching the highboard divers or the parallel bar gymnasts on the television coverage of an Olympic Games – he would become an instant expert on that particular sport. And so it was with the Biathlon. It did not take at all long for me to realise that it was test of skill and stamina and nerve and, probably, that it had had an important role in the military capabilities of (amongst others) Norway, Sweden and Russia. The international field was wide-ranging, however: the flags of China, Canada, Germany and Britain were amongst the two dozen or so fluttering against the blue sky. In their haphazard turns, the practicing competitors swept into the stadium, lay down to assume their shooting positions, fired at the distant target, and then arose quickly to resume their journey. I admired their poise and grace.

The main part of the study visit was a presentation by the stadium director to his guests – about 30 of us from across Europe – on the development of the stadium, the financing that had gone into it and the plans for the future. He was a young man of about 30 years of age and he was very impressive: excellent English, well informed, realistic and, above all, clearly committed to ensuring that Ostersund held off the competition from elsewhere in Sweden and the wider Baltic region to take its turn in hosting these types of event. The planning seemed to have been meticulously thought through, even extending to the stadium authorities manufacturing their own snow during the previous winter and storing it (under sawdust apparently) in order to ensure that they had enough of it for the competition and that it was of the right quality. The director duly reported on how the EU funding had been used: to improve the stadium communications, to add to the spectator capacity and to introduce electricity into the television commentators' boxes. At this point, for some reason, the unfortunate mental image of a sheepskin-coated John Motson, holding a microphone and standing in a blizzard, came to mind.

By the following day – having had a three-legged flight back to Edinburgh – I was back in Milngavie. I switched on the Eurosport channel on the television in my living room to watch one of the women's events in the 2009 World Cup Biathlon from Ostersund in Sweden. I saw the whiteness of the snow and the black circles on the shooting targets (which turned white when they were hit) and, in one of the camera's panoramic sweeps, the large VIP marquee in which the stadium director had given his presentation. I also saw the thousands of spectators on the banking of the terraces – all fully wrapped up against the bitter cold – cheering each and every competitor as she set off on her outward journey. Good luck to them, I thought – competitors and spectators and organisers alike – for their enthusiasm and fortitude and determination.

One year after the trip to Sweden – in December 2010 – I spent a few days in London on my way to Prague for another EU conference, the last I would attend before my retirement from the civil service in March 2011. There were no sporting events in the Czech Republic for me to take in during the short period I was there, unfortunately, but London was different. The Oxford versus Cambridge varsity rugby match at Twickenham was quickly followed by West Ham United versus Manchester City at Upton Park (or the Boleyn Ground as the venue is formally called). I had been keen to attend both events as means of closing off a couple of longstanding sporting circles: my last spectating Blue at the Varsity Match had been in 1979; and the unpleasant experience of observing and hearing the overt racism at West Ham's home match with West Bromwich Albion had taken place in 1982.

In some respects, the Varsity Match was unchanged from what I recalled from over 30 years earlier. It was played at a frenetic pace and littered with mistakes, mainly by Cambridge, the pre-match favourites. Once Oxford had broken the deadlock with two well-taken tries midway through the first half, Cambridge were chasing the game and, notwithstanding the overwhelming superiority of their forwards in the second half scrums, they fell short by 21 points to 10.

What had changed was the venue itself, of course. Successive phases of expansion and development had produced a rugby cathedral in south west London that is clear testimony to the wealth and ambition of the Rugby Football Union. Inside the stadium, only the lowest of the three tiers of seating was in use for the game and, even though this was far from fully occupied, the attendance was still a healthy 27,000 plus. The stadium complex itself – with its wide external concourse, the heroic statue that greets those arriving from the direction of Twickenham station and its extensive historical references (The Carling Room, The Beaumont Room, Obolensky's Restaurant, Wakefield's Restaurant) – presents an uneasy combination of size and tradition. And money-making capacity, of course: witness the RFU shop, the World Rugby Museum, the corporate hospitality suites and the plethora of bars. It was a pleasant afternoon, however – cold and clear – and I enjoyed watching the match from my (cramped) seat at the back of the East Stand, the play in front of me illuminated by the bright sunshine filtering through the glass panels on the roof in the south west corner of the ground. At the end of the game, I made a mental note that the better side had won and that I had been fairly indifferent about the outcome: another difference from the spectating experience that I had had as a student.

Two days later, I laid to rest the ghost of Upton Park in 1982. West Ham United – bottom of the league and with their manager, Avram Grant, under obvious pressure to gather much-needed points – played host to the Manchester City side that had been assembled with hundreds of millions of pounds from their Middle East backers. City's own manager, Roberto Mancini, faced his own pressures: to qualify for the Champions League (at least) and, according to regular reports in the football media, to stave off the unrest of some of his exorbitantly paid playing squad.

The match went according to form and status. City won 3–1 and dominated the play through the midfield duo of the powerful Yaya Toure and the skilful David Silva. It was a measure of their superior resources that Mancini was able to bring on two England internationals – Adam Johnson and James Milner – as second half substitutes and it was Johnson who scored the third goal after running on to a perfectly timed pass from Silva. I noted the way that Mancini took off his temperamental Italian forward, Mario Balotelli, after he had been booked for dissent and when I would have laid odds that a second yellow card would inevitably follow. The petulant Balotelli walked straight past his manager and down the tunnel to the changing room. That aside, however – and with Carlos Tevez absent through suspension – it did strike me that City looked to be more than a collection of individual football mercenaries: they played like a team with some impressive passing and movement. By contrast, West Ham looked lightweight as an attacking force, notwithstanding the continual prompting of the energetic Scott Parker, and I judged that the second half of their season might be something of a struggle. (It duly was, of course, and relegation to the Championship followed).

This was the first match I had ever attended in the Barclays Premier League and, in some respects at least, it was not what I had expected. It was a tribute to the West Ham club – and the spectators around me in the West Stand – that I did not hear any foul language or see any anti-social behaviour. Perhaps the hooligans and the loudmouths were elsewhere, but, for me, it was a pleasant experience to watch the game in the company of genuine supporters displaying the full range of emotions – initially hope and expectation, later disappointment and resignation – in a way that seemed almost old-fashioned. As the final minutes of the game approached, the middle-aged West Ham supporter next to me commented on how the differences in the clubs' respective resources was reflected in the quality of players on the pitch, but he seemed to do so without bitterness and with a full appreciation of Manchester City's strengths: "I love watching David Silva".

My neighbour left before West Ham scored their late consolation goal. I wished him a safe journey home with a silent hope that his team might somehow avoid relegation. Later, as I left my seat, I looked over the roof on the far side of the ground to the wastelands of east London. West Ham United struck me as a good club which is attempting to uphold traditions for family support off the pitch (reflected in the family-related ticket deals being offered for the Christmas and New Year matches and the national anthem-like renditions of "I'm Forever Blowing Bubbles" for which everybody stood at the start of each half) as well as for skilful play on it (as recognised in the naming of the Sir Bobby Moore and Sir Trevor Brooking stands).

And, for the record, there was not a hint of racism in sight. The major changes in the top tier of English football over the last 30 years – and the social mores that both accompany and reflect them – include the acceptance of it being a global sport operating in a worldwide labour market. The 22 players starting this particular match came from no fewer than 15 different countries. And, in the overall West Ham squad for the season, as given in the official programme, all five players in the forward line were black. It was with some satisfaction that I saw that Clyde Best's successors were being given the crowd's unequivocal support.

Chapter 22

Firhill and Fir Park

My graduation to the Age of the Affluent Reflective did not inhibit my selective interest in the local sporting occasions. However, although I had ventured out to see games featuring the Old Firm – Celtic (versus Dunfermline) and Rangers (versus Leeds United) – and the Scottish international side (versus Germany and Italy) relatively soon after arriving in Scotland in 1992, it was many years before I added any other football matches to this list. In the Spring of 2009, I decided to rectify this by taking in a few games, in quick succession, in the west: Partick Thistle versus Greenock Morton in Division One, Queen's Park versus Ayr United in Division Two, Motherwell versus Dundee United in the Scottish Premier League and Albion Rovers versus East Stirlingshire in Division Three.

There were both "push" and "pull" elements behind this. The "push" was the desire – on a couple of the Saturday afternoons – to avoid watching the television coverage of what was shaping up to be the worst England rugby side for almost 20 years suffer (possible) humiliating defeat in the Six Nations championship: I decide that I would record the England matches and, depending on the results, watch them later. The "pull" – entirely more positive – was the wish to see these famous teams, whose names had jumped off the football pages of the newspapers and magazines of my sporting childhood and adolescence and whose fortunes had been updated on the Saturday evening radio and television as the weekly ritual of the "classified check" had been performed on my mother's pools coupon. It occurred to me that, in a minor form – and substituting the trains of the west of Scotland as my preferred mode of transport – this was, at least in part, the fulfilment of my childhood promise that, in later life, I would cycle the country and track down the soccer matches available for viewing at all the various grounds.

I had been to the Partick Thistle ground at Firhill on several previous occasions, of course, to watch the Glasgow rugby union side take on different types of European opposition and the Scotland rugby league team play a couple of matches. I knew, therefore, that my seat in the Jackie Hubbard Stand would provide an excellent view of the whole pitch and that all of the home support would be congregated there, leaving the Morton fans to occupy (fully as it turned out) the covered stand behind one of the goals and the remaining two sides of the ground completely untenanted.

I had often heard that the experience of matches at Partick Thistle was more enjoyable than at their much larger counterparts at Celtic or Rangers[51] and that, accordingly, it was more suitable for family viewing. Indeed, this theme was developed by the home side's chairman in the match programme: "[W]e try to ensure that each spectator has a pleasant and safe couple of hours here at Firhill... in the family atmosphere... [compared with] the unpleasantness so often evident at Old Firm matches". I wasn't sure that "family atmosphere" was quite the right description in the second half, when Morton were pushing for an equaliser and the referee and linesmen made a succession of contentious decisions, as the abuse that poured down on the officials was not for the faint-hearted. But I could see the general point. There was no sectarian chanting or unremitting hostility and I had to smile when, after the hitherto despised linesman had flagged for offside against a Morton goal, he received a polite round of applause as he ran back to the half way line. The chatter of the Partick supporters behind me included favourable references to the skilful defending by one of the Morton centre backs and the robust presence of both their front line forwards.

I knew that part of my reasoning for attending this fixture – reflecting so many of my interests and allegiances in other sports – was the acknowledgement of the long history of the Partick Thistle club and of its presence and role in this part of Glasgow. In front of the stand, a long sign running next to the touchline announced that this was the centenary of playing at Firhill. The club itself had formed in 1876 and, after a nomadic existence for the first 30 years, had moved to Firhill in 1909. For the Morton match, the team played in yellow shirts, with red hoops on the front, and black shorts. That this colour combination is the same as the West of Scotland rugby side is no coincidence – the latter donated their strips to the soccer team in 1936 – though I was given to understand that there had been some disquiet amongst supporters about the club's recent choice of colour (pink) for the team's away fixtures.

A week later, I was in one of the two adjacent blocks of seating at Hampden Park that had been allocated for the supporters of Queen's

Park and Ayr United. The latter made up a sizeable proportion of the 1,100 attendance and, from the block to my left, the roar that greeted the spectacular volley that brought the first of their side's goals did justice to the famous venue. I sat back with the comfort of the empty seats around me and another full view of the whole pitch as the home supporters politely encouraged Queen's Park to respond. But the two teams' respective positions in the league table – with the home side second from bottom and the visitors challenging for promotion – were fully reflected on the pitch and the 3–0 outcome was a fair reflection of Ayr's midfield competitiveness and striking prowess.

For me, the final score was only part of the story, of course. The bigger picture was the occasion and the venue. As with the Firhill stadium in Partick, I had been to Hampden Park before, but for a rugby match: Scotland versus Australia in November 2004. This was different. This was Queen's Park, formed in 1867 with a strict amateur ethos – the club's website confirms that no-one had ever received money for playing for the club – and whose pre-eminence in the last quarter of the nineteenth century had brought no fewer than 10 Scottish Cup wins between 1874 and 1893. They had even been FA Cup runners-up in 1884 and 1885. This success had been based on a style of play which was the foundation of the modern game of football: i.e. ball control, passing and team work, rather than individualistic dribbling, kick and rush, and hacking. It left quite a legacy.

I caught up with modern Scotland on my walk back to Mount Florida railway station to catch the local train into the centre of Glasgow. In my usual way, I had waited for a few minutes for the stadium to clear, so that I could take in a final view, before setting off. Climbing up the hill, I could hear that I was being followed by a small knot of "Super Ayr United" supporters – perhaps 15 to 20 in total – heading for the same destination and some thirty or forty yards behind. There was some singing and swearing, but nothing more serious. I reached the station platform first and stood to one side as the group came through in dribs and drabs, heading for the end of the platform and, when it arrived, the front of the train. Whilst taking care to avoid eye contact, I studied some of them as the group walked by. There seemed to be a common pattern: they were teenage boys – wiry, grim-faced, hair brushed forward, thin jackets or shirts sodden with earlier rain – who interrupted further chanting with harshly accented curses or repeated spitting on to the platform or track. When we reached Central Station, I followed behind as they loudly exited from the main platform and turned to the left to head for the train to Ayr. I went down the escalator for the lower level train to Milngavie. As I did so, it occurred to me that the same scenes, with the same casts, were probably being played out across the country: from Brechin to Stranraer, and from Carlisle to Gillingham come to that. I wondered about the participants. And their futures.

Like Partick Thistle and Queen's Park, the Motherwell football club also has a proud history, having been founded in 1886. The "official matchday magazine" – I retain the right to refer to it as a "programme" – had the heading "Steelmen" blazed across the top of the front cover: a reference to earlier and different times, steel production having ceased at the huge Ravenscraig works in 1992. At the end of a direct rail journey of exactly an hour from Milngavie, a 20 minute walk took me to the ground, Fir Park. I progressed quickly through a nondescript shopping precinct, along a main road flanked by several well-patronised public houses and past the soulless blocks of council offices. I was fully aware that the decline of industrial employment had hit Motherwell hard, as it had the other tough Lanarkshire towns, and the route to the ground provided easy confirmation of the doleful legacy. Later, when I retraced my route after the match, I looked in vain for a Starbucks to pick up a "latte to go", fully realising that the dilettante Nils Crane in *Frasier* would have been proud of me.

The game was entertaining enough, however, particularly in the second half, which had six bookings and a winning goal for Motherwell that was scored seconds after the visitors had had what appeared to be an obvious penalty award turned down. I stretched out across a couple of seats in the main Phil O'Donnell Stand and enjoyed the enthusiasm of the supporters around me – "Come on, The 'Well" – including the two young women behind me, who were kicking every ball and making every tackle for the home side. On the way home, I read the programme in detail, and admired its comprehensive coverage and presentation. One sign of the times stood out from the summary of the Dundee United first team squad: of its 22 members, 10 came from Scotland and the other dozen were comprised of 10 different nationalities.

The Albion Rovers versus East Stirlingshire fixture was a good one for me to choose for two reasons. First, I had recently completed Jeff Connor's *Pointless: A season with Britain's Worst Football Team*, the respectful but uncompromising description of the East Stirlingshire club's 2004–05 season, in which they had finished bottom of the league for the third (of five) successive seasons. Connor had captured the grim reality of football life in the lowest reaches of the Scottish Football League, not only in its standard of play and its lack of finances, but in the general poverty of its overall ambience: "The sheer impoverishment of some of the arenas visited remains difficult to describe; the appearance and demeanour of some of the fans encountered still haunt my dreams". More specifically, Connor had not pulled his punches in describing his visit to "the derelict square known as Cliftonhill [the home of Albion Rovers]. The forsakenness of the whole place is best summed up by the main sponsors' advertising hoarding on the empty covered area opposite the main stand: Reigart Demolition".

Second, there was a family link to the home club. My father had once mentioned to me that, as a young man, he had regularly visited his aunt and uncle when they had lived in nearby Coatdyke. His uncle, John Bain, had run the sports club of Stewart and Lloyds Ltd, an engineering company that later became part of the then British Steel Corporation. Shortly after moving up to Scotland in 1992, I followed this up by locating the Stewart and Lloyds sports ground, though it was by then derelict, apart from a bowling club, with its tennis courts and football pitches overgrown and in disrepair. A housing estate, with its new cars and satellite dishes, rose up the hill on the other side of the ground. Albion Rovers had been my great uncle's local club and he and his friends had been regular supporters. I felt that I had a connection, however tenuous, with the locality.

For East Stirlingshire, things had moved on (by almost four seasons) since the events covered in *Pointless*. The club had sold its former ground and was now ground-sharing with Stenhousemuir. The chairman and manager had departed, as had all but one of the players whose season Connor had chronicled. Moreover, the new regime was having considerable success, with the side now challenging for promotion and handily placed for a play-off position at the end of the season. By contrast, for their part, Albion Rovers were struggling, notwithstanding the continued support of Reigart as their main sponsors: third from bottom of the league, defeated in their last home game by Elgin City (who were bottom), and without a win in 11 games. It was no surprise, therefore, that the visitors won 2–0, especially after Albion Rovers had had a defender sent off midway through the first half, slightly harshly I thought, for denying an opposition forward what the referee judged to have been a clear run on goal. East Stirlingshire were sound in defence and neatly industrious in midfield and I could fully understand – based on my newly acquired expertise on Scottish Third Division football – why they were doing well.

The game itself was brisk and enjoyable, played on a good pitch in the bright May sunshine by players who were committed and energetic. As ever, however, I was interested in the surroundings and the context. The spectators – all 346 of us – were confined to the narrow stretch of terracing or the main stand that ran along one side of the pitch. The East Stirlingshire fortunes being on the rise, the visitors had brought some vocal support, duly kitted out in replica shirts and/or scarves with an old fashioned design of thick dark blue and white stripes. Their supporters' chanting was led by 20 or 30 youths (including some girls) who traded insults with a dozen of their host counterparts who were standing only slightly further down the terrace. There was no trouble, however: three members of the police were able to stand idly nearby and the two bands of young supporters cheerily swapped their respective positions on the terrace at half time.

There was much to admire about the game's presentation. With it being the last home game of 2008–09, pre-match awards were made for the Albion Rovers player of the season and the goal of the season, the latter being generously given to a player who was no longer at the club. I was particularly impressed by the matchday programme "sponsored by the Horseshoe Bar" which, at £1-50p, represented the best value I seen for such a publication for some time. In addition to articles reporting on the two awards and a tribute to the progress that the visitors had made over the last couple of seasons, the programme had interesting pieces about football club finances and the future of lower level Scottish football. The club also took the opportunity to thank, by name, all those who had assisted over the course of the season: ticket sellers, stewards, programme sellers, the ladies in the pie shop...

Before the kick-off, as I took up my position on the terrace, I was approached by a man with a young boy. "Excuse me", the man asked, "Are you the man for the book?". I said no, of course, not quite understanding what the question was, though I wondered if the man might have thought I was Jeff Connor.

As the game unfolded, I learned at first hand what hopes and expectations the home supporters might have. "We need a completely new midfield for next season", said one plump middle-aged lady, perhaps optimistically, bedecked in a blue and yellow replica shirt. At a more practical level, "that's another ball lost", as a powerful defensive clearance was blasted over the high corrugated fence on the far side of the Cliftonhill Stadium. In the second half, having retreated to a seat at the edge of the main stand, my attention was taken by a heavily built middle-aged man sitting by himself a few rows in front of me. "Come on, Rovers", he shouted every few minutes. "Come on, Rovers". His season would soon be over. I silently wished him better success for the next year.

When I got home, I read again the passage roughly half way through *Pointless* in which Connor described his visit to Cliftonhill Stadium as a member of the East Stirlingshire entourage. He had begun by summarising the general characteristics of the locale: "[t]he ground is next door to the district magistrates' court and opposite a distillery. Football, 'beaks' and cheap blends; the abstract of Saturdays in Coatbridge". There had followed graphic depictions of the dressing rooms, toilets and home supporters: "Albion Rovers fans brought up amid this squalor are not noted for their subtlety. The level of abuse had to be heard to be believed… Many of the home fans were already drunk…" I thought back to the question that had been posed to me on the terrace before the kick-off and was relieved that I might have given the correct answer.

Meanwhile, the West of Scotland football (i.e. rugby) club had recovered from its period in the doldrums. At the end of the 2006–07 season, coached by the former Scotland international John Beattie, they were promoted from the third division and reached the semi-final of the cup. In March 2007, after an absence of 5 years, I took my place in the stand and watched the expertly-drilled home forwards – led by the returned Gordon Bulloch and the loyal Guy Perrett – overwhelm the Murrayfield Wanderers pack. The following month, Bulloch and his front row colleagues did the same to first division opposition: firstly Dundee HSFP – an echo of my first visit to Burnbrae 15 years earlier – in the cup quarter-final and then Glasgow Hawks. The encounter with the latter was the semi-final, which the Hawks held on to win narrowly after opening up a sizeable first half lead and, fortuitously for them, persuading the referee that their front row injuries meant the scrums in the last 10 minutes should be uncontested.

The West of Scotland club was on a roll. A second successive promotion followed in 2007–08. The match programme – my indicator of rugby club prosperity – was neat and glossy and well patronised by local advertisers. The junior section was thriving. The First XV was infiltrated by some impressive teenagers, including the 18 year-old Conor Davis at fly-half – who, according to one programme, joined the club when he was 6 – and the 17 year-old Robert Harley in the back row. I enjoyed taking up my position in the stand, whether on afternoons of gusty rain or crisp sunshine, and watching the progress that the side was making under Beattie's tutelage and Bulloch's leadership.

West of Scotland's first match back in the Premier Division, in August 2008, was – inevitably – at Burnbrae against the Glasgow Hawks. There was no narrow finish this time, nor any uncontested scrums, as the home side won comfortably. Later, I checked in the respective match programmes and discovered that only 4 West and 3 Hawks players had survived from the cup semi-final of 16 months earlier plus one other (Rory Kerr), who had moved back from the latter to the former. A fortnight later, West of Scotland played a steady game in persistent drizzle to defeat Hawick, another traditionally difficult opponent. By winning 6 of the first 7 home fixtures, the side built up a cushion of league points that saw it well on its way to mid-table respectability: a notable achievement.

Other young players came to the club or were promoted through the junior ranks: the tall 19 year-old Richie Gray in the second row, the excellent Roddy Grant as openside flank forward, who was quickly promoted to the Scotland sevens squad, and 18 year-old Peter Horne, a confident full back. These players were not just making up the numbers by getting experience of high level club rugby; they were decisively influencing the course of matches. It was Horne's 5 penalties and conversion, in difficult conditions, that won the match against Hawick. The 17 year-old Robert Harley of the previous season – now the 18 year-old Robert Harley – also featured in the early games. I watched him with interest, partly because, as a commanding blindside flank forward, he was clearly a player of immense promise, but also because my non-rugby playing son – Tom – had casually mentioned that he had been in his class at the Douglas Academy in Milngavie and that he was a really nice lad.

As so it was, as I watched one of the West of Scotland games from my excellent vantage point at the back of the stand, that it finally occurred to me that I had turned into my father. The realisation came when I heard this disembodied voice shout something in the general direction of the pitch. I cannot recall exactly what it was: words of encouragement for the home team, or advice to the referee that he had missed an opposition forward pass, or some such. I do remember that it was polite and restrained – and in line with the reminder from the West of Scotland chairman, printed in every match programme, that the referee and touch judges were volunteers and should be treated with respect – and I can clearly recollect what it sounded like. It was this 50-something man, shouting out in a Leeds accent, and encouraging the progress and success of the players in his team, some of whom were more than 30 years younger than he was. It was me.

And it was not only me. It was also my father, watching his beloved Hunslet, perhaps in their last seasons at Parkside or as tenants at the Elland Road Greyhound Stadium.

In Autumn 2005, I saw the Scotland play at Murrayfield for the first time since their match against South Africa in the 1999 World Cup. I purchased my £60 ticket for the West Stand two days before it was announced the All Blacks were to make 13 changes from the side that had beaten England at Twickenham on the previous Saturday. In other words, despite the fact that this game could give New Zealand only their second grand slam against the four home countries in the 100 years that they had been touring the British Isles, they were, in effect, looking ahead two years to the next World Cup and treating the match as a high-level trial for some of their fringe first team players,. If I had been a Scottish rugby player – or official or supporter – I think I would have found this somewhat patronising.

The New Zealand team was not entirely a second XV, however. The tour captain Tana Umaga played in the centre, the devastating Richie McCaw was in the back row and the consistently impressive Chris Jack played in the second row. The presence of McCaw in the squad, together with two MacDonalds – Angus in the back row and Leon on the replacements' bench – was a reminder of the Celtic ancestry of a sizeable portion of the All Blacks team, even though this share was diminishing as the New Zealand authorities took advantage of their unfair ability to hoover up the best of the playing talent from Samoa and Fiji to include in their ranks.

Notwithstanding the absence of several front-line players – including, disappointingly, Daniel Carter, Doug Howlett and Aaron Mauger – New Zealand were too strong for Scotland. By the half hour mark, they had taken a 22 points to 3 lead and another potential half century for the All Blacks (possibly even reaching the 69 points they had scored against Scotland in Dunedin in 2000) was on the cards. However, Scotland looked to have far more spirit and organisation about them than had been apparent against Australia at Hampden Park 12 months earlier and that, combined with the All Blacks' reluctance to move out of second gear for any length of time, prevented the score being increased until the last ten minutes. Scotland even fashioned a fine try of their own when, after a period of sustained pressure on the New Zealand line, a neat kick behind the defence by the replacement fly half, Phil Godman, produced a well-worked try for the swiftly supporting Simon Webster. The Scots in the crowd went delirious, basking in the triumphant finale that their side's determined second half performance had brought. However, I did wonder about the validity of the celebrations when the scoreboard revealed who had come off distinctly second best – the final tally was 10–29 – although I could understand the collective relief after such a long period of under-achievement by the Scotland side. It was a curious echo of the other Murrayfield crowd's reaction after Scotland had scored their two late consolation tries against England in 1998, having been heavily outscored earlier in the match.

As usual, I did my best to take in the whole event, beginning, before the match, with a couple of laps of the outside of the stadium. As with a cricket test match, there was a varied supporting cast: the attractive girls attempting to persuade spectators to buy the audio link to the referee's comments to the players; the queue of children waiting to have their faces painted in the black of New Zealand or the blue and white of the Scottish saltire; the neat array of franchised fast food outlets. I stood like a groupie in the funnel of spectators that clapped the New Zealand players and coaches as they walked the short distance from the team bus through to the entrance to the changing rooms. I watched as the massed pipe and drum bands warmed up for their entrance into the stadium with a rehearsal of *A Scottish Soldier*. As I did so, my mind raced back to a news item I had heard on the radio shortly after the British Army had entered Basra in Iraq in 2003. The reporter had said that the sound of bagpipes had led the advance. From my sheltered civilian perspective, I can only imagine the emotional stimulus that that would have given me if I had been in one of the Scottish regiments preparing for action on that day: I do know, however, that I would have had an emphatic psychological upper hand.

My neighbours in the expensive seats in the West Stand seemed to be predominantly Scottish. The young man on my right – mid 20s, I would have guessed – spent the whole match shouting passionately for his side apart from during the extensive periods when he was berating the Welsh referee, Nigel Whitehouse, for every decision that was not in Scotland's favour. "How can that be a knock on?", shouted my neighbour from a distance of sixty yards after the referee, from a distance of five yards, had blown his whistle and awarded a scrum. By contrast, on my left sat a rotund man, probably in his 60s, whose commentary on the events on the field offered a more than reasonable parody of a retired brigadier. "With intent, Scotland", he bellowed, as the forwards gathered for a line out. "With intent". Later, after the ball had clearly rolled over the touchline, the players had stopped for a breather and the official had raised his flag: "A little lackadaisical there, touch judge". Later still, a more direct exhortation, when a Scottish passing movement had crabbed across the field: "Run at the bastards, Scotland".

When I managed to block out the nonsense coming from both sides, I was struck by the defining characteristics of the All Blacks' play, especially their physical aggression in the defensive tackle and the ability of both forwards and backs to offload to a supporting player when in contact. It was Scotland's good fortune that New Zealand did not capitalise on a couple of sweeping handling movements, including one directly from the opening kick off, when space was created for Joe Rokocoko to make ground down the left wing: it was only a dropped pass on the inside that prevented Scotland going 0–7 down within the first 60 seconds. I was also impressed by both the scrum halves used by New Zealand: Piri Weepu, with his powerful hand-off and quick pass, and Jimmy Cowan, a confident and skilful player, who dealt with one threatening moment by running at full speed on to a loose ball in front of his posts and scooping it up with one hand before clearing to touch. The crowd gave generous rounds of applause to Richie McCaw, when he retired injured during the second half, and to the hooker, Anton Oliver, when he was also replaced late in the game. The match programme described Oliver as a "veteran", which he undoubtedly was at the age of 30 and having played over 100 times in the Super 12 competition. It was salutary to recall that I had seen his father, Frank Oliver, play for the All Blacks in the 1978 match against England at Twickenham, when I had looked down on his scrappy try, following a line-out on the England line, from my place on the terraces of the South Stand.

The rejuvenation of the Scotland team's fortunes in the 2006 Six Nations championship was both surprising and welcome. The opening match was against France and, a few days before the game, I decided to invest the necessary tidy sum (another £60 plus the internet booking fee) for another prime seat in the West Stand on the halfway line with an uninterrupted view of the whole pitch. I was amply rewarded. Scotland approached the match with passion and commitment, in contrast with their visitors who, in the jargon used by many sports commentators, did not "turn up". The acclaimed fly-half, Frederic Michalak, had a poor game, repeatedly drifting laterally across the pitch when he had the ball and crowding the room required by his centres. One of the latter, Ludovic Valbon, had only come into the side because the French captain, Yannick Jauzion, had picked up a late injury. This was a telling blow for France. I did not disagree with the assessment in the match programme that Jauzion could be bracketed with Daniel Carter as the world's best all-round player, and it was a considerable disappointment for me (and for France) that he did not play. His unfortunate replacement had an even worse game than Michalak, dropping the ball several times.

The growing belief of the home supporters that an unlikely victory might be on the cards was given added credence in the second half when, to general astonishment, the Scottish forwards won a line out on the French 22 and proceeded to drive a rolling maul all the way over the try line. The huge roar around the stadium – which grew in intensity as the drive progressed – reflected a combination of elation and disbelief. The conversion to the try extended the Scottish lead to 17 points. As the minutes passed, the sense of excitement and tension within the home support around me rose inexorably, as Scotland appeared to be on the brink of unexpected victory. It was a matter of the home side maintaining a disciplined and well-organised defensive line, led from the front by the impressive Jason White. France did score a couple of tries, but it was not sufficient to prevent a deserved Scottish win by 20 points to 16.

After the match, I joined the vast army of supporters walking back up the main road towards the centre of Edinburgh. This is a ritual occurrence after every Murrayfield international, when the massed battalions set off from Roseburn Crescent and stride out for Haymarket Station and beyond, reducing any traffic unfortunate enough to be attempting the reverse journey to a standstill. A glance at the significant numbers looking to enter the station and go down to the platforms (one of which would hold my train back to Glasgow) was enough to persuade me to keep going up West Maitland Street and towards Waverley Station. By the time I approached Princes Street, the numbers had thinned out slightly, but they were still sizeable. A few feet in front of me, a group of four French supporters – stocky middle-aged men, easily identifiable with their team's scarves – walked past a gaunt-looking youth who was standing in a shop doorway. The youth dropped his cigarette to the ground and stubbed it out. Looking down at his boot, he murmured audibly: "Fucking gubbed you, didn't we?". The Frenchmen kept walking without breaking their stride: they were either indifferent to the provocative comment or, more likely, unable to translate from the local vernacular.

For the next visit of the All Blacks to Murrayfield in September 2007, the going rate for a ticket in the West Stand had risen exponentially. The £85 I invested for a seat at the end of the stand in the corner of the ground was, at that time, the most I had ever paid to see a sporting event: a record which would itself be beaten (indeed, shattered) less than a month later, as I have described elsewhere. This was a group match in the Rugby World Cup and, adhering to my longstanding philosophy of having no excuse for not being part of a major sporting event when the opportunity presented itself on my doorstep, I decided that my attendance would be mandatory.

The Scottish team management took the game seriously. So seriously, in fact, that they decided to field a near-second XV, so that the first-choice players could avoid injury and be ready for the crucial group encounter with Italy the following weekend. I thought that this was an absolutely appalling decision. Not only was it an insult to the spectators that had paid considerable sums to watch the match – and mine was by no means the most expensive ticket – it was hugely disrespectful to the opposition and to the tournament itself. Moreover, it betrayed the psychology of defeatism. The Scots were effectively saying that their first XV had no chance of beating New Zealand. I read the comments of the distinguished former All Black captain, Sean Fitzpatrick, in that morning's *Sunday Times* – that the margin of New Zealand victory could be 80 points and that that would be what Scotland deserved – in total agreement.

It turned out to be half that margin. By a neat symmetry, New Zealand led 20–0 at half time and won the match 40–0, scoring six tries in the process. I was pleased to have seen Dan Carter and Richie McCaw and I was impressed by the power of the New Zealand scrum and the long range sprints for tries by Carter and Doug Howlett. The Scots defended bravely, as everyone knew they would, led by some courageous tackling by the full back Hugh Southwell, and they were keenly cheered on by their supporters. But virtually the whole game was played in the Scotland half and the match was over as a contest after a few minutes when, from a scrum on the Scottish line, McCaw took a simple inside pass and strolled over unopposed for the first try.

I reflected on the occasion on the train back to Glasgow. This was the way it now was. The professionalisation – and corporatisation – of the sport's foremost international event meant that ticket prices were exploding, the two sides had played in blue and grey shirts that were virtually indistinguishable, and the Scottish coach had decided that any slight advantage that would assist his team to reach a quarter-final place should be given precedence over attempting to lead a Scotland team to a first-ever victory over New Zealand. In retrospect, the irony was that this was not a great New Zealand team: later events in Cardiff, when France defeated them in the quarter-final, showed what was possible when they were confronted by a team with commitment and determination. Of course, the record books show that Scotland duly reached their desired quarter-final place – thereby securing whatever performance-related rewards to which the management and players might have been entitled – but they lost there to Argentina and, accordingly, left no mark on the competition.

Happily, other aspects of the encounter were more in keeping with the traditions of rugby spectating. The group of four lads next to me in the stand were New Zealand supporters, who had come over for the tournament and hired a camper van to transport themselves around Britain and France. We stayed in our seats after the game and shared a beer.

A different generation of representative players was on show at the West of Scotland ground at Burnbrae at the end of the 2006–07 season. The Under 18 Six Nations championship took place in and around Glasgow that year and I took the opportunity to watch England's matches against Scotland and Ireland. The main stand was full for both games and there seemed to be plenty of England support, not at all of which was comprised of the parents and other family members of the players of the squad.

The games had certain similarities. Both were won by England, though far from comfortably. Both were fast and furious, particularly in their respective first halves, and very physically demanding. As with the club matches on the ground, there was an unremittingly committed scramble for possession at the breakdown. All this was wholly admirable, of course. Amongst the individual performances, I was impressed by the athleticism of Courtney Lawes in the England second row and the all-round excellence of David Lewis at scrum half. However, it did not take me long to realise that, although it was the Under 18 side in front of me, this was not dissimilar to watching how the full England team went about its task: a powerful scrum (with, it has to be said, some very big lads for 18, not least Lawes and his second row partner, Graham Kitchener) and a well-drilled technique in the "pick and go" routine of grinding out the hard yards. But there was very little evident flair. I thought back to the skills and panache shown by the best of my near-contemporaries – John Horton and David Richards – when they had been of a similar age to these players and I had watched them at the Llanelli Schools Sevens tournaments all those years ago. Where were their successors?

I think the simple answer to that question is that the game of rugby union is different to what it had been when Horton and Richards were coming through. By this, I do not only mean the changes in the professional/amateur relationship or the rules of the game or the fitness of the players or the media exposure. The system through which the young talent emerges has also been overhauled. I noticed from the match programme that all bar three of the 26 players listed in the England squad were attached to clubs in the English Premiership as well as, in some cases, to a school or college. Many – if not most – of these players were either on the pathway to becoming professional players or had reached that status already. At club and representative level, they were part of an elite that, I feared, might be in danger of being coached to death.

The Glasgow Warriors' gradual improvement in the Heineken Cup was confirmed in the 2007–08 season when, relocated back to the Partick Thistle ground at Firhill, they needed to beat Saracens in the last round of pool matches, with a bonus point, to qualify for the quarter finals. It was not to be. Saracens scored two soft tries – one when a Glasgow player waited too long for a kick to go dead in-goal and the other from an interception from an inside pass at the scrum near the half way line – and the visitors held on to win 21–17. It was a similar story in the following year's competition, when narrow pool defeats were incurred in the home fixtures against strong teams from Toulouse and Bath. There was a consistent pattern: Glasgow competed strongly in defence, particularly in the skirmishes at the break-down – where the young back-row forwards John Barclay and Johnnie Beattie were consistently outstanding – but did not have the firepower or the nous to win the tight matches. Glasgow's subsequent victory in the away fixture in Toulouse – impressive and deserved though it was – came after their chances of qualification for the quarter-final stage of that year's competition had disappeared.

As ever, in these games, there were certain individual players who caught the eye. The principal reason for my going to watch Saracens was undoubtedly to catch a final glimpse of Richard Hill, one of my favourite of all England rugby players over the long period I have been watching the sport. I spent some time following his movements around the pitch and admiring how his reading of the game compensated, at least in part, for his reduction in pace. I made a point of applauding him when he left the field after 50 minutes. Saracens also fielded Andy Farrell, who played a strong game in the centre. Here was a classic echo: I had first seen Farrell 15 years earlier, when, as an 18 year-old, he had played for the Great Britain rugby league team against New Zealand at Headingley.

In the case of Toulouse, there was a range of top line performers to admire: the aggression of Byron Kelleher, the skill of Clement Poitrenaud, the weary experience of Fabien Pelous. Not that I would necessarily have learned this from the glossy match programme, which devoted precisely one of its 72 pages to the opposition. But it didn't matter. The star performer was Yannick Jauzion in the centre. His general excellence – in his running, passing and leadership, for he was also the captain of his side – reminded me why I had forsaken the comfort of the domestic fireside for the huddled intimacy of the Jackie Husband Stand on a dank and chilly October evening.

The final of the 2008–09 Heineken Cup – Leicester Tigers versus Leinster – was played at Murrayfield and, in line with my usual philosophy for "local" sporting events of this type, there was no excuse not to go. Following a late purchase of a ticket from the Scottish Rugby Union internet site, I took up my place at the back of the West Stand, above one of the corner flags, and looked out over the roof of the opposite stand towards Edinburgh Castle and, to its left, the imposing towers of the former Donaldson's School for the Deaf. It was a pleasant Saturday afternoon in late May and it was a good place to be. This was the first time I had seen an Irish provincial side since Ulster's visit to Scotstoun to play Glasgow in 1997. As for Leicester, I had last watched them in 1981, the year that the teenage Brian Moore had lined up in the front row for Roundhay in a John Player Cup tie and I had stood on the terracing on the lower side of Chandos Park wondering if that particular game would turn out to be the biggest match of his life.

The Heineken Cup final was an uplifting experience, not only due to the tension of the occasion, the closeness of the scores and the predictably fierce commitment of the players. Nor just for the excellence of Brian O'Driscoll and Georden Murphy or the calm maturity of the young Johnny Sexton, whose late penalty goal won the trophy for Leinster. Nor, even, for the prosaic nature of the "sin bin", to which one of the Leinster prop forwards found himself banished for 10 minutes on either side of half time, and which comprised a little plastic chair on he was obliged to sit all by himself near the touchline. Rather, it was the whole occasion and, in particular, it was the respectful way in which both sets of supporters gave vent to their fervency. The Leinster supporters – with their waves of blue and white flags and in a 4 to 1 majority – kept up the tradition, developed by those following the provincial teams in Ireland, of maintaining an immaculate silence when an opponent was lining up a kick at goal. The Leicester supporters did likewise. Then, when the game had been lost and the presentation podium was being prepared for the formal ceremonies, the Leicester supporters remained *en bloc* in order to acknowledge the efforts of both sets of players when they received their medals. Although I had seen similar behaviour by the respective supporters at countless rugby league Challenge Cup finals over the years, I was touched by this for some reason. I suppose that I had a mental image of the television coverage of any corresponding football cup final, in which the evacuation of one half of the stadium usually commences the moment that the final whistle is blown. The echoes of the distant rugby league finals at Wembley also returned during the Leinster lap of honour, when the chorus of U2's *Beautiful Day* thundered around the ground and brought back clear memories of the Wigan supporters' similarly stirring rendition of Tina Turner's *Simply the Best*.

The West of Scotland club found it harder in the Premier Division of the Scottish Rugby Union in 2009–10 and 2010–11. In the former, the loss of 8 of the opening 10 games gave weight to my pre-season suspicion that this would be a battle against relegation and that my long-established propensity for following the fortunes of "yo-yo" teams – New Hunslet RLFC in the 1970s, Fulham RLFC in the 1980s – would be continued. The loss of the some of the young turks from the previous season – Richie Vernon, Richie Gray, Peter Horne and Roddy Grant – to the professional Glasgow and Edinburgh sides (with Vernon and Gray quickly graduating to full Scotland caps) left a considerable gap, whilst the pack was not as formidable as it had been a couple of seasons earlier. In a reversal of the events of the cup quarter-final of April 2007, the powerful Dundee HSFP forwards bullied and out-muscled the home side in a match at Burnbrae in September 2009. The club did well to retain its divisional status at the end of the season, thanks to a useful run of 6 wins out of 8 from mid-season, as Edinburgh Academicals and Stewart's Melville FP were condemned to the relegation places.

But relegation was not avoided in 2010–11. The retirements of John Beattie as coach and Gordon Bulloch as talismanic leader on the pitch, combined with the usual turnover of playing staff, left some gaps that were apparently too big to fill. A generally fragile defensive record saw West of Scotland win only 2 of the 11 games against the other sides in the division, conceding an average of 45 points per match, including 92 points at Dundee, the side that seemed to constitute the bellwether for assessing the team's state of health. This meant that they entered a play-off system involving the bottom 4 sides in the Premier Division and the top 4 sides in the division below, who played each other to determine the remaining 4 places in the following season's top league. West of Scotland lost all 7 play-off matches.

Curiously, it was on the occasion of one of West of Scotland's rare wins in the early part of the 2009–10 season that I experienced a sense of something that I had not come across before. A fine – albeit narrow – win it was too, away to the Glasgow Hawks, whose young outside-half, Duncan Weir, just failed to land a long-range penalty goal with the last kick of the match. I watched the first half from the touchline near the half-way line on the far side of the pitch from the clubhouse at the neat ground at Glasgow High School and was reminded, at close quarters, of the committed ferocity of the close contact play. West of Scotland built up a healthy lead and, when the visitors scored again at the beginning of the second half, I changed my position to take up a vantage point deeper into the Glasgow Hawks half, expecting that that would be where the bulk of the play would take place.

Needless to say, apart from a couple of unproductive skirmishes near the Glasgow line, that turned out not to be the case. The home side fought back with a couple of tries of their own. What struck me, however, was not my physical distance of much of the play from my new vantage points – firstly from the small banking of terrace near one of the corners and then from behind the dead ball line at the end of the ground – but what seemed to be an emotional detachment from the events on the pitch. It was almost as if I was not actually there; or, given that I obviously was, that it was as a ghostly presence without any attachment to the earthly conflict that I was witnessing. Perhaps it was simply my choice of second half venue, detached from the bulk of the spectators and looking across the ground in response to the roars of the home supporters in front of the clubhouse and the competing cheers of the West of Scotland support to one side and, to my left, the incoherent shouting of a couple of individual barrackers with pint glasses in their hands. Or perhaps, it was a sense of foreboding of something to come. After the penultimate passage of play – which ended prematurely when the referee stopped play and blew for the scrum that would lead to the Glasgow Hawks's final penalty attempt – one of the West of Scotland players remained on the ground to receive prolonged attention before being carried off on a stretcher. I could not see who it was to start with, but a check of those standing confirmed that it was Robert Harley.

Although Harley was out of action for several weeks, he made a full recovery to come back strongly later in the season. In the reverse fixture against Glasgow Hawks at Burnbrae, he seemed to be the single home player who kept going determinedly right to end of a match in which West of Scotland were heavily defeated. Later, at Firhill, I saw him play with distinction in another losing cause, this time for Scotland Under 20s against their English counterparts.

I reflected on the feeling I had had at the first Glasgow Hawks game for some time afterwards. Was it a sense of being unwelcome at the ground? Absolutely not. Was it, as my wife tentatively suggested later, an indication of finding the game of rugby, in general, not to be as attractive or enjoyable to watch as it previously had been? Possibly. Was it – more profoundly – a psychological reflection of any hidden stresses brought about by work-related business or family concerns or a mid-life recognition of the sense of my place in the world? Possibly again, though I suspected that these were somewhat deeper waters.

Chapter 23

South Leeds Stadium

The sporting encounters recorded in this volume cover the 50 year period through to 2011. However, in one sense, an earlier conclusion to the overall story takes place in the summer of 2004. On a Friday evening in June, my sister Rosemary and I went to the South Leeds Stadium to watch the Hunslet Hawks play the Gateshead Thunder in the LHF National League division two. A few days earlier, our father had been laid to rest in the Lawnswood Cemetery in Leeds, where he shares a plot with our mother, whose battle with the effects of Alzheimer's Disease had finally ended in April 2000.

Dad had been diagnosed with a malignant mesothelioma – the growth in the lining between the lung and the chest brought about by exposure to asbestos dust – in the autumn of 2002. At the time, we thought that his condition had been brought about by the close proximity in Armley of the building firm for which he had been employed for most of his working life to the notorious JW Roberts Ltd company, as the two businesses had been near neighbours in Canal Road. Although the Roberts asbestos factory had closed down in 1959, the time lag between exposure to the dust and evidence of the mesothelioma can be substantial and, indeed, can run into decades. My father had begun working in the area at the end of the 1940s. He had said that he had often walked through the Roberts factory as a short cut on his way to work and he could remember the dust lying thick on the ground.

The West Yorkshire Coroner was to take a different view, however. On the basis of the advice of a cancer expert, he concluded that dad's exposure to asbestos dust had occurred because of the nature of many of the jobs at which he had been present in his routine work as a joiner and foreman, where these had involved the removal of asbestos from old buildings prior to their destruction or renovation. In my father's case, therefore, the mesothelioma had most probably been brought about, not by the specific proximity to JW Roberts Ltd, but through an aspect of his job that constituted a routine part of his everyday work. It is a salutary thought to consider the implications of the Coroner's conclusion for those thousands of others in the building industry who, whilst working for similar small building companies throughout the country, have also undertaken this type of activity. My sister and I attended the inquest in November 2004. It was the day of my fiftieth birthday.

My father had been pleased when the Hunslet rugby league club had taken up residence at the South Leeds Stadium in Middleton in November 1995. He looked forward to my occasional visits to the ground with him, so that he could confirm the club's progress and speculate on the future. From the main stand, he liked the view over the pitch and across to the city, albeit, in the near distance, with some poignancy at the fate of the former Parkside home. My father was also aware that, for other reasons, Middleton had a historical significance which extended far beyond the boundaries of South Leeds.[52] It was entirely proper that the club should again be permanently based in a location with such a rich industrial history.

The downside was that the South Leeds Stadium had seating on only one side of the ground and a fairly limited capacity. As a result, when Hunslet won the Northern Ford Premiership final at the end of the 1999 season, they were denied promotion into the Super League by the rugby league authorities. The effects of this were entirely predictable and, whilst not exactly constituting the death knell of the club, firmly established what its status would be in the succeeding years. Most of the better players in this side, naturally seeking to play at the highest level, sought their opportunities elsewhere. The period since 1999 has been one of continual struggle for the club as, with limited resources and a small supporter base, it has had to rely on a combination of seasoned veterans and raw youngsters.

My sister and I had to go to the Gateshead Thunder match, of course. Rosemary, at her first ever Hunslet game, wore the Hawks scarf that Dad had bought for her as a Christmas present some years earlier; I wore the same myrtle, white and flame scarf that I had worn nearly 40 years earlier, when Alan Preece scored under the Headingley posts against Wakefield Trinity in the 1965 Challenge Cup semi-final. Before the game, on entering the main stand, we took a (not entirely accidental) wrong turning and ended up in the directors' suite where, unchallenged, we relaxed and had a quiet drink. The game itself was evenly contested to start with, before Hunslet took control and Gateshead fell away. The home side had rattled up a half century of points before the end of the match. A Hunslet player making his debut against Gateshead was a young centre called Gareth Murrell, whose father, Bryan, Dad and I had seen playing for Hunslet at Elland Road a generation earlier; he acquitted himself well and had a tidy game.

Reflecting on the match – and the overall circumstances – later, I was struck by the symmetry with which events had unfolded, as determined by the rugby fates. In 2004, the Hunslet club was in the lower reaches of the professional ranks, just as they had been when my father had first taken me to see them play Whitehaven at Parkside in August 1961. By contrast, the leading club in the rugby league was now Leeds, who had won the Championship for the first time in 1961 and who, as emphatically the best side in Britain in 2004, would go on to win the Super League Grand Final for the first time in October of that year.

My father had been taken by his grandfather to watch his first Hunslet match at Parkside whilst at primary school. Given that his support had therefore lasted for over 70 years, I thought it appropriate to write to the chairman of the club in July 2004. It was a two page letter, which set out dad's recollections of the Hunslet triumphs of the 1930s – the Challenge Cup win in 1934 and the Championship victory in 1938 – and his memories of his favourite players of that era, Jack Walkington and Oliver Morris. It went on to describe how Dad had taken me to Parkside when I was six and how I had watched my first match sitting on his shoulders at the back of the main stand. I mentioned dad's loyalty to the club, as their home fixtures moved from Parkside to the Leeds Greyhound Stadium and then to Elland Road and the South Leeds Stadium. I concluded by referring to my father's pride in his roots in south Leeds and the values that he had learned there from his own parents and grandparents. The Hunslet rugby league club had been an important reference point for him from an early age and his affection for the club, and his respect for its traditions, had remained with him throughout his life. After thanking the club on dad's behalf, I referred to the cheque that I had enclosed as a contribution towards an end-of-season drink for the players and staff, when they might perhaps raise a glass to my father.

The cheque was cashed a month later. I did not receive a reply to the letter.

My valedictory attendances at sporting events in Leeds – the city in which I had served my apprenticeship as an ordinary sports spectator – took place via three separate visits in 2010 and 2011. In the first of these, in March 2010, a long weekend gave me the opportunity to watch the home fixtures fulfilled on successive days by the Leeds Rhinos rugby league club, Leeds United AFC and the Leeds Carnegie rugby union side.

On the Friday evening, the Leeds Rhinos hosted Harlequins RL in a Super League fixture. It was five days after Leeds had narrowly lost the World Club championship match to the Melbourne Storm at Elland Road, the home side having won their third successive Super League title – and their fourth in six years – the previous October. Notwithstanding their uncertain early season league form – won two, lost two – it was clear that Leeds were now the pre-eminent rugby league club side in Britain.

I took my place on the 20 metre line at the western end of the North Stand. It was very close to where I had been seated for the Wigan match on my only previous Super League visit four years earlier and, therefore, in the same part of the ground as my 7 year-old self had watched, transfixed, as Denis Hartley dropped a goal for Hunslet in the 1962 Yorkshire Cup Final against Hull Kingston Rovers. In my mind's eye, I could picture the ball's low skimming trajectory as Hartley's kick scraped over the bar and crashed into the crowded spectators behind the goal posts.

Leeds took the lead when Brent Webb – one of five internationals from Australia or New Zealand in their squad for this match – sprinted over for a try after four minutes: 4–0. Harlequins levelled the scores when the young debutant Leeds winger, Tom Bush, was outjumped by his opposite number when reaching for a high kick into the corner: 4–4. Bush had the last word, however, pouncing on a low grubber kick behind the Harlequins line to register a try just as the hooter was sounding for the end of the match. It has to be said that his try was slightly academic in the grand scheme of things, as it took the score to 62–4.

Leeds had stuttered to a 14–4 half-time lead, but there was no stopping them in the second half. Their 48 unanswered points came at my end of the pitch and I watched in admiration as the combination of skill, power and speed proved too much for the opposition. Harlequins did not give up, but, once they had started to miss the occasional tackle, the floodgates were bound to open. The forward dominance of Kylie Leuluai and Jamie Peacock provided the space in which Leeds's main distributors – Danny Buderus and Matt Diskin – could move the ball quickly and allow the half-backs Rob Burrow and Danny McGuire to search for the gaps in the Harlequins defence. McGuire scored the try of the evening, taking the ball at speed on the half way line, chipping over the defence and gathering the ball and then chipping again, this time over the full back, to collect the ball again and dive under the posts. However, it was Burrow who was my favourite player in this Leeds team: small, brave, quick and skilful. He is the modern rugby league era's Roger Millward, without question. He is also, I would have thought, excellent value for his personal sponsors. As he successfully notched each of his 7 conversions to Leeds's 12 tries, the excitable stadium announcer dutifully confirmed that Burrow was sponsored by ASC Stainless Steel Holdings.

I expected that this would be the last time that I would watch a rugby league match at Headingley. It was inevitable, therefore, that, during the steady procession of Leeds's second half tries, I would cast my eyes around the ground to remember it as it was and as it had been. One thing that struck me was how much less grass there was on the pitch. I had remembered it as being lush and green and, from walking over the ground at the end of a game with my father on more than one occasion, slightly undulating. From the stand, the pitch now looked bare and hard and, by allowing a higher bounce of the ball, was a contributory factor in enabling McGuire to score his excellent try.

The main addition to the infrastructure in recent seasons has been the huge Carnegie Stand at the eastern end, which has replaced the open terracing. But the basic shape and look of the ground had not really changed much. The North Stand seats remain uncomfortably cramped but provide a good view of the action unless – and it is a crucial caveat – the seat is located behind one of the stand's tall steel pillars. The South Stand also looked to be much the same, albeit with the roof freshly be-decked in the club's yellow and blue with the name of the primary club sponsors – the Leeds Building Society – predominantly displayed. It remains standing room only, heavily populated by the Leeds die-hards and, I am sure, an intimidating atmosphere in front of which to perform for any visiting club's centres and wingers. The main change to the stand, compared with my earliest visits, had been the removal of the narrow spiral steel staircase, which the television commentary team had to negotiate in order to reach their broadcasting gantry, invariably to the cat-calls of the spectators below. A victory for the health and safety brigade, I suspect.

The match programme had also changed in some respects and not others. It extended to over 80 pages and was a glossy description of the range of activities occurring in this well-organised club – charity events, Diskin's testimonial, the work of the backroom staff, the age-group teams, cheerleaders – as well as more immediate matters in hand such as reports on recent Leeds matches and introductions to the current opposition. I looked out for one particular feature and I was not disappointed. The "Flashback – Caught on Camera" page featured a Leeds game against Dewsbury from February 1991 and, amazingly, it was a match that Leeds had won: 40–20 on this occasion.

When the final whistle sounded and the players left the pitch, I stood for a few moments near a dividing wall in the North Stand and cast my mind back. The Hartley drop goal in 1962; the ferocious Great Britain-Australia international of 1963; John Bevan's triumphant run back to his position after scoring a try against Australia in 1978; Max Krilich and Brett Kenny sprinting in under the posts for the Australians in 1982; Jonathan Davies's long-range interception try for Great Britain against New Zealand in 1993; and, not least, in 1965, the bouncing ball, near the Wakefield Trinity try line, that Alan Preece pounced on prior to sending my father's beloved Hunslet into the Challenge Cup final at Wembley.

Two days later, on a sunny Sunday afternoon, I was at Headingley again, standing behind one of the barriers in the South Stand and watching Leeds Carnegie play Saracens in the Guinness Premiership.

The days of the Roundhay and Headingley rugby union clubs had long passed. They had been amalgamated to form Leeds RUFC in 1992 in the expectation (or perhaps merely the hope) that there should be strong rugby union side in Yorkshire to match the likes of Leicester and Wasps and Gloucester. It is probably valid to conclude that it had been only a partial success. The Pilkington Cup had been won (as Leeds Tykes) at Twickenham in 2005 and there had been forays into European competition, but recent seasons had been typified by the "yo-yo" status that I had seen characterise other teams in other sports. Leeds had been either relegated from the Premiership or promoted to it in each of the last four years.

Relegation having apparently been their clear fate for much of the 2009–10 season, Leeds were still desperately clinging on to their Premiership status, a couple of recent victories having brought them level on points with Sale at the foot of the table with seven league matches left to play. On the evidence of this performance against Saracens – a side lying third in the table – it was difficult to see why Leeds were in this position. Their forwards gained the upper hand in the scrum and the defence was sound and it was only by missing some kickable penalty goal opportunities that the margin of victory was restricted to 19–12. For their part, Saracens – with six South Africans in their starting line-up and the All Black Justin Marshall coming on late in the game as a replacement – looked limited in ambition, seeming to rely on the place-kicking and drop-kicking skills of the fly-half, Derick Hougaard, and lacking the attacking threat that they had demonstrated to Glasgow at Firhill in the Heineken Cup two years earlier. But what did I know? At the end of the season, it was the same Saracens who were contesting the Guinness Premiership final against the Leicester Tigers at Twickenham and whose grasp on the trophy was only prised away by a last minute Leicester try.

It had been a long time since I had watched a rugby match from the South Stand, but it seemed that, even though this was the union rather than league code, the cycloptic vision of most of its inhabitants had not changed a great deal. In the open space in my part of the terrace, the middle-aged man standing next to me complained incessantly about the referee's incompetence or bias and his views were loudly choroused by another man and his daughter behind us to our right and another couple in front. I decided that there was no point in changing my viewing position, however, as their counterparts were certain to be found all over the stand. It has to said, however, that the Leeds supporters gave huge encouragement to their side throughout the match – they were the proverbial sixteenth man – and there was a delighted, almost joyous, atmosphere at the final whistle when it was realised that, with Sale's defeat that afternoon, their side had lifted itself off the bottom of the table. On more than one occasion, the resounding chant of "Yorkshire, Yorkshire" rang through the stand. Perhaps the initial aims of the club's founders were coming to fruition after all. Relegation was duly avoided – by both Leeds and Sale – at the end of the season, as Worcester Warriors were demoted from the Premiership.[53]

On leaving the ground, I realised that my rugby union spectating in Leeds had ended at this point. I also knew that, in truth, it had ended many years before – probably around 1981 – either when I had paid my last visit to Chandos Park to see a Roundhay match or gone with my father down to Clarence Field in Kirkstall to watch Headingley. My best memories would be of bright evenings in March or April, watching the ferocious club battles in the later rounds of the Yorkshire Cup, or of the autumn matches in the County Championship, admiring the skilful three-quarters in the Yorkshire side. Those days had long gone, particularly at Roundhay, where the former Chandos Park is now a housing estate.

I was gratified, however, to see that the first team pitch at the Headingley club has met with a more satisfactory fate. The Leeds Carnegie RUFC website reports that, when Headingley had been given the opportunity to buy the pitch after the First World War for the sum of £2,500, the money had been raised by club members as a memorial to those that had lost their lives in that terrible conflict. A pre-Leeds Carnegie/Saracens walk down the hill into Kirkstall confirmed that the pitch is now part of the complex of the Leeds Rugby Academy – servicing both the league and union teams – with the clubhouse itself remaining intact as the Academy's offices and changing rooms. The terraces on which my father and I had stood near the entrance to the ground and the two covered stands that had been on either side of the pitch were no longer there, replaced by tall wire fencing and some scraggly bushes, but the ground itself looked to be well-maintained with the thick padding in the clubs' colours at the bases of the tall goalposts and the playing surface of green and lush grass. I walked back up the hill with a sense of satisfaction at the unbroken connection with that earlier – and lost – generation. An important sense of local continuity has remained in place.

Sandwiched between the two rugby fixtures in March 2010 was Leeds United versus Brentford at Elland Road. As I arrived early, I took a walk away from the ground to the site of the former Leeds Greyhound Stadium, a few hundred yards from the soccer ground, where the New Hunslet rugby league club had played for a short time in the 1970s after the closure of the Parkside ground. I knew that the stadium had been demolished in the early 1980s, though I was somewhat surprised that no real economic use was being made of it, apart from as an overspill car park for the football club. I looked around the desolate space, with its banking on the far side supporting a line of tall, flimsy trees, and the rough surface of broken asphalt. Again, it was difficult to avoid the memories: the narrow, cramped rugby pitch with its unusual goalposts, the noise of the crowd echoing eerily around the high stands, and Steve Pitchford of Leeds being sent off the field during a Hunslet victory against their local rivals, their last to date in a competitive fixture between the clubs.

I walked back to the Elland Road football ground and took my place in the paddock of the John Charles Stand near the half way line. This was Leeds United's third season in the third tier of English football – formally League One but really, for sporting Luddites such as me, League Division Three – and their desperation for promotion was keenly evident in the tense impatience of the spectators around me. As things stood, Leeds were handily placed in the second of the two automatic promotion places, but their recent league form had been patchy – two wins in nine matches – and the spectre of two unsuccessful play-off campaigns at the end of the previous seasons clearly hung over the proceedings. Leeds's cause was not greatly helped here: a 1–1 draw against spirited mid-table opponents, whose travelling support of 2,000 in the far corner of the ground clearly enjoyed their afternoon.

The Leeds manager, Simon Grayson, spent the whole game standing in his technical area, just in front of us, and he could not have avoided the sense of dissatisfaction that came from the crowd behind him at his side's inability to dispatch their allegedly inferior opposition. For some reason, I thought of Winston Churchill's famous dictum about standing at the Dispatch Box in the House of Commons and having concern about his own backbenchers: "The Opposition is in front of you. The Enemy is behind". Notwithstanding Leeds's good season to date – including an FA Cup win against Manchester United at Old Trafford – the expectations on the manager clearly constituted Grayson's biggest problem. In this regard, I had been struck by a comment in the "YEP Jury" column of the previous day's *Yorkshire Evening Post*, in which five Leeds supporters had offered their views on the forthcoming match. It was predictable enough that all of them had forecast Leeds to win, with a cumulative score of 13–0, but what jumped off the page was the view of one correspondent – a 36 year-old from Shadwell – that "Brentford, and all the mediocrity they stand for, come to the home of football this weekend". Not every supporter will have respect for the opposition, of course – including for a side that had undergone a remarkable recovery after looking to be heading out of the Football League only two seasons earlier – though I did wonder just how much intolerance a newspaper of repute might be prepared to sustain from its contributors.

The crowd's immediate feedback to Grayson and his team would have been different, of course, if a Leeds shot in the closing minutes had not rebounded back into play from the inside of a Brentford post. As ever in sport, there is a small margin between hero and villain. For my part, I was impressed by the calm authority and skilful touches of Jonathan Howson and Toumani Diagouraga in the respective midfields and, in particular, the commanding presence of Wojciech Szczesny – a 19 year-old on loan from Arsenal, albeit already a Polish international – in the Brentford goal.

It had been over 40 years since my first visit to Elland Road to see a Leeds United match (Charlton Athletic in 1968) and nearly 30 since my last (Liverpool in 1981). The Lowfields Roads stand and the terraces in front it, from which I had seen that first game, had long gone – demolished in 1992 according to an article in the Brentford match programme – and been replaced by the huge East Stand. Even before that, in the mid 1970s, the infamous Scratching Shed had been demolished and replaced by the South Stand, whilst, at the other end of the ground, the Gelderd End or Kop was now the Don Revie Stand. I liked the arena. Each of the stands had its own character and, in their disjointed fashion, they combined to provide the ground with atmosphere and intimacy. Clearly, it was a case of two down and two to go. John Charles and Don Revie had booked their permanent memorials – as had Billy Bremner with his vibrant statue outside the ground at the corner of Lowfields Road and Elland Road – and that only left the East and South stands to give their names to two future heroes.

My second visit to Leeds in 2010 took the form of two days cricket at Headingley in July, firstly for a Twenty-20 match between Yorkshire and Warwickshire – or Yorkshire Carnegie and the Warwickshire Bears in the modern vernacular – and then for the first day of the 4-day County Championship match between the same two sides.

It was my first Twenty-20 match, though, in truth, I was probably more interested in the ground than the cricket. I had seen that the Headingley cricket ground was changing significantly from my visits to watch the Leeds

Rhinos rugby league matches in 2006 against Wigan and, earlier in 2010, Harlequins, so I knew what to expect. But this was the first cricket I had seen at this venue since Sachin Tendulkar and Sourav Ganguly put England to the sword on the Saturday of the 2002 England-India test match.

The main change in the ground was that it had grown taller. The stiff breeze still blew in from behind the wide expanses of the former Western Terrace, now the West Stand – sufficiently strongly at the Twenty-20 match to send the hat of one of the umpires cascading across the square – but it was now confronted by the high barriers of the new East Stand, the double-decked North East stand, the huge replay screen cum scoreboard and the towering Carnegie Pavilion behind the bowler's arm at the Kirkstall Lane end of the ground. Apart from the Main Stand (or Football Stand) and the re-designed Old Pavilion building, the construction work of the last two years had completed the removal of virtually all the familiar landmarks of my earlier spectating years at Headingley: the creaking Kirkstall Lane turnstiles set in the solid brick wall next to the main road, the entrance to the cycle track past the newspaper vendor's little kiosk, the scoreboard framed in the trees, the Winter Shed, the functional 1960s-built pavilion and offices and the low bank of terracing that had once guarded the Bowling Pavilion and greens. On the other hand, the shape and size of the ground were unchanged – as when I first viewed it (when attending the 1962 Yorkshire Cup final at the adjacent rugby ground), it still seemed a long way from one side to the other – its parameters set by the length of the Football Stand, itself unchanged apart from a new roof and the removal of the clock.

I realised that the new look to Headingley – the Headingley Carnegie Cricket Ground, to give it the full title – was a sign of the times. The years of under-investment had had to be rectified if it were to retain its status as a test match ground against the increased competition presented by the greater number of alternative venues than in years past. The characteristics of the "old" Headingley – a certain charm and quirkiness to complement its tradition and history (though emphatically without its being picturesque or even attractive) – were no longer sufficient to meet the requirements of modernity and efficiency and (basic) comfort that are now the pre-requisites for hosting major sporting events. The Yorkshire club – which had only purchased the freehold of the ground as recently as 2005 – had had to make a significant capital outlay in the hope of a higher stream of future revenues. It is a risky venture.

I headed for the new Members' Long Room in the East Stand: a delightfully proportioned room in a gentle arc overlooking the ground and a proper home for the Yorkshire members after all these years. Before play started, I looked at the various pieces of memorabilia that decorated the room, including the tributes to Lord Hawke and Hedley Verity, and spent some time studying the test match honours boards, which covered the wall at one end with the details of all the centuries and 5-wicket bowling feats that had occurred in Headingley test matches. To date, the ground had witnessed 96 test match centuries, beginning with that of the Hon FS Jackson for England against Australia in 1905. I reckoned that I had seen at least part of 25 of these innings, beginning with Geoff Boycott for England against New Zealand in 1973 and ending with Ganguly in 2002. I sat at a small table with my pre-match coffee and I thought of my father – with his simple pleasures – who would have revelled in the ambience of this splendid location. A young girl came round selling raffle tickets for an autographed bat. After she had passed, the elderly man next to me muttered to his wife: "It's about time they changed the prize".

On the pitch, Yorkshire restricted Warwickshire to 155 for 8 – a total that was slightly below par, I judged – and then got off to a flying start as the impressive Adam Lyth stroked 34 off only 16 deliveries. Thereafter, the batting fell away, with only the West Indian fast bowler Tino Best, batting at number 9, managing to score at more than a run a ball thanks to the innings's single six hit. Another of Yorkshire's overseas players was Herschelle Gibbs, whose expensive failure to catch Steve Waugh in a World Cup match on the same ground in 1999 is one of the "nano-dramas" recorded earlier in this volume; he managed only 17 off 19 balls, despite being dropped twice.

I have not checked the details of the win-loss account of the visits to watch Yorkshire play one-day cricket at Headingley or Bradford Park Avenue in my late teenage years, but my guess is that the overall balance would have been in deficit, as successive Yorkshire batting line-ups generally failed to reach the required totals. If so, skipping from that generation to this, nothing much had changed on the playing side. I sat in the East Stand in the bright late afternoon sunshine as Yorkshire fell further behind the required run rate, their weak batting performance eventually petering out into defeat by 34 runs. The current custodians of the white rose appeared to be no more adept at convincingly winning a Sunday afternoon one-day game than their predecessors had been. But, as the inevitable outcome unfolded, I realised that the final result probably meant less to me than those corresponding disappointments had registered at the earlier age. I had seen a Twenty-20 game – with its snatches of pop music and pubescent acrobatic dancers and coloured clothing and white ball – played before a sizeable crowd on a pleasant afternoon. I did wonder about the popularity of this form of the game, however, and whether it would be sustained beyond the short term.

The following day was the first of the corresponding County Championship match. Yorkshire batted through the day to reach 325 for 4 off 96 overs, Adam Lyth again leading from the front with 84 and Gerard Brophy, the wicket-keeper, accelerating his innings nicely after tea to reach 92 not out. The Warwickshire attack was not particularly menacing, but it kept going throughout the day, tying the Yorkshire batsmen down in mid-afternoon.

I reflected on the scene around me and confirmed – or re-confirmed – that I will always like the rituals of County Championship cricket. I like applauding the good shots and the fine pieces of fielding and the tight maiden overs and the individual or team landmarks. I like being part of the ruddy-faced crowd with its tightly packed holdalls and its cushions and its newspapers and its sensible clothing for all weathers. I like the rhythm of the day – beginning on this occasion with the dismissal of Yorkshire's acting captain, Jacques Rudolph, without scoring and ending with a bright partnership between Brophy and Adil Rashid in the evening sunshine – with its formal interruptions for lunch and tea. I liked the way in which, having taken Rudolph's wicket and retreated to his fielding position on the boundary, the Warwickshire bowler Neil Carter modestly raised his hand to acknowledge the respectful applause given by the half dozen spectators seated in a single row of seats on the other side of the boundary rope.

I moved around the ground over the course of the day: the lower tier of the Football Stand, the East Stand, the new Carnegie Pavilion – though not the Western Terrace, from where in 1966 I had seen the vintage Yorkshire side of Close, Trueman, Illingworth *et al* for the first time, but which is no longer open to spectators for County Championship matches – before watching the last session from the balcony of the Football Stand. It was from here that my father and I had watched our last day at a test match: England versus India in 2002. In my mind's eye, I could see Tendulkar launching a delivery from Andrew Caddick into the corporate hospitality boxes over to my right and Ganguly despatching Ashley Giles over the old pavilion. And, all the time, the lights on the old scoreboard had been alerting the umpires that it was getting too dark to play.

The third and final visit to Leeds took place in August 2011, principally to watch a Hunslet rugby league match, though the County Championship cricket fixture list also enabled me to make a detour to attend the fourth day of Yorkshire versus Sussex at Scarborough.

It had been 24 years – since the day of Jack Simmons's match-winning performance for Lancashire in a Refuge Assurance League game in August 1987 to be precise – since I had seen Yorkshire play at Scarborough. I was reminded of even earlier times when I walked up to the ground from the railway station and passed Trafalgar Square, around which Brian Stevens and I had patiently queued for a couple of hours before taking two of the final places at the Gillette Cup semi final against Nottinghamshire in 1969.

The venue did not seem to have changed very much. Its size, proportions and characteristics were much as I remembered them: the protective framing given by the two straight terraces of bed and breakfast boarding houses meeting at an angle on North Marine Drive; the gentle slope of the raised West Stand; the rows of wooden seating in front of the main entrance; the small section for Yorkshire Members in front of the elegant pavilion. A man waiting to dry his hands in one of the gents' toilets told me that "they've spent 3 million on the ground... and there still isn't any bloody soap next to the wash basins". But I would not complain. The ground looked neat and clean and, on this day, in the warm sunshine and with a sizeable crowd in attendance, there was plenty of entertainment on a good batting pitch.

My expert opinion of the state of the pitch was based on the evidence that, during the day, a total of 519 runs were scored for the loss of 9 wickets, the Sussex nightwatchman James Anyon batted for over two hours for his maiden first-class 50, and the Sussex captain Michael Yardy compiled his second century of the match with apparent ease. Yardy's skilfully timed declaration left Yorkshire to score 344 runs to win in a minimum of 51 overs; they managed 312 for 6 before the sides agreed on the draw.

The early overs of both innings followed a similar pattern in that – after virtually every ball – there were the continual sounds of clapping and shouts of encouragement from several of the fielders to the bowler. I had noticed this many years earlier – in particular, I recalled a Yorkshire versus Middlesex match at Headingley ("Well bowled, Cat") – but here the effects seemed to be amplified by the bowl of the ground created by the banked seating and the brigade of boarding houses. The Yorkshire fielders started things off – "Great pressure", "We'll get our rewards", "250 all out" (at 201 for 4) – though they were realistic enough to make suitable amendments as events unfolded. I had a wry smile when "The first half hour is vital" was subtly replaced by "The first hour is vital" and "One wicket opens the door". Meanwhile Sussex progressed serenely to score 154 runs for the loss of one wicket in the two hours before lunch. By that time, there were signs that Yorkshire's aggression was becoming more self-directed. When Steve Patterson misjudged a piece of fielding and conceded three runs towards the boundary to my right, the curses of the bowler, Ryan Sidebottom, were again amplified by the ground's acoustics.

When it came to their turn, the Sussex fielders went through their corresponding repertoire of oral gymnastics. I know that all this energetic shouting is part and parcel of the modern game – in club cricket as well as in the County Championship and beyond[54] – and that it is usually accompanied by various forms of graceless sledging of the batsmen, but I did wonder, not for the first time, how effective it actually was. It seemed to part of a routine – along with the mandatory shouts of "catch it", whenever the ball bounced up near a close fielder – that everyone took for granted and, effectively, ignored. It certainly did not seem to affect Yorkshire's opening batsmen, as Jacques Rudolph and Joe Sayers rattled up a partnership of 174.

In amongst the high scoring, – and whilst intrigued, as usual, by the way in which a County Championship game steadily evolved towards its conclusion – I was keen to register the feats of individual skill. Rudolph scored 120, thereby atoning for his early dismissal in the match against Warwickshire which I had attended at Headingley the previous year: a lovely innings of classic cover driving and, when Yorkshire accelerated their run chase, some big hitting into the crowd. Monty Panesar bowled a long spell of left arm spin. Jonathan Bairstow batted aggressively with a mixture of powerful strokes and Twenty-20 type improvisation. And, most impressively, Wayne Parnell took an astonishing catch from a towering Bairstow hit on the boundary near the pavilion. Running towards the boundary rope, Parnell got under the ball and, on receiving it, tossed it up immediately so that it wasn't in his possession when he crossed the rope. He then turned back immediately and re-caught the ball on the right side of the boundary. A remarkable combination of skill, agility and clear-headed quick thinking.

During the lunch and tea intervals, the Scarborough outfield was crowded with lots of other cricket matches: smaller events with young boys (and girls), their paunched fathers and uncles, and mothers and, in some instances, grandparents. Some had proper wickets; others made do with a rucksack. One ginger-haired boy – aged perhaps 8 or 9 – spent the whole of the lunch break bowling to an older brother from a distance of about 12 yards. He had a good bowling action, great energy and boundless enthusiasm. He was as I had been at his age.

At the close of the match, I wandered over the outfield to inspect the wicket. It was heavily marked with the bowlers' footmarks and the scoring of the batsmen's studs where they had taken guard. The footmarks had left a pronounced indentation in the pitch that, no doubt, Panesar had been aiming to hit. It gave even greater weight to the quality of Rudolph's innings.

I took a last look around the ground and conjured up the fond memories of previous visits: Don Wilson's massive six, Gary Sobers's dismissal, Ray Illingworth's captaincy, Jack Simmons's warming-up exercises (and bowling) and my dad's reaction when we were strolling around the ground and we walked past the great Les Dawson.

And so to August 21st 2011. Fifty years (and two days) had passed since my first visit to Parkside to watch Hunslet play Whitehaven at the beginning of the 1961–62 season. I took my place in the second tier of the South Leeds Stadium to await the Hunslet Hawks's vital home game with the Barrow Raiders in the rugby league Cooperative Championship. With summer rugby having been introduced several seasons before, the August and September fixtures had taken on some significance in Hunslet's battle to avoid relegation. Hunslet needed to win at least one (and possibly both) of their two remaining fixtures to avoid the drop.

At lunchtime, I had taken the bus from the centre of Leeds up the Dewsbury Road and alighted at Parkside Lane, which, all those years before, my father had driven down on his way to the large roughly surfaced car park outside the Parkside rugby stadium. I walked down the road and into the Parkside Industrial Estate, which, since the mid 1970s, has occupied the spacious grounds in which the stadium, the adjacent cricket ground and the car park had once stood. It being a Sunday, there seemed to be no-one around, apart from the driver of a white van, who passed me on the road and preceded me into the estate. The estate itself was no different (though no worse) than a thousand others across the country – a combination of warehouses and industrial units – though I noticed that one of the units was boarded up and a sign outside another announced that its tenants had relocated elsewhere. I walked through the estate and up to the top of a short mound of scrubby grass and bushes, where I was almost level with some of the units' roofs. The estate stretched out below me and, in my mind's eye, I pictured what had stood there in an earlier time.

In the South Leeds Stadium, I sat more or less in the same place that I had for the Hunslet Hawks versus Gateshead Thunder match in the summer of 2004. The warehouses of the Parkside Industrial Estate stood in the near distance to my left beyond which towered the prominent offices and hotels of central Leeds. Looking out to the right, the green and hilly part of Middleton rose above the railway line. Beyond the fencing on the opposite side of the ground stood a large wind turbine.

I had a good feeling about Hunslet's prospects when, introducing the teams before the kick-off, the stadium announcer welcomed everyone to the "Stade de South Leeds". After a combative and evenly-matched start to the game, the home side took control and stretched out into a 26–0 half time lead. A couple of the tries were long range efforts, cheered all the way by me, both in my own right and as my dad's proxy. Barrow recovered temporarily at the start of the second half, but Hunslet held out comfortably and, towards the end, the winger Waine Pryce's fourth try, converted by Jack Latus to give him his seventh successful goal kick, took the score to 42–12. At the end of the game, Hunslet were applauded from the field by the home supporters and, to their credit, by the hard core of a committed and noisy Barrow following.

I sat in my seat for some time after those around me had departed. I could feel a welling in my eyes and that I was shaking slightly. It had been the perfect script.

It was now fifty years – and counting – and it was time to move on.

Chapter 24

Reflections

I return to the questions that were posed in the Preface to this book? What have I derived from all these years of sports spectating? What has drawn me back to the live event, whether cup final or test match or routine club game? What is it that sport has meant to me over the fifty years that I have been sitting in the stand or watching from the touchline?

These issues are complex, and it would undoubtedly take an analyst far more skilled – as well as more detached – than I am to discern the key factors that have lain behind my spectating behaviour over this long period. It is clear, however, given all that has been presented in this volume, that watching sport has not simply been a uniformly positive experience. My emotional responses to sports spectating have been characterised by lows as well as highs. In particular, it is noticeable that there are references throughout the book to the feelings of anti-climax that have been experienced immediately after watching a sporting encounter or on later reflection. And yet, I have still returned to that stand or that touchline.

I would suggest that any interpretation of my sports spectating career should include at least the following strands.

First – and, perhaps, most obviously – there has been an attraction to sporting excellence. At one level, this means techniques and skills. More specifically, it means skills performed in the heat of the competitive environment. As Ed Smith notes in *What Sport Tells Us About Life*, if it were skill *per se* that brings us to sports matches, we would enjoy exhibition matches more than competitive games. Instead, we are drawn to "the battle to win within a context where the rules actually work".

Smith's only reference to rugby league in his thought-provoking book is that it is "a famously hard game... not a game for fancy theories or over-intellectualism". It was precisely within this environment that I was taught at an early age to appreciate the individual skills of the players I was watching – beginning with the Hunslet full back Billy Langton catching the ball over the touchline with his feet still in the field of play and the centre Geoff Shelton demonstrating how to draw his opponent and deliver the pass to send his winger down the touchline – and this lesson has been successively applied across the range of other sporting occasions that I have witnessed. Moreover, I was aware from the very first that such skills were being displayed in a formidably competitive environment that, in this particular case, was underpinned by the harsh reality of the players' success being rewarded by a higher financial return.

Admiration for performers at the top of their profession has been a continual theme running through this volume – from Ray Illingworth to Sachin Tendulkar, Reg Gasnier to Ellery Hanley, Gareth Edwards to Yannick Jauzion, Bobby Moore to David Silva. To have seen these players in the flesh has been more than just registering another famous name on the field in front of me, although I readily acknowledge that this is a factor that cannot be ignored. I have also sought to recognise – and to see the reasons for – their place at the top of their particular sporting tree. In this regard, I think it has probably helped that I played some sport myself – predominantly rugby at school and college and cricket at a good club standard, but also, to various low standards at various times, tennis, badminton, squash, athletics, golf, football and rowing. This has made me appreciate the skills being demonstrated in front of me even more, especially by those who, as described in earlier chapters, made their sport seem so easy – Alan Old playing at fly half for Yorkshire against Edinburgh, for example, or Alvin Kallicharran batting for Warwickshire against Yorkshire in a Benson and Hedges Cup semi final. I played enough sport to know that it is far from easy.

Sporting excellence extends beyond technical skills, of course. It also incorporates the quality of leadership which is usually, though not always, reflected on the sports field by the captaincy in team events. The styles of effective leadership that I have observed have varied considerably – physical and cerebral, flamboyant and calm – and it has been a continual fascination to watch the successful practitioners at work. Not surprisingly, the game of cricket has provided a high proportion of these (Brian Close, Ray Illingworth, Mike Brearley, Imran Khan, Mark Taylor), but there have also been good examples elsewhere (Bobby Moore, Bill Beaumont, Bobby Skinstad, Ellery Hanley). I have been regularly surprised at how the styles of different captains – or, indeed, of the same captain at different times – can contribute to their side's success.

This aspect of sport has always interested me, probably because I was captain of my age-group rugby and cricket teams at school, and, in a sense, the burden of captaincy has never been shaken off. Over the long years as a spectator, rather than practitioner of sport, I could empathise completely with CLR James's comment in *Beyond a Boundary* that "From as far back as I can remember I have captained the fielding side of every match I have seen". However, it should be reported that, even when I did have the formal responsibility, my own application of the principles I thought I was learning was not always successful. During a period in which I was adopting the robust approach favoured by the Brian Close school of captaincy – at around Under 14s level – I was given a rebuke by the cricket master in charge of one of our opponents, who stated that I was being too brusque in asking (or ordering) my fielders to change their positions in the field; I am not sure that, even today, I know what the problem was.

Excellence also means courage. The most obvious example of this is the physical courage that is required in the major contact sports, where the risk of blood being shed or serious injury being incurred is ever present. It takes courage to play international rugby – league or union – in today's climate of confrontation and collision, just as it always has done. It took courage to play club rugby in Yorkshire in the 1970s – again in both codes – before the all-seeing video camera and other methods of detecting foul play became more widely available. In cricket, it took courage for any batsman to face the world's fastest bowlers in the long period in the game's history – now barely credible – before the batsman's helmet offered some protection against the misjudged rising ball and the potentially fatal blow on the temple. As with all cricket followers in 1975, I was particularly struck by the brazen courage of David Steele marching out to face the rampant Dennis Lillee and Jeff Thomson and being rewarded with a sizeable haul of runs and a firm place in our affections. Other examples of courageous behaviour take different forms, perhaps determined by the broader circumstances of the occasion or, as on that unpleasant afternoon at Upton Park at the beginning of 1982, in the players' dignified response to the direct provocation by a significant proportion of the spectators. Step forward Cyrille Regis and Brendon Batson.

The second reason for my longstanding spectating behaviour will be obvious from the earlier discussion: the appeal of the dramatic. I am aware that this is well-trodden territory, not least by CLR James who, in *Beyond a Boundary*, took the analysis back to the birth of democracy in ancient Greece and the critical roles played by both the tragic drama of the stage and the games of the early Olympics. James brought his compelling story up to date by noting the "[t]he state of the city, the nation or the world can invest a sporting event with dramatic intensity such as is reached in few theatres" so that "[w]hen the democrat Joe Louis fought the Nazi Schmeling [in the rematch of 1938 for the world heavyweight boxing title] the bout became a focus of approaching world conflict". James's focus was principally on the drama inherent in cricket, of course, particularly the way in which the conflict between individuals (the batsman and the bowler) represents that between the larger groups (their respective teams): "The batsman facing the ball does not merely represent his side. For that moment, to all intents and purposes, he is his side".

From the examples I have given, it is clear that drama on the sports field covers the full range of activity. In duration, it can be in the build up to the event (the Wales versus England rugby union international in 2005); it can last for the entirety of the contest itself (several of the rugby league Challenge Cup finals described earlier); or it can in that split-second of action, sometimes preceded by the anticipation of the outcome of that action, that has defined each of the nano-dramas summarised in Chapter 21 above. The drama can be based on the individual's decisive contribution to the match's outcome (Botham and Willis at Headingley in 1981) or a team's brooding dominance of the occasion (the Australian rugby league sides in 1982 and 1986). The drama can be poetic (Tiger Woods's chip to the first green at Troon in 1997) or ugly (the Casey-Tamati fight in the Great Britain-New Zealand rugby league test at Headingley in 1980). The drama can also be symbolic, or even iconic, as illustrated by the baggy green caps of successive Australian cricket XIs (no sponsored headgear for them) or the roar of the crowd as the greyhounds' traps opened at Catford. The drama can be in the unexpected result of the contest itself – and the emerging realisation that a shock is on the cards – as in the victories in the Challenge Cup finals of 1983 and 1998 by Featherstone Rovers and Sheffield Eagles, respectively. It can be when the visiting team, faced with overwhelming home support and playing on the away territory, emerges triumphant for its own small band of followers: West Ham United at Elland Road in 1971, Cadiz at Espanyol in 2005, Wigan Warriors at Leeds Rhinos and the Tennessee Titans at the Washington Redskins in 2006 and the Minnesota Vikings at the Chicago Bears in 2007. It can also be when the home side itself wins the contest, against prior expectations, and the dominant mass of its supporters enjoys an unanticipated success: Great Britain versus Australia at Wembley in 1990, Scotland versus France at Murrayfield in 2006.

The underlying case is made, I think. Sport *is* drama and conflict. Sport is the battle for honour (and honours). And an important part of the enjoyment in watching sport is to see the resolution of that battle and its effect on the winners and losers.

At the personal level, part of the drama can be in simply getting things wrong. A rhetorical question that has appeared on several occasions throughout this volume has been the plaintive: What did I know? On the primary school trip to the rugby league Challenge Cup final at Wembley in 1966, I confidently predicted to my class-mates that Wigan would win – St Helens won 21–2 – and my self-respect was only restored when, in the essay that our teacher made us write on the train back to Leeds, I offered the (correct) view that the St Helens winger, Len Killeen, should win the Lance Todd Trophy as the man-of-the-match. As the 1970s turned into the 1980s, I was of the view that the state of British rugby league was generally healthy, based on the robust and skilful contests that I had been seeing between the leading clubs of the time: in the next Ashes test match to be played on British soil (at Hull in 1982), Australia won 40–4. Later in the decade, after I had seen Widnes convincingly beat Leeds in the third round of the 1989 Challenge Cup, I was absolutely convinced that they would reach the Wembley final: St Helens defeated them in the semi final. (Never underestimate St Helens seems to be a emerging theme here).

Likewise in other sports. After Ian Botham made his one-day international debut for England (against the West Indies in 1976), I wondered if he would have a successful career at the highest level: Botham retired from Test cricket in 1992 having played in 102 matches and with 5,200 runs, 383 wickets and 120 catches to his name. After seeing Espanyol limp to defeat at home to Cadiz in 2005, I judged that they were likely candidates for relegation from the premier division of La Liga: Espanyol subsequently retained their league status, won the Copa del Reys in the same season, and reached the final of the following year's UEFA Cup. At the Ryder Cup at Walton Heath in 1981, I wondered why the world's top golfers – including Jack Nicklaus and Tom Watson in that year's contest – required to take the advice of their playing partners when deciding on the nature of a particular putt. I still wonder about this, incidentally. But what do I know?

Third, I am attracted to tradition and continuity. It is probably no coincidence that the teams I have watched for any length of time have had long and distinguished histories: Yorkshire CCC (founded 1863), Hunslet RLFC (a founder member of the Northern Rugby League in 1895, the rugby club having been formed in 1883), West of Scotland FC (1865), Leeds United (1920). Similarly, other sporting events I have visited, albeit only occasionally, have excellent pedigrees: the Lawn Tennis Championship at Wimbledon (1877), the Open Championship (1860). The Ryder Cup dates from 1927, the Cambridge University Amateur Boxing Club from

1897, the New York Knickerbockers from the formation of the Basketball Association of America in 1946, the Washington Redskins from 1937 and the Chicago Bears from 1922.

I like the idea that the players I have watched, and with whom I have occasionally identified, were continuing the lines that had been established in the distant past. I saw Justin Leonard on the Saturday of his victory in the 1997 Open Championship at Troon; the following day, his name joined the list of previous winners which stretched back from Jack Nicklaus and Bobby Jones all the way to Old Tom Morris. On a similar theme, I admired the way that, through the actions of Willie Haughey at the Christie's auction in 1994, the medal collection acquired over a ten year career at the club by Tommy Gemmell was kept intact and retained by Celtic FC (founded 1888). The extreme case of sporting longevity, of course, is the London Marathon. Whilst I was present at the first running of this particular event in 1981, the distance itself has a considerably longer derivation as a feat of athletic endurance – dating back to 490 BC – though I appreciate that this particular historical link is rather forcing the point.

There are caveats here, of course. Whilst it is salutary to consider that Geoff Gunney was following in the footsteps of Albert Goldthorpe as a Hunslet rugby league player respected by his contemporaries throughout the game, or that Shane Warne was bowling on the same Headingley square that Wilfred Rhodes had tormented earlier generations of batsmen, I have already noted that the sports themselves have changed, in most cases out of all recognition. The continuity card can be overplayed. I recognise, also, that my attachment to history has been heavily influenced by the fact that, for those sports to which I was introduced by my father at an early age – rugby league and cricket, and especially the former – the spectating tradition within the family had already been established through him and his own father, uncles and grandfather. A strong element of continuity and tradition was, therefore, provided by default. However, whilst the history of these sports (and their teams) has always been of interest, having been imposed on me in this benign way, I do not think I have made a conscious decision to rule out the new and untried. There is no reason why I should not enjoy watching sports of more recent vintage. For the present, however, I remain untested on live spectating of the triathlon or synchronised swimming or beach volleyball.

After a while, of course – and I have probably long passed this point – the longevity of my spectating career itself contributes to the role of tradition as a factor determining that same spectating behaviour. In effect, the causality becomes circular. I have some satisfaction in those examples of sporting continuity of which I have been an active constituent in my own right, for example the many consecutive years of attending the Challenge Cup final and the Headingley test match or the visits to see successive touring Australian and New Zealand rugby league sides. As part of this personal contribution to the continuity of sports spectating – and following the concept of the "echo" noted earlier – I have particularly liked the way that individual players have entered and exited the story and then re-appeared again at a later date.

Sometimes, it has been at a much later date: Lawrence Dallaglio (Wasps second XV and England rugby union sevens team, later England rugby captain in a Calcutta Cup match at Murrayfield); Ray Illingworth (Yorkshire, then Leicestershire, then Yorkshire again); Phil Sanderson (a fashionably long-haired teenager with the pre-1973 Hunslet rugby league club, later a bald-headed prop forward with Bradford Northern); Roger Millward (a teenage rugby league sensation with Castleford, later the respected player-coach masterminding Challenge Cup success for Hull Kingston Rovers); Brian Clough (the "dynamic young manager" with Derby County, later the experienced European Cup winner with Nottingham Forest); Mark Hateley (a raw teenage centre forward with Coventry City, later the hardened professional with Rangers); Andy Farrell (another teenage prodigy, this time representing Great Britain at rugby league, later the dominant Saracens centre in an important Heineken Cup match); Jason Robinson (the young try-scoring tearaway – in every sense – for Wigan in a Challenge Cup final, later to lead out the England rugby union team against Wales at the Millennium Stadium); and, not least, Jim Love (Leeds Schools Under 14s cricket XI through to the Yorkshire first XI, the England one-day international XI and, later, captain of the Scotland XI).

A related attraction of watching sport is one that is probably only provided retrospectively through the selective prism of memory, of which the contents of this volume have been an example. It is through conducting this exercise in sporting recollection that I have confirmed – or, perhaps, realised for the first time – the role that spectating has played in defining the various stages of my life to date. These life stages have been easily identifiable and fairly conventional: childhood and school in Leeds (to 1974), university in Cambridge (1974 to 1980), employment in London (1981 to 1992), marriage (from 1988) and life in Scotland (from 1992). As has been described, each of these stages (and locations) can be associated with a particular set of sporting connections, covering either regular visits to particular venues (Parkside, Headingley Cricket Ground, Grange Road, Craven Cottage, Burnbrae, Wembley) or one-off attendances at specific events (Ryder Cup, Wimbledon, Open Championship).

Moreover, the direction of association again goes both ways: from the life stage to sporting recollection, and vice versa. If I think of my time at primary school, for example, it is a natural step to recollect my second year project on "Rugby League" or my alternate Saturday afternoons watching Hunslet; by contrast, if I recall my visits to sporting events at the Sydney Cricket Ground or Madison Square Garden, the link is made logically to my employment with the London-based firm of economic consultants and the spectating opportunities that I was able to take on business trips overseas.

It can be seen that – in my case, at least – the "conventional" life stages have overlapped, to a considerable extent, with my Seven Ages of Watching Sport. I should emphasise, however, that the latter do not simply represent the chronological passage of time and place. The Seven Ages have characteristics of their own – naiveté, enthusiasm, affluence, experience, cynicism, bewilderment – that not only define the individual (in this case, me) at each particular stage, but, critically, affect the perspective with which the sporting event is viewed.

Of course, the stages of my life are associated, by memory, with more than just a mono-dimensional link to sports spectating. They are also linked to cohorts of friends or colleagues or other associates as well as to the other components of lifestyle, as represented by the houses in which I have lived or the routine journeys to my place of study or work or the income I have had at my disposal or the thousand other constituents that define the nature and quality of daily life. However, it has been noticeable how even these characteristics of everyday existence have had some sporting connections. I have mentioned the number of good friends – some of whom I am unfortunately no longer in contact with – who, at different times, shared my spectating interests: Brian Stevens, Andrew Carter, Stephen Hunter, Llyr James, Robert Gausden. I am also struck by the regular references to music – especially pop music – that I have made in this volume: the Jam, Madness, the Piranhas, Bonnie Tyler, Tina Turner, Tony Hadley, Hear'Say, Atomic Kitten. Not all of these were my particular favourites (an understatement), but each has a resonance with a particular sporting occasion – ranging from the Jam at a Cambridge United home football league fixture in 1979 through to Atomic Kitten at the rugby league Challenge Cup final of 2002 – that, for me, provides an unbreakable connection.

At the end of the journey through life comes death. I have mentioned previously that, in many ways, the climax of this book comes not with any sporting events which I attended in 2011 to mark the fiftieth anniversary of my first spectating experience, but with my father's passing in 2004. After that, everything is postscript.

When my father died, I was a few months short of my fiftieth birthday and, my mother having died four years earlier, I was now the oldest in the direct line of my family. There was nothing particularly unusual in that, of course: I would guess that it was broadly in line with the normal pattern of demographic averages. But, for the individual reflecting on his or her circumstances, those averages do not matter. Again, I suspect, in common with most other people in that situation, it was from that period that my thoughts on the inevitability of decline and death became more pronounced.

This sounds morbid and – I emphasise – is not intended to be. I think that, in the sixth of my Seven Ages, I still retain the optimism of life – and for life – that I have always had, though I have reached the point of realisation that the fitness and vitality of my youth will probably never return. But there is no doubt that, in recent years, I have paid more attention to the passing of those whose sporting exploits I had had occasion to view with such attention and respect.

Some of those whom I had seen in action during one of my earlier Ages had already passed away many years before, of course. From the ranks of the cricketers, for example, Ken Barrington, Tony Nicholson and (as I first learned from that newspaper vendor's headline outside Blackfriars Underground station) Wilf Slack had died in the 1980s with Barrington the oldest of these at 50. In the following decade, amongst others across the sporting spectrum whom I had seen on the field of play: Bobby Moore, Billy Bremner, David Bairstow, Malcolm Marshall, Sylvester Clarke, Payne Stewart and Walter Payton. Each shocking and saddening in its own way.

After 2004, my mental list of the departed contained two types of entry: those that had been in their peak or veteran years during the period of my earliest interest in sport and who, therefore, tended to be former cricketers or rugby league players in their 70s or 80s (Freddie Trueman, Vic Wilson, Jeff Stevenson, Eric Ashton, Don Fox); and those who were either younger than I or only slightly older (Mike Gregory, Keith Smith, Ray Gravell, David Topliss, Graham Dilley). All of the names mentioned here have featured earlier in this narrative and the passing of each prompted some deep reflection on my part of what their roles in that narrative had been. A surrogate member of the former type of entry was my uncle Vic – the loyal companion for Dad and me, whether watching successive Challenge Cup finals at Wembley or his beloved Leeds RLFC in the annual Boxing Day morning fixtures or on my first visit to watch Yorkshire and Lancashire in a Roses cricket match – who died in Hampshire in 2006.

Let me now move from the personal to the general. A further reason for my chronic interest in sports spectating undoubtedly relates to sport's innate ability to act as a barometer of the society around it. Again, there is nothing original in this view, of course: the principle has been clearly established for a long time. Mike Brearley summarises it admirably in *The Art of Captaincy*: "Games, like art, achieve their impact in the way they reflect and symbolise life outside the frame, the stage, the arena". Similarly, in the introduction to his authoritative *Rugby's Great Split: Class, Culture and the Origins of Rugby League Football*, Tony Collins states that "sporting culture reflects the society in which it is rooted and can offer us a window through which to study that society". The distinguished journalist WF Deedes – whose long career covered major events in war, politics and international affairs – noted, with specific reference to cricket, that "it has an awkward way of reflecting what is wrong with us. It is the mirror on the wall".[55] More generally, in *The Meaning of Sport*, Simon Barnes concludes that: "In a sense, sport means everything, because it is a giant, ever-changing, all-purpose metaphor".

I am attracted to the sports event and all that is attached to it – the behaviour of the participants, the involvement of the spectators, the nature of the media coverage (if any), and so on – as a reflection of the much deeper currents that are all around us. The events that I have watched have reflected the various components of a heady cocktail – comprising nationalism, hedonism, short-termism, consumerism, individualism and/or media-driven celebrity – each of which has sought to extend a powerful grip on at least part of Britain's sporting psyche. On that day at Upton Park in the early 1980s, there was a manifestation of the unsubtle racism that was still widely prevalent at that time. But things move on, and generally for the better. It had only been in November 1978 that Viv Anderson had become the first black footballer to play for England; by the time that England defeated Germany in a friendly international in November 2008, no fewer than seven black Englishmen featured in the game. Similarly, as Barnes has noted, by the middle of the decade, a number of British Muslims – including the boxer Amir Khan and the cricketers Nasser Hussain and Sajid Mahmood – had acquired the understanding and admiration of the broader public: "Our Boys. That's the best weapon against the tensions of division that has ever been devised".

The shifts in the broader societal context means that the sports themselves have to evolve, sometimes at apparently bewildering speed, in order to maintain their respective places in the metaphorical sun. More specifically, whether by the accident of play or the design of administration, most sports have recognised the need to take action so that they can keep their share of the crowded market in which they are competing for the leisure pound. To give an obvious example, the game of cricket that I first went to see at the Yorkshire versus Lancashire Roses match at Headingley in 1966 – or even at the Yorkshire versus Worcestershire one-day John Player League game in 1969 – is not the same as the game being played today. In the mid 1960s, we would have looked on in shocked disbelief at fielding circles, batting helmets, coloured clothing, numbered shirts, reverse sweeps, Twenty-20 cricket, and so on.

Even within the narrower confines of test cricket, the game has moved on at a dramatic pace. Compare and contrast. On a good batting wicket at Headingley in 1968, in a drawn game over 5 days, England and Australia scored a total of 1,159 runs over 519 overs: 2.23 runs per over. In 2001, in the corresponding match that also went to the last session on the final day (albeit after some time was lost to rain), the two sides scored 1,247 runs in 307 overs: 4.06 runs per over. The tempo of test cricket has changed, perhaps for ever, as the overs are bowled more slowly and the runs scored far more quickly. The latter has partly resulted from the influence of one-day cricket, but also because of the increased weight that has been given to the concept of aggressive batting for its own sake, which was brought back to test cricket by successive Australian sides in the mid 1990s as a means of generating the time in the field to bowl the opposition out twice and, thereby, to win more matches. It has been a wholly refreshing development.

I have little sympathy with those who would wish to constraint any sport within a time warp and prevent its development. At the same time, however, I believe that there is also a heavy burden on the custodians of the sport to ensure that its intrinsic qualities are retained. In the case of cricket, for example, this presented a formidable challenge after the great success of the 2005 Ashes series. Depending on what exactly the claim meant, to have heard that "cricket is the new football" was not necessarily something to be welcomed. Similarly, the enthusiasm of the sport's administrators for Twenty-20 cricket has set some alarm bells ringing. Simon Barnes, in *The Meaning of Sport*, summarised the risk: "Cricket is doing all it can to bring in the fickle, the sensation-seekers: assuming that the heartland audience will always be there. The truth of the matter is that a betrayed heartland is perfectly capable of moving on, while people who enjoy the favours of the fickle should not be surprised when the fickle find something more amusing".

The concept of sport as a barometer for society applies on a far wider canvas than the domestic context on which I have generally focused in this volume. It is clear that the overseas sporting events that I have described also provide more than sufficient confirmation, if that were needed, of the integral role of sport within different societies and of the ways in which sport assists in presenting the nature of those societies to the observer from outside. Several examples have been reported: at the Madison Square

Garden in 1987, I was struck by both the slick corporate presentation of the New York Knickerbockers basketball team and by the relaxed atmosphere in which the local supporters could consume their beer and frankfurters whilst watching the game; at the Sydney Cricket Ground in 1986, I observed the young toughs who supported the St George and Parramatta rugby league sides as they eyed each other up for the possible post-match confrontation; in successive visits to the France-England rugby union internationals in Paris in the 1980s, I listened to the bands playing in the stands as the released cockerels strutted down the touchline; at the FedEx Field in Maryland in 2006, I was struck by the references – both subtle and explicit – to patriotism and support for the US military's operations in Iraq and Afghanistan.

In addition, everywhere, there have been the spectators' concerns (and passions) about the result of the contest they were seeing, ranging from the disappointed reactions of the downbeat Bayern Munich supporters after the Dynamo Kiev win in Munich's Olympic Stadium in 1975 through to the small knot of ecstatic Cadiz fans celebrating their away win at Espanyol in 2005 and the booing meted out to the Washington Redskins by their own fans in 2006. And – also everywhere – there has been the general contact that sport provides which, at its height, can encourage complete strangers to engage with one another on common ground. There is something reassuringly familiar about being informed by a New Zealand rugby league enthusiast – in a remote tea shop in the mountains of Nepal – about the tactical prowess of his side's scrum half. Or, on the same trip, in a small village, being drawn into conversation with a Ghurka and his family on the basis of my chance observation of an action photograph from a rugby league match in a newspaper on the wall at the back of a shop. Sport can do all this. It is both parochial and universal. And each of these characteristics is a virtue.

In deriving this upbeat interpretation of the role of sport, I do not neglect the negative connotations that are often associated with sporting activity, especially at the level of elite competition. In this context, reflecting on the long period covered in this volume, it is not an original thought to state that sport has lost its naiveté. Two contrasting sports news events from the summer and autumn of 2006 offered apparent confirmation of this point of view. First, in the space of a few days in July, it was reported that both that month's winner of the Tour de France, Floyd Landis, and the world record holder at the 100 metres sprint, Justin Gatlin, had failed drug tests due to the unacceptably high levels of testosterone that had been found within their systems. In other words, the custodians of two of world sport's flagship – indeed, iconic – titles were found to be grievously flawed. Three months later, in October, the death was announced of Don Thompson at the age of 74. I read Thompson's obituaries with particular interest, as he had been a hero of my mother's when I was a very young boy, not so much for his sporting accomplishment – he was the gold medal winner in the 50 kilometre walk at the Rome Olympics of 1960 – but for the incredible way in which he had prepared for the excessively humid conditions in which he knew the event would take place. Thompson had practised on a treadmill in his bathroom, the temperature and humidity of which he had raised through continuously boiling kettles and pans of water.

A stark contrast, therefore, between the innocence of then (epitomised by Thompson) and the cynicism of now (revealed by Landis/Gatlin)? Perhaps. In an interesting commentary in July 2011 on the use of performance-enhancing drugs by some high-profile modern American sportsmen (prompted by the judge's declaration of a mistrial in the trial for perjury of the former Major League Baseball pitcher Roger Clemens), Bruce Arthur suggested in the Canadian *National Post* that "late in the 20th century professional sports became such a roaring bonfire of money that some athletes pushed themselves further than ever before, even when already assured of generational greatness... [and] that science allowed for more and more complex ways to push bodies further and faster and more carefully".

On the other hand, perhaps not. In the *Sunday Times* article following the Landis/Gatlin drug test failures, the excellent Rob Hughes reminded his readers that in the 1960s – even before the systematic drug abuse by the former East German state athletes of the following decade – some of the world's leading practitioners in athletics and cycling had been benefiting from pharmaceutical assistance: "Forty years on, only the names of drugs and the appliance of science have changed. The cheats, the dopes, the liars are still running". In other words, not all the champions of yesteryear were as imaginative and purist as Don Thompson.

Let us now fast forward to the autumn of 2009 when, it appeared, another rash of news stories converged to focus on the seamier side of sporting endeavour: the acknowledgement by the Renault organisation that it had ordered Nelson Piquet Jr to crash his car during the previous year's Singapore Grand Prix in order to bring about a favourable race outcome for its other driver; the full details of rugby union's "Bloodgate", in which a Harlequins player had bitten on a fake blood capsule towards the end of the Heineken Cup quarter-final, six months earlier, so as to facilitate his replacement by another player; several instances of high profile footballers being judged guilty of simulation (or, to avoid the euphemism, diving) in the penalty area; Thierry Henry's blatant hand-ball in the build up to the decisive goal in France's World Cup play-off match with Ireland; allegations of match-fixing against high-ranking snooker players... Was this the moral universe in which most – if not all – top-level sport was to be found?

In one respect, this issue might seem detached from my immediate terms of reference. I did not see Landis cycle or Gatlin run, still less Thompson walk; I have never attended a motor racing Grand Prix. On the other hand, the Landis and Gatlin and Renault stories are obviously part of the general context in which I continue to watch sport. They are – or were – part of the cast list of potential players who might have trodden on the sports field at a time I was observing. Moreover, in the case of Harlequins, I was directly affected – in two ways. First, the match in question was against Leinster, whose eventual success in this particular game was later rewarded with a place in the Heineken Cup final at Murrayfield: the thunderous contest with Leicester and the joyous occasion in the sunshine of a late May afternoon in Edinburgh, to which I have made reference earlier. How close was I – and 70,000 others – to being deprived on this experience by a club determined to take their place at that event by fair means or foul?

Second, the most prominent man of rugby whose reputation and career were shredded by the fake blood revelations was Dean Richards. For an English rugby follower of my generation – who, apart from the solitary success of Bill Beaumont's side in 1980, had to wait until 1991 for a Grand Slam success in the Five Nations Championship – I would offer the view that Richards was one of the three iconic players (along with Martin Johnson and Johnny Wilkinson) of our spectating careers. I have a vivid memory of him smashing his way into the Scottish 22 to set up the position from which Nigel Heslop, on the right wing, scored the only try of the 1991 Calcutta Cup match at Twickenham. I was there, sitting next to the late Stephen Hunter in the East Stand, as Richards powered through the Scottish defence. And now it had come to this. There were feelings of sadness and despondency, as well as incredulity and anger, in the fall-out from Bloodgate.

In all of the above examples, it is near impossible, therefore, to ignore the relationship between the specific episodes of triumph and downfall and the broader circumstances in which those episodes were conducted. And – it is important to emphasise – it is not all villainy. Consider the summer of 2009 again. What drama and virtue – both individual and collective – was to be found elsewhere: the electrifying performances of the sprinter Usain Bolt at the World Athletics Championships; the triumph of the returning mother, Kim Clijsters, at the US Open Tennis Championship; the agonising closeness with which the 59 year-old Tom Watson came to winning the Open Championship; the success of England's cricketers on the deciding final day of the Ashes series. As Neil Drysdale of *The Herald* perceptively reported in September 2009, when trying to make sense of that summer's events, "...the reality is that one of the things which lures us towards field of dreams is that the protagonists are fallible flesh and blood, not angelic cardboard cut-outs". And, of course, those protagonists reflect the environment from which they come. We return to sport as a barometer for society, with the virtues and faults of both clear to see.

Before leaving the "sport as a barometer of society" theme, I am aware that I need to hedge my bets somewhat in using it as an explanation for my continued interest in sports spectating. The reason for this is that the explanation understates the expanding role which sport itself – elite sport, in particular – plays within society. This is a huge subject in its own right, of course, and one that extends considerably beyond the scope of this volume.[56] It is stating the obvious to note that the globalisation of the media for marketing and promotion means that, for the major events, the professional participants and their various entourages, sport is very big business indeed. However, what interests me is the impact that this has had on my personal relationship with the sports event and its players.

In particular, I am interested in the reduced incidence of my attendance at elite sporting events in the UK over the latter part of the half-century that this volume has covered. At the time of the 50th anniversary of my first rugby match (in August 2011), I had attended precisely one Premiership football match, I had not seen a cricket test match or a rugby league Challenge Cup final since 2002, and I had not been to a rugby union international since 2007 or a soccer international since 1993. The Open Championship visit had been in 1997 and the expeditions to Wimbledon and the Ryder Cup in the 1980s. By contrast, in recent years, my attention has generally focused on smaller scale events at home (at West of Scotland, for example) or on the opportunities provided by family holidays overseas (in Barcelona, Washington and Chicago).

Whilst part of the explanation undoubtedly relates to the changing family circumstances of the last few years, I think there is more too it than that. There has certainly not been a budget constraint, as my status as The Affluent Reflective has confirmed. Rather, I suspect that there has been a change in the relationship between me (as an "ordinary spectator") and the nature of the elite sporting event and its participants. There is a greater distance between us.

The nature of the changed relationship between spectator and event varies with each of the major sports – football, rugby and cricket – on which I have focused in this volume. In the case of football, my personal relationship with individual teams – including Leeds United in the 1960s and 1970s – was always fairly limited, if not threadbare. Nonetheless, the Leeds team of my early spectating years was built around a core of players that remained unchanged for many seasons and whose individual names – Bremner, Charlton, Hunter... – were not only identifiable, but apparently set in stone. Moreover, most of them had a local identity: they lived in recognisable houses (albeit large ones) and they were occasionally to be seen socialising in the local pubs and restaurants. It was inevitable, therefore, that the team's success (and, probably, its notoriety) provided me with a type of reflected glory by association that occasionally proved useful, especially after I had moved away from the city to live in Cambridge and London.

In the modern era of multi-million pound annual salaries and gated mansions, I do wonder if the supporters of the current equivalents of that Leeds United team – Arsenal or Manchester City, for example – relate to their team in the way that the crowd around me did when I first went to Elland Road to see Leeds play Charlton Athletic in the autumn of 1968. The size and passion of their home attendances suggests that, perhaps, they do.[57] But, for me, there has been a shift. I have no relationship with any club team, even from a distance. Moreover, somewhat to my regret, I now also have a diminishing attachment to the England team. This has nothing to do with living in Scotland for nearly 20 years; it has everything to do with the performances (and conduct) of successive generations of England players and the remoteness from me that this has generated.

The dynamics of the changing spectator-event relationship in rugby union are different, if for no other reason that the sport officially became a professional one for the elite participants in 1995. Two decades on – and, in the England context, greatly assisted by the Rugby World Cup success of 2003 – the top players have global recognition and the salary (and sponsorship) rewards to match, albeit not at the stratospheric levels now attained by the highest paid footballers. Again, it is not surprising that this has affected the relationship between the ordinary spectator (me) and the spectacle itself. Previously, there was undoubtedly something honourable (if not romantic) about the idea of someone performing as a hospital surgeon or working in a steelworks from Monday to Friday and then going out to play in an England-Wales rugby international on the Saturday. In the era of the full-time professional, those days have gone, though I would not begrudge those with particularly high levels of rugby skill taking advantage of the financial opportunities that are available. Besides, the club level still provides ready examples of the skilled layman. If I want to see rugby played by students, lawyers, teachers and doctors (though perhaps not steelworkers), I can take a five minute walk to Burnbrae to watch West of Scotland.

My diminished attraction to international rugby union probably emanates from two factors, one general and one specific. First, I do not think that the game is as interesting as it was when I first watched Wales play England in the 1970s. Of course, the overall standards – of fitness, skills, organisation – have improved with professionalism. Moreover, it is easy to overstate the quality and excitement of matches from the distant past. But professionalism – combined with a succession of changes to the laws of the game – also seems to have brought greater conformity and predictability at the expense of finesse and subtlety. (The Under 18 international matches I saw at Burnbrae in 2007 confirmed that the new values were being firmly inculcated into the next generation of elite players). Willie John McBride, writing in 2004 (in *Willie John: The Story of My Life*), stated that: "It's not a game for the likes of Gerald Davies, Barry John or Phil Bennett today... [as] now all we have is a game played by huge men, whether they are forwards or three-quarters, all trying to bash into each other and win a bruising physical contest". McBride perhaps overstates his case slightly – recent years have seen room for the likes of Jason Robinson and Shane Williams – but he is fundamentally correct.

The second factor goes back to the Scotland versus New Zealand group match at Murrayfield in the 2007 World Cup. I am afraid that – several years on – the cynical approach of the Scotland team management to those spectators (including me) who had paid handsomely for their tickets still rankles. The Scottish second team was fielded, in order to preserve the fitness of the First XV who would subsequently play in the later qualifying match against Italy. The predictable one-sided contest ensued with New Zealand dominating the match and winning comfortably. That decision told me all I needed to know about where I fitted into the grand scheme of things when it came to watching the Scottish national team play rugby. It was my last visit to Murrayfield to watch a rugby international.

It is the watching of test match cricket that perhaps provides the richest seam for discussing the changing relationship between the ordinary spectator and the event. In presenting the earlier discussion about the ways in which the sport has evolved during my spectating lifetime, I was aware that the focus of the description was on the playing of the game: the laws, clothing, tempo, and so on. For the spectator, improvements off the pitch – in the level of comfort provided – have been more haphazard.

In some respects, there have been some changes for the better. I noted earlier the rotten wooden benches at the Headingley Cricket Ground, with their accompanying insect life, that gave considerable importance to the choice of seat on the Western Terrace in my early years of watching Yorkshire or England; these were thankfully purged during one of the ground's development phases. Likewise, the test match authorities do at least now provide some financial compensation in the event of an entire day's play being rained off (unlike my experience at the Oval for the Saturday of the England-West Indies test match in 1980). In general, also, umpires seem rather more sensitive to the requirement for play to continue into the evening to make up for earlier lost time (c.f. the England-Australia test matches at Lord's and Headingley in 1981).

On the other hand, I do wonder if – in the modern marketing-speak – the overall quality of the spectator "experience" has not struggled to match the rising cost of attendance. An instructive benchmark is provided by the upper balcony of the Football Stand at Headingley. I referred earlier, not only to the rudimentary and narrow seating, which remained unchanged each year, but also, at different times, to the risks or inconvenience provided by angry wasps, incontinent pigeons and loud radio reporters (quite apart from the ramblings of Jonathan and Jocelyn, for which I appreciate the ground authorities were not responsible.[58])

All this did not prevent my father and me attending the Headingley test match for all those years, of course. There was never any suggestion that we would not: it was as fixed a part of the annual routine as Christmas or Easter. But our attendance was in spite of the facilities, not encouraged by them. Moreover, it became more expensive. A seat in the Football Stand balcony cost £27 for the Saturday of the South Africa test match of 1994; for the same visitors in 2012, the price is £65.[59]

It is of interest, I think, that the value for money of watching test match cricket raised its media profile in 2011 in the wake of the lower than anticipated attendances at the England-Sri Lanka tests at Cardiff and Southampton. Moreover, much of this comment was generated by some of those high profile media pundits, whose transition from test match player to national newspaper correspondent and/or television commentator had provided them with a cocooned experience of test match involvement several stages removed from that of the "ordinary spectator".[60] However, whilst it is to their credit that this issue has been raised for discussion, there is also a sense of Establishment concern at the factors affecting the finances of English cricket, especially within the counties. As usual, it is a broad societal trend – in this case, the general uncertainty about the state of the economy – that is the key driving force.

I will leave the reader to judge whether I have answered the questions that were posed in the Preface. From the spectrum of reasons for sport's appeal, as identified by Ed Smith in *What Sport Tells Us About Life*, have my motivations been nearer to the "scholastic" or the "happy clapper"?

For my part, I was struck by Smith's identification of what he labelled "sport's silent majority" and his description of this group's main characteristics. "[T]hese quiet, serious, feeling fans... are not the shouting members of the mob. Nor are they the aesthetes or strategists who take the pieces of sport and fit them into their own philosophies... They may very much want one team to win, but they aren't blind to the sadness of wishing defeat on the opposition. They seek rather than demand victory, admire brilliance, sympathise with humiliation and crave sportsmanship. They constantly find in sport new versions of old stories – the oldest and deepest stories of all". These are admirable qualities and I would be content to be part of this group.

This leads, I think, to the final reason for my attraction to watching sport. It takes me full circle. I go back to that first Saturday afternoon at Parkside in August 1961, when my father took me to watch Hunslet play Whitehaven. From that particular day, watching sport has been part of the overall context within which I have been able to look out on to the world. It has helped me to shape my place in that world – both social and locational – and, accordingly, it has also helped me to address the challenges and opportunities that are faced or made available on an everyday basis. In short, watching sport has assisted in dealing with life.

More specifically – and as the central part of this overall role which watching sport has played – the act of spectating has been a key constituent of my being a member of my particular family. By this, I do not simply mean that I went to many sporting events with my father, though this was clearly an important component of the family fabric. I am also conscious that, on those occasions when I have watched sport by myself – a sizeable proportion of those detailed in this volume – I will have done so from my family's (especially my father's) perspective as well as my own. It was if, on every one of these occasions, he was standing at my side.

It will have been clear from the descriptions in this book that I was fortunate in being part of a loving and caring family, in which the principles and standards of behaviour – honesty, compassion, hard work, a sense of humour – were reflective of the values that my parents had derived from their own families. The original sources of those influences had a wide geographical distribution – North Yorkshire and Scotland, London and Germany – and so there has been an inevitable complexity in the way that my own values were shaped. My parents provided the filter for these influences, of course. And in my father's case, as I was keen to state in my letter to the chairman of the Hunslet rugby league club, the principles that he passed on to me – and which I was happy to take – incorporated the values that had been absorbed in his own childhood in south Leeds, including on the terraces at Parkside.

The Seventh Age

The Childlike Sage

This is – as yet – uncharted territory. As noted in the Preface, it might correspond exactly to Shakespeare's "second childishness and mere oblivion, sans teeth, sans eyes, sans taste, sans everything". More optimistically, the final stage will be characterised by the wisdom of old age compensating for the inevitable mental and physical deterioration.

To be continued…

Notes

Preface

1   *All the world's a stage,*
    And all the men and women merely players;
    They have their exits and their entrances;
    And one man in his time plays many parts.
    His acts being seven ages.
    William Shakespeare, *As You Like It*, Act 2, Scene 7

Chapter 1

2   These observations were broadcast in a Channel 4 television documentary – *More Trees in Hunslet* – which Richard Hoggart wrote and presented in 1988.

3   *Born on the Wrong Side* is the inspirational account of how Cec Thompson – a young black man from a background of poverty and unable to write his name – not only revealed an excellence in professional rugby but also, following a long struggle to get an education, enjoyed a successful career in teaching and business.

4   The company, for which my father began working shortly after the Second World War, was based in Armley, also in south Leeds. It was close to where JW Roberts Ltd was located before it closed in the 1950s. Roberts manufactured asbestos boiler mattresses for locomotives. Armley residents of the time have reported that the asbestos dust covered the rooftops of the surrounding houses and that children used to make "snowballs" from the dust in the street. My father was later to recall that he would take a short-cut through the Roberts site on his way to and from work.

5   The feat of playing and scoring in every match of a rugby league season was first accomplished by Jim Hoey of Widnes in 1932–33.

6   The rugby league historian Les Hoole's publication about this game – *The All Leeds Final: The Story of the 1938 Rugby League Championship Final* – reproduces the heights and weights of the two sides from the match programme and confirms that, at 13 stone 12 pounds, Vic Hey was heavier than any member of the Hunslet team, including the forwards; Oliver Morris was 10 stone 2 pounds. However, Morris's task was made easier when Hey was injured and went out on to the wing for much of the second half.

7   In his meticulously researched account of this achievement, *Four Cups to Fame*, Bryan Smith makes an interesting point concerning the Terrible Six: "With the exception of [Tom] Walsh, who was a police constable, the rest were, or had been, colliers... [The] miners developed tremendous upper body strength by virtue of the fact that they spent most of their working day on their knees – they were burly men with hefty shoulders".

8   One of the Terrible Six – John Willie Higson – was later transferred to Huddersfield,

with whom he repeated the feat of winning all four trophies in 1914–15.

9   At the outbreak of the First World War, there about 5,000 British subjects living in Germany. The horseracing course at Ruhleben, near Spandau in Berlin, was turned into a prisoner-of-war camp for the male civilians of enemy countries, mostly British. The National Library of Scotland website, which has reported on the Library's purchase of various editions of the *Ruhleben Camp Magazine* as part of its rare books acquisitions strategy, notes that, after a while, the prisoners began to manage their own internal affairs with no objection from the Germans, who strictly adhered to the Geneva Convention. This included the use of a printing press.

10 Dennis Hartley is one of the players described in the former Great Britain coach Maurice Bamford's affectionate *Play to Win: Rugby League Heroes*. The career details record that Hartley made exactly 200 appearances for Hunslet, in which he scored 23 tries and one goal. This was that goal. The figure jumped off the page when I read the book in 2005 and as I recalled with affection the events surrounding it over 40 years earlier.

11 For many of the older generation of Leeds supporters, Lewis Jones is the club's greatest ever player. It has been pointed out to me that, if this is the case, he forms of unique partnership with John Charles – perhaps less controversially, the greatest footballer ever to play for Leeds United – in that they were born within five miles of each other in Swansea.

Chapter 2

12 In *We've Swept the Seas Before Boys: An Illustrated Record of Hunslet's 1907–08 All Four Cups Season*, Les Hoole reproduces a newspaper report describing the return of the team to Parkside after the victory over Oldham in the Championship Final replay. The report states that: "throughout the rejoicing the crowds sang chorus after chorus of 'We've swept the seas before boys' ".

13 A spirited rendition of "We've swept the seas before boys" – all one and a quarter minutes of it – is given on the CD accompanying Brian Smith's *Four Cups to Fame*, published in 2008. The song might be just about unknown today, but it lasted the course for 60 years.

14 The attendance at the 1966 Challenge Cup final between St Helens and Wigan was 98,536 according to the official records. This is the largest ever attendance for a rugby league match in the UK, apart from the replayed Warrington-Halifax Challenge Cup final at Odsal Stadium in Bradford in 1954. It also remains the biggest sporting crowd of which I have been a part.

Chapter 3

15 The Yorkshire all-rounder Roy Kilner, who died at the age of 37 in 1928, summarised the tension of the Roses match in this pre-sledging era: "We'll say 'Good morning', then never speak again for three days". (Quote take from John Marshall's *Headingley*, 1970).

Chapter 4

16 The detailed and scholarly *The Encyclopaedia of Rugby League Football*, compiled by AN Gaulton and published in 1968, has, as its front cover, a photograph of a Leeds player tackling (and landing on top of) a Wakefield Trinity opponent in that year's waterlogged Challenge Cup final. The accompanying punch on to the back of the head is clearly evident.

17 My recollection of the Bramley-Hull KR game was another to be prompted by Maurice Bamford's *Play to Win: Rugby League Heroes*, published in 2005, in which his description of Arthur Beetson's "abrasive style and hard no-nonsense tackling" represents something of an understatement. It is extraordinary how memories are triggered. Bamford's text, with the accompanying photograph of Beetson – a *doppelganger* of Joe Don Baker in the 1980s television thriller *Edge of Darkness*, incidentally – took me straight back to that banking at McLaren Field and the shared experience with my uncle Bob.

18 The most passionately articulated exposition of the dislike for a neighbouring club – in this case, football – is probably that given by Colin Shindler, a Manchester City supporter, in *Manchester United Ruined My Life*. The perspective that Dad and I had on the Leeds rugby league club had nothing like the level of desperate antagonism experienced by Shindler, but we still enjoyed the *schadenfreude* of those occasions on which Leeds failed to justify their "top club" status, of which there were many in later years.

Chapter 6

19 Ian McGeechan played in the Headingley first XV for 16 years until his retirement in 1980. In *Lion Man: The Autobiography*, published in 2009, he reflects on the social composition of the club during his early years there: "I was just a lad from the local secondary modern school. Headingley drew most of its players from the major northern public schools, such as Leeds Grammar, Sedburgh and Ampleforth College". He also notes that, within the elite groups of clubs to which Headingley belonged, there was a distinct pecking order: "We… had a northern chip on the shoulder about clubs that looked down on us. We could only play Gloucester at Gloucester… because they refused to come north to play us at home. Bristol didn't deign to come to Headingley either". McGeechan writes movingly of the Headingley club's contribution in the First World War, when over 200 men enlisted, more than 50 were killed and 21 gained military honours.

20 A fascinating description of the origins of the Yorkshire Cup competition is given in Chapter 1 of Tony Collins's *Rugby's Great Split: Class, Culture and the Origins of Rugby League Football*.

Chapter 7

21 The *Yorkshire Post*'s ability to give near-equal weight to world geopolitics and the county's sports news was reflected in the headline in the immediately adjacent column on that day's front page: "Illingworth can go, says Mr Sellers". The chairman of the

Yorkshire CCC selection committee, Brian Sellers, was reported as confirming that the club did not offer contracts and that Ray Illingworth, if he wished to move to another county, was free to go elsewhere. Unlike for the main story, however, the timing of the pronouncement was not given.

Chapter 8

22 The famous Wren Library of Trinity College, Cambridge, holds AA Milne's original manuscript for *Winnie-The-Pooh*, the book that had consoled me during my enforced absence from the Hunslet versus Leeds Challenge Cup quarter final tie of 1965. Such is the occasionally obscure nature of the connections and echoes identified in this volume.

23 Steve Warlow's philosophy had been handed down through the student generations. In his excellent *A Game for Hooligans: The History of Rugby Union*, Huw Richards refers to the rumpus provoked by the Welsh international winger, Rowe Harding, who, in what Richards describes as the first British player memoir, stated that his Cambridge teams were "professional gladiators, devoting all our time and energies to winning the varsity match". Harding won four Blues between 1924–27.

Chapter 9

24 This was part of a long-running jinx that I seemed to place on Mike Brearley whenever I saw him bat. In 8 completed innings, in various forms of cricket for Middlesex and England, he scored 93 runs at an average of 11.6. Brearley is in good company, however. A generation later, I was to see Andrew Flintoff in two test matches at Headingley: South Africa in 1998 and India in 2002. He registered a pair in both games and took a total of one wicket.

25 An interesting historical perspective on this particular Middlesex vs Yorkshire Benson and Hedges Cup game is provided by Terry Brindle's match report in the following day's *Yorkshire Post*. He deemed it worthy of mention that Kevin Sharp, the Yorkshire batsman, "went in helmeted". This was a sensible move by Sharp, who was facing the fearsome West Indian fast bowler, Wayne Daniel, on a lively pitch. However, even allowing for these particular circumstances, Sharp's additional protection was regarded as unusual at the time.

Chapter 11

26 For the television coverage of the Barbarians-New Zealand match of January 1973, the skills on the pitch were complemented by those behind the microphone. My friend Llyr James has pointed out to me that, in the following week's *New Statesman*, the television critic stated that Cliff Morgan had turned rugby commentary almost into an art form. The BBC's DVD, released in 2005 – *Barbarians v All Blacks, 1973: The Greatest Rugby*

Match Ever Played – uses Morgan's match commentary. It also contains, as a special feature, an informative commentary from Edwards and two of his teammates, Phil Bennett and David Duckham.

Chapter 12

27 A summary of the allegations of attempted match-fixing involving Leeds United in the early 1970s is given in Stuart Sprake and Tim Johnson's *Careless Hands: The Forgotten Truth of Gary Sprake*, which also details the painful rift that was created between the Leeds United goalkeeper and many of his former team-mates after the newspaper articles were published.

28 I had suspected that this was something of an urban myth, until Brian Clough, who signed Duncan McKenzie during his short period as Leeds United manager, provided confirmation in *Clough: The Autobiography*: "McKenzie was an extrovert who, apart from puffing forty fags a day and being one of the most popular entertainers on the pitch, had mastered the rare art of jumping over Minis in the car park".

29 There was a remarkable echo over 30 years later. A feature article on current war artists in the *Sunday Times Magazine* in July 2009 referred to Nick Bashall's work in Kosovo, Afghanistan and Iraq. A motorbike accident in his twenties had cost Bashall the use of his right arm and he had subsequently learned to draw and paint with his left hand.

30 The England squad listed in the match programme for the England-Luxembourg ladies volleyball encounter included the 18 year-old Joan Quigley from the Kirkby club. Although I did not realise this at the time, she was the first international sportsman/woman I had seen in action who was my age or younger, notwithstanding that she was already a veteran of 20 previous internationals. The squad also contained three 19 year-olds. This is perhaps a suitable note on which to end the discussion of the Age of the Absent Player, albeit that my participation in ladies volleyball was not a practical option.

Chapter 13

31 In his meticulously researched history of the rugby international matches between England and Wales – *The Red and the White* – Huw Richards records that Brynmor Williams's tactic had been used in exactly the same way 79 years earlier by the Welsh scrum-half Dickie Owen in the closing stages of the 1902 fixture at the Rectory Field, Blackheath. "[F]ull-back John Strand-Jones – who would go on to take up a chaplaincy in Karachi – drop-kicked the goal" from the penalty award to give Wales a 9–8 win.

32 By the time of the Lord's test match of 1981, Ian Botham was only being appointed England captain on a match-by-match basis. In *Botham, My Autobiography*, he relates how, going into the match, "I had decided that my time was up as captain. I simply did not know whether I was coming or going... The uncertainty was demoralising for me and the team". The stony silence that greeted Botham as he walked through the

MCC members' enclosure, following his first-ball dismissal in the second innings, did not encourage him to revise this decision.

33 When watching Australia bat, I could not but be impressed – that is to say, astounded – by the latest design of head protection, as revealed by Graham Yallop. The large transparent visor on his helmet appeared to be several inches away from the lower part of his face. Did this really represent the latest technological progress, following on from Mike Brearley's use of the skull-cap against the West Indies in 1976 and Kevin Sharp's crash helmet when facing Wayne Daniel in 1979? If so, it looked incredibly unwieldy, as well as ugly. I did recognise, of course, that I could not challenge Yallop's right to protect himself in all ways possible. It was simply – and literally – the modern face (1981 vintage) of the game of cricket.

34 Ian Botham described the rationale for his approach to this innings in *Head On – Botham: The Autobiography*: "Given the state of the wicket, which made even survival something of a lottery, I decided to swing the bat. It had failed miserably at Lord's, but here it paid off".

35 A fascinating perspective of the final day's play – and of the thought processes that the England captain went through in deciding who should bowl and what the field placings should be – is to be found in Mike Brearley's excellent *The Art of Captaincy*.

36 In the 1985 edition of his book, Mike Brearley mistakenly reports that the Australian captain was Greg Chappell, rather than Kim Hughes. My pencilled annotation in the margin of the page in my copy represents a trivial note of oneupmanship on this cerebral and successful England captain. Elsewhere in the book, Brearley acknowledges the uncertainty he faced in deciding what to do on winning the toss at the Oval test match, eventually opting to put Australia in to bat: "When the score reached 120 for no wicket, the sun was blazing and the pitch had eased, I wondered if I had done the right thing". My thoughts were not dissimilar, on that first day, as I watched the Australian batsmen despatch the ball to all parts of the ground. The decision was vindicated by the end result, however; the match was drawn and England consolidated their 3–1 series win.

Chapter 14

37 In his excellent *The Chicago Bears and Super Bowl XX: The Rise and Self-destruction of the Greatest Football Team in History*, John Mullin provides an interesting insight into why the American football authorities thought that the market opportunities in Britain had improved at that time. In particular, he notes the low point reached by soccer in the UK due to hooliganism and/or stadium deaths (at the Heysel Stadium and Valley Parade).

38 The post-1980s paths of these clubs are interesting. I kept track of them only very loosely, but it is clear that, for the committed supporter of either club, the vagaries of success and failure would have been strikingly evident. Cambridge United were fifth in the old Second Division in 1991–92 and thus qualified for the play-offs to decide on a founding place in the inaugural season of the Premier League. They subsequently declined to bottom place

in the Football League in 2004–05 and relegation to the (then) Nationwide Conference. At the end of the 2010–11 season, they remained in the fifth tier of the English league system. Wimbledon, having initially vacated Plough Lane for Crystal Palace's ground at Selhurst Park, morphed into the Milton Keynes (MK) Dons. After relegation into League Two, they were promoted back into League One for 2008–09 and reached the play-offs in that division in 2010–11. Meanwhile, AFC Wimbledon – the spiritual heirs of the former club in south west London, founded in 2002 by supporters opposed to the Milton Keynes move – enjoyed five promotions in nine seasons, culminating in entry into the Football League via the Conference play-offs at the end of the 2010–11 season.

Chapter 17

39 As with the Geoff Boycott century in the Headingley test match of 1977, highlights of Graham Gooch's innings in the Headingley test matches of 1991 and 1992 are included on the *Cricket's Entertainers* video released by the BBC in 1993.

40 Paul Smith confirms in *Wasted?* that it was in this year – 1984 – that he first took cocaine, although it was not until the following decade that his desperate descent into serious drug addiction, loss of family and eventual homelessness gathered momentum. His subsequent attempt to re-build his life in the UK and USA makes for reading that is both fascinating and disquieting.

41 Several years later, when I finally caught up with CLR James's classic *Beyond a Boundary*, I read his description of the preparatory routine followed by the great West Indian batsman, George Headley, on the morning of big matches. James gives rather more detail than we would perhaps wish to know – including Headley's bowel movements as well as his early rise and his chain-smoking – but then reaches the point at which Headley enters the stage: "[O]nce he starts to walk down the pavilion steps he would not be able to recognise his father if he met him halfway. Everything is out of his mind except batting". When I read this line, I instantly thought back to that summer's day in the mid 1980s and the focused stare in Wilf Slack's eyes as he walked through the Long Room at Lord's.

Chapter 18

42 West of Scotland FC was the only one of Scotland's 8 founding rugby clubs to be open; 3 were university sides, the others for schools' former pupils.

43 "First Minister reveals he's backing teams that have Scottish-based players", *The Scotsman* (news.scotsman.com), 25 May 2006.

Chapter 20

44 The concept of "competition balance" within a sporting league is noted in Ed Smith's *What Sport Tells Us About Life*. Smith refers to US-based research which suggests

that the most important factor in keeping leagues balanced is ensuring a breadth of talent coming into the sport – encouraged by an unprejudiced and proactive attitude to recruiting young players – rather than imposing wage or other labour restrictions on the sport's current high earners.

45 This represented something of an echo. Two years earlier, in 1995, my father and I had watched in eager anticipation as Darren Gough strode out to bat in the first innings against the West Indies on the same ground. If anything, the welcome for the local hero was even more rapturous. Gough attempted to hook his first ball from Ian Bishop and was caught in the outfield.

46 I have noted elsewhere in this volume how some cricketers – Mike Brearley, Darren Gough, Andrew Flintoff – could hardly score a run on those occasions I saw them play; for the last of these, this was literally the case. With Steve Waugh, the position was somewhat different. I saw all or part of four of his innings at Headingley – in three test matches (1989, 1993 and 1997) and the 1999 Cricket World Cup – during which he scored 458 runs and was dismissed only once.

47 Between them, Mike Atherton and Alec Stewart produced only one test match century at Headingley – the latter's 170 against Pakistan in 1996 – over this period.

Chapter 21

48 The updated edition of Jason Robinson's *Finding my Feet: My Autobiography* was published two years later, in 2007. Chapter 17 is entitled: "How a boy from Hunslet became England captain".

49 Lluis Companys was the president of the Generalitat of Catalonia – the provincial government – during the Spanish Civil War. He was shot by a firing squad in 1940.

50 My inability to assess the latent strengths of Spanish soccer teams was confirmed the following season, when Espanyol followed up their Copa del Reys success by reaching the final of the UEFA Cup, losing on penalties to Sevilla at Hampden Park, Glasgow. Five players from the starting line-up against Cadiz were in the team.

Chapter 22

51 The crowd of 3,348 for the Partick Thistle versus Morton game was only slightly less than the highest of the season to that date at Firhill. On the same day, 50,301 watched Rangers play Kilmarnock at Ibrox.

Chapter 23

52 The Middleton Railway – established by Act of Parliament in 1758 and, since 1960, run by a Preservation Society – claims to be the oldest railway in the world. The first commercially successful revenue-earning steam locomotives (as opposed to experimental

operations) entered service in 1812.

53 The "yo-yo" syndrome returned at the end of the 2010–11 season, when Leeds Carnegie were relegated and Worcester Warriors promoted to take their place in the Premiership.

54 Harry Pearson comments on the use of sledging in club cricket in his revealing *Slipless in Settle: A Slow Turn Around Northern Cricket*, which describes a tour around the north's most celebrated leagues in 2009: "Beckwithshaw are easily the most voluble team I have come across all season, and frankly that is saying something".

Chapter 24

55 "Has England lost its Days of Grace?", *Daily Telegraph*, July 1989. Reprinted in *Words and Deedes: Selected Journalism*, 1931–2006.

56 An interesting discussion is provided by Tim de Lisle in "How Did Sport Get so Big?", *Intelligent Life*, Summer 2010, pp72–78.

57 Tim de Lisle offers a plausible psychological explanation for this – "As life becomes more atomised, people yearn to be part of a crowd" – noting the parallel boom in live music at a time of diminishing record sales.

58 See Chapter 20 above.

59 The total increase in the nominal price between 1994 and 2012 is therefore 141%. This far exceeds the rise in the general price level, whether measured by the Retail Price Index (RPIX, excluding mortgage interest payments) or the All Items Consumer Price Index (CPI). Given a reasonable assumption about inflation in the year to August 2012, these indices will have increased by approximately 69% and 48%, respectively, between 1994 and 2012. In the jargon of economists, the real price increase of the Football Stand balcony ticket – i.e. over and above the general inflation rate – will have been between 43–63%, depending on whether RPIX or the CPI is used as the measure of general inflation.

60 See, for example, Mike Atherton, "Testing time for short-changed spectators", *The Times*, 30 June 2011.

Acknowledgements

Sports spectating is a communal activity. It requires the participation of others – as organisers, administrators, players, coaches and, of course, fellow spectators – as well as of the individual spectator himself or herself. My thanks are due, therefore, to all those with whom I have shared the sporting events that are described in the pages of this book. I might have watched sport with family or friends or, most often, as an individual, but I have always been aware that the opportunity to attend these events – large or small, professional or amateur, international or local – is dependent on the efforts of many other people.

I am most grateful for the work done on the production of this book by the team at SilverWood Books. In particular, Helen Hart has consistently provided positive and constructive support and I have drawn extensively on her experience and expertise. Sarah Newman has undertaken the page layouts and presentation with great skill.

Before deciding to proceed with publication, I was appreciative of the warm enthusiasm given to the book's underlying concept by Alison Baverstock of Kingston University at a writers' workshop she convened at the 2011 Edinburgh Book Festival.

I have benefited significantly from the feedback given by Llyr James to a draft of the early chapters of the book. In addition to some valuable ideas about placing the experiences of my first years of sports spectating within the social and literary contexts of the time, he suggested a number of factual corrections to the text. Any errors that remain are entirely my responsibility.

Several acknowledgements are due in relation to the photographs used in this book. The photograph of the author was taken at Trevor Graham Photography in Milngavie; I am grateful to Trevor Graham for its use in both the book and the related marketing and, more generally, for his assistance in the presentation of all the photographs.

The photograph of Barry Davies is reproduced by kind permission of the BBC. My thanks are due to Barry Davies, not only for agreeing to the use of the photograph, but for his generosity in allowing the reproduction of a letter he wrote to me some 45 years ago.

The photograph on the cover of the Hunslet RLFC match programme is of a similar vintage. It was taken by J Hickes in 1965. Permission to use it in this book has been kindly given by his son, David Hickes, of David Hickes Photography, Pool in Wharfedale.

The photographs of the menu for the 1973 Roundhay School First

XV annual dinner include the menu cover, which itself reproduced the school's badge and motto. Their use in this book is by kind permission of Neil Clephan, Headteacher of Roundhay School, Leeds.

Other photographs, taken by the author, include images associated with various sporting institutions. I am most grateful for the permissions given for reproduction by West Ham United FC, the Chicago Bears Football Club and the Washington Redskins.

All reasonable efforts have been made to contact copyright holders. If anyone feels that their copyright has been breached, I should be very happy to address that in any future reprint.

The jacket design is based on an original idea and artwork by Katherine Rigg. It captures exactly the book's central theme: the perspective of an individual (and "ordinary") sports spectator within a larger and anonymous crowd. At SilverWood Books, Adrian Hart was responsible for the stylish and eye-catching final design

Finally, to Angela, Tom and Katherine, who indulge me in my frequent enthusiasms and (occasional) rants – my love and thanks.

John Rigg
Glasgow
May 2012

Bibliography

Books and Booklets

American Football
John Mullin, *The Chicago Bears and Super Bowl XX: The Rise and Self-destruction of the Greatest Football Team in History*, Triumph Books, Chicago, 2005.

Association Football
The World Book of Football Champions, [no publisher given], 1962.
Brian Clough (with John Sadler), *Clough: The Autobiography*, Partridge Press, London, 1994.
Jeff Connor, *Pointless: A Season With Britain's Worst Football Team*, Headline Book Publishing, 2005.
Tommy Gemmell and Graham McColl, *Tommy Gemmell: Lion Heart*, Virgin Books Ltd, 2004.
Peter Lorimer and Phil Rostron, *Peter Lorimer: Leeds and Scotland Hero*, Mainstream Publishing Ltd, 2002.
Frank McLintock, *True Grit: The Autobiography*, Headline Book Publishers, 2005.
David Peace, *The Damned Utd*, Faber and Faber Limited, 2006.
Colin Shindler, *Manchester United Ruined My Life*, Headline Book Publishing, 1998.
Stuart Sprake and Tim Johnson, *Careless Hands: The Forgotten Truth of Gary Sprake*, Tempus Publishing Limited, 2006.

Cricket
Michael Atherton, *Opening Up: My Autobiography*, Hodder and Stoughton, 2003.
Dickie Bird (with Keith Lodge), *Dickie Bird: My Autobiography*, Hodder & Stoughton, 1997.
Derek Birley, *A Social History of English Cricket*, Aurum Press Ltd, 1999.
Ian Botham, *Botham: My Autobiography*, CollinsWillow, London, 1994.
Ian Botham, *Head On – Botham: The Autobiography*, Ebury Press, 2007.
Geoff Boycott, *Boycott: The Autobiography*, Macmillan London Ltd, 1987.
Mike Brearley, *The Art of Captaincy*, Hodder and Stoughton, 1985.
Ken Dalby, *Headingley Test Cricket 1899–1975*, Olicana Books Limited, 1976.

CLR James, *Beyond a Boundary*, Hutchinson, 1963.

JM Kilburn, *A Century of Yorkshire County Cricket*, Yorkshire Post, 1963.

The Lifebuoy book of the test series: England versus Australia 1962–63, Grosvenor Press (England) Ltd, 1963.

John Marshall, *Headingley*, Pelham Books, 1970.

Harry Pearson, *Slipless in Settle: A Slow Turn Around Northern Cricket*, Little, Brown, 2010

Playfair Cricket Annual, especially 1970–73 (editor: Gordon Ross) and 1996 (editor: Bill Frindall), The Dickens Press (1970–73) and Headline Book Publishing (1996).

Jack Pollard (editor), *Cricket: the Australian Way*, Newnes Books, 1968

Paul Smith, *Wasted*, Know the Score Books Ltd, 2007.

Vera Southgate, *The Story of Cricket*, A Ladybird "Easy-Reading" Book, Wills & Hepworth Ltd, 1964.

Alec Stewart, *Playing for Keeps*, BBC Books, 2003.

Herbert Sutcliffe, *How to Become a First Class Batsman*, Herbert Sutcliffe Ltd publisher, 1949.

Michael Vaughan, *Time to Declare: My Autobiography*, Hodder and Stoughton, 2009.

Steve Waugh, *Out of My Comfort Zone: The Autobiography*, Penguin Books Ltd, 2005.

Wisden Cricketers' Almanack 2002 (editor: Graeme Wright), John Wisden & Co. Ltd, 2002.

Yorkshire County Cricket Club: American Tour (compiled by Phil Sharpe), Martin Black Publications Ltd, 1964.

Rugby League

Maurice Bamford, *Play to Win: Rugby League Heroes*, London League Publications Ltd, 2005.

Trevor Delaney, *The Grounds of Rugby League*, Trevor R Delaney publisher, 1991.

AN Gaulton, *The Encyclopaedia of Rugby League Football*, Robert Hale Limited, 1968.

Dave Hadfield, *Up and Over: A Trek Through Rugby League Land*, Mainstream Publishing, 2004.

Les Hoole, *The All Leeds Final: The Story of the 1938 Rugby League Championship Final*, Les Hoole publisher, 1988.

Les Hoole and Mike Green, *The Parksiders: A Brief History of Hunslet RLFC, 1883–1973*, Mike Green publisher, 1988

Les Hoole, *We've Swept The Seas Before Boys: An Illustrated Record of Hunslet's 1907–08 All Four Cups Season*, Rugby League Heritage publisher, 1991.

Barrie McDermott and Peter Smith, *Made for Rugby*, Pan Books, 2005.

Keith Macklin, *The Rugby League Game*, Stanley Paul & Co Ltd, 1967.

Geoffrey Moorhouse, *At The George: and other essays on Rugby League,* Hodder and Stoughton Ltd, 1989.

Jason Robinson, *Finding my Feet: My Autobiography* (updated edition), Hodder & Stoughton, 2007.

Rothmans Rugby League Yearbook, 1983–84, edited by David Howes and Raymond Fletcher, Queen Anne Press, 1983.

Bryan Smith, *Four Cups to Fame*, Delta Design and Print Ltd, Leeds, 2008.

Cec Thompson, *Born on the Wrong Side*, Acadia Books Ltd, 2006.

Eddie Waring Rugby League Annual, White Rose Publications, (Nos. 5–7; 1963, 1964, 1965) and MB Publications (No. 8, 1968).

Windsors Rugby League Annual, 1962–63, compiled and edited by Ken J Adams, Windsors (Sporting Investments) Ltd publisher, 1962.

Rugby Union
Bill Beaumont, *Bill Beaumont: The Autobiography*, CollinsWillow, 2003.

Willie John McBride, *Willie John: The Story of My Life*, Piatkus Books Ltd, 2004.

Ian McGeechan, *Lion Man: The Autobiography*, Simon and Schuster UK Ltd, 2009.

Brian Moore, *Brian Moore: The Autobiography*, Transworld Publishers Ltd, 1995.

Huw Richards, *A Game for Hooligans: The History of Rugby Union*, Mainstream Publishing, 2006.

Huw Richards, *The Red and the White*, Aurum Press Ltd, 2009.

Rugby League and Rugby union
John Bentley, *John Bentley: My Story*, Andre Deutsch Limited, 1999

Tony Collins, *Rugby's Great Split: Class, Culture and the Origins of Rugby League Football*, Frank Cass Publishers, 1998.

Ray French, *My Kind of Rugby: Union and League*, Faber and Faber Limited, 1979.

Sport (general)
Simon Barnes, *The Meaning of Sport*, Short Books, 2006.

Ed Smith, *What Sport Tells Us About Life*, Penguin Books, 2009.

Other
WF Deedes, *Words and Deedes, Selected Journalism, 1931–2006*, Macmillan, 2006.

Harold Fullard ed., *Philips' Modern School Atlas*, 65th edition, George Philip & Son Limited, 1967.

Richard Hoggart, *The Uses of Literacy: aspects of working class life with special references to publications and entertainments*, Chatto and Windus, 1957.

Clive James, *Unreliable Memoirs*, Picador, 1980.

A.A. Milne, *Winnie-the-Pooh*, Methuen & Co Ltd edition, 1965.

The Reader's Digest Association, *The Reader's Digest Great Encyclopaedic Dictionary*, Oxford University Press, 1964.

William Shakespeare, *Complete Works*, HarperCollins, 1994.

David Storey, *This Sporting Life*, Longmans, 1960.

Keith Waterhouse, *City Lights: A Street Life*, Hodder and Stoughton, 1994.

Murray Watson, *Being English in Scotland*, Edinburgh University Press, 2003.

DVD

Barbarians v All Blacks, 1973: The Greatest Rugby Match Ever Played, BBC Worldwide Ltd, 2005.

Film

This Sporting Life, directed by Lindsay Anderson, Independent Artists Productions, 1963.

Magazines

1964 Cricket Spotlight, edited by Robert Baker, Mercury Press, 1964

Intelligent Life, Summer 2010.

Newspapers (various editions)

UK

Cambridge Evening News; Daily Express; Daily Mail; Daily Telegraph; The Herald; New Statesman; Rugby Leaguer; The Scotsman; Sunday Express; Sunday Times; The Times; Wales on Sunday; Yorkshire Evening Post; Yorkshire Post

World
Canada: *National Post*
Spain: *La Vanguardia*
USA: *Chicago Sun-Times; Washington Post*

Television

More Trees in Hunslet, written and presented by Richard Hoggart, Brook Productions for Channel 4, 1988.

Video

101 Top Rugby League Tries, BBC Enterprises, 1989.
Century of Rugby League, BNT/Andy Dobson Production, 1995
Cricket's Entertainers, BBC Enterprises, 1993.
Going for the Line: The Official Centenary Video – A Century of Rugby League. Micron Video, 1995.

Index

Barstow, Stan   4
Bashall, Nick   165, 381
Bates, Mick   107
Bath Rugby   208, 334
Batley RLFC   24, 30, 189
Batson, Brendon   189, 357
Batty, David   268
Baxter, Jim   258
FC Bayern Munich   158, 210, 366
Beal, Nick   255
Beardmore, Kevin   226
Beardmore, Robert   226
Bearsden & Milngavie Highland
Games   272–3, 296
Beattie, John   327, 336
Beattie, Johnny   334
Beaumont, Bill   144, 151, 154, 188–
9, 356, 368
Beckenbauer, Franz   210
Bedser, Alec   40
Beetson, Arthur   65, 379
Beijing   216
Belle Vue, Wakefield   58
Benaud, Richie   3
Bennett, Phil   121, 371, 381
Benson and Hedges Trophy (cricket)
133, 242, 244, 271, 356, 380
Bentley, John   195–6, 229
Best, Clyde   111, 189, 320
Best, Tino   349
Bevan, Brian   22–4, 146
Bevan, Derek   211
Bevan, John   147, 344
Biley, Alan   xiv, 162
Binks, Jimmy   49, 78, 89
Bird, Dickie   87, 289
Birethanti, Nepal   217, 234
Birley, David   129
Birmingham University   19
Bironas, Rob   311–2
Bishop, Ian   289, 384
Black, Tim   260
Blackheath FC   117
Blackpool Borough RLC   22–23, 61,
72, 208

Blair, Steve   253
Bland, Colin   45, 128
Blofeld, Henry   290
Blokhin, Oleg   210–1
Bolt, Usain   368
Bonneval, Eric   211
Boon, David   285
Boothferry Park, Hull   219–20
Borde, CG   41
Border, Alan   285, 287
Borough Park, Blackpool   61, 72
Boston, Billy   16, 33, 227
Botham, Ian   89, 128, 135, 183, 185–
7, 242–3, 296, 358–9, 381–2
Bowden, Reg   176
Bowes, Bill   53
Bowles, Stan   162
Boyce, Max   152
Boycott, Geoff   xiv, 48, 50–2, 75, 78,
81–2, 84–8, 124–8, 131, 133–4, 137,
183, 186–8, 214, 241–2, 245, 275,
304, 349, 383
Boyd, Tommy   265
Bradford City FC   40
Bradford Northern/Bradford Bulls
RLFC   34, 69, 142, 145–7, 151, 174,
188, 225, 227–8, 231, 271, 279–83
Bradford Park Avenue cricket ground
85–6, 88, 135, 236, 262, 349
Bradford Park Avenue AFC   106
Bradman, Sir Donald   47, 132, 216
Braine, John   4
Bramall Lane, Sheffield   160, 162
Bramley RLFC   58, 65, 230–1, 277,
379
Brazil (football)   182
Brearley, Mike   85, 126–7, 132, 188,
238, 356, 364, 380, 382, 384
Bremner, Billy   103–4, 107, 158, 347,
363, 370
Brentford FC   346
Bridges, Keith   146, 233
Bright, Ray   126–7
Brindle, Terry   380
Bristol RFC   379

Qadir, Abdul 243
Queen Mary College, London
University 171, 177, 189–90
Queen's Park FC 321–3
Queens Park Rangers FC 162
Quigley, Joan 381

Ramadhin, Sonny 77
Ramprakash, Mark 239, 289, 291
Ramsey, Alf 102
Ramsey, Bill 32, 34, 59
Randall, Derek 126, 128–9, 131, 304
Rangers FC 265–9, 304, 321–2, 384
Rasari, Mesake 255
Rashid, Adil 350
Rayne, Keith 207
Rayne, Kevin 207
Reaney, Paul 103
Redknapp, Harry 111
Redpath, Brian 254
Regis, Cyrille 189, 357
Reiffel, Paul 285
Reilly, Malcolm 226
Revie, Don 103, 109, 157–9, 347
Rhodes, Harold 78
Rhodes, Wilfred 47, 53, 77, 360
Rice, Jerry 191
Richards, Barry 85
Richards, David 97, 334
Richards, Dean 368
Richards, Huw 380–1
Richards, John 159
Richards, Maurice 70
Richards, Viv 89, 134, 136, 294
Richmond FC 91, 117, 151
Rigg, Bob (uncle) 20, 30–2, 35, 57–60, 65, 69–70, 102, 163
Rigg, John (author)
        employment 171, 189–90, 192, 212, 251, 316–7, 361
            learning about cricket 39, 43
            learning about rugby league 9–11, 25, 146
            playing sport xvii–xviii, 28, 50, 52, 64, 96, 122, 124–5, 156, 161, 356–7

        schooling 27–8, 36–8, 50, 67, 90, 100, 361
            university 88, 115–6, 161, 163, 361
Rigg, John (grandfather) 6, 165
Rigg, Peggie (mother) 17–20, 27, 46, 49, 65, 70–3, 103, 128, 131, 200, 248, 277–8, 282, 363, 367
Rigg, William (father)
        childhood/youth 6–7, 14–6, 57, 104, 141, 325, 341, 360, 373
        cricket 40, 48–50, 76, 80, 84, 88, 125, 186–7, 236–40, 243–8, 284–5, 292, 295–6, 349–50, 353
        employment/retirement 8, 57, 192–3, 230, 339–40
        and family 6–8, 15, 18, 64, 81, 163, 208, 282
        football 108, 171–2, 231–2
        rugby league 8–10, 13–6, 20–1, 23–4, 30–2, 34–5, 38, 57–8, 60–2, 67–70, 138–41, 143–6, 173–5, 188, 222–3, 225, 227–8, 276–84, 340–1, 353, 373
        rugby union 14, 91–2, 94–5, 97, 119, 156, 172–3, 196, 253–5, 257, 302, 372
        other xviii, 116, 197, 317, 328, 362–3
Riggins, John 311
Riley, George 162
Ringer, Paul 154, 194
Ripley, Andy 118
Risman, Bev 63, 77
Rivett, Leroy 282
Robbie, John 120–1
Roberts, Andy 132–3
JW Roberts Ltd 339–40, 377
Roberts, Mike 150
Roberts, Rachel 5
Robertson, John 206, 268, 275
Robinson, Jason xiv, 279–80, 302, 316, 361, 371, 384
Robson, Bryan 182, 217
Rodber, Tim 255

Sydney Cricket Ground   xiv, 36,
214–5, 362, 366
Szczesny, Wojciech   347

Tait, Alan   228, 271, 280
Tait, Matthew   302
Tamati, Kevin   147, 358
Tate, Dennis   29
Taylor, Bob   243
Taylor, Jack   160, 210
Taylor, Ken   40, 52, 78
Taylor, Mark   287, 356
Taylor, Simon   254
Tees, Eddie   63, 221
Tendulkar, Sachin   285, 295, 348,
350, 356
Tennessee Titans   310–4, 358
Tevez, Carlos   319
Theismann, Joe   311
Thomas, Arwel   263
Thompson, Cec   7, 15, 377
Thompson, Don   367–8
Thompson, Garry   171
Thompson, Hunter S   xv
Thompson, Tommy   61
Thomson, Jeff   126, 129–30, 185,
291, 357
Thorpe, Graham   286, 289
Tipping, Simon   196
Tollett, Tulsen   282
Topliss, David   140, 145, 175, 233, 363
Torrance, Sam   179
Tottenham Hotspur FC   107, 158, 206
Toulouse (rugby)
        see Stade Toulousain
Toure, Yaya   319
Traill, Ken   30–1
Trent Bridge cricket ground   125
Trevino, Lee   xiv, 179
Trinity College, Cambridge   xvii, 115,
380
Troon golf course   273, 305
Trotter, Dennis   174
Trueman, Freddie   40, 42, 44–5,
48–9, 53, 78, 350, 363

Tuffnell, Phil   247
Tuffs, Neil   xvii, 176
Tuigamala, Va'aiga   261
Turner, Derek   17
Turner, Glenn   76
Turner, Tina   282, 335, 362
Twenty–20 cricket   3, 75, 347, 349,
365
Twickenham Stadium   xiv, 117–9,
150–2, 193–6, 223–4, 244, 283, 318–
9, 331, 368
Tyler, Bonnie   284, 362

Ulster (rugby union)   98, 189, 262,
335
Umaga, Tana   329
Underwood, Derek   52, 79, 88–9
Underwood, Rory   195
United States Eagles (rugby union)
121
Upton Park, London   111, 189, 318–
20, 357, 364
Ustinov, Peter   227
Uttley, Roger   95

Vaealiki, David   308
Valbon, Ludovic   331
Vale of Lune RUFC   94
Van Vollenhoven, Tom   3
Van der Westhuizen, Jost   259
Vanier, C   178
Varsity Match
        boxing   164–6
        rugby union   117–20, 123, 318
Vaughan, Michael   xiv, 272, 294
Verity, Hedley   47, 53, 77, 132
Vernon, Richie   336
Vines, Don   17
Viollet, Dennis   270
Volleyball   166–8, 210, 381

Wakefield RFC   91, 93, 98, 255
Wakefield Trinity RLFC   16, 24, 30–31,
59–60, 68, 72, 140, 142, 144–5, 151,
163, 175–6, 225, 233, 304, 340, 344

Lightning Source UK Ltd.
Milton Keynes UK
UKOW021140130612

194329UK00003B/3/P

9 781781 320051